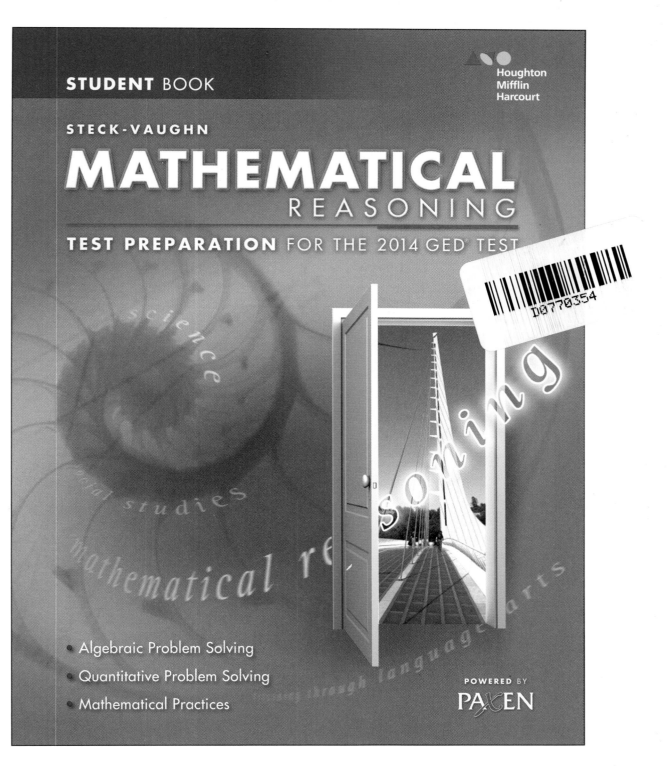

STUDENT BOOK

Houghton
Mifflin
Harcourt

STECK-VAUGHN

MATHEMATICAL
REASONING

TEST PREPARATION FOR THE 2014 GED° TEST

- Algebraic Problem Solving
- Quantitative Problem Solving
- Mathematical Practices

POWERED BY
PAXEN

Houghton
Mifflin
Harcourt

POWERED BY
PAXEN

Acknowledgments

For each of the selections and images listed below, grateful acknowledgement is made for permission to excerpt and/or reprint original or copyrighted material, as follows:

Images

Cover (bg) © Tetra Images/Corbis: **cover (inset)** © John Elk/Lonely Planet Images/Getty Images. **xii** Used with permission of Texas Instruments. **BLIND** Used with the permission of Gil Coronado. **1 (paying bills online)** iStockphoto © YinYang. **24** Used with the permission of Christopher Blizzard. **25 (police officer using computer)** GettyImages © Thinkstock. **48** Used with the permission of Philip Emeagwali. **49** Shutterstock © RDaniel. **92** Used with the permission of Huong McDoniel. **93 (man using software)** iStockphoto.

Mathematical Reasoning

Student Book

Table of Contents

About the GED® Test

Welcome to the first day of the rest of your life. Now that you've committed to study for your GED® credential, an array of possibilities and options—academic, career, and otherwise—awaits you. Each year, hundreds of thousands of people just like you decide to pursue a GED® credential. Like you, they left traditional school for one reason or another. Now, just like them, you've decided to continue your education by studying for and taking the GED® Test.

Today's GED® Test is very different from previous versions of the exam. Today's GED® Test is new, improved, and more rigorous, with content aligned to the Common Core State Standards. For the first time, the GED® Test serves both as a high-school equivalency credential and as a predictor of college and career readiness. The new GED® Test features four subject areas: Reasoning Through Language Arts (RLA), Mathematical Reasoning, Science, and Social Studies. Each subject area is delivered via a computer-based format and includes an array of technology-enhanced item types.

The four subject-area exams together comprise a testing time of seven hours. Preparation can take considerably longer. The payoff, however, is significant: more and better career options, higher earnings, and the sense of achievement that comes with a GED® credential. Employers, colleges, and universities accept the GED® credential as they would a high school diploma. On average, GED® graduates earn at least $8,400 more per year than those with an incomplete high school education.

The GED® Testing Service has constructed the GED® Test to mirror a high school experience. As such, you must answer a variety of questions within and across the four subject areas. For example, you may encounter a Social Studies passage on the Reasoning Through Language Arts Test, and vice versa. Also, you will encounter questions requiring varying levels of cognitive effort, or Depth of Knowledge (DOK) levels. The following table details the content areas, number of items, score points, DOK levels, and total testing time for each subject area.

Subject-Area Test	Content Areas	Items	Raw Score Points	DOK Level	Time
Reasoning Through Language Arts	**Informational Texts—75%** **Literary Texts—25%**	*51	65	80% of items at Level 2 or 3	150 minutes
Mathematical Reasoning	**Algebraic Problem Solving—55%** **Quantitative Problem Solving—45%**	*46	49	50% of items at Level 2	115 minutes
Science	**Life Science—40%** **Physical Science—40%** **Earth and Space Science—20%**	*34	40	80% of items at Level 2 or 3	90 minutes
Social Studies	**Civics/Government—50%** **U.S. History—20%** **Economics—15%** **Geography and the World—15%**	*35	44	80% of items at Level 2 or 3	90 minutes

*Number of items may vary slightly by test.

Because the demands of today's high school education and its relationship to workforce needs differ from those of a decade ago, the GED® Testing Service has moved to a computer-based format. Although multiple-choice questions remain the dominant type of item, the new GED® Test series includes a variety of technology-enhanced item types: drop-down, fill-in-the-blank, drag-and-drop, hot spot, short answer, and extended response items.

The table to the right identifies the various item types and their distribution on the new subject-area exams. As you can see, all four tests include multiple-choice, drop-down, fill-in-the-blank, and drag-and-drop items. Some variation occurs with hot spot, short answer, and extended response items.

2014 ITEM TYPES

	RLA	Math	Science	Social Studies
Multiple-choice	✓	✓	✓	✓
Drop-down	✓	✓	✓	✓
Fill-in-the-blank	✓	✓	✓	✓
Drag-and-drop	✓	✓	✓	✓
Hot spot		✓	✓	✓
Short answer			✓	
Extended response	✓			✓

Moreover, the new GED® Test relates to today's more demanding educational standards with items that align to appropriate assessment targets and varying DOK levels.

- **Content Topics/Assessment Targets** These topics and targets describe and detail the content on the GED® Test. They tie to the Common Core State Standards, as well as state standards for Texas and Virginia.
- **Content Practices** These practices describe the types of reasoning and modes of thinking required to answer specific items on the GED® Test.
- **Depth of Knowledge** The DOK model details the level of cognitive complexity and steps required to arrive at a correct answer on the test. The new GED® Test addresses three levels of DOK complexity.
  - **Level 1** You must recall, observe, question, or represent facts or simple skills. Typically, you will need to exhibit only a surface understanding of text and graphics.
  - **Level 2** You must process information beyond simple recall and observation to include summarizing, ordering, classifying, identifying patterns and relationships, and connecting ideas. You will need to scrutinize text and graphics.
  - **Level 3** You must explain, generalize, and connect ideas by inferring, elaborating, and predicting. For example, you may need to summarize from multiple sources and use that information to develop compositions with multiple paragraphs. Those paragraphs should feature a critical analysis of sources, include supporting positions from your own experiences, and reflect editing to ensure coherent, correct writing.

Approximately 80 percent of items across most content areas will be written to DOK Levels 2 and 3, with the remainder at Level 1. Writing portions, such as the extended response item in Social Studies (25 minutes) and Reasoning Through Language Arts (45 minutes), are considered DOK Level 3 items.

Now that you understand the basic structure of the GED® Test and the benefits of earning a GED® credential, you must prepare for the GED® Test. In the pages that follow, you will find a recipe of sorts that, if followed, will guide you toward successful completion of your GED® credential.

GED® Test on Computer

Along with new item types, the 2014 GED® Test also unveils a new, computer-based testing experience. The GED® Test will be available on computer and only at approved Pearson VUE Testing Centers. You will need content knowledge and the ability to read, think, and write critically, and you must perform basic computer functions—clicking, scrolling, and typing—to succeed on the test. The screen below closely resembles a screen that you will experience on the GED® Test.

The **INFORMATION** button contains material vital to the successful completion of the item. Here, by clicking the Information button, you would display a map about the American Revolution. On the Mathematical Reasoning exam, similar buttons for **FORMULA SHEET** and **CALCULATOR REFERENCE** provide information that will help you answer items that require use of formulas or the TI-30XS calculator. You may move a passage or graphic by clicking it and dragging it to a different part of the test screen.

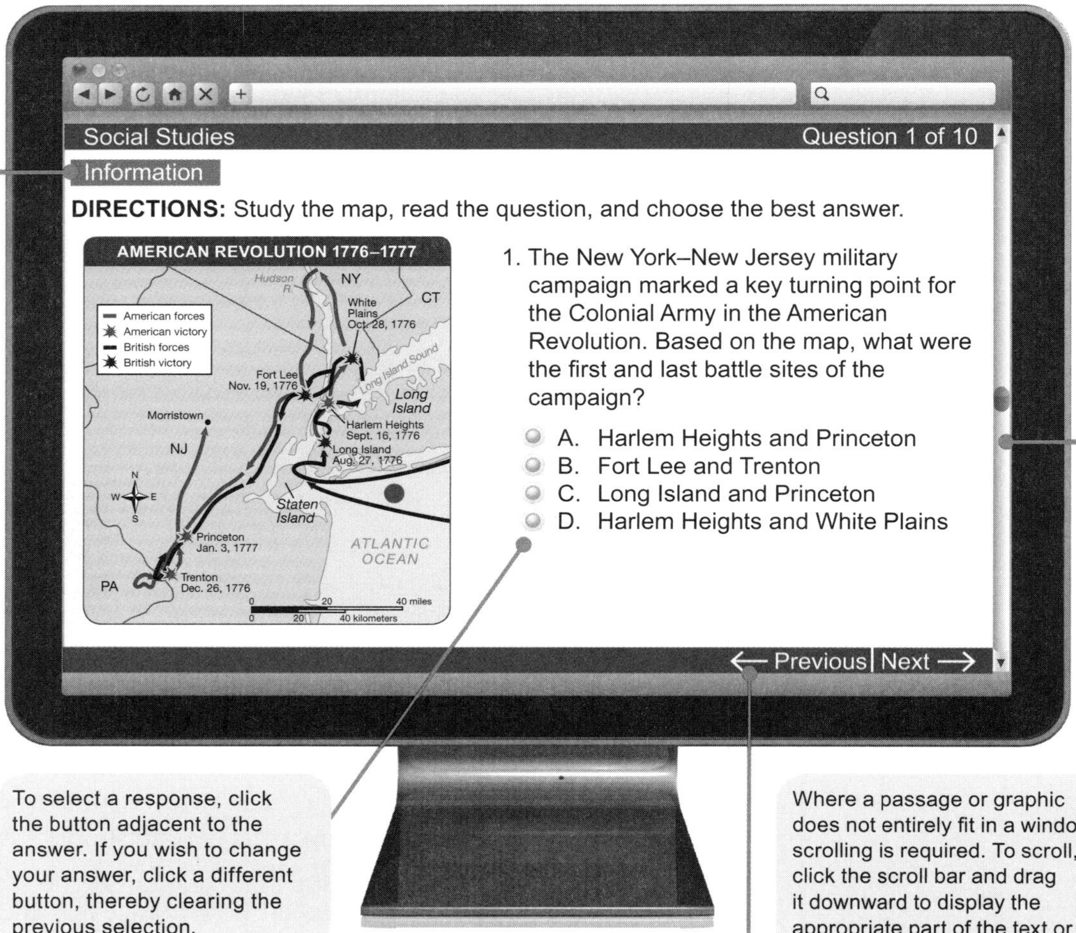

Social Studies

Question 1 of 10

Information

DIRECTIONS: Study the map, read the question, and choose the best answer.

AMERICAN REVOLUTION 1776–1777

- American forces
- American victory
- British forces
- British victory

Hudson R.
NY
White Plains Oct. 28, 1776
CT
Fort Lee Nov. 19, 1776
Long Island Sound
Long Island
Morristown
Harlem Heights Sept. 16, 1776
NJ
Long Island Aug. 27, 1776
Staten Island
Princeton Jan. 3, 1777
ATLANTIC OCEAN
PA
Trenton Dec. 26, 1776

0   20   40 miles
0   20   40 kilometers

1. The New York–New Jersey military campaign marked a key turning point for the Colonial Army in the American Revolution. Based on the map, what were the first and last battle sites of the campaign?

   - A. Harlem Heights and Princeton
   - B. Fort Lee and Trenton
   - C. Long Island and Princeton
   - D. Harlem Heights and White Plains

← Previous | Next →

To select a response, click the button adjacent to the answer. If you wish to change your answer, click a different button, thereby clearing the previous selection.

Where a passage or graphic does not entirely fit in a window, scrolling is required. To scroll, click the scroll bar and drag it downward to display the appropriate part of the text or graphic. The light gray portion of the scroll bar shows the amount of text or graphic that you cannot presently see.

To return to the prior screen, click **PREVIOUS**. To advance to the next screen, click **NEXT**.

Some items on the new GED® Test, such as fill-in-the-blank, short answer, and extended response questions, will require you to type answers into an entry box. In some cases, the directions may specify the range of typing the system will accept. For example, a fill-in-the-blank item may allow you to type a number from 0 to 9, along with a decimal point or a slash, but nothing else. The system also will tell you keys to avoid pressing in certain situations. The annotated computer screen and keyboard below provide strategies for entering text and data for fill-in-the-blank, short answer, and extended response items.

The passage below is an excerpt from *Common Sense*, a pamphlet written by Thomas Paine prior to the American Revolution. In it, Mr. Paine argues for the American colonists to set up a new government separate from the British monarchy.

We have boasted the protection of Great Britain, without considering, that her motive was *interest* not *attachment*; that she did not protect us from *our enemies* on *our account*, but from *her enemies* on *her own account*, from those that had no quarrel with us on any *other account*, and who will always be our enemies on the SAME ACCOUNT. Let Britain waive her pretentions to the continent, or the continent throw off the dependence, and we should be at peace with France and Spain were they at war with Britain.

Write a summary of how Thomas Paine's position in this excerpt reflects the enduring issue of American independence from Great Britain. Incorporate relevant and specific evidence from the excerpt, and your own knowledge of the issue and the circumstances surrounding the events leading to the American Revolution. This task may require 25 minutes to complete.

✂ Cut   📋 Copy   📋 Paste   Undo   Redo

← Previous | Next →

When writing an extended response, you may need to move words from one position to another. If so, first select the relevant words and then click **CUT**. Next, move the cursor to the appropriate part of the typing window and click **PASTE**. If you're unsure about whether to move text, you may select **COPY**, which will allow you to keep text in its original position while trying it elsewhere in the document. If you make an edit and then change your mind, you can click **UNDO** to reverse it. If you decide that you do want the edit, click **REDO** to keep it.

The **NUMBERS 0 THROUGH 9** are located here. They can be used in combination to form larger numbers, depending on your needs.

You may need to use some second-level characters on the keyboard. If so, hold down the **SHIFT** key and type the second-level key, such as a question mark.

Use the **DELETE** key to remove what you typed, and then type in a new answer.

About *Steck-Vaughn Test Preparation for the 2014 GED® Test*

Along with choosing to pursue your GED® credential, you've made another smart decision by selecting *Steck-Vaughn Test Preparation for the 2014 GED® Test* as your main study and preparation tool. Our emphasis on the acquisition of key reading and thinking concepts equips you with the skills and strategies to succeed on the GED® Test.

Two-page micro-lessons in each student book provide focused and efficient instruction. For those who require additional support, the companion workbooks, provide *twice* the support and practice exercises. Most lessons in the series include a *Spotlighted Item* feature that corresponds to one of the technology-enhanced item types that appear on the GED® Test.

The **LEARN THE SKILL** section provides information about the skill to be studied.

Each lesson includes correlations to **ASSESSMENT TARGETS** that will help focus your studies.

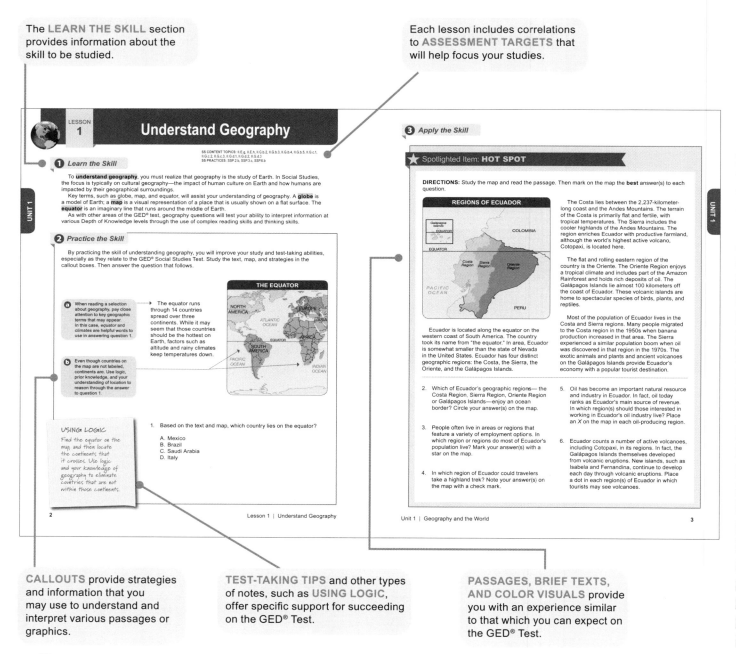

CALLOUTS provide strategies and information that you may use to understand and interpret various passages or graphics.

TEST-TAKING TIPS and other types of notes, such as **USING LOGIC**, offer specific support for succeeding on the GED® Test.

PASSAGES, BRIEF TEXTS, AND COLOR VISUALS provide you with an experience similar to that which you can expect on the GED® Test.

Student Book

Every unit in the student book opens with the feature GED® Journeys, a series of profiles of people who earned their GED® credential and used it as a springboard to success. From there, you receive intensive instruction and practice through a series of linked lessons, all of which tie to Content Topics/Assessment Targets, Content Practices (where applicable), and DOK levels.

Each unit closes with an eight-page review that includes a representative sampling of items, including technology-enhanced item types, from the lessons that comprise the unit. You may use each unit review as a posttest to gauge your mastery of content and skills and readiness for that aspect of the GED® Test.

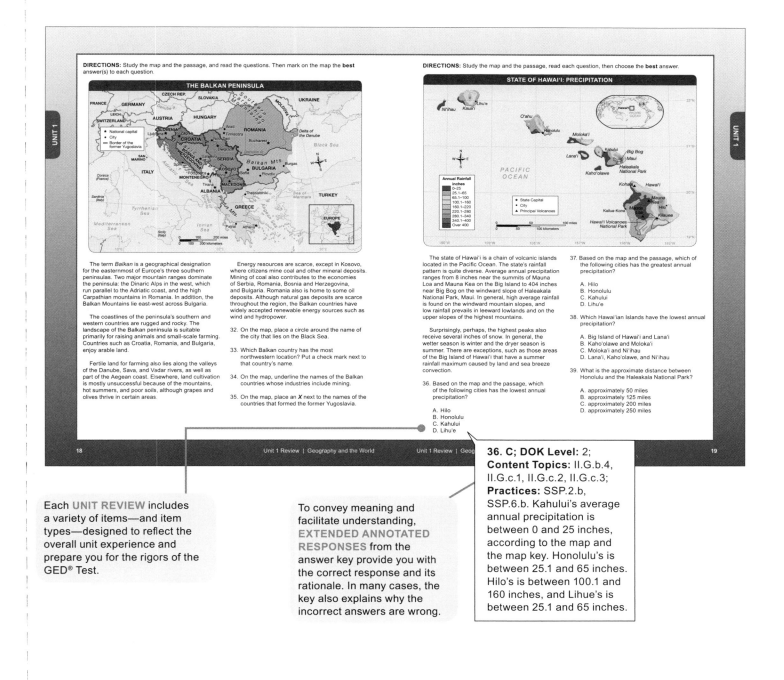

Each UNIT REVIEW includes a variety of items—and item types—designed to reflect the overall unit experience and prepare you for the rigors of the GED® Test.

To convey meaning and facilitate understanding, EXTENDED ANNOTATED RESPONSES from the answer key provide you with the correct response and its rationale. In many cases, the key also explains why the incorrect answers are wrong.

36. C; DOK Level: 2; **Content Topics:** II.G.b.4, II.G.c.1, II.G.c.2, II.G.c.3; **Practices:** SSP.2.b, SSP.6.b. Kahului's average annual precipitation is between 0 and 25 inches, according to the map and the map key. Honolulu's is between 25.1 and 65 inches. Hilo's is between 100.1 and 160 inches, and Lihue's is between 25.1 and 65 inches.

About the GED® Mathematical Reasoning Test

The new GED® Mathematical Reasoning Test is more than just a set of math items. In fact, it reflects an attempt to increase the rigor of the GED® Test to better meet the demands of a 21st-century economy. To that end, the GED® Mathematical Reasoning Test features an array of technology-enhanced item types. All of the items are delivered via computer-based testing. The items reflect the knowledge, skills, and abilities that a student would master in an equivalent high school experience.

Multiple-choice questions remain the majority of items on the GED® Mathematical Reasoning Test. However, a number of technology-enhanced items, including drop-down, fill-in-the-blank, drag-and-drop, and hot spot questions, will challenge you to master and convey knowledge in deeper, fuller ways. For example:

- Multiple-choice items assess virtually every content standard as either discrete items or as a series of items. Multiple-choice items on the new GED® Test will include four answer options (rather than five), structured in an A./B./C./D. format.
- Drop-down items include a pull-down menu of response choices, enabling you to choose the correct math vocabulary or numerical value to complete statements. In the example below, the terms *greater than*, *equal to,* and *less than* allow for comparisons between two quantities:

$$\sqrt{65} \qquad \begin{matrix} \text{greater than} \\ \text{equal to} \\ \text{less than} \end{matrix} \qquad 7^2$$

- Fill-in-the-blank items allow you to type in a numerical answer to a problem using keyboard symbols or a character selector. You also may use fill-in-the-blank items to express one-word or short answers to questions about mathematical reasoning.
- Drag-and-drop items involve interactive tasks that require you to move small images, words, or numerical expressions into designated drop zones on a computer screen. You may use drag-and-drop options to organize data, order steps in a process, or move numbers into boxes to create expressions, equations, and inequalities.
- Hot spot items consist of a graphic with virtual sensors placed strategically within it. They allow you to plot points on coordinate grids, number lines, or dot plots. You also may create models that match certain criteria.

You will have a total of 115 minutes in which to answer about 46 items. The GED® Mathematical Reasoning Test is organized across two main content areas: quantitative problem solving (45 percent of all items) and algebraic problem solving (55 percent). Half of the items will be written at Depth of Knowledge Level 2. The TI-30XS calculator and a formulas page, such as that on p. xiv in this book, will be embedded within the test's interface.

About *Steck-Vaughn Test Preparation for the 2014 GED® Test: Mathematical Reasoning*

Steck-Vaughn's student book and workbook help unlock the learning and deconstruct the different elements of the test by helping you build and develop core mathematics skills. The content of our books aligns to the new GED® math content standards and item distribution to provide you with a superior test preparation experience.

Our *Spotlighted Item* feature provides a deeper, richer treatment for each technology-enhanced item type. On initial introduction, a unique item type—such as drag-and-drop—receives a full page of example items in the student book lesson and three pages in the companion workbook lesson. The length of subsequent features may be shorter depending on the skill, lesson, and requirements.

A combination of targeted strategies, informational callouts and sample questions, assorted tips and hints, and ample assessment help clearly focus study efforts in needed areas.

In addition to the book features, a highly detailed answer key provides the correct answer and the rationale for it so that you know exactly why an answer is correct. The *Mathematical Reasoning* student book and workbook are designed with an eye toward the end goal: success on the GED® Mathematical Reasoning Test.

Along with mastering key content and reading and thinking skills, you will build familiarity with alternate item types that mirror in print the nature and scope of the technology-enhanced items included on the GED® Test.

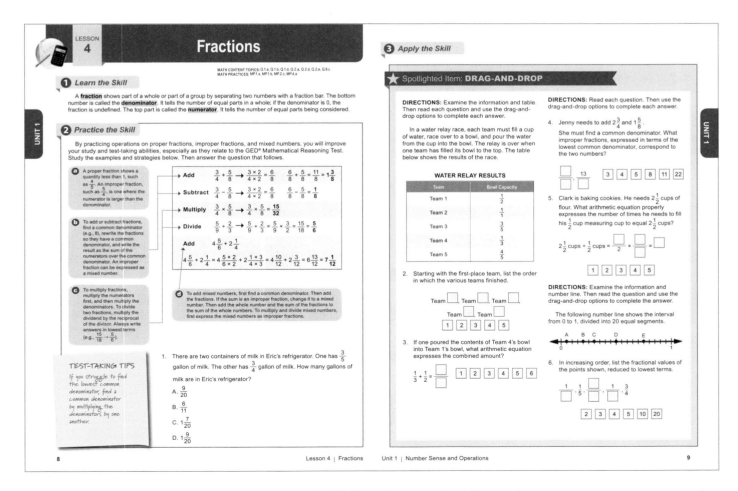

Calculator Directions

Certain items on the GED® Mathematical Reasoning Test allow for the use of a calculator to aid in answering questions. That calculator, the TI-30XS, is embedded within the testing interface. Students may also bring their own TI-30Xs MultiView calculator to use on the test. The TI-30XS calculator will be available for most items on the GED® Mathematical Reasoning Test and for some items on the GED® Science Test and GED® Social Studies Test. The TI-30XS calculator is shown below, along with callouts of some of its most important keys. A button that enables the calculator reference sheet is located in the upper right corner of the testing screen.

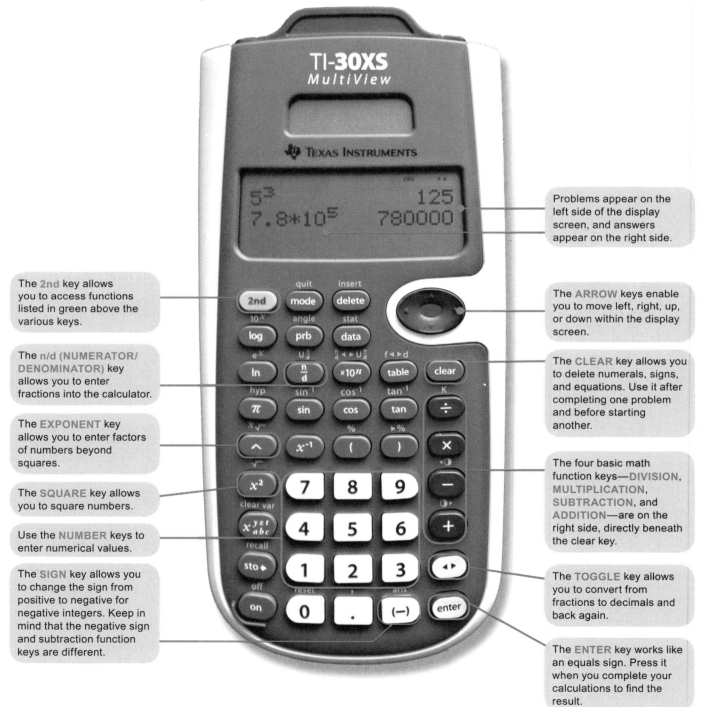

Problems appear on the left side of the display screen, and answers appear on the right side.

The 2nd key allows you to access functions listed in green above the various keys.

The n/d (NUMERATOR/DENOMINATOR) key allows you to enter fractions into the calculator.

The EXPONENT key allows you to enter factors of numbers beyond squares.

The SQUARE key allows you to square numbers.

Use the NUMBER keys to enter numerical values.

The SIGN key allows you to change the sign from positive to negative for negative integers. Keep in mind that the negative sign and subtraction function keys are different.

The ARROW keys enable you to move left, right, up, or down within the display screen.

The CLEAR key allows you to delete numerals, signs, and equations. Use it after completing one problem and before starting another.

The four basic math function keys—DIVISION, MULTIPLICATION, SUBTRACTION, and ADDITION—are on the right side, directly beneath the clear key.

The TOGGLE key allows you to convert from fractions to decimals and back again.

The ENTER key works like an equals sign. Press it when you complete your calculations to find the result.

Getting Started

To enable the calculator for a question that allows it, click the upper left portion of the testing screen. If the calculator displays over the top of a problem, you may move it by clicking it and dragging it to another part of the screen. Once enabled, the calculator will be ready for use (no need to push the **on** key). The directions below are for using the calculator in *mathprint* mode. Classic mode can be used by pressing the mode key and selecting *classic*.

- Use the **clear** key to clear all numbers and operations from the screen.
- Use the **enter** key to complete all calculations.

2nd Key

The green **2nd** key is located in the upper left corner of the TI-30XS. The **2nd** key enables a second series of functions, which are located above the keys and noted in green type. To use the 2nd-level function, click the **2nd** key, and then click the key with the 2nd-level function you need.

Fractions and Mixed Numbers

To enter fractions, such as $\frac{3}{4}$, click the **n/d (numerator/denominator)** key, followed by the numerator quantity [**3**]. Next, click the **down arrow** button (upper right corner of the calculator), followed by the denominator quantity [**4**]. To calculate with fractions, click the **right arrow** button and then the appropriate function key and other numerals in the equation.

To enter mixed numbers, such as $1\frac{3}{8}$, first enter the whole number quantity [**1**]. Next, click the **2nd** key and the **mixed number** key (1st level **n/d**). Then enter the fraction numerator [**3**], followed by the **down arrow** button and then the denominator [**8**]. If you click **enter**, the mixed number will convert to an improper fraction. To calculate with mixed numbers, click the **right arrow** button and then the appropriate function key and other numerals in the equation.

Negative Numbers

To enter a negative number, click the **negative sign** key (located directly below the number **3** on the calculator). Keep in mind that the **negative sign** key differs from the **subtraction** key, which is found in the far right column of keys, directly above the **addition (+)** key.

Squares, Square Roots, and Exponents

- **Squares:** The x^2 key squares numbers. The **exponent** key (^) raises numbers to powers higher than squares, such as cubes. For example, to find the answer to 5^3 on the calculator, first enter the base number [**5**], then click the exponent key (^), and follow by clicking the exponent number [**3**] and then the **enter** key.
- **Square Roots:** To find the square root of a number, such as 36, first click the **2nd** key, then click the **square root** key (1st-level x^2), then the number [**36**], and finally **enter**.
- **Cube Roots:** To find the cube root of a number, such as **125**, first enter the cube as a number [**3**], followed by the **2nd** key and ^ key. Finally, enter the number for which you want to find the cube [**125**], followed by **enter**.
- **Exponents:** To perform calculations with numbers expressed in scientific notation, such as 7.8×10^9, first enter the base number [**7.8**]. Next, click the **scientific notation** key (located directly beneath the **data** key), followed by the exponent level [**9**]. You then have 7.8×10^9.

Formulas for the GED® Mathematical Reasoning Test

Following are formulas that will be used on the new GED® Mathematical Reasoning Test. A button that will enable a formula reference sheet will appear in the upper left corner of the testing screen itself.

Area of a:

square	$A = s^2$
rectangle	$A = lw$
parallelogram	$A = bh$
triangle	$A = \frac{1}{2}bh$
trapezoid	$A = \frac{1}{2}h(b_1 + b_2)$
circle	$A = \pi r^2$

Perimeter of a:

square	$P = 4s$
rectangle	$P = 2l + 2w$
triangle	$P = s_1 + s_2 + s_3$
Circumference of a circle	$C = 2\pi r$ OR $C = \pi d$; $\pi \approx 3.14$

Surface area and volume of a:

rectangular/right prism	$SA = ph + 2B$	$V = Bh$
cylinder	$SA = 2\pi rh + 2\pi r^2$	$V = \pi r^2 h$
pyramid	$SA = \frac{1}{2}ps + B$	$V = \frac{1}{3}Bh$
cone	$SA = \pi rs + \pi r^2$	$V = \frac{1}{3}\pi r^2 h$
sphere	$SA = 4\pi r^2$	$V = \frac{4}{3}\pi r^3$

(p = perimeter of base with area B; $\pi \approx 3.14$)

Data

mean	mean is equal to the total of the values of a data set, divided by the number of elements in the data set
median	median is the middle value in an odd number of ordered values of a data set, or the mean of the two middle values in an even number of ordered values in a data set

Algebra

slope of a line	$m = \dfrac{y_2 - y_1}{x_2 - x_1}$
slope-intercept form of the equation of a line	$y = mx + b$
point-slope form of the equation of a line	$y - y_1 = m(x - x_1)$
standard form of a quadratic equation	$y = ax^2 + bx + c$
quadratic formula	$x = \dfrac{-b \pm \sqrt{b^2 - 4ac}}{2a}$
Pythagorean theorem	$a^2 + b^2 = c^2$
simple interest	$I = Prt$ (I = interest, P = principal, r = rate, t = time)
distance formula	$d = rt$
total cost	total cost = (number of units) × (price per unit)

Test-Taking Tips

The new GED® Test includes more than 160 items across the four subject-area exams of Reasoning Through Language Arts, Mathematical Reasoning, Science, and Social Studies. The four subject-area exams represent a total test time of seven hours. Most items are multiple-choice questions, but a number are technology-enhanced items. These include drop-down, fill-in-the-blank, drag-and-drop, hot spot, short answer, and extended response items.

Throughout this book and others in the series, we help you build, develop, and apply core reading and thinking skills critical to success on the GED® Test. As part of an overall strategy, we suggest that you use the test-taking tips presented here and throughout the book to improve your performance on the GED® Test.

> **Always read directions thoroughly so that you know exactly what to do.** As we've noted, the 2014 GED® Test has an entirely new computer-based format that includes a variety of technology-enhanced items. If you are unclear of what to do or how to proceed, ask the test provider whether directions can be explained.

> **Read each question carefully so that you fully understand what it is asking.** For example, some passages and graphics may present information beyond what is necessary to correctly answer a specific question. Other questions may use boldfaced words for emphasis (for example, "Which statement represents the **most** appropriate revision for this hypothesis?").

> **Manage your time with each question.** Because the GED® Test is a series of timed exams, you want to spend enough time with each question, but not *too* much time. For example, on the GED® Mathematical Reasoning Test, you have 115 minutes in which to answer approximately 46 questions, or an average of about two minutes per question. Obviously, some items will require more time and others will require less, but you should remain aware of the overall number of items and amount of testing time. The new GED® Test interface may help you manage your time. It includes an on-screen clock in the upper right corner that provides the remaining time in which to complete a test.

Also, you may monitor your progress by viewing the **Question** line, which will give you the current question number, followed by the total number of questions on that subject-area exam.

> **Answer all questions, regardless of whether you know the answer or are guessing.** There is no benefit in leaving questions unanswered on the GED® Test. Keep in mind the time that you have for each test, and manage it accordingly. If you wish to review a specific item at the end of a test, click **Flag for Review** to mark the question. When you do, the flag will display in yellow. At the end of a test, you may have time to review questions you've marked.

> **Skim and scan.** You may save time by first reading each question and its answer options before reading or studying an accompanying passage or graphic. Once you understand what the question is asking, review the passage or visual for the appropriate information.

> **Note any unfamiliar words in questions.** First attempt to re-read the question by omitting any unfamiliar word. Next, try to use other words around the unfamiliar word to determine its meaning.

> **Narrow answer options by re-reading each question and re-examining the text or graphic that goes with it.** Although four answers are *possible* on multiple-choice items, keep in mind that only one is *correct*. You may be able to eliminate one answer immediately; you may need to take more time or use logic or make assumptions to eliminate others. In some cases, you may need to make your best guess between two options.

> **Go with your instinct when answering questions.** If your first instinct is to choose **A** in response to a question, it's best to stick with that answer unless you determine that it is incorrect. Usually, the first answer someone chooses is the correct one.

GED® JOURNEYS

Gil Coronado

After earning his GED® certificate, Gil Coronado embarked on a succesful career in the military and, later, as head of the Selective Service System.

"The military opened more doors in my life than I ever thought existed. It's truly one of the best experiences a young person can have ..."

Gil Coronado has a knack for numbers. Coronado, who left high school to enlist in the United States Air Force, earned his GED® certificate and went on to a distinguished 30-year career in the military. During that time, he earned more than 35 awards, including the prestigious Bronze Star for his service during the Vietnam War.

After retiring from the military, Coronado continued to serve his country as deputy assistant secretary at the Department of Veterans Affairs. In 1994, Coronado accepted a position requiring a knowledge of mathematics and a talent for organization when he was appointed the ninth director of the Selective Service System. Each year, federal law requires all men, about 1.8 million per year, to register with Selective Service within 30 days of turning 18 years of age.

As director of the Selective Service, Coronado managed 180 federal employees; 11,000 board members; more than 50 appointed state heads; and 450 reserve officers. He also provided leadership to regional directors and the Data Measurement Center. As the agency's first Hispanic director, Coronado modernized the system so that men may register online.

Throughout his career, Coronado remained true to his roots. He advocated for creation of Hispanic Heritage Month, established by Congress in 1988. He also founded and chaired the group "Heroes and Heritage" and served as a member of the National Consortium for Education Access.

CAREER HIGHLIGHTS: *Gil Coronado*

- Born and raised in San Antonio, Texas
- Earned his college degree from Our Lady of the Lake University
- Graduated from several military service schools

- Served in Southeast Asia during the Vietnam War
- Named European Commander of the Year
- Inducted into the U.S. Army Officer Candidate School Hall of Fame

Number Sense and Operations

Unit 1: Number Sense and Operations

You are surrounded by numbers. Whether paying bills, negotiating a car loan, budgeting for rent or groceries, depositing a check, or withdrawing money, you use basic math skills such as addition, subtraction, multiplication, and division to perform a variety of everyday tasks.

In the same way, number sense and operations play an important part on the GED® Mathematical Reasoning Test. In Unit 1, you will study whole numbers, operations, integers, fractions, ratios and proportions, decimals, and percent, all of which will help you prepare for the GED® Mathematical Reasoning Test.

Table of Contents

LESSON	PAGES
1: Whole Numbers	2–3
2: Operations	4–5
3: Integers	6–7
4: Fractions	8–9
5: Ratios and Proportions	10–11
6: Decimals	12–13
7: Percent	14–15
Unit 1 Review	16–23

People use essential math skills to complete everyday tasks such as budgeting, paying bills, and saving and investing money.

Whole Numbers

MATH CONTENT TOPICS: Q.1.d, Q.6.c
MATH PRACTICES: MP.1.a, MP.1.b, MP.1.e, MP.2.c, MP.5.c

UNIT 1

1 Learn the Skill

Whole numbers are written with the digits 0 through 9. The value of a digit in a whole number depends on its place. The value of a whole number is the sum of the values of its digits. When you write a whole number, place commas every three digits counting from the right.

Write a whole number in words just like you read it (for example, *two hundred twelve* would be written numerically as *212*). To compare and order whole numbers, compare digits that have the same place value. In some problems, you may need to round whole numbers to a certain place value.

2 Practice the Skill

To successfully solve problems on the GED® Mathematical Reasoning Test, you must understand place value, how to read and write whole numbers, how to compare and order whole numbers, and how to round whole numbers. Read the example and strategies below. Then answer the question that follows.

(a) Tables make information easier to compare by organizing it in labeled rows and columns. Most tables, including this one, present information from left to right and from top to bottom.

Millions			Thousands			Units		
hundreds	tens	ones	hundreds	tens	ones	hundreds	tens	ones
				4	3	0	6	2

(b) The value of a whole number is the sum of the values of its digits. For example, the value of the *4* is actually *40,000* because it is in the ten thousands place.

$$4 \times 10{,}000 = 40{,}000$$
$$3 \times 1{,}000 = 3{,}000$$
$$0 \times 100 = 000$$
$$6 \times 10 = 60$$
$$2 \times 1 = 2$$
$$= \mathbf{43{,}062}$$

(c) When you compare whole numbers, the number with the most digits is greater. If two numbers have the same number of digits, compare the digits from left to right. Understanding these symbols will aid in comparing whole numbers:
= means *equals*
> means *is greater than*
< means *is less than*

$43{,}0\underline{6}2 > 43{,}0\underline{4}1$

The number *43,062* is read and written in words as **forty-three thousand, sixty-two.** When rounded to the hundreds place, 43,062 is **43,100.**

TEST-TAKING TIPS

Circle the digit you want to round. If the digit to the right of the circled digit is 5 or more, add 1 to the circled digit. If it is less than 5, do not change the circled digit.

1. Carrie needs to round her income to the thousands place. What is $56,832 rounded to the thousands place?

A. $56,000
B. $56,800
C. $56,900
D. $57,000

DIRECTIONS: Read each question, and choose the **best** answer.

2. Meredith wrote a check for $182 to pay a bill. How is 182 written in words?

   A. one hundred eight-two
   B. one hundred eighty-two
   C. one hundred and eighteen-two
   D. one-hundred eighty and two

3. Mr. Murphy rounds his students' test scores to the tens place. Jonathan's test score is 86. What is his test score rounded to the tens place?

   A. 80
   B. 86
   C. 90
   D. 100

4. Each book in a historical library is given a number. The books are arranged on shelves according to their numbers. The range of numbers for shelves I through L is shown below.

   Shelf I   1337–1420
   Shelf J   1421–1499
   Shelf K   1500–1622
   Shelf L   1623–1708

   On which shelf would you find a book numbered 1384?

   A. Shelf I
   B. Shelf J
   C. Shelf K
   D. Shelf L

5. Michael swam 2,450 yards on Monday, 2,700 yards on Tuesday, and 2,250 yards on Wednesday. What is the order of his daily swim yardage from least to greatest?

   A. 2,450; 2,700; 2,250
   B. 2,250; 2,700; 2,450
   C. 2,250; 2,450; 2,700
   D. 2,700; 2,450; 2,250

6. Michael swam an additional 2,500 yards on Thursday. Place his swim yardages in order by day from greatest to least.

   A. Monday, Tuesday, Wednesday, Thursday
   B. Tuesday, Thursday, Monday, Wednesday
   C. Wednesday, Monday, Thursday, Tuesday
   D. Tuesday, Thursday, Wednesday, Monday

7. A professional cyclist bicycled 22,755 miles in 2005; 20,564 miles in 2006; and 23,804 miles in 2007. If the three years are listed in order of the miles bicycled, from least to greatest, how would the years be listed?

   A. 2006, 2005, 2007
   B. 2006, 2007, 2005
   C. 2005, 2007, 2006
   D. 2007, 2005, 2006

DIRECTIONS: Study the information and table, read each question, and choose the **best** answer.

The table below shows a sporting goods store's monthly sales for the first six months of the year.

Monthly Sales	
January	$155,987
February	$150,403
March	$139,605
April	$144,299
May	$149,355
June	$148,260

8. Based on the table, in which month did the store have its highest promotion to increase sales?

   A. January
   B. February
   C. March
   D. May

9. In which month might the store want to run a special promotion to increase sales?

   A. March
   B. April
   C. May
   D. June

10. Based on the table, what sales trend can you determine?

   A. People purchased the most sporting goods equipment during early spring.
   B. Sales were at their highest in winter months.
   C. Monthly sales remained the same from January through June.
   D. People purchased more sporting goods as summer approached.

Operations

MATH CONTENT TOPICS: Q.1.b, Q.2.a, Q.2.e, Q.7.a
MATH PRACTICES: MP.1.a, MP.1.b, MP.2.c, MP.3.a, MP.4.a, MP.5.c

1 Learn the Skill

The four basic math operations are addition, subtraction, multiplication, and division. Add quantities to find a **sum**, or total. Subtract to find the **difference** between two quantities.

Multiply quantities to find a **product** when you need to add a number many times. Divide when separating a quantity into equal groups. The **dividend** is the initial quantity. The **divisor** is the number by which you divide. The **quotient** is the answer.

Factors are numbers that can be multiplied together to get another number. Factors of a whole number refer to other whole numbers that divide into the original whole number with no remainder.

2 Practice the Skill

To successfully solve problems on the GED® Mathematical Reasoning Test, you must determine the correct operation(s) to perform and the proper order in which to perform them. Read the examples and strategies below. Then answer the question that follows.

a Add the numbers in each column, working from right to left. If the sum of a column of digits is greater than 9, regroup to the next column on the left.

b To subtract, align digits by place value. Subtract the numbers in each column, working from right to left. When a digit in the bottom number is greater than the digit in the top number, regroup.

a **Addition**

$$\begin{array}{r} \overset{1}{482} \\ + 208 \\ \hline 690 \end{array}$$

b **Subtraction**

$$\begin{array}{r} \overset{7\,12}{4\cancel{8}\cancel{2}} \\ - 208 \\ \hline 274 \end{array}$$

c **Multiplication**

$$\begin{array}{r} \overset{2}{\overset{3}{482}} \\ \times \;\; 34 \\ \hline \overset{1}{1,928} \\ \times 14,460 \\ \hline 16,388 \end{array}$$

c Multiply the ones digit of the bottom number by all the digits in the top number. Align each result, or partial product, under the digit by which you multiplied. Use zeros as placeholders. After you've multiplied digits in the top number by all the digits in the bottom number, add the partial products.

d **Division**

$$\begin{array}{r} 517 \text{ R12} \\ 14\overline{)7250} \\ -70 \\ \hline 25 \\ -14 \\ \hline 110 \\ -98 \\ \hline 12 \end{array}$$

d

$$\begin{array}{r} 517 \text{ R12} \\ 14\overline{)7250} \\ 14 \times 5 = -70 \\ \hline 25 \\ 14 \times 1 = -14 \\ \hline 110 \\ 14 \times 7 = -98 \\ \hline 12 \end{array}$$

1. Shirley has $1,256 in her bank account. She withdraws $340. How much money is left in her bank account?

   A. $816
   B. $916
   C. $926
   D. $996

⭐ Spotlighted Item: **FILL-IN-THE-BLANK**

DIRECTIONS: Read each question. Then write your answers in the boxes below.

2. Alex drove from Denver, Colorado, to Chicago, Illinois, in two days. The first day he drove 467 miles. The second day he drove 583 miles. What is the total distance that Alex drove?

3. During a word game, Alicia had 307 points. She was unable to use all of her letters, so she had to subtract 19 points at the end of the game. What was Alicia's final score?

4. Juan works 40 hours per week. He earns $9 per hour. How much does Juan earn in one week?

5. Carl pays $45 per month for car insurance. How much does he spend on car insurance in 1 year?

6. Four friends went out for pizza. The total cost for appetizers, pizza, and drinks was $64. If the friends split the cost equally, how much did each friend pay?

7. Not including 1 and 60, how many whole numbers are factors of the number 60?

8. Each month, Anna pays $630 in rent. How much rent does she pay over the course of 18 months?

9. The quarterback on Scott's favorite football team is closing in on a 4,000-yard passing season. He has thrown for 3,518 yards with two games remaining. How many yards would the quarterback need to average during the final two games to reach his goal of 4,000 yards?

10. Which whole number is the largest common factor of both the numbers 36 and 20?

11. What is the smallest whole number that has both 6 and 9 as factors?

DIRECTIONS: Study the diagram. Then write your answer in the box below.

504 sq ft

12. Claire is purchasing bags of mulch to cover her vegetable garden. One bag of mulch will cover 12 square feet. How many bags of mulch will Claire need?

Integers

MATH CONTENT TOPICS: Q.1.d, Q.2.a, Q.2.e, Q.6.c
MATH PRACTICES: MP.1.a, MP.1.b, MP.1.c, MP.2.c, MP.3.a, MP.4.a

UNIT 1

① Learn the Skill

Integers include positive whole numbers (1, 2, 3, ...), their opposites, or negative numbers (−1, −2, −3, ...), and zero. Positive numbers show an increase and may be written with or without a plus sign. Negative numbers show a decrease and are written with a negative sign. Integers can be added, subtracted, multiplied, and divided. There are specific rules for adding, subtracting, multiplying, and dividing integers.

In some cases, you may need to determine an integer's **absolute value**, or its distance from 0. Absolute values are always greater than or equal to zero, never negative. So the absolute value of both 9 and −9 is 9.

② Practice the Skill

Many mathematics problems relating to real-world situations use integers. You must understand and follow the rules for adding, subtracting, multiplying, and dividing integers to solve such problems on the GED® Mathematical Reasoning Test. Read the examples and strategies below. Then answer the question that follows.

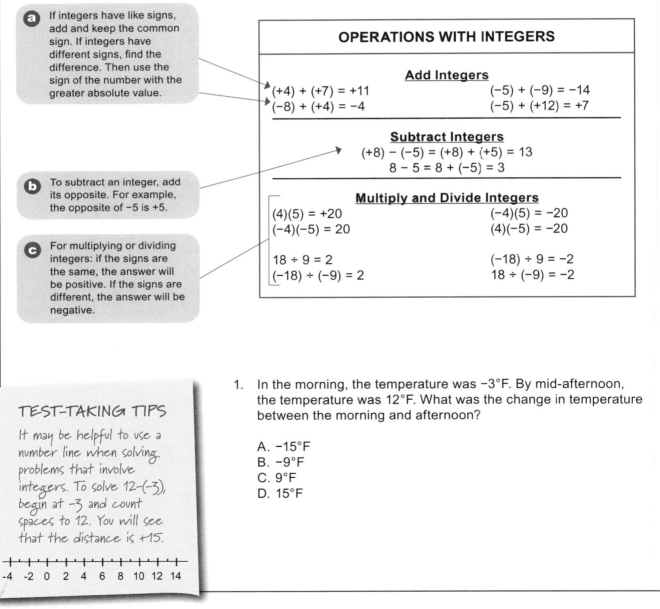

ⓐ If integers have like signs, add and keep the common sign. If integers have different signs, find the difference. Then use the sign of the number with the greater absolute value.

ⓑ To subtract an integer, add its opposite. For example, the opposite of −5 is +5.

ⓒ For multiplying or dividing integers: if the signs are the same, the answer will be positive. If the signs are different, the answer will be negative.

OPERATIONS WITH INTEGERS

Add Integers

$(+4) + (+7) = +11$ $(−5) + (−9) = −14$

$(−8) + (+4) = −4$ $(−5) + (+12) = +7$

Subtract Integers

$(+8) − (−5) = (+8) + (+5) = 13$

$8 − 5 = 8 + (−5) = 3$

Multiply and Divide Integers

$(4)(5) = +20$ $(−4)(5) = −20$

$(−4)(−5) = 20$ $(4)(−5) = −20$

$18 ÷ 9 = 2$ $(−18) ÷ 9 = −2$

$(−18) ÷ (−9) = 2$ $18 ÷ (−9) = −2$

TEST-TAKING TIPS

It may be helpful to use a number line when solving problems that involve integers. To solve 12−(−3), begin at −3 and count spaces to 12. You will see that the distance is +15.

-4 -2 0 2 4 6 8 10 12 14

1. In the morning, the temperature was −3°F. By mid-afternoon, the temperature was 12°F. What was the change in temperature between the morning and afternoon?

    A. −15°F
    B. −9°F
    C. 9°F
    D. 15°F

★ Spotlighted Item: **FILL-IN-THE-BLANK**

DIRECTIONS: Read each question, and write your answer in the box below.

2. Uyen has a balance of $154 in her savings account. She withdraws $40 from a cash machine. What is her new balance?

3. In a board game, Dora moves forward 3 spaces, back 4 spaces, and forward again 8 spaces in one turn. What is her net gain or loss of spaces?

There were 3,342 students enrolled at a university. Of those students, 587 graduated in May. Over the summer, 32 students left the university, and 645 new students enrolled in the fall.

4. How many students were enrolled in the fall?

5. What is the change in the number of students enrolled between May and the following fall?

DIRECTIONS: Read the question, and choose the **best** answer.

6. Sasha's home is 212 feet above sea level. She participated in a scuba dive in which she descended to 80 feet below sea level. Which integer describes Sasha's change in position from her home to the lowest point of her dive?

   A. −292
   B. −132
   C. 132
   D. 292

DIRECTIONS: Study the number line, read the question, and choose the **best** answer.

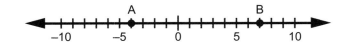

7. The absolute value of the difference between two numbers is the distance between the two numbers on the number line. What is the absolute value of the difference between points *A* and *B*?

   A. −11
   B. −3
   C. 3
   D. 11

DIRECTIONS: Study the information and table, read each question, and choose the **best** answer.

Melanie played a game and kept track of her score. The table shows her points earned for each round.

MELANIE'S POINTS SCORED

Round	Points Scored
1	8
2	−6
3	−4
4	3
5	4

8. What was Melanie's score at the end of Round 5?

   A. 25
   B. 15
   C. 7
   D. 5

9. Melanie played a sixth round and scored −8 in that round. What was her overall score?

   A. −13
   B. −3
   C. 13
   D. 18

Fractions

MATH CONTENT TOPICS: Q.1.a, Q.1.b, Q.1.d, Q.2.a, Q.2.d, Q.2,e, Q.6.c
MATH PRACTICES: MP.1.a, MP.1.b, MP.2.c, MP.4.a

UNIT 1

1 Learn the Skill

A **fraction** shows part of a whole or part of a group by separating two numbers with a fraction bar. The bottom number is called the **denominator**. It tells the number of equal parts in a whole; if the denominator is 0, the fraction is undefined. The top part is called the **numerator**. It tells the number of equal parts being considered.

2 Practice the Skill

By practicing operations on proper fractions, improper fractions, and mixed numbers, you will improve your study and test-taking abilities, especially as they relate to the GED® Mathematical Reasoning Test. Study the examples and strategies below. Then answer the question that follows.

a A proper fraction shows a quantity less than 1, such as $\frac{4}{5}$. An improper fraction, such as $\frac{5}{4}$, is one where the numerator is larger than the denominator.

b To add or subtract fractions, find a common denominator (e.g., 8), rewrite the fractions so they have a common denominator, and write the result as the sum of the numerators over the common denominator. An improper fraction can be expressed as a mixed number.

c To multiply fractions, multiply the numerators first, and then multiply the denominators. To divide two fractions, multiply the dividend by the reciprocal of the divisor. Always write answers in lowest terms (e.g., $\frac{15}{18} \to \frac{5}{6}$).

Add $\frac{3}{4} + \frac{5}{8} \to \frac{3 \times 2}{4 \times 2} = \frac{6}{8}$ $\frac{6}{8} + \frac{5}{8} = \frac{11}{8} = 1\frac{3}{8}$

Subtract $\frac{3}{4} - \frac{5}{8} \to \frac{3 \times 2}{4 \times 2} = \frac{6}{8}$ $\frac{6}{8} - \frac{5}{8} = \frac{1}{8}$

Multiply $\frac{3}{4} \times \frac{5}{8} \to \frac{3}{4} \times \frac{5}{8} = \frac{15}{32}$

Divide $\frac{5}{9} \div \frac{2}{3} \to \frac{5}{9} \div \frac{2}{3} = \frac{5}{9} \times \frac{3}{2} = \frac{15}{18} = \frac{5}{6}$

Add $4\frac{5}{6} + 2\frac{1}{4}$

$4\frac{5}{6} + 2\frac{1}{4} = 4\frac{5 \times 2}{6 \times 2} + 2\frac{1 \times 3}{4 \times 3} = 4\frac{10}{12} + 2\frac{3}{12} = 6\frac{13}{12} = 7\frac{1}{12}$

d To add mixed numbers, first find a common denominator. Then add the fractions. If the sum is an improper fraction, change it to a mixed number. Then add the whole number and the sum of the fractions to the sum of the whole numbers. To multiply and divide mixed numbers, first express the mixed numbers as improper fractions.

TEST-TAKING TIPS

If you struggle to find the lowest common denominator, find a common denominator by multiplying the denominators by one another.

1. There are two containers of milk in Eric's refrigerator. One has $\frac{3}{5}$ gallon of milk. The other has $\frac{3}{4}$ gallon of milk. How many gallons of milk are in Eric's refrigerator?

   A. $\frac{9}{20}$

   B. $\frac{6}{11}$

   C. $1\frac{7}{20}$

   D. $1\frac{9}{20}$

⭐ Spotlighted Item: **DRAG-AND-DROP**

DIRECTIONS: Examine the information and table. Then read each question and use the drag-and-drop options to complete each answer.

In a water relay race, each team must fill a cup of water, race over to a bowl, and pour the water from the cup into the bowl. The relay is over when one team has filled its bowl to the top. The table below shows the results of the race.

WATER RELAY RESULTS

Team	Bowl Capacity
Team 1	$\frac{1}{2}$
Team 2	$\frac{1}{1}$
Team 3	$\frac{3}{5}$
Team 4	$\frac{1}{3}$
Team 5	$\frac{4}{5}$

2. Starting with the first-place team, list the order in which the various teams finished.

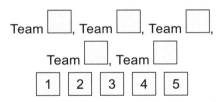

3. If one poured the contents of Team 4's bowl into Team 1's bowl, what arithmetic equation expresses the combined amount?

DIRECTIONS: Read each question. Then use the drag-and-drop options to complete each answer.

4. Jenny needs to add $2\frac{3}{4}$ and $1\frac{5}{8}$.
   She must find a common denominator. What improper fractions, expressed in terms of the lowest common denominator, correspond to the two numbers?

5. Clark is baking cookies. He needs $2\frac{1}{2}$ cups of flour. What arithmetic equation properly expresses the number of times he needs to fill his $\frac{1}{2}$ cup measuring cup to equal $2\frac{1}{2}$ cups?

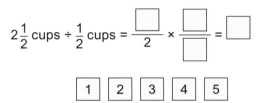

$$2\frac{1}{2} \text{ cups} \div \frac{1}{2} \text{ cups} = \frac{\square}{2} \times \frac{\square}{\square} = \square$$

| 1 | 2 | 3 | 4 | 5 |

DIRECTIONS: Examine the information and number line. Then read the question and use the drag-and-drop options to complete the answer.

The following number line shows the interval from 0 to 1, divided into 20 equal segments.

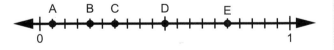

6. In increasing order, list the fractional values of the points shown, reduced to lowest terms.

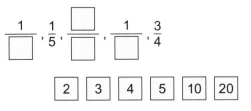

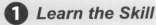

LESSON 5

Ratios and Proportions

MATH CONTENT TOPICS: Q.2.a, Q.2.e, Q.3.a, Q.3.c
MATH PRACTICES: MP.1.a, MP.1.b, MP.1.e, MP.2.c, MP.4.a

UNIT 1

1 Learn the Skill

A **ratio** is a comparison of two numbers. You can write a ratio as a fraction, using the word *to*, or with a colon (:). A **proportion** is an equation with a ratio on each side. The ratios are equal. You can use proportions to solve problems involving equal ratios.

2 Practice the Skill

By practicing the skill of solving ratios and proportions, you will improve your study and test-taking abilities, especially as they relate to the GED® Mathematical Reasoning Test. Study the information below. Then answer the question that follows.

a A ratio is different from a fraction. The bottom or second number of a ratio does not necessarily represent a whole. Therefore, you do not need to rename improper fractions as mixed numbers. However, ratios still should be simplified.

b A **unit rate** is a ratio with the denominator of 1. It can be expressed using the word *per*.

c In a proportion, the cross products are equal. Use cross products to solve proportions. If one of the four terms is missing, cross-multiply and divide the product by the third number (the number uninvolved in the cross-product) to find the missing number.

Ratio

Jonathan earns $10 in 1 hour.

The ratio of dollars earned to hours is $\frac{10}{1}$, 10 to 1, or 10:1.

This also can be written as $10 per hour.

Proportion

$\frac{3}{4} = \frac{6}{8}$

$4 \times 6 = 8 \times 3$
$24 = 24$

$\frac{9}{12} = \frac{3}{x}$ $\longrightarrow$ $9x = 12 \times 3$
$9x = 36$
$x = 4$

USING LOGIC

When you write a proportion to solve a problem, the terms in both ratios need to be written in the same order. In problem 1, the top numbers can represent gallons and the bottom numbers can represent cost.

1. Carleen bought 3 gallons of milk for $12. How much would 4 gallons of milk cost?

A. $9
B. $12
C. $16
D. $18

10

Lesson 5 | Ratios and Proportions

DIRECTIONS: Read each question, and choose the **best** answer.

2. Sam averages 65 miles per hour on a road trip. How many hours will it take him to drive 260 miles?

    A. 3
    B. 4
    C. 5
    D. 6

3. The Jammers basketball team had a win-to-loss ratio of 5:1 during their season. They won 25 games. How many games did they lose?

    A. 5
    B. 6
    C. 7
    D. 8

4. A store sold 92 pairs of pants and 64 shirts. What is the ratio of the number of pants sold to the number of shirts sold?

    A. 23:16
    B. 16:23
    C. 64:92
    D. 16:92

5. Amanda traveled 558 miles in 9 hours. What is the unit rate that describes her travel?

    A. 52 miles per hour
    B. 61 miles per hour
    C. 62 miles per hour
    D. 71 miles per hour

6. Jill mixed 2 cups of sugar with 10 cups of water to make lemonade. What ratio of sugar to water did she use?

    A. $\frac{1}{5}$
    B. $\frac{2}{10}$
    C. $\frac{5}{1}$
    D. $\frac{10}{2}$

DIRECTIONS: Read each question, and choose the **best** answer.

7. The GED® preparation class has a teacher-to-student ratio of 1:12. If there are 36 students in the class, how many teachers are present?

    A. 2
    B. 3
    C. 4
    D. 6

8. Sarah can ride 4 miles in 20 minutes on her bike. How many miles can she bike in 120 minutes?

    A. 12
    B. 15
    C. 24
    D. 480

9. The ratio of adults to children on a field trip is 2:7. If there are 14 adults on the trip, how many children are there?

    A. 1
    B. 7
    C. 28
    D. 49

10. The ratio of cars to trucks at an auto dealership is $\frac{3}{2}$. If there are 144 cars at the dealership, how many trucks are there?

    A. 288
    B. 240
    C. 216
    D. 96

11. In the recent college football season, Max threw 32 touchdowns and only 12 interceptions. In the most simplified form, what was his ratio of touchdowns to interceptions thrown?

    A. 16:6
    B. 8:3
    C. 8:2
    D. 4:1

Decimals

MATH CONTENT TOPICS: Q.1.a, Q.2.a, Q.2.e, Q.6.c
MATH PRACTICES: MP.1.a, MP.1.b, MP.1.e, MP.2.c, MP.3.c, MP.4.a

UNIT 1

1 Learn the Skill

A **decimal** is another way to write a fraction. It uses the base-ten place value system. You can compare and order decimals using place value. Decimals include place values such as tenths, hundredths, and thousandths. Decimals can represent amounts much smaller than 1. You can round decimals as you do whole numbers.

As with fractions, you can add, subtract, multiply, and divide decimal numbers. When you perform operations with decimals, you must pay close attention to the placement of the decimal point. For example, when you add or subtract, write the numbers so that the place values and decimal points align.

2 Practice the Skill

By practicing the skill of operations with decimals, you will improve your study and test-taking abilities, especially as they relate to the GED® Mathematical Reasoning Test. Study the table and information below. Then answer the question that follows.

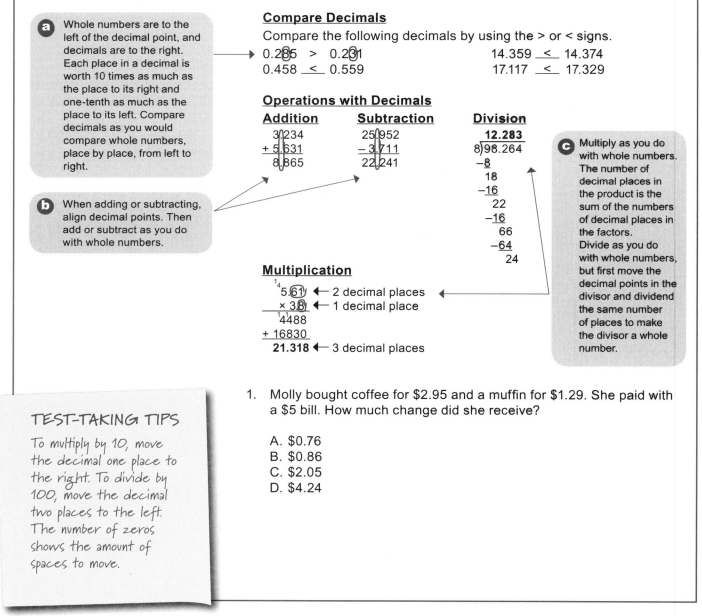

a Whole numbers are to the left of the decimal point, and decimals are to the right. Each place in a decimal is worth 10 times as much as the place to its right and one-tenth as much as the place to its left. Compare decimals as you would compare whole numbers, place by place, from left to right.

b When adding or subtracting, align decimal points. Then add or subtract as you do with whole numbers.

Compare Decimals

Compare the following decimals by using the > or < signs.

0.285 > 0.231   14.359 _<_ 14.374
0.458 _<_ 0.559   17.117 _<_ 17.329

Operations with Decimals

Addition
```
  3.234
+ 5.631
  8.865
```

Subtraction
```
  25.952
−  3.711
  22.241
```

Division
```
      12.283
  8)98.264
   −8
    18
   −16
     22
    −16
     66
    −64
     24
```

c Multiply as you do with whole numbers. The number of decimal places in the product is the sum of the numbers of decimal places in the factors.
Divide as you do with whole numbers, but first move the decimal points in the divisor and dividend the same number of places to make the divisor a whole number.

Multiplication
```
    1 4
   5.61   ← 2 decimal places
 ×  3.8   ← 1 decimal place
  1 4
   4488
+ 16830
  21.318  ← 3 decimal places
```

TEST-TAKING TIPS

To multiply by 10, move the decimal one place to the right. To divide by 100, move the decimal two places to the left. The number of zeros shows the amount of spaces to move.

1. Molly bought coffee for $2.95 and a muffin for $1.29. She paid with a $5 bill. How much change did she receive?

   A. $0.76
   B. $0.86
   C. $2.05
   D. $4.24

DIRECTIONS: Study the information and table, read each question, and choose the **best** answer.

Coach Steve needed to purchase new soccer equipment for the upcoming season.

Equipment	Price	Quantity
Soccer ball	$12.95	6
Shin guards	$10.95	12
Knee pads	$8.95	12
Uniforms	$17.00	12

2. How much will Coach Steve spend on uniforms and soccer balls?

   A. $47.95
   B. $97.80
   C. $211.77
   D. $281.70

3. How much more will Coach Steve spend on shin guards than knee pads?

   A. $16.00
   B. $24.00
   C. $36.00
   D. $48.00

DIRECTIONS: Study the information and table, read each question, and choose the **best** answer.

Sliced deli meat is sold by the pound. Shana bought four different meats at the deli.

Deli Meat	Weight
Chicken	1.59 pounds
Turkey	2.07 pounds
Ham	1.76 pounds
Roast beef	2.15 pounds

4. Which package of deli meat weighed the least?

   A. Chicken
   B. Turkey
   C. Ham
   D. Roast beef

5. How many packages of deli meat weighed less than 2.25 pounds?

   A. 1
   B. 2
   C. 3
   D. 4

DIRECTIONS: Read the question, and choose the **best** answer.

6. Paper Plus sells reams of paper for $5.25 each. Discount Paper sells the same reams of paper for $3.99 each. How much would you save by purchasing 15 reams of paper at Discount Paper instead of at Paper Plus?

   A. $1.26
   B. $18.90
   C. $78.75
   D. $138.60

DIRECTIONS: Study the information and table, read each question, and choose the **best** answer.

The Warriors softball team had five players competing for the league's batting title.

Player	Batting Average
Jennifer	.3278
Ellen	.3292
Krysten	.3304
Marti	.3289

7. Marti believes that if the season were to end today, she would have the highest batting average. Which explains the error in her reasoning?

   A. She found the lowest batting average.
   B. She compared digits in the tenths place.
   C. She rounded all batting averages to the nearest thousandth.
   D. She compared the digits moving right to left.

8. Which player had the highest batting average?

   A. Jennifer
   B. Ellen
   C. Krysten
   D. Marti

UNIT 1

Percent

MATH CONTENT TOPICS: Q.2.a, Q.2.e, Q.3.c, Q.3.d
MATH PRACTICES: MP.1.a, MP.1.b, MP.1.e, MP.2.c, MP.4.a

1 Learn the Skill

As with fractions and decimals, **percents** show part of a whole. Recall that, with fractions, a whole can be divided into any number of equal parts. With a decimal, the number of equal parts must be a power of 10. Percent always compares amounts to 100. The percent sign, %, means "out of 100."

There are three main parts of a percent problem—the base, the part, and the rate. The **base** is the whole amount. The **part** is a piece of the whole or base. The **rate** tells how the base and whole are related. The rate is always followed by a percent sign. You can use proportions to solve percent problems.

2 Practice the Skill

By practicing the skills of finding percents and solving percent problems, you will improve your study and test-taking abilities, especially as they relate to the GED® Mathematical Reasoning Test. Study the table and information below. Then answer the question that follows.

a To convert a fraction to a decimal, divide the numerator by the denominator. To convert a decimal to a fraction, write the decimal digits as the numerator and the place value of the last digit as the denominator. Simplify. To write a decimal as a percent, multiply by 100. Do the reverse to write a percent as a decimal. To write a percent as a fraction, write the percent as the numerator of a fraction with denominator 100, then simplify.

Fraction	Decimal	Percent
$\frac{1}{5}$	$1 \div 5 = 0.2$	$0.2 \times 100 = 20 \rightarrow 20\%$
$\frac{1}{4} = \frac{25}{100}$	$25 \div 100 = 0.25$	25%
$\frac{1}{2} = \frac{50}{100}$		50%

Use a Proportion

Zach answered 86% of the questions on a math exam correctly. If there were 50 questions, how many questions did Zach answer correctly?

$$\frac{\text{Part}}{\text{Base}} = \frac{\text{Rate}}{100} \quad \frac{?}{50} = \frac{86}{100} \quad 50 \times 86 = 4300 \rightarrow 4300 \div 100 = \textbf{43 questions}$$

b To find a percent of change, subtract the original amount from the new amount to find the amount of change. Divide the difference by the original amount. Convert the decimal to a percent. To compute interest (*I*), multiply the amount borrowed (*p*) by the rate (*r*), written as a decimal, and the time (*t*), written in years.

Find Percent Increase or Decrease

Last year, Kareem paid $750 a month in rent. This year he pays $820 a month. What's the percent increase?

$820 − $750 = $70.00
$70.00 ÷ $750 = 0.09
0.09 × 100 = **9%**

Interest Problems

Kelly took out a $20,000 loan for 4 years at 3% interest. How much interest (*I*) will she pay?

$I = prt$
$I = \$20{,}000 \times 0.03 \times 4$
$I = \textbf{\$2,400}$

USING LOGIC

Recall that a fraction is a ratio of part to whole. A percent is a ratio with a denominator of 100. When using a proportion, set the rate over 100 to equal the part over the base.

1. In a neighborhood, 27 of the 45 children are in elementary school. What percent of children in the neighborhood are in elementary school?

    A. 20%
    B. 40%
    C. 60%
    D. 166%

⭐ Spotlighted Item: **DROP-DOWN**

DIRECTIONS: Read each situation, and choose the option that **best** completes each sentence.

2. Shelly's Boutique is advertising 25% off all merchandise.

   Customers will save [Drop-down] off the original price during the sale.

   A. $\frac{1}{4}$ B. $\frac{1}{2}$ C. $\frac{2}{3}$ D. $\frac{3}{4}$

3. City Electric provides electricity for $\frac{1}{8}$ of the homes in Center City.

   City Electric provides electricity for [Drop-down] % of homes.

   A. 8   B. 10.5   C. 12.5   D. 80

4. In a survey, 0.22 of the respondents answered "Yes" to the question, "Would you consider voting for a candidate from a third party?"

   [Drop-down] of respondents answered "No."

   A. $\frac{11}{50}$ B. $\frac{39}{50}$ C. $\frac{78}{10}$ D. $\frac{22}{100}$

5. The Strikers girls soccer team won 9 of its 13 games.

   The Strikers won approximately [Drop-down] % of the games.

   A. 61.5   B. 66.7   C. 69.2   D. 76.9

6. At Bright Minds Learning, 75% of employees work as instructors. There are 300 employees at Bright Minds Learning.

   [Drop-down] employees work as instructors.

   A. 150
   B. 175
   C. 200
   D. 225

DIRECTIONS: Read each situation, and choose the option that **best** completes each sentence.

7. Tia earns $552 per week. Of this amount, 12% is deducted for taxes.

   $ [Drop-down] is deducted each week.

   A. 6.62   B. 55.20   C. 66.24   D. 485.76

8. Andrew received a raise from $24,580.00 per year to $25,317.40 per year.

   He received a raise of [Drop-down] %.

   A. 2   B. 3   C. 7.4   D. 29

9. Isabelle paid $425 plus 6% sales tax for a new bicycle.

   She paid a total of $ [Drop-down].

   A. 25.50   B. 27.50   C. 450.50   D. 457.50

10. A sofa is regularly priced at $659 but is on sale for 20% off.

    The sale price of the sofa is $ [Drop-down].

    A. 639.00   B. 527.20   C. 450.80   D. 131.80

11. A computer company received 420 customer service calls in one day. Forty-five percent of the calls were about software issues.

    [Drop-down] of the calls were about software.

    A. 19   B. 189   C. 229   D. 231

12. Daria invested $5,000 in an account that earns 5% interest annually.

    She will earn $ [Drop-down] in interest over nine months.

    A. 5,250.00
    B. 1,875.00
    C. 250.00
    D. 187.50

Unit 1 Review

DIRECTIONS: Read each question, and choose the **best** answer.

1. Two-thirds of Mrs. Jensen's class passed the science exam. If there are 24 students in her class, how many passed the exam?

   A. 13
   B. 14
   C. 15
   D. 16

2. Dina purchased a new dining room table for $764.50 and four new chairs for $65.30 each. What was the cost of the whole set?

   A. $829.80
   B. $895.10
   C. $1,025.70
   D. $1,091.00

3. The Martins drove 210.5 miles on the first day of their trip and 135.8 miles the second day. How many more miles did they drive the first day than the second day?

   A. 74.7
   B. 149.4
   C. 271.6
   D. 346.3

4. Erin must add $4\frac{1}{2}$ cups of flour to her cookie batter using a $1\frac{1}{2}$-cup measuring cup. How many times will she need to fill the measuring cup with flour?

   A. one
   B. two
   C. three
   D. four

5. What is the smallest whole number that has both 6 and 8 as factors?

   A. 14
   B. 18
   C. 24
   D. 48

DIRECTIONS: Read each question, and choose the **best** answer.

6. A new movie has opening-day ticket sales of $21,343,845. How is 21,343,845 written in words?

   A. Twenty-one million, three hundred and forty-three thousand, eight hundred forty-five
   B. Twenty-one million, three hundred forty-three thousand, eight hundred forty-five
   C. Twenty-one million, three forty-three thousand, eight hundred forty-five
   D. Twenty-one million, three hundred forty-three thousand, eight four-five

7. Not including 1 and 24, how many whole numbers are factors of 24?

   A. 4
   B. 5
   C. 6
   D. 7

DIRECTIONS: Study the information and table below, read each question, and choose the drop-down option that **best** answers each question.

The table shows the breakdown of after-school options for students at Oak Ridge Elementary School.

WHAT STUDENTS DO AFTER SCHOOL

Option	Number of Students
Parent pickup	118
Walk	54
Bus	468
After-school programs	224

8. What fraction of students walk home? Drop-down

   A. $\frac{1}{48}$ B. $\frac{1}{32}$ C. $\frac{1}{16}$ D. $\frac{3}{16}$

9. What fraction of students take the bus or stay after school? Drop-down

   A. $\frac{56}{117}$ B. $\frac{468}{864}$ C. $\frac{117}{216}$ D. $\frac{173}{216}$

DIRECTIONS: Read each question, and choose the **best** answer.

10. Kara invested $1,250 in the production of a friend's music CD. Her friend paid her back at 6% simple annual interest after 36 months. How much money did Kara get back?

    A. $225
    B. $1,025
    C. $1,325
    D. $1,475

11. Ken needs a cable that is $4\frac{3}{4}$ meters long. He has a cable that is $5\frac{1}{3}$ meters long. What fraction of a meter will Ken need to cut off?

    A. $\frac{1}{2}$
    B. $\frac{7}{12}$
    C. $\frac{2}{3}$
    D. $\frac{3}{4}$

12. Evan is developing a table of population data for cities in his state and is rounding the numbers to the nearest hundred. What would he enter for a city with a population of 93,548?

    A. 93,500
    B. 93,550
    C. 93,600
    D. 94,000

13. Fred receives a phone call from his accountant and is told that his investments gained one hundred three thousand, seven hundred fifty dollars in value during the past 12 months. What number would Fred write down?

    A. $103,705
    B. $103,715
    C. $103,750
    D. $130,750

DIRECTIONS: Read the question, and choose the **best** answer.

14. Tracy bought two pretzels for $1.95 each and two soft drinks for $0.99 each. If she paid with a $10 bill, how much change did she receive?

    A. $4.12
    B. $5.11
    C. $5.88
    D. $7.06

DIRECTIONS: Study the information and table below, read each question, and choose the drop-down option that **best** answers each question.

A number of women participate in five different intramural college sports. The fraction of women who participate in each sport is shown in the table.

WOMEN'S INTRAMURAL SPORTS

Sport	Fraction of Women
Basketball	$\frac{1}{6}$
Volleyball	$\frac{1}{20}$
Soccer	$\frac{1}{3}$
Ultimate frisbee	$\frac{1}{5}$
Lacrosse	$\frac{1}{4}$

15. In which sport do the greatest number of women participate? | Drop-down |

    A. Basketball
    B. Volleyball
    C. Soccer
    D. Lacrosse

16. What fraction of women participate in lacrosse and basketball? | Drop-down |

    A. $\frac{2}{10}$ B. $\frac{5}{12}$ C. $\frac{1}{2}$ D. $\frac{1}{3}$

17. What percent of women participate in volleyball and ultimate frisbee? | Drop-down |

    A. 4% B. 5% C. 20% D. 25%

DIRECTIONS: Read each question. Then write your answer in the box below.

18. Benjamin drove a distance of 301.5 miles in 4.5 hours. If Benjamin drove at a constant rate, how many miles per hour did he drive?

19. Scarlett purchased 20 shares of AD stock at $43 per share. She sold the 20 shares at $52 per share. How much money did Scarlett make on her investment?

20. A group of 426 people is going to a rally. Each bus can take 65 people. What is the minimum number of buses needed?

21. What is $[(-1) \times 2 \times (-3) \times 4 \times (-5)]$ divided by 6?

22. The proportion of students to chaperones for a school trip is required to be no more than 7 to 1. If 45 students go on the trip, what is the minimum number of chaperones that must accompany the students?

23. Donovan rode 135 miles on his bike at a unit rate of 27 miles per hour. How many hours did he spend riding?

24. Steak on sale at the local grocery store costs $8 per pound. How many dollars would $3\frac{1}{2}$ pounds cost?

DIRECTIONS: Read the question. Then write your answer in the box below.

25. What number is the largest common factor of both 18 and 42?

DIRECTIONS: Study the information and table below, read each question, and choose the **best** answer.

Kurt and his family went to the state fair. They ate lunch at a wild game restaurant. The menu is shown below.

MENU AT THE STATE FAIR

Item	Price
Walleye fillet	$5.89
Elk sandwich	$9.65
Wild boar barbecue	$9.19
Salmon on a stick	$5.45
Kid's buffalo platter	$3.50

26. What is the most expensive item on the menu?

A. Walleye fillet
B. Elk sandwich
C. Wild boar barbecue
D. Salmon on a stick

27. Kurt ordered 1 wild boar barbecue, 1 walleye fillet, and 3 kid's buffalo platters. If he brought $50 with him to the fair, how much does he have left?

A. $18.58
B. $24.42
C. $25.58
D. $31.42

28. How much more do 2 elk sandwiches cost than 3 kid's platters?

A. $6.15
B. $7.88
C. $8.80
D. $15.80

29. Alice typed her income into tax-preparation software. If her income was fifty-six thousand, two hundred, twenty-eight dollars, which series of digits did she type?

    A. 5, 6, 2, 2, 0, 8
    B. 5, 0, 6, 2, 2, 8
    C. 5, 6, 2, 0, 8
    D. 5, 6, 2, 2, 8

30. Delaney has $198 in her checking account. She deposits $246 and writes checks for $54 and $92. How much is left in her account?

    A. $98
    B. $298
    C. $482
    D. $590

31. The ratio of men to women in a chorus is 2:3. If there are 180 women in the chorus, how many men are in the chorus?

    A. 72
    B. 108
    C. 120
    D. 270

32. Anna can knit a scarf in $1\frac{2}{3}$ hours. How many scarves can she knit in 4 hours?

    A. $2\frac{2}{5}$

    B. $2\frac{3}{3}$

    C. 3

    D. $3\frac{1}{5}$

33. Eighty-four percent of student athletes attended a preseason meeting. If there are 175 student athletes, how many attended the meeting?

    A. 28
    B. 84
    C. 128
    D. 147

34. Thirty-five percent of residents surveyed were in favor of creating a new road. The remaining residents objected. If 1,200 people were surveyed, how many objected to the new road?

    A. 780
    B. 420
    C. 360
    D. 35

35. Tom makes $200 per week working a part-time job. He pays $300 per month for his share of the rent where he lives. How much money does he have left for other expenses in one year?

    A. $1,200
    B. $5,200
    C. $6,000
    D. $6,800

DIRECTIONS: Study the table below, read each question, and choose the best answer.

BICYCLE TRAINING OVER THE WEEKEND

Miles Biked	
Jackson	26.375
Ben	$25\frac{4}{5}$
Stefan	32.95

36. How many more miles did Stefan ride than Ben?

    A. 7
    B. 7.15
    C. $7\frac{3}{5}$
    D. 7.25

37. The distance Stefan rode is greater than the distance Jackson rode by about what percent?

    A. 23%
    B. 24%
    C. 25%
    D. 26%

DIRECTIONS: Study the information and table below, read each question, and choose the **best** answer.

During an election year, 200 people were surveyed about their political affiliation. The results are shown in the table.

VOTERS' POLL

Party Affiliation	Number of People
Democratic	78
Republican	64
Independent	46
Green	10
Libertarian	2

38. What is the ratio of Green Party supporters to Libertarian Party supporters?

A. 5 to 1
B. 1 to 5
C. 10 to 1
D. 2 to 10

39. If 400 people were surveyed, how many would you expect to affiliate themselves with the Democratic Party?

A. 278
B. 156
C. 78
D. 39

40. What percentage of those surveyed was neither Democrat nor Republican?

A. 71%
B. 59%
C. 41%
D. 29%

DIRECTIONS: Read each question, and choose the **best** answer.

41. The population of a city grew from 43,209 to 45,687 in just five years. What was the percent increase in the population to the nearest whole percent?

A. 4%
B. 5%
C. 6%
D. 7%

42. Fifty-four percent of customers at a grocery store bought milk on Friday. What fraction of the customers is this?

A. $\frac{27}{50}$

B. $\frac{14}{25}$

C. $\frac{9}{17}$

D. $\frac{3}{5}$

43. Rodrigo pays $165.40 per month on his car loan. How much does he pay on his loan in 1 year?

A. $992.40
B. $1,654.00
C. $1,984.80
D. $3,969.60

44. A muffin recipe calls for $1\frac{3}{8}$ cups of oil. If Sean triples the recipe, how many cups of oil does he need?

A. $3\frac{1}{8}$ cups

B. $4\frac{1}{8}$ cups

C. $4\frac{1}{4}$ cups

D. $4\frac{3}{8}$ cups

45. A certain type of cheese sells for $8.99 per pound. What is the cost of a 1.76-pound block of cheese?

A. $5.10
B. $14.38
C. $15.80
D. $15.82

46. If the cost of a home mortgage is $324,000 over 15 years, how much does one have to pay each month (not including interest)?

    A. $1,800
    B. $2,160
    C. $3,600
    D. $21,600

DIRECTIONS: Study the information and table, read each question, and choose the **best** answer.

The following table lists the average daily receipts for a seafood restaurant during a typical week.

CATCH-BY-THE-SEA RESTAURANT SALES

Restaurant Receipts	
Monday	$14,960
Tuesday	$14,610
Wednesday	$13,430
Thursday	$16,420
Friday	$21,100
Saturday	$29,280
Sunday	$25,460

47. List in decreasing order of receipts the five days with the greatest sales.

    A. Saturday, Sunday, Friday, Thursday, Monday
    B. Saturday, Sunday, Friday, Monday, Thursday
    C. Saturday, Sunday, Friday, Thursday, Tuesday
    D. Saturday, Sunday, Friday, Monday, Tuesday

48. Which day has the lowest receipts?

    A. Monday
    B. Tuesday
    C. Wednesday
    D. Thursday

49. Based on the table, what sales trend can you identify?

    A. Sales decrease steadily during the weekdays.
    B. People are more likely to eat at the restaurant on the weekends.
    C. Sales increase steadily from Friday through Sunday.
    D. Weekend specials help boost the profits of the restaurant.

DIRECTIONS: Read each question, and choose the **best** answer.

50. Fred and Mary take Joe out to lunch for his birthday. Fred's meal costs $13, Mary's meal costs $15, and Joe's meal costs $16. If Fred and Mary split the entire cost and a $10 tip evenly between them, how much do they each pay?

    A. $18
    B. $22
    C. $27
    D. $54

51. At a school bake sale, students sold 125 chocolate cookies, 89 oatmeal cookies, 32 sugar cookies, and 56 coconut cookies. How would the cookie types be listed if ordered from least sold to most sold?

    A. Chocolate, oatmeal, coconut, sugar
    B. Chocolate, oatmeal, sugar, coconut
    C. Sugar, coconut, chocolate, oatmeal
    D. Sugar, coconut, oatmeal, chocolate

52. Justina deposits $2,000 per month into her checking account. Payments for mortgage, car loan, utilities, and property taxes totaling $2,300 per month are withdrawn automatically. If she makes no other transactions, what is the change in her checking account balance (and not including any bank fees or penalties) after one year?

    A. −$3,600
    B. −$300
    C. $300
    D. $3,600

53. A plane drops 300 feet, rises 240 feet, drops 180 feet, and rises 130 feet. What is the height of the plane now relative to its initial height?

    A. −410 feet
    B. −190 feet
    C. 190 feet
    D. 410 feet

DIRECTIONS: Read each question, and choose the **best** answer.

54. If −15 is subtracted from a number, the result is −12. What is that number?

   A. −27
   B. −3
   C. 3
   D. 27

55. Sara has $1,244 in her checking account. She deposits a check for $287 and withdraws $50 cash. What is her new balance?

   A. $1,294
   B. $1,481
   C. $1,531
   D. $1,581

56. Ellie has a pass that allows her to drive through tolls without stopping to pay. The amount of the toll is automatically charged to her credit card. She pays a fee of $5 per month for this service. Each toll she pays is $1.25. She budgets $65 a month for her total toll bill. What is the maximum number of tolls she can pass through each month and still stay within her budget?

   A. 12
   B. 24
   C. 48
   D. 60

57. A skier takes a chairlift 786 feet up the side of a mountain. He then skis down 137 feet and catches a different chairlift 542 feet up the mountain. What is his position when he gets off the chairlift relative to where he got on the first chairlift?

   A. −1,191 feet
   B. −381 feet
   C. +381 feet
   D. +1,191 feet

DIRECTIONS: Read the question, and choose the **best** answer.

58. Each day for three days, Emmit withdrew $64 from his account. Which number shows the change in his account after the three days?

   A. −$192
   B. −$128
   C. $128
   D. $192

DIRECTIONS: Study the information and table, read each question, and choose the **best** answer.

The following table lists the monthly expenses for a small business.

SOMETHING'S BREWING COFFEE SHOP

Monthly Expenses	
Salaries	$38,400
Rent	$3,600
Utilities	$800
Supplies	$1,200
Misc	$1,600

59. What are the total monthly expenses for the business?

   A. $31,200
   B. $38,400
   C. $44,000
   D. $45,600

60. What are the total monthly expenses excluding employee salaries?

   A. $3,600
   B. $7,200
   C. $31,200
   D. $38,400

61. What percent of the expenses are used for supplies and miscellaneous expenses, to the nearest tenth of a percent?

   A. 15.8%
   B. 7.3%
   C. 6.1%
   D. 2.6%

DIRECTIONS: Study the information and table, read each question, and choose the **best** answer.

The following table lists what Morgan, Tom, and Dana scored in each round of a game.

SCORE FOR EACH ROUND

Round	1	2	3	4	5	6	7	8	9
Morgan	1	0	3	1	−1	1	−1	0	1
Tom	0	−1	1	0	2	1	−1	2	0
Dana	2	1	2	0	1	0	−1	−1	−2

62. What was Morgan's final score?

   A. 2
   B. 3
   C. 4
   D. 5

63. List the three friends in order of their final scores, from lowest to highest.

   A. Morgan, Tom, Dana
   B. Morgan, Dana, Tom
   C. Dana, Tom, Morgan
   D. Dana, Morgan, Tom

DIRECTIONS: Examine the information and number line, read each question, and write your answer in the box below.

The number line shown below represents the temperatures at three different times during the day.

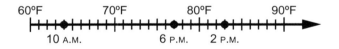

64. What was the change in temperature from 10 A.M. to 6 P.M.?

[ ]

65. What was the change in temperature from 2 P.M. to 6 P.M.?

[ ]

DIRECTIONS: Read each question, and use the drag-and-drop options to complete each answer.

66. Select two numbers that render the following fractional expression undefined. Note that there may be more than one possible answer.

$$\frac{5 - \boxed{}}{(2)\boxed{} - 6}$$

| 2 | 3 | 4 | 5 | 6 |

67. A grocery store stocker places 15 gallons of whole milk, 20 gallons of 2% milk, 20 gallons of 1% milk, and 20 gallons of skim milk in the case. What fraction of the milk stocked was whole milk?

$$\frac{\boxed{}}{\boxed{}}$$

| 1 | 3 | 5 | 7 | 10 | 20 |

68. In increasing order, list the fractional values of the three points, reduced to lowest terms.

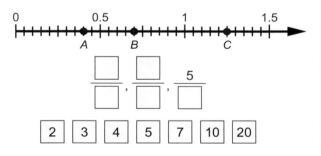

$$\frac{\boxed{}}{\boxed{}}, \frac{\boxed{}}{\boxed{}}, \frac{5}{\boxed{}}$$

| 2 | 3 | 4 | 5 | 7 | 10 | 20 |

69. What is the magnitude of the difference between $\frac{7}{10}$ and $\frac{5}{4}$, expressed as a fraction reduced to lowest terms?

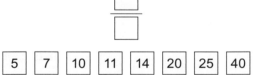

$$\frac{\boxed{}}{\boxed{}}$$

| 5 | 7 | 10 | 11 | 14 | 20 | 25 | 40 |

70. Four thousand circuits underwent electrical testing. Ninety three of every one hundred circuits tested passed inspection. Write a proportional relationship that could be used to find the number of circuits that passed.

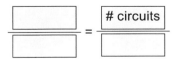

$$\frac{\boxed{}}{\boxed{}} = \frac{\text{\# circuits}}{\boxed{}}$$

| 93 | 100 | 4,000 |

GED® JOURNEYS

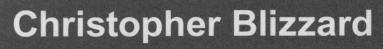

Christopher Blizzard

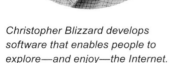

Christopher Blizzard develops software that enables people to explore—and enjoy—the Internet.

"Computing is an increasingly important part of the way that we create our lives—online and off. The rights that we enjoy in society are ... closely tied with how we interact with software and hardware."

Christopher Blizzard likes to cast a wide—and free—'Net. As a leading expert in the math-heavy world of Web-based software development, Blizzard believes that the Internet should remain a public resource accessible by all. To that end, Blizzard, who earned his GED® certificate in 1994, helps develop software that allows people to explore the Internet.

For years, Blizzard served as the Director of Web Platform at Mozilla, a leading developer of open-source software. There, he helped lead the Internet's migration from an online document storage compartment into an array of dynamic software that today runs on computers, mobile phones, tablets, and even televisions.

Blizzard has been a longtime contributor to various open-source projects, most notably for Mozilla and the One Laptop per Child (OLPC) project. Mozilla's best-known product, the Internet browser Firefox, launched in 2005. Since then, it has been downloaded more than 1 billion times worldwide.

The goal of One Laptop per Child involves demonstrating the effectiveness of laptops as learning tools for children in developing countries. In the effort, Blizzard sought to create an engaging social environment in which children could both learn and share together.

A longtime believer in and practitioner of social media, Blizzard in 2012 brought his talents to Facebook and its 1 billion monthly users. At Facebook, Blizzard serves as the company's Developer Relations lead.

CAREER HIGHLIGHTS: *Christopher Blizzard*

- Worked for one of the leading providers of open-source software
- Contributes to open-source projects, such as One Laptop per Child
- Worked previously as systems engineer and software developer
- Served on Mozilla Foundation's Board of Directors

Measurement/Data Analysis

Unit 2: Measurement/ Data Analysis

Each time you step on a scale, plan a trip, or cook a meal, you use skills related to measurement and data analysis. The growing use of computers and the Internet has assisted in the collection, storage, and interpretation of large sets of data. Such information often is presented in graphs.

Skills used to measure and analyze data are important both to your everyday life as well as to your success on the GED® Mathematical Reasoning Test. In Unit 2, you will study different measurement systems and forms of measurement, along with probability and visual ways of displaying data. Such skills will help you prepare for the GED® Mathematical Reasoning Test.

Table of Contents

UNIT 2

Professionals across various industries use electronic databases and the Internet to collect, store, and interpret data.

Measurement and Units of Measure

MATH CONTENT TOPICS: Q.2.a, Q.2.e, Q.3.a, Q.3.c, Q.6.c
MATH PRACTICES: MP.1.a, MP.1.b, MP.1.d, MP.1.e, MP.2.c, MP.3.a, MP.4.a

❶ Learn the Skill

When solving measurement problems, you either will use the U.S. customary system or the metric system. Units of measure in the **U. S. customary system** include inch and foot (length), ounce and pound (weight), and pint and quart (capacity). Units of measure in the **metric system** include centimeter and meter (length), gram and kilogram (mass), and milliliter and liter (capacity).

Time is a universal measure that is measured in standard units such as seconds, minutes, hours, days, weeks, months, and years. The **elapsed time** time between two events is the amount of time that has passed from one time to another. Many problems involving time use the formula **distance = rate × time**.

❷ Practice the Skill

By practicing the skill of using measurement systems and converting among units of measure within each system, you will improve your study and test-taking abilities, especially as they relate to the GED® Mathematical Reasoning Test. Read the information and strategies below. Then answer the question that follows.

U.S. CUSTOMARY UNITS OF MEASURE

Length	**Liquid Capacity**	**Weight**
1 foot (ft) = 12 inches (in.) 1 yard (yd) = 3 feet 1 mile (mi) = 5,280 feet 1 mile = 1,760 yards	1 cup (c) = 8 fluid ounces (fl oz) 1 pint (pt) = 2 cups 1 quart (qt) = 2 pints 1 gallon (gal) = 4 quarts	1 pound (lb) = 16 ounces (oz) 1 ton (t) = 2,000 pounds

METRIC UNITS OF MEASURE

ⓐ When you convert and rename a unit in the metric system, multiply or divide by 10, 100, or 1,000. The following prefixes can help in making metric conversions:

milli- means $\frac{1}{1,000}$

centi- means $\frac{1}{100}$

deci- means $\frac{1}{10}$

deca- means 10
hecto- means 100
kilo- means 1,000

Length
1 kilometer (km) = 1,000 meters (m) 1 meter = 100 centimeters (cm) 1 centimeter = 10 millimeters (mm)

Capacity	**Mass**
1 kiloliter (kL) = 1,000 liters (L) 1 liter = 100 centiliters (cL) 1 centiliter = 10 milliliters (mL)	1 kilogram (kg) = 1,000 grams (g) 1 gram = 100 centigrams (cg) 1 centigram = 10 milligrams (mg)

TIME

Time
1 hour (h) = 60 minutes (min) 1 minute = 60 seconds (s)

TEST-TAKING TIPS

When converting from a lesser unit (e.g., deciliter) to a greater unit (e.g., liter), divide by 10 for each step on the ladder. When converting from a greater unit to a lesser unit, multiply by 10 for each step.

1. Dante mixes 30 milliliters of one liquid with 2 centiliters of a second liquid. How many centiliters of liquid does he have altogether?

   A. 5 cL
   B. 32 cL
   C. 50 cL
   D. 302 cL

UNIT 2

Spotlighted Item: **FILL-IN-THE-BLANK**

DIRECTIONS: Read each question, and then write your answer in the box below.

2. Samantha is building a miniature maze for a science experiment. She determines that she needs 6 yards of wood for the exterior walls and 12 feet of the same wood for the interior walls. How many feet of wood must she buy in order to build her maze?

3. A 40 g ball of yarn is 125 m long. What is the mass of a ball of the same yarn that is 2 km long?

4. Over a two-day track meet, Jason ran in one 2-kilometer race, two 1,500-meter races, and five 100-meter races. How many meters did Jason run over the two days?

5. In August of 2012, Usain Bolt was named the fastest man in the world when he completed a 200-meter race in 19.32 seconds. Assuming he traveled at a constant speed, how much time did he take to run 1 meter?

DIRECTIONS: Read each question, and choose the **best** answer.

6. Mr. Trask wants to fill his four hummingbird feeders with liquid food. Two feeders hold 6 fluid ounces each. One larger feeder holds 1 cup of liquid. The largest feeder holds 1 pint. How many fluid ounces of liquid food does Mr. Trask need to fill the four bird feeders?

   A. 14 fl oz
   B. 28 fl oz
   C. 30 fl oz
   D. 36 fl oz

7. Additive Manufacturing uses 3-D printers to build 3-D solids by adding material layer by layer. If plastic flows from the printer at a rate of 10 mL per second, what is the total amount of plastic released after 1 hour?

   A. 3.6 L
   B. 10 mL
   C. 36 L
   D. 100 mL

DIRECTIONS: Study the table, read each question, and choose the **best** answer.

The table below shows approximate data for three oil spills over the past two decades.

Oil Spill	Duration of Spill	Quantity of Oil Spilled
A	5 hrs	287,000 kL
B	8 hrs	260,000 L
C	30 min	292,000 L

8. Which disaster had the highest spill rate?

   A. Oil Spill A
   B. Oil Spill B
   C. Oil Spill C
   D. They all had equal rates of spill.

9. At the end of the first 30 minutes, what was the greatest quantity of oil leaked into the sea by oil spill A, B, or C?

   A. 287,000 kL
   B. 292,000 L
   C. 260,000 L
   D. 28,700 kL

Length, Area, and Volume

MATH CONTENT TOPICS: Q.2.a, Q.2.e, Q.4.a, Q.4.c, Q.4.d, Q.5.a, Q.5.f
MATH PRACTICES: MP.1.a, MP.1.b, MP.1.c, MP.1.e, MP.2.c, MP.3.a, MP.4.a

1 Learn the Skill

The distance around a polygon, such as a triangle or rectangle, is its **perimeter**. To determine the perimeter of a polygon, measure and add the lengths of its sides. **Area** is the amount of space that covers a two-dimensional figure. Area is measured in square units. The area of a rectangle is the product of its width and length.

Three-dimensional figures have **volume**, or the amount of space that exists inside a figure. Volume is measured in cubic units. A rectangular prism is a three-dimensional figure with rectangular sides, shaped like a box. The volume of a rectangular prism is the product of its length, height, and width. The **surface area** of a rectangular prism is the sum of the areas of its six sides. A **cube** is a special kind of rectangular prism that has six square, congruent sides.

2 Practice the Skill

By practicing the skills of measuring lengths and finding the perimeter, area, and volume, you will improve your study and test-taking abilities, especially as they relate to the GED® Mathematical Reasoning Test. Read the example and strategies below. Then answer the question that follows.

Workers at Aqua Construction Company have designed a backyard pool surrounded by a tiled area. The dimensions of the pool are: 5 cm (width), 2 cm (length), and 4 cm (depth). Each centimeter on the blueprint represents 3 feet on the actual structure.

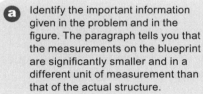

a Identify the important information given in the problem and in the figure. The paragraph tells you that the measurements on the blueprint are significantly smaller and in a different unit of measurement than that of the actual structure.

b The volume of a rectangular prism, or a square prism, is the area of the base times the height. The formula for volume of a rectangular prism is length × width × height ($l × w × h$). Since all sides of a cube measure the same length, the volume of a cube is $l × l × l$.

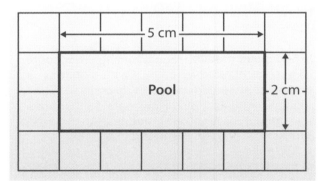

1. What is the **actual** volume of the swimming pool?

   A. 40 cubic feet
   B. 90 meters squared
   C. 1,080 cubic feet
   D. 10 centimeters squared

INSIDE THE ITEMS

Always check the units you are working with carefully. Remember, measures of area are always given in square units, while measures of volume are given in cubic units.

DIRECTIONS: Study the figures, read each question, and choose the **best** answer.

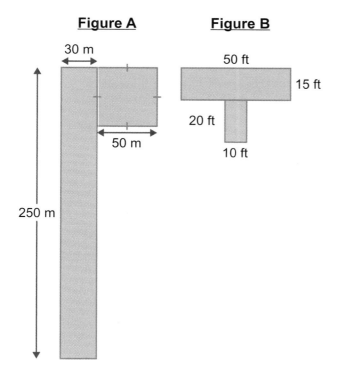

Figure A   **Figure B**

2. What is the area of Figure A?

    A. 750 square meters
    B. 310 square meters
    C. 1 square kilometer
    D. 10,000 square meters

3. What is the perimeter of Figure A?

    A. 360 m
    B. 460 m
    C. 560 m
    D. 660 m

4. What is the area of Figure B?

    A. 1,700 sq ft
    B. 950 sq ft
    C. 150 sq ft
    D. 95 sq ft

5. If 1 meter = 3.28 feet, find the difference in perimeter between Figure A and Figure B.

    A. 1994.8 ft
    B. 1328.8 ft
    C. 280 ft
    D. 640 ft

6. If Figure B is the top view of a storage container that is 30 feet deep, what is the volume of the water tank?

    A. 2,250 cubic feet
    B. 5,100 cubic feet
    C. 13,800 cubic feet
    D. 28,500 cubic feet

DIRECTIONS: Read each question, and choose the **best** answer.

7. A rectangular prism has a volume of 600 cubic feet. If the length is 20 feet, and the width is 15 feet, what is the height of the prism?

    A. 2 ft³
    B. 2 ft
    C. 300 ft
    D. 300 ft²

8. Mary uses 56 inches of yarn to form a rectangle. If the rectangle is 4 inches wide, what is its length?

    A. 4 inches
    B. 8 inches
    C. 48 inches
    D. 24 inches

9. A cube has volume of 27 cubic feet. What is the length of its base?

    A. 9 ft
    B. 6 ft
    C. 3 ft
    D. 1 ft

10. Mr. Peters recently opened a new distribution center for his company. The floor has an area of 2 square kilometers, and the volume is 1 cubic kilometer. What is the height of the distribution center?

    A. 5 km
    B. 0.5 km
    C. 2 km
    D. 2.5 km

Mean, Median, and Mode

MATH CONTENT TOPICS: Q.2.a, Q.2.e, Q.6.c, Q.7.a
MATH PRACTICES: MP.1.a, MP.1.b, MP.1.c, MP.1.e, MP.2.c, MP.3.a

① Learn the Skill

Mean, median, mode, and range are values used to describe a set of data. The **mean** is the average value of a data set. The **median** is the middle number in a set of data when the values are ordered from least to greatest. In the number set 23, 24, 28, 30, and 75, the median is 28—meaning it's greater than half of the numbers in the set and less than the other half. Note that the median was unaffected by the number 75, which is much larger than the other numbers in the set. In this case, the median more accurately describes the set than the does the mean (36).

The **mode** is the value that occurs most frequently in a set of data. In the number set 23, 24, 24, 28, 30, and 75, 24 is the mode. The **range** is the difference between the greatest value and the least value in a set of data. In the above example, the range is 52.

② Practice the Skill

By practicing the skills of finding mean, median, mode, and range, you will improve your study and test-taking abilities, especially as they relate to the GED® Mathematical Reasoning Test. Read the example and strategies below. Then answer the question that follows.

ⓐ To find the median of a data set, list the values in order from least to greatest. The number 65 is listed three times in the table. When ordering numbers, be sure to list 65 three times.

ⓑ When a number set consists of an odd number of values, the middle number is the median. When the set consists of an even number of data points, find the mean of the two middle numbers. Note that the median may not be a number in the set of data. It could be a different whole number, or a decimal.

Felipe measured and recorded the heights of runners participating in a neighborhood relay race.

HEIGHTS OF RELAY RACE RUNNERS

Runner	Height (inches)
Carol	63
Steven	68
Pedro	65
Julia	65
Chantell	67
Camille	64
Frank	72
William	71
Jane	65
Jake	72

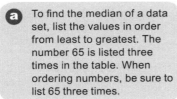

USING LOGIC

There are 10 values in the table. When listing values from least to greatest, check that you listed a total of 10 values, including repetitions of the same value.

1. What is the median height of the runners?

   A. 65 inches
   B. 65.2 inches
   C. 66 inches
   D. 67 inches

DIRECTIONS: Study the information and table, read each question, and choose the **best** answer.

The running times of a YMCA-sponsored 100-meter race are shown below.

TIMES FOR THE 100-METER RACE

Runner	Time (seconds)
David	13.5
Sanya	16
Jeremy	12.6
Erica	15.2
Chen	12.8
Yusuf	11.8
Matt	17.2
Sarah	12.1

2. What is the range of the runners' times in the 100-meter race?

   A. 4.2 s
   B. 5.4 s
   C. 6.4 s
   D. 13.9 s

3. What is the median time in the race?

   A. 5.4 s
   B. 12 s
   C. 13.15 s
   D. 13.9 s

4. What is the difference between Sarah's time and the mean time of the runners?

   A. 1.35 s
   B. 1.8 s
   C. 13.9 s
   D. 13.15 s

5. Describe the relationship between the median and mean in the above race times.

   A. The median was slightly less than the mean.
   B. The median was slightly greater than the mean.
   C. The median and mean were the same.
   D. The mode was greater than both the median and the mean.

DIRECTIONS: Study the information and table, read the question, and choose the **best** answer.

The owner of Ice Cream Palace listed the number of milk shakes sold each day for one week.

DAILY MILK SHAKE SALES

Day	Mon.	Tues.	Wed.	Thurs.	Fri.	Sat.
Milk Shakes Sold	22	16	20	26	24	85

6. Which value best describes the number of milk shakes sold at Ice Cream Palace on a typical summer day?

   A. 20
   B. 21.6
   C. 23
   D. 32.16

DIRECTIONS: Study the information and table, read the question, and choose the **best** answer.

Sneaker sales at Sneaker World were recorded each day for one week.

SNEAKER WORLD SALES

Day	Total Sales
Monday	$5,229
Tuesday	$3,598
Wednesday	$6,055
Thursday	$3,110
Friday	$3,765
Saturday	?

7. The mean sales for this one week were $4,443. The manager misplaced her records for Saturday. What were the sales on Saturday?

   A. $458
   B. $4,901
   C. $4,987
   D. $9,344

DIRECTIONS: Read the question, and choose the **best** answer.

8. Dex scores 80%, 75%, 79%, and 83% percent on his final exams. Which of the following represents his mean score in percent form?

   A. 79.25%
   B. 79.5%
   C. 83%
   D. 317%

Probability

MATH CONTENT TOPICS: Q.1.b, Q.2.e, Q.8.b
MATH PRACTICES: MP.1.a, MP.1.b, MP.1.e, MP.2.c, MP.3.a

1 Learn the Skill

When you flip a coin, you have an equal chance of flipping heads or tails. The chance of it landing on heads can be expressed as 1:2, where 1 represents the number of favored outcomes (flipping heads) and 2 represents the number of possible outcomes. This ratio expresses the **theoretical probability** of the event. In theory, each time you flip a coin, you have a 50% chance of flipping heads. You can express theoretical probability as a fraction ($\frac{1}{2}$), ratio (1:2), or percent (50%).

Probability based on the results of an experiment is called **experimental probability**. As with theoretical probability, you can express experimental probability as a fraction, ratio, or percent. If you toss a quarter 10 times and get heads 6 times, the experimental probability is $\frac{6}{10}$, which simplifies to $\frac{3}{5}$.

2 Practice the Skill

By practicing the skill of probability, you will improve your study and test-taking abilities, especially as they relate to the GED® Mathematical Reasoning Test. Read the example and strategies below. Then answer the question that follows.

a By choosing a striped marble from the bag during the first event and not replacing it, Marc affected the outcome of the second event. The two events are said to be **dependent**. When events are dependent, the number of outcomes changes.

If Marc had replaced the marble after the first event, the first event would not have affected the outcome of the second event. In this case, the first event and the second event would have been **independent**.

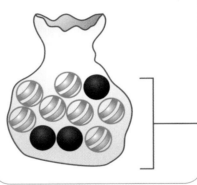

A bag of 10 marbles contains 7 striped marbles and 3 black marbles.

b Probability can be expressed as a ratio. If the bag contained two black marbles and three striped marbles, the probability of drawing a black marble would be 2:5, meaning that there are two black marbles and five possible outcomes. The same probability can be expressed as a fraction ($\frac{2}{5}$), as a decimal (0.4), and as a percent (40%).

a

1. In the first event, Marc draws a striped marble. He does not replace it. In the next three events, Marc draws 2 striped marbles and 1 black marble. He does not replace those marbles, either. What is the probability that he will select a black marble on the fifth event?

   A. 1:10
   B. 1:3
   C. 2:7
   D. 2:3

DIRECTIONS: Study the spinner, read each question, and choose the **best** answer.

Maude uses this spinner to conduct a probability experiment.

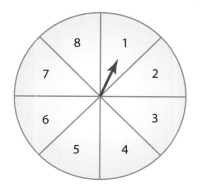

2. On the first spin, what is the probability that the spinner will land on 6?

   A. 1:8
   B. 1:7
   C. 1:6
   D. 6:8

3. On the second spin, what is the probability that the spinner will land on 4 or 8?

   A. 0.48
   B. 0.28
   C. 0.25
   D. 0.16

4. Maude spins the spinner twice. She lands on 4 and 6. So far, what is her experimental probability of spinning an odd number?

   A. $\frac{0}{2}$
   B. $\frac{1}{6}$
   C. $\frac{1}{8}$
   D. $\frac{1}{1}$

5. Maude spins the spinner two times. What is the probability she lands on an odd number and then the number 2?

   A. 0.5
   B. 0.0625
   C. 0.5
   D. 0.625

DIRECTIONS: Examine the information and table, read each question, and choose the **best** answer.

A large chain store keeps track of its daily customer complaints.

COMPLAINT CALLS

Department	Number of Complaints
Electronics	6
Housewares	4
Automotive	2
Clothing	3

6. What is the probability that the next complaint call to the store will concern the clothing department?

   A. 20%
   B. 25%
   C. 30%
   D. 50%

7. What is the probability that the next complaint call will concern the electronics department or the housewares department?

   A. $\frac{4}{15}$
   B. $\frac{1}{2}$
   C. $\frac{3}{5}$
   D. $\frac{2}{3}$

8. What is the probability that the next call will concern a department other than electronics?

   A. 0.2
   B. 0.4
   C. 0.6
   D. 1

DIRECTIONS: Read the question, and choose the **best** answer.

9. Ian read in the newspaper that there is a 40% chance of rain tomorrow. What is the probability that it will **not** rain tomorrow?

   A. $\frac{1}{25}$
   B. $\frac{3}{50}$
   C. $\frac{3}{5}$
   D. $\frac{1}{1}$

Bar and Line Graphs

MATH CONTENT TOPICS: Q.6.a, Q.6.c
MATH PRACTICES: MP.1.a, MP.2.c, MP.3.a, MP.4.c, MP.5.a

1 Learn the Skill

Graphs organize and present data visually. **Bar graphs** use vertical or horizontal bars to show and often compare data. **Line graphs** often show how a data set changes over time. Graphs may include scales and keys that give detail about the data.

Scatter plots are a type of line graph that show how one set of data affects another. The relationship between data sets is known as its **correlation.** A correlation may be positive (extending upward from the origin to *x*- and *y*-points), or negative (extending downward from the *y*-axis to the *x*-axis), or it may not exist at all.

2 Practice the Skill

By practicing the skill of interpreting bar and line graphs, you will improve your study and test-taking abilities, especially as they relate to the GED® Mathematical Reasoning Test. Read the example and strategies below. Then answer the question that follows.

ⓐ Multiple sets of data can appear on a bar graph or a line graph. When it occurs in a line graph, such as this one, you will see two or more line patterns. The lines usually will appear in different colors, as they do in this graph.

ⓑ When using a graph, first examine its different parts. The title describes the topic of the graph. Labels along the vertical and horizontal axes describe the data. The scale of the vertical axis shows the interval being used. You will find categories along the horizontal axis. This line graph also has a key that shows the color code used for the two different parks.

This line graph shows the monthly rainfall through the spring and summer at two state parks.

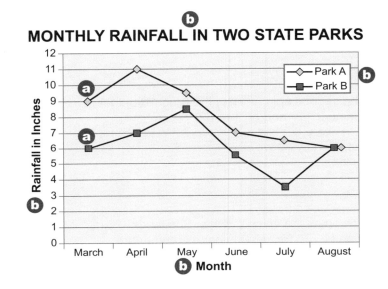

1. During which month was the difference in rainfall between the two parks the greatest?

A. March
B. April
C. June
D. July

TEST-TAKING TECH

Some of the questions on the GED® Mathematical Reasoning Test will require you to interact on-screen with a graph or grid by clicking on it to select the correct answer. These items are called hot spots.

Spotlighted Item: **HOT SPOT**

DIRECTIONS: Study the information and graph, and read each question. Then mark on the graph the **best** answer to each question.

Fred records the long jump results in a track meet. He creates the following bar graph to show the results online.

LONG JUMP RESULTS

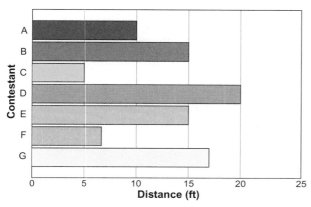

2. Which contestant jumped exactly half as far as the contest winner? Circle that bar on the graph.

3. Katie and Alana jumped the same distance. How far did they jump? Circle the distance in the scale on the graph.

4. Place an **X** on the name of the participant that disproves the statement "No contestant jumped farther than 18 feet."

5. Contestant C significantly improved his long jump on his next attempt. In fact, he tripled his previous distance. Record Contestant C's new distance on the graph by extending his bar to the proper distance.

6. Contestant D foot-faulted on his last attempt, so he reverts to his previous best distance of 17 feet. Adjust Contestant D's result by drawing a line on his bar at the correct new long distance.

DIRECTIONS: Study the information and scatter plot, and read the question. Then mark on the scatter plot the **best** answer to each question.

An educational company compared student scores on the GED® Mathematical Reasoning Test with the amount of hours they prepared for it. Their findings are shown in the scatter plot below.

STUDY TIME FOR GED® MATH TEST

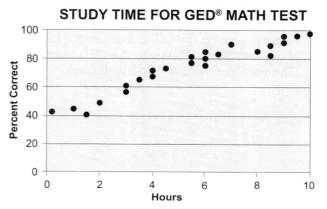

7. Anton hopes to earn at least an 80% on the GED® Mathematical Reasoning Test. Circle on the scale the amount of hours that Anton should plan to study for the test.

DIRECTIONS: Study the information and graph, and read the question. Then mark on the graph the **best** answer to each question.

The following graph shows the effect that increasing levels of education have on earnings.

8. Circle on the graph the levels of education that resulted in unemployment below the national average in 2012.

EDUCATION PAYS

Unemployment rate in 2012 (%) | Median weekly earnings in 2012 ($)

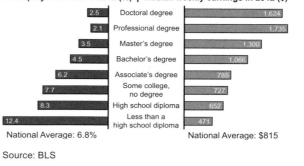

National Average: 6.8%   National Average: $815

Source: BLS

UNIT 2

Circle Graphs

MATH CONTENT TOPICS: Q.6.a
MATH PRACTICES: MP.1.a, MP.1.b, MP.2.c, MP.3.a, MP.4.c

1 Learn the Skill

Like bar and line graphs, circle graphs show data visually. Whereas a line graph shows how data changes over time, a **circle graph** shows how parts of data compare to a whole. For example, a circle graph of sales from each department in a store can show at a glance the most productive department, as well as how each department's sales compares to that of the whole store.

Values of circle graph sections may be expressed as fractions, decimals, percents, or even as whole numbers. In some cases, you may need to convert from one form to another, such as from fractions to percents.

2 Practice the Skill

By practicing the skill of interpreting circle graphs, you will improve your study and test-taking abilities, especially as they relate to the GED® Mathematical Reasoning Test. Study the graph and information below. Then answer the question that follows.

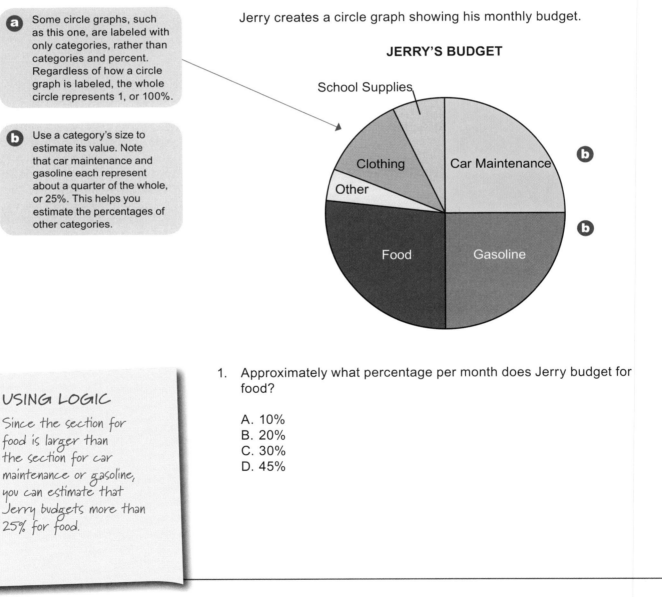

a Some circle graphs, such as this one, are labeled with only categories, rather than categories and percent. Regardless of how a circle graph is labeled, the whole circle represents 1, or 100%.

b Use a category's size to estimate its value. Note that car maintenance and gasoline each represent about a quarter of the whole, or 25%. This helps you estimate the percentages of other categories.

Jerry creates a circle graph showing his monthly budget.

JERRY'S BUDGET

USING LOGIC

Since the section for food is larger than the section for car maintenance or gasoline, you can estimate that Jerry budgets more than 25% for food.

1. Approximately what percentage per month does Jerry budget for food?

A. 10%
B. 20%
C. 30%
D. 45%

⭐ Spotlighted Item: **DRAG-AND-DROP**

DIRECTIONS: Study the graph and table. Then complete the graph by writing the labels in the correct sections of the graph.

2. **SOURCES OF TUITION MONEY**

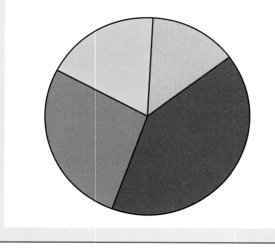

Financial Aid	45%
Salary	30%
Scholarships	20%
Parents	15%

DIRECTIONS: Study the information and graph, read the question, and choose the **best** answer.

The circle graph below shows the methods of transportation that employees use to get to work.

HOW EMPLOYEES GET TO WORK

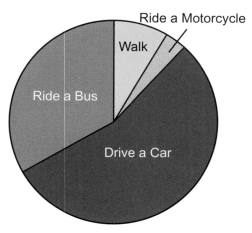

3. About what part of the employee population drives a car to work?

A. 25%
B. 30%
C. 50%
D. 60%

DIRECTIONS: Study the information and graph, read the question, and choose the **best** answer.

A library creates a circle graph of the types of books checked out by readers last September.

WHAT PEOPLE READ LAST SEPTEMBER

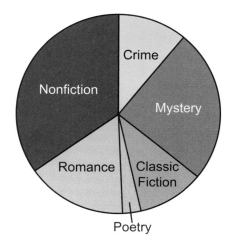

4. Which categories of books could a librarian make the best argument to order this August?

A. nonfiction and mystery
B. mystery and romance
C. nonfiction and crime
D. classic fiction and poetry

Dot Plots, Histograms, and Box Plots

MATH CONTENT TOPICS: Q.2.a, Q.2.e, Q.6.b, Q.7.a
MATH PRACTICES: MP.1.a, MP1.b, MP.1.e, MP.2.c, MP.3.a, MP.4.a, MP.4.c

1 Learn the Skill

Dot plots provide a quick and easy way of organizing sets of data with modest numbers of values (e.g., those less than 50). They consist of a number line on which each occurrence of a value is noted by a dot; the number of dots associated with each value indicates the frequency of that value in the data set. **Histograms** are made up of adjoining bars of equal width. A histogram's bars have lengths that correspond to an associated scale. Unlike dot plots, histograms may be used with any size data set and are used to show frequency.

Box plots are a convenient way of showing and comparing sets of numerical data using five characteristics of each data set: the median value, the lower (25%) and upper (75%) quartile values, and the maximum and minimum values.

2 Practice the Skill

By practicing the skills of representing, displaying, and interpreting data using dot plots, histograms, and box plots, you will improve your study and test-taking abilities, especially as they relate to the GED® Mathematical Reasoning Test. Study the information and plots below. Then answer the question that follows.

ⓐ A dot plot contains detailed information about a data set and allows for determination of quantities such as mean, mode, and range. For example, since there is an odd number of students (33), the median score value will be the 17th value (8), counting in from either end. This appears as the mid-line in the box plot.

ⓑ Since the median value is an actual data point, that data point is not considered to be part of the upper or lower halves of the data set. The *lower quartile* is the median of the lower half of the data set. The *upper quartile* is the median of the upper half of the data set. Since there are 16 points in each half, the quartile values will be half-way between the 8th and 9th data values. In the case of the upper quartile, both values are 9; the upper quartile value then is 9. This appears as the upper bound of the box in the box plot.

A class of 33 students takes a 10-point quiz. The following dot plot (top) and box plot (bottom) represent the distribution of student scores.

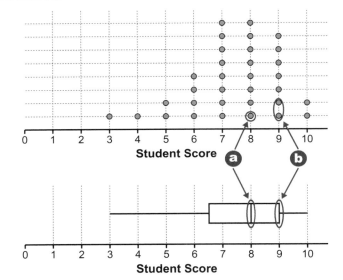

USING LOGIC

The circled points were found by counting from left to right, starting at the top of each column of dots. You can check your work by counting from right to left, also starting at the top of each column of dots.

1. Using the dot plot, what is the lower quartile student score for this quiz?

A. 6
B. 6.5
C. 7
D. 7.5

DIRECTIONS: Study the information and dot plot, read each question, and choose the **best** answer.

A sleep study is conducted on 40 people for one week. The average number of hours of sleep per night per subject is rounded to the nearest hour. The tabulated results are shown in the following dot plot.

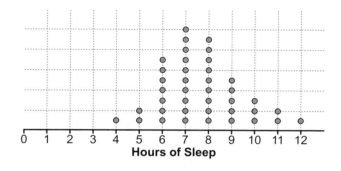

Hours of Sleep

2. What is the median value of the hours of sleep reported in this study?

    A. 6.5 h
    B. 7 h
    C. 7.5 h
    D. 8 h

3. What is the mode value of the distribution?

    A. 6.5 h
    B. 7 h
    C. 7.5 h
    D. 8 h

4. What is the range of the distribution?

    A. 4 h
    B. 5 h
    C. 7 h
    D. 8 h

5. How many subjects had 9 hours of sleep?

    A. 5
    B. 6
    C. 7
    D. 9

DIRECTIONS: Study the information and histogram, read the question, and choose the **best** answer.

A new prime-time animated television comedy recently aired its first episode. Although targeted to young adults, the new show excited network officials because of its broader appeal across age groups. The histogram below illustrates the new show's ratings popularity—as measured in millions of viewers—across various age groups.

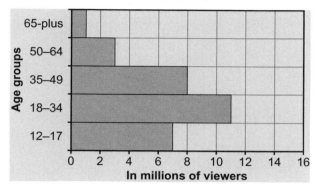

In millions of viewers

6. What pattern can you identify based on the viewership data?

    A. The show was equally popular among all age groups.
    B. The show was most popular among the 35–49 age group.
    C. The show enjoyed high ratings among teens and adults under 50.
    D. The show had little popularity among young viewers.

DIRECTIONS: Study the information and dot plot, read the question, and choose the **best** answer.

A teacher's class roster shows her students have the following ages.

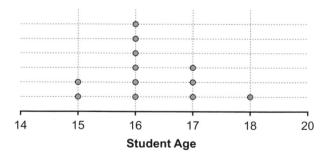

Student Age

7. What is the range of the data?

    A. 3
    B. 4
    C. 6
    D. 16

DIRECTIONS: Read each question, and choose the **best** answer.

1. An artist needs 840 feet of ribbon for an outdoor work of art. The company that manufactures the ribbon only sells it in large rolls of 100 yards. Given the information in the table, how many yards of ribbon does the artist want to use?

Length

1 foot (ft) = 12 inches (in.)
1 yard (yd) = 3 feet
1 mile (mi) = 5,280 feet
1 mile = 1,760 yards

A. 70 yd
B. 280 yd
C. 300 yd
D. 2,520 yd

2. A shoelace has a mass of 1 gram. A textbook has a mass of about 1 kilogram. Given the information in the table, how many shoelaces would you need to gather to have mass equal to that of two textbooks?

Mass

1 kilogram (kg) = 1,000 grams (g)
1 gram = 100 centigrams (cg)
1 centigram = 10 milligrams (mg)

A. 100
B. 200
C. 1,000
D. 2,000

3. A gardener is planting flowers along the edge of two triangular sections of a large garden, as shown below. Both triangular plots are the same size. What is the total perimeter of the two triangular garden plots?

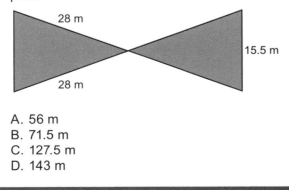

A. 56 m
B. 71.5 m
C. 127.5 m
D. 143 m

DIRECTIONS: Read each question, and choose the **best** answer.

4. An architect designs a dividing wall with three moveable sections, shown below, for a conference room at a large hotel. The two triangular shapes are the same size. When the three pieces fit together, what is the area of the dividing wall?

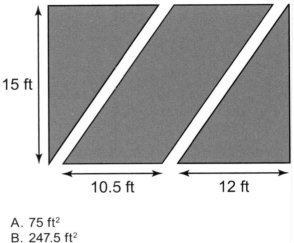

A. 75 ft²
B. 247.5 ft²
C. 337.5 ft²
D. 1890 ft²

5. Jane is making an ornament that consists of powders of different colors. She wants 250 grams of blue powder, 250 grams of silver powder, 300 grams of red powder, and 375 grams of green powder. How many kilograms of powder will Jane need altogether?

A. 1.175 kg
B. 11.75 kg
C. 117.5 kg
D. 1,175 kg

6. The flight distance between Boston and Chicago is approximately 850 miles. A commercial airliner leaves Boston at 11:30 A.M. The average speed of the plane is 500 mph. The time in Boston is one hour ahead of the time in Chicago. What time will it be in Chicago when the plane lands?

A. 12:12 P.M.
B. 1:12 P.M.
C. 1:42 P.M.
D. 2:12 P.M.

DIRECTIONS: Read the question, and choose the **best** answer.

7. Contractors installing a wire fence around two tennis courts need to find the perimeter so that they know how much fence to order. Each tennis court is 60 feet wide and 120 feet long. How much fencing do the contractors need to order to enclose the tennis courts with the margins shown?

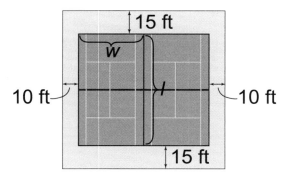

A. 290 ft
B. 360 ft
C. 520 ft
D. 580 ft

DIRECTIONS: Study the figures below, read each question, and choose the **best** answer.

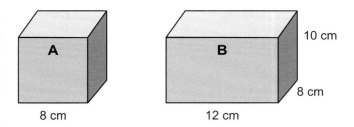

8 cm   12 cm

8. Container A is a cube. What is the volume of Container A in cubic centimeters?

A. 24 cm³
B. 64 cm³
C. 512 cm³
D. 384 cm³

9. Henry fills the two containers with water. How much water will he use?

A. 1,472 cm³
B. 1,024 cm³
C. 968 cm³
D. 54 cm³

DIRECTIONS: Study the information and table, read each question, and choose the **best** answer.

A cable television company asks a family to keep track of the number of hours they spend watching television. They record weekly data for two months.

WEEKLY TELEVISION VIEWING

Week	Hours Watched
1	21.5
2	28
3	15.5
4	23
5	29
6	34
7	27
8	35

10. To the nearest tenth, what is the mean number of hours watched each week by the family?

A. 26
B. 26.6
C. 27
D. 27.5

11. Which statement best describes the mean and the median?

A. The median is slightly greater than the mean.
B. The median and mean are equal.
C. The mean is slightly greater than the median.
D. The mean is significantly greater than the median.

12. What is the range of the weekly hours watched for the family?

A. 15.5
B. 18.5
C. 19.5
D. 35

DIRECTIONS: Study the information and figure below, read each question, and choose the **best** answer.

The die has one of the digits 1 through 6 on each side.

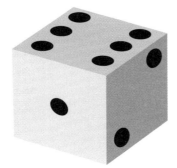

13. What is the probability of rolling an even number?

    A. 25%
    B. 33%
    C. 50%
    D. 66%

14. What is the probability of rolling a 2 or a 4?

    A. 25%
    B. 33.3%
    C. 50%
    D. 66.6%

15. A pair of die are rolled together. What is the probability, expressed as a fraction, of a roll that totals 2 or 4?

    A. $\frac{1}{18}$
    B. $\frac{1}{9}$
    C. $\frac{1}{6}$
    D. $\frac{1}{3}$

DIRECTIONS: Read each question, and choose the **best** answer.

16. Devaughn averages 45 mph driving along a mountain road. How many miles, expressed as a decimal, can Devaughn travel in 45 minutes?

    A. 60
    B. 52.5
    C. 45
    D. 33.75

17. Every evening, Mrs. Jackson walks around her neighborhood for a distance of about 1.25 miles. The walk usually takes her about 25 minutes. About how fast does she walk?

    A. 0.5 mph
    B. 1 mph
    C. 3 mph
    D. 5 mph

18. A hockey team traveling in a bus left one school at 11:50 A.M. They arrived at another school in the same time zone at 2:10 P.M. How long was the trip?

    A. 2 hours 20 min
    B. 2 hours 10 min
    C. 2 hours 00 min
    D. 1 hour 50 min

DIRECTIONS: Study the information and line graph, read each question, and choose the **best** answer.

A company keeps track of the bonuses its employees receive each year.

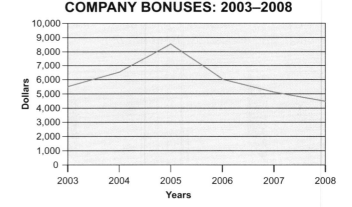

COMPANY BONUSES: 2003–2008

19. Between which two years did the amount of bonuses awarded show the greatest increase?
    Drop-down

    A. 2003–2004   C. 2005–2006
    B. 2004–2005   D. 2006–2007

20. During which year was the amount of bonuses awarded less than $5,000? Drop-down

    A. 2005   B. 2006   C. 2007   D. 2008

DIRECTIONS: Study the information and table, read each question, and use the drag-and-drop options to choose the **best** answer.

Four basketball players try shooting baskets from distances ranging from 5 feet to 30 feet, shooting 10 times at each distance. The table below shows how many times the different players made the shots.

Distance (ft)	Player 1	Player 2	Player 3	Player 4
5	10	9	10	8
10	10	8	9	7
15	9	7	8	5
20	6	7	5	2
25	3	1	2	0
30	1	0	0	0

21. A scatter plot of the results is shown below. Is the correlation positive or negative?

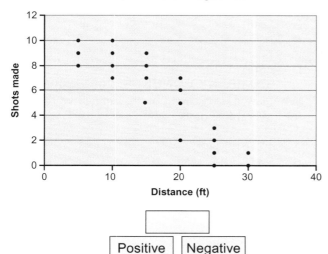

Positive | Negative

22. For which distance is the spread in performance the greatest?

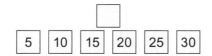

5 | 10 | 15 | 20 | 25 | 30

DIRECTIONS: Read each question, and choose the **best** answer.

23. A cardboard box has the dimensions shown below. If the length, width, and height were each doubled, what would be the new volume?

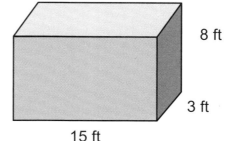

8 ft
3 ft
15 ft

A. 2,880 ft³
B. 1,440 ft³
C. 720 ft³
D. 52 ft³

24. A single six-sided die is rolled, and two coins are tossed at the same time. What is the probability, expressed as a fraction, of coming up with a three on the die, and two heads on the coins?

A. $\frac{1}{4}$

B. $\frac{1}{6}$

C. $\frac{1}{10}$

D. $\frac{1}{24}$

25. There are two green boxes and two red boxes. How many possible ways are there of arranging the boxes in a row?

A. 4
B. 6
C. 12
D. 24

26. If three six-sided dice are thrown, what is the probability, expressed as a fraction, that they will all come up with the same number?

A. $\frac{1}{6}$

B. $\frac{1}{12}$

C. $\frac{1}{36}$

D. $\frac{1}{216}$

DIRECTIONS: Read the question, and choose the **best** answer.

27. A pair of coins have been tossed two times and come up both heads each time. What is the probability, in percent, that the next time they are tossed, they will come up both heads?

    A. 1.56%
    B. 6.25%
    C. 12.5%
    D. 25%

DIRECTIONS: Study the diagram and information, read each question, and choose the **best** answer.

   The most popular game at a carnival is *Spin for Fortune*, shown below. The "Sorry" outcome means that the player does not win a prize.

28. What are the chances, expressed as a decimal, that a player spinning the wheel will win a prize?

    A. 0.5
    B. 0.375
    C. 0.25
    D. 0.125

29. Suppose a player really wants to win a cake. What are the chances of that player winning a cake, expressed in percent?

    A. 50%
    B. 37.5%
    C. 25%
    D. 12.5%

DIRECTIONS: Study the information and table, read each question, and choose the **best** answer.

   A public radio station is having a week-long fund drive. The results for the first five days are shown below.

RADIO STATION FUNDRAISER

Fund Drive Results	
Monday	$5,400
Tuesday	$6,200
Wednesday	$4,900
Thursday	$4,400
Friday	$7,600
Saturday	
Sunday	

30. What is the range of the daily fund-drive results so far?

    A. $1,600
    B. $3,200
    C. $4,400
    D. $7,600

31. What is the daily mean of the fund-drive results for the first five days?

    A. $4,750
    B. $5,400
    C. $5,700
    D. $7,125

32. What is the median of the fund-drive result for the first five days?

    A. $4,400
    B. $4,900
    C. $5,400
    D. $7,600

33. If the goal of the fund drive is $45,000, what must be the mean of the funds raised on Saturday and on Sunday?

    A. $16,500
    B. $8,250
    C. $6,430
    D. $5,110

DIRECTIONS: Study the information and table, read each question, and write the answer in the box below.

The following table lists what Morgan, Tom, and Dana scored on each round of a game.

SCORE FOR EACH ROUND

Round	1	2	3	4	5	6	7	8	9
Morgan	1	0	3	1	−1	1	−1	0	1
Tom	0	−1	1	0	2	1	−1	2	0
Dana	2	1	2	0	1	0	−1	−1	−2

34. Considering the scores of all three players together, what is the mean score to the nearest tenth?

35. Considering the scores of all three players together, what is the mode of the score distribution?

36. Construct a dot plot for the scores of the three players.

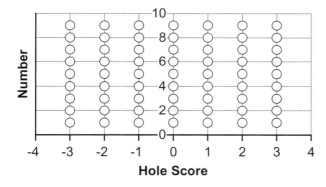

Hole Score

37. Construct a box plot for the scores of the three players.

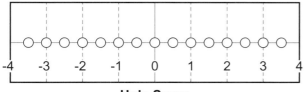

Hole Score

DIRECTIONS: Study the diagram and information, read each question, and write the answer in the box below.

The playing area of a football field is 100 yards long and 160 feet wide, as shown below.

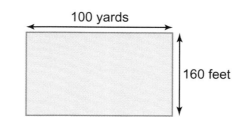

38. To the nearest tenth, how many times would one have to walk the length of the football field to have walked one mile?

39. To the nearest tenth, how many times would one need to walk around the perimeter of the football field to have walked one mile?

DIRECTIONS: Read the question, and choose the **best** answer.

40. Suppose one is given four cards, numbered 1 through 4. The cards are shuffled and dealt one at a time. What is the probability, expressed as a fraction, that they will be dealt in order, 1 first, then 2, then 3, and then 4?

   A. $\frac{1}{4}$

   B. $\frac{1}{6}$

   C. $\frac{1}{12}$

   D. $\frac{1}{24}$

DIRECTIONS: Study the information, then use the drag-and-drop options to complete each answer.

A banquet hall receives the following orders for a 60-person dinner.

DINNER ORDERS

Meal	Number
Steak	17
Fish	15
Pasta	12
Chicken	11
Vegetarian	5

41. Write the names of the various meals in the appropriate place in the bar graph below:

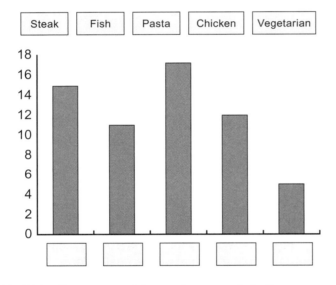

Steak   Fish   Pasta   Chicken   Vegetarian

42. Write the names of the various meals in the appropriate place in the circle graph:

Steak   Fish   Pasta   Chicken   Vegetarian

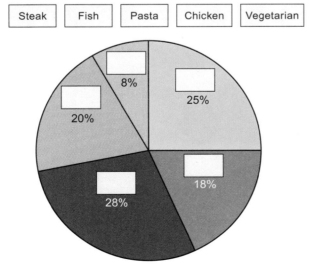

43. Which kind of graph is best for comparing the numbers of each kind of meal ordered with each other, and which is best for comparing the number of each kind of meal ordered with the total number of meals ordered? Write each graph in the proper box.

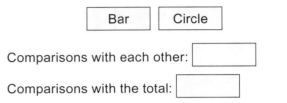

Bar   Circle

Comparisons with each other: _____

Comparisons with the total: _____

DIRECTIONS: Study the information and line graph, read each question, and choose the **best** answer.

The heights of three people during the first 20 years of their lives are plotted in the graph below.

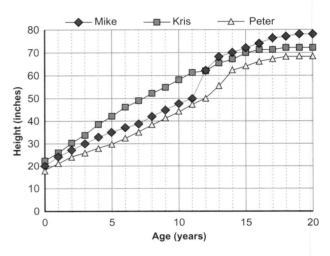

44. What is the order of the three people at age 10, from greatest to least height?

A. Mike, Kris, Peter
B. Mike, Peter, Kris
C. Kris, Mike, Peter
D. Kris, Peter, Mike

45. Which of the people experience the greatest change in height in one year, and at what age does that occur?

A. Peter in the year following his 13th birthday
B. Mike in the year following his 11th birthday
C. Kris in the year following her 10th birthday
D. Kris in the year following her 11th birthday

DIRECTIONS: Study the information and graphs, read each question, and choose the **best** answer.

The ethnic make-up of students at two different high schools is shown in the following circle graphs.

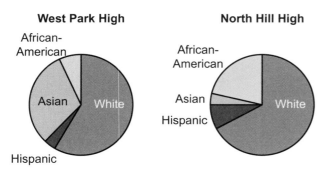

West Park High   **North Hill High**

46. What is the second largest ethnic group at West Park High?

   A. African-American
   B. Asian
   C. Hispanic
   D. White

47. What is the approximate ratio of the percentage of Hispanic students at West Park to the percentage of Hispanic students at North Hill?

   A. 1:2
   B. 1:3
   C. 2:1
   D. 3:1

DIRECTIONS: Study the information, and complete the plots indicated.

A basketball player scores the following points over the course of 25 games, ordered from least to greatest: 14, 14, 16, 16, 17, 17, 18, 18, 18, 19, 20, 20, 21, 21, 21, 22, 22, 23, 24, 24, 26, 27, 29, 30, 35.

48. Create a dot plot of the data.

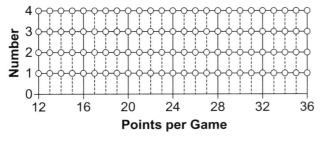

49. Create a histogram of the data, grouping data in four-point intervals indicated on the x-scale below.

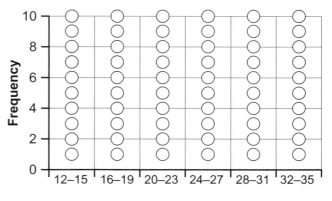

Points per Game

DIRECTIONS: Study the information and box plot, read each question, and choose the **best** answer from the drop-down choices given.

The diameters of four different batches of $\frac{1}{8}$-inch bolts are measured, and the distributions of the diameters are shown in the box plot below.

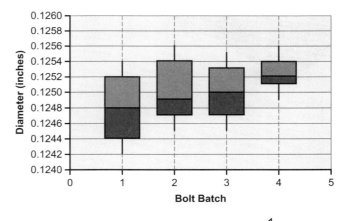

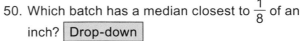

50. Which batch has a median closest to $\frac{1}{8}$ of an inch? | Drop-down |

   A. 1   B. 2   C. 3   D. 4

51. If the diameters are required to be between 0.1242 inch and 0.1252 inch in order to fit the corresponding nuts produced by the manufacturer, which batch will have the lowest reject rate? | Drop-down |

   A. 1   B. 2   C. 3   D. 4

GED® JOURNEYS

Philip Emeagwali

Philip Emeagwali used his success on the British version of the GED® Test as a springboard to multiple college degrees and a career in the field of supercomputing.

Philip Emeagwali is known as the "Bill Gates of Africa." It's easy to see why. As with Gates, the famed founder of Microsoft, Emeagwali left school before receiving his high school diploma. Like Gates, Emeagwali has enjoyed tremendous success in the computer industry.

Emeagwali, a native of Nigeria, left school when his family no longer could afford to pay for his education. He instead taught himself subjects such as mathematics, physics, chemistry, and English. Such efforts enabled Emeagwali to pass the General Certificate of Education exam (the British version of the GED® Test) and earn a scholarship to Oregon State University. It was only after Emeagwali arrived in the United States that he first used a telephone, visited a library, or saw a computer. Emeagwali graduated from Oregon State and went on to earn master's degrees in civil engineering, marine engineering, and mathematics.

Emeagwali's determination served as a springboard to his success in the field of supercomputing. In 1989, a computer program that he developed became the first to perform 3.1 billion calculations per second. Emeagwali used this program to help scientists understand how oil flowed underground. For his efforts, Emeagwali was awarded the prestigious Gordon Bell Prize, considered the Nobel Prize of computing.

"I find supercomputing to be a fascinating, challenging, and critical technology that can be used to solve many societal problems, such as predicting the spread of AIDS ..."

CAREER HIGHLIGHTS: *Philip Emeagwali*

- Invented a program for the Connection Machine, the fastest computer on Earth

- Designed a system of parallel computers used by search engines such as Yahoo

- Developed the Hyperball computer, which can forecast global-warming patterns

- Conducted research to help solve problems in the areas of meteorology, energy, health, and the environment

Algebra, Functions, and Patterns

Unit 3: Algebra, Functions, and Patterns

Algebra builds upon the core areas of mathematics, such as number sense, measurement, and data analysis, by translating everyday situations into mathematical language.

We use algebra to solve complex problems and to explore more sophisticated areas of mathematics. Certain jobs, such as those in high-tech fields, require strong backgrounds in algebra and other forms of higher mathematics.

Algebraic items make up 55 percent of questions on the GED® Mathematical Reasoning Test. In Unit 3, you will study algebraic expressions, equations, squares, cubes, exponents, factoring, graphing, slope, and other skills that will help you prepare for the GED® Mathematical Reasoning Test.

Many high-tech jobs today require advanced mathematics skills, especially in the area of algebra.

Table of Contents

Algebraic Expressions and Variables

MATH CONTENT TOPICS: Q.2.a, Q.2.e, A.1.a, A.1.c, A.1.g
MATH PRACTICES: MP.1.a, MP.1.b, MP.2.a, MP.4.a, MP.4.b

1 Learn the Skill

A **variable** is a letter used to represent a number. Variables are used in algebraic expressions. An **algebraic expression** has numbers and variables, sometimes connected by an operation sign.

A variable may change in value, which allows the expression itself to have different values. When you evaluate an algebraic expression, you substitute a number for the variable and solve. For example, if $b = 3$, then $b + 12 = 15$. If $b = -1$, then $b + 12 = 11$.

2 Practice the Skill

By practicing the skills of using variables and simplifying and evaluating algebraic expressions, you will improve your study and test-taking abilities, especially as they relate to the GED® Mathematical Reasoning Test. Study the example and strategies below. Then answer the question that follows.

a Order is important for division and subtraction. For example, "6 less than 3" is $3 - 6$, but "the difference between 6 and 3" is $6 - 3$.

b To simplify an expression, add like terms. Like terms have the same variable or variables raised to the same power. For example, $2x$ and $4x$ are like terms.

If an expression has parentheses, use the distributive property to simplify.

To evaluate an expression, substitute the given values for the variables, and then follow the order of operations.

Words	Symbols
4 more than a number	$x + 4$
5 less than a number	$x - 5$
3 times a number	$3x$
A number times itself	x^2
The product of 8 and a number	$8x$
The product of 6 and x added to the difference between 5 and x	$6x + (5 - x)$
The quotient of 6 and x	$\frac{6}{x}$ or $6 \div x$
One-third of a number increased by 5	$\frac{1}{3}x + 5$

Simplify $4x(5x + 7) - 2x$

$$(4x)(5x) + (4x)(7) - 2x$$
$$20x^2 + 28x - 2x$$
$$20x^2 + 26x$$

TEST-TAKING TIPS

Multiplication can be written in several ways. In algebraic expressions, a number next to a variable means multiplication. The expression $3y$ is the same as 3 times y. Parentheses and a dot also indicate multiplication: $3(y)$ and $3 \cdot y$ are the same as $3y$.

1. Gabe's current age is 3 times his sister's current age. If x is his sister's current age, which expression represents Gabe's current age?

   A. $3x$

   B. $\dfrac{x}{3}$

   C. $x - 3$

   D. $x + 3$

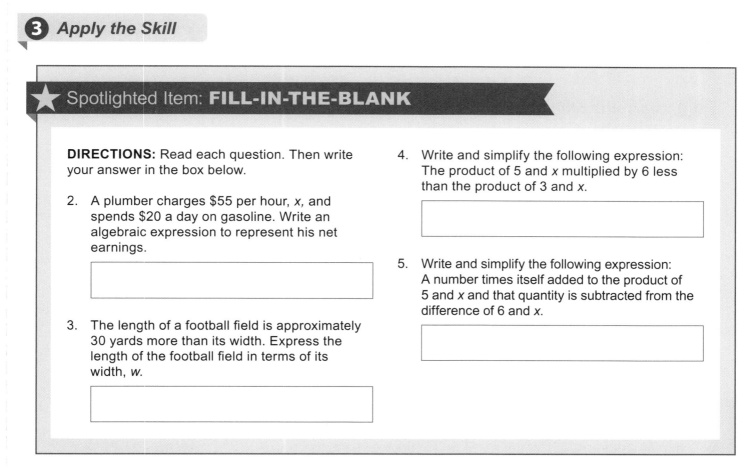

⭐ Spotlighted Item: **FILL-IN-THE-BLANK**

DIRECTIONS: Read each question. Then write your answer in the box below.

2. A plumber charges $55 per hour, *x,* and spends $20 a day on gasoline. Write an algebraic expression to represent his net earnings.

3. The length of a football field is approximately 30 yards more than its width. Express the length of the football field in terms of its width, *w*.

4. Write and simplify the following expression: The product of 5 and *x* multiplied by 6 less than the product of 3 and *x*.

5. Write and simplify the following expression: A number times itself added to the product of 5 and *x* and that quantity is subtracted from the difference of 6 and *x*.

DIRECTIONS: Study the information and figure, read each question, and choose the **best** answer.

The rectangle below has a length and width defined in terms of a variable, *w*, as shown.

$2w - 3$

6. Which expression represents the perimeter of the rectangle?

   A. $3w - 3$
   B. $w(2w - 3)$
   C. $5w - 3$
   D. $6w - 6$

7. Which expression represents the area of the rectangle?

   A. $w + 2w - 3$
   B. $w(2w - 3)$
   C. w^2
   D. $w + 2w - 3 + w + 2w - 3$

DIRECTIONS: Read each question, and choose the **best** answer.

8. The width of Kevin's yard is 10 feet more than twice the width of his garage. Which expression below describes the width of his yard if *g* represents the width of the garage?

   A. $2g(10)$
   B. $\frac{2g}{10}$
   C. $2g + 10$
   D. $2g - 10$

9. Michael's score on a math quiz was 8 more than one-half of his score on his science quiz. If *s* is his score on the science quiz, which expression below describes Michael's score on his math quiz?

   A. $\frac{s}{2} + 8$
   B. $\frac{s}{8} + 2$
   C. $\frac{1}{2}s - 8$
   D. $\frac{1}{2}(8) + s$

UNIT 3

Equations

MATH CONTENT TOPICS: Q.2.a, Q.2.e, A.1.b, A.1.c, A.2.a, A.2.c
MATH PRACTICES: MP.1.a, MP.1.b, MP.1.e, MP.2.a, MP.2.c, MP.4.a

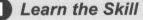

① Learn the Skill

As you recall, an algebraic expression uses numbers and variables, sometimes connected by an operation sign. However, expressions do not include equal signs. An **equation,** though, is a mathematical statement that shows an algebraic expression on each side of an equal sign. An equation may or may not contain variables.

To solve an equation, find the value of the variable that makes the statement true. To do this, isolate the variable on one side of the equation. Perform inverse operations to isolate the variable. Remember, addition and subtraction are inverse operations, as are multiplication and division.

② Practice the Skill

By practicing the skill of solving equations, you will improve your study and test-taking abilities, especially as they relate to the GED® Mathematical Reasoning Test. Study the information below. Then answer the question that follows.

ⓐ Perform inverse operations on *both* sides of the equation. When performing an operation on one side of an equation, do the same to the other side. Perform the inverse operations for addition and subtraction first and then for multiplication and division. When finished, substitute your solution for the variable into the equation to check your answer.

ⓑ Notes on solving equations:
- Some equations can be simplified before you solve. Combine like terms on either side of the equation.
- Some equations have two variables on both sides. In this case, group all of the variables on one side.

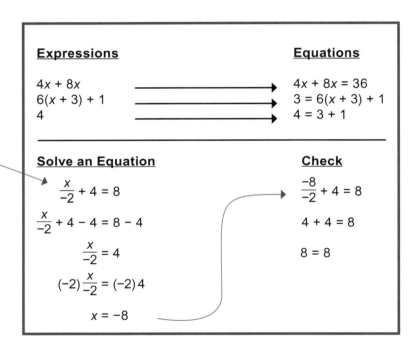

Expressions

$4x + 8x$
$6(x + 3) + 1$
4

Equations

$4x + 8x = 36$
$3 = 6(x + 3) + 1$
$4 = 3 + 1$

Solve an Equation

$$\frac{x}{-2} + 4 = 8$$

$$\frac{x}{-2} + 4 - 4 = 8 - 4$$

$$\frac{x}{-2} = 4$$

$$(-2)\frac{x}{-2} = (-2)4$$

$$x = -8$$

Check

$$\frac{-8}{-2} + 4 = 8$$

$$4 + 4 = 8$$

$$8 = 8$$

CONTENT TOPICS

If a situation has two unknown quantities or variables, you will need two equations to solve the problem. Solve one of the equations to find one of the variables, then substitute for that variable in the second equation.

1. Levi paid two bills. The cost of the two bills was $157. The second bill was $5 more than twice the amount of the first bill. Which of the following equations could be used to find the amount of the first bill?

   A. $5 - 2x = 157$
   B. $2x - 5 = 157$
   C. $x - (2x + 5) = 157$
   D. $x + (2x + 5) = 157$

DIRECTIONS: Read each question, and choose the **best** answer.

2. The sum of two consecutive integers is 15. Which equation could be used to find the first number?

   A. $x + 2x = 15$
   B. $2x + 1 = 15$
   C. $x - 1 = 15$
   D. $\frac{1}{2}x - 1 = 15$

3. The cost of an adult ticket to the ballet is $4 less than 2 times the cost of a child's ticket. If an adult ticket is $20, how much is a child's ticket?

   A. $8
   B. $10
   C. $12
   D. $14

4. Stephanie's age is 3 years greater than half of her sister's current age. If her sister is 24 years old, what is Stephanie's age?

   A. 12
   B. 15
   C. 17
   D. 21

5. The number of cellos in an orchestra is equal to 2 more than one-third of the number of violins. If there are 24 violins in the orchestra, how many cellos are there?

   A. 6
   B. 8
   C. 9
   D. 10

6. Caroline has twice as many yoga classes as aerobics classes. If she is taking 3 yoga and aerobics classes, which of the following equations could be used to find the number of aerobics classes she is taking?

   A. $3x = 3$
   B. $3x - 1 = 3$
   C. $2x - 1 = 3$
   D. $x = 3$

DIRECTIONS: Study the information, read the question, and choose the **best** answer.

The perimeter of the triangle is 16.5 feet.

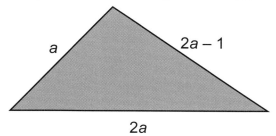

7. Which equation can be used to find the value of a?

   A. $5a - 1 = 16.5$
   B. $2a - 1 - a - 2a = 16.5$
   C. $a(2a - 1)(2a) = 16.5$
   D. $4a - 1 = 16.5$

DIRECTIONS: Read each question, and choose the **best** answer.

8. Four times a number is four less than two times the number. What is the number?

   A. -4
   B. -2
   C. 2
   D. 4

9. Julian collects rare political party convention pins. The number of Democratic Party pins he has is 14 less than 3 times the number of Republican Party pins he has. If he has 98 pins in all, how many Republican Party pins does he have?

   A. 14
   B. 28
   C. 42
   D. 70

10. If $y = 2.5$, what does x equal in the equation $10y - 4(y + 2) + 3x = 5(3 - x)$?

    A. 2
    B. 1
    C. -1
    D. -2

UNIT 3

Squaring, Cubing, and Taking Roots

MATH CONTENT TOPICS: Q.2.a, Q.2.b, Q.2.c, Q.2.d, Q.2.e, A.1.e
MATH PRACTICES: MP.1.a, MP.1.b, MP.1.e, MP.2.c, MP.3.a, MP.4.a, MP.4.b, MP.5.a, MP.5.b, MP.5.c

1 Learn the Skill

When a number or a variable is multiplied by itself, the result is called the **square** of that number or variable. Squaring the number 5, for example, is finding the product $5 \times 5 = 25$; this product is written as 5^2, where the ^{2} indicates that the product is composed of two factors of 5.

When a number or variable is multiplied by itself an additional time, the result is called the **cube** of the number or variable. For example the cube of 5 is $5 \times 5 \times 5 = 125$; this product is written as 5^3.

To find the **square root** of a number, find the number that, when squared, equals the given number. The **cube root** of a number is that number which, when cubed, equals the given number. Square and cube roots are indicated by radical signs, $\sqrt{25}$ and $\sqrt[3]{125}$ respectively.

2 Practice the Skill

By practicing the skills of squaring, cubing, and taking the corresponding roots of quantities, you will improve your study and test-taking abilities, especially as they relate to the GED® Mathematical Reasoning Test. Study the information below. Then answer the question that follows.

a The square of a negative number is positive; if two numbers differ only in their sign, their squares are both positive and equal. The square root of a positive number can, as a result, have two values. Since there are no real numbers that, when multiplied by themselves, give a negative number, square roots of negative numbers are undefined when dealing with real numbers.

b The cube of a negative number is negative. As a result, the cube root of a negative number exists, is negative, and is equal in magnitude to the cube root of the absolute value of the number.

$1^2 = 1 \times 1 = 1$	$1^3 = 1 \times 1 \times 1 = 1$
$2^2 = 2 \times 2 = 4$	$2^3 = 2 \times 2 \times 2 = 8$
$(-1)^2 = (-1) \times (-1) = 1$	$(-1)^3 = (-1) \times (-1) \times (-1) = -1$
$(-2)^2 = (-2) \times (-2) = 4$	$(-2)^3 = (-2) \times (-2) \times (-2) = -8$

$\sqrt{1} = 1, -1$	$\sqrt[3]{1} = 1$
$\sqrt{4} = 2, -2$	$\sqrt[3]{8} = 2$
$\sqrt{9} = 3, -3$	$\sqrt[3]{27} = 3$
$\sqrt{-9} = $ undefined	$\sqrt[3]{-27} = -3$

TEST-TAKING TIPS

Taking the square root of a number is different from dividing a number by 2. When finding the square root of x, consider: what number times itself equals x? When dividing x by 2, think: what number plus itself equals x?

1. The length of a square can be determined by finding the square root of its area. If a square has an area of 81 m², what is the length of the square?

A. 8 m
B. 8.5 m
C. 9 m
D. 9.5 m

UNIT 3

③ Apply the Skill

DIRECTIONS: Examine the information. Then read each question and use the drag-and-drop options to complete each answer.

2. Complete the following, assuming that $x < 0$.

x^2 [＿＿＿＿＿] x^3 [＿＿＿＿＿]

$\sqrt{x}$ [＿＿＿＿＿] $\sqrt[3]{x}$ [＿＿＿＿＿]

[> 0] [< 0] [is undefined]

3. Choose the solution (or solutions) of the equation $x^3 = 512$ from the list provided. The equation may have one solution, more than one solution, or no solution at all.

Solution(s): [＿＿]

[−16] [−8] [8] [16] [32]

DIRECTIONS: Read each question, and choose the **best** answer.

4. Carlos completed x^3 squats as part of his football workout. If $x = 5$, how many squats did he complete?

    A. 10
    B. 15
    C. 25
    D. 125

5. The length of a side of a cube can be determined by finding the cube root of its volume. If a cube has a volume of 64 cm³, what is the length of a side?

    A. 4 cm
    B. 8 cm
    C. 16 cm
    D. 32 cm

6. To determine the length of yarn needed for a project, Josie must solve $\frac{\sqrt{x}}{4}$ for $x = 64$. What is the solution?

    A. 2
    B. 4
    C. 8
    D. 16

7. Mark multiplied a number by itself. He found a product of 30. What is the number, rounded to the nearest tenth?

    A. 4.5
    B. 5.4
    C. 5.5
    D. 15

8. A square has an area of 50 square feet. What is the perimeter of the square, rounded to the nearest foot?

    A. 7 ft
    B. 28 ft
    C. 49 ft
    D. 100 ft

9. A student is told that a moving car travels a distance x, where x, expressed in miles, is the solution of the equation $(8 − x)^2 = 64$. The student argues that the car can't be moving, since x must equal zero. Which of the following describes the distance, x?

    A. The student is correct; x must equal zero.
    B. The student is incorrect; x can also be 8.
    C. The student is incorrect; x can also be 16.
    D. The student is incorrect; x can also be −8.

10. A gallon has a volume of 231 cubic inches. If a gallon of milk was sold in a perfectly cubical container, to the nearest tenth of an inch how high would the container be?

    A. 6 inches
    B. 6.1 inches
    C. 6.2 inches
    D. 6.3 inches

Exponents and Scientific Notation

MATH CONTENT TOPICS: Q.1.c, Q.2.a, Q.2.b, Q.2.c, Q.2.d, Q.2.e, Q.4.a, A.1.d, A.1.e, A.1.f
MATH PRACTICES: MP.1.a, MP.1.b, MP.1.e, MP.2.c, MP.3.a, MP.3.c, MP.4.a, MP.4.b, MP.5.c

1 Learn the Skill

Exponents are used when a number, called the base, is multiplied by itself many times. The exponent shows the number of times that the base appears in the product. When a quantity is given an exponent of n, it is said to be raised to the nth **power**; for example, 2^5 is the same as 2 raised to the 5th power. There are rules for adding, subtracting, multiplying, and dividing quantities with exponents.

Scientific notation uses exponents and powers of 10 to write very small and very large numbers in a compact form that simplifies calculations. Scientific notation requires that the decimal point be located just to the right of the first nonzero digit.

2 Practice the Skill

By practicing the skill of working with exponents and scientific notation, you will improve your study and test-taking abilities, especially as they relate to the GED® Mathematical Reasoning Test. Study the examples below. Then answer the question that follows.

a A number or quantity raised to the first power equals itself. A number or quantity (except zero) raised to the zero power equals one. When a number is raised to a negative power, write the reciprocal and change the negative exponent to a positive.

b Terms can be added and subtracted if they are alike, meaning they must have the same variable raised to the same exponent.

c To multiply terms with the same base, keep the base and add the exponents. Do the opposite for division. If the bases are not the same, simplify using the order of operations.

$5^1 = 5$	$5^0 = 1$ **a**	$5^{-2} = \dfrac{1}{5^2} = \dfrac{1}{25}$ **a**
$2x^2 + 4x^2 + 1 = 6x^2 + 1$ **b**		$4x^2 - x^2 = 3x^2$ **b**
$(3^2)(3^3) = (3)^{2+3} = 3^5$ **c**		$\dfrac{6^5}{6} = 6^{5-1} = 6^4$ **c**
$4.2 \times 10^7 = 42{,}000{,}000$		$5{,}800{,}000 = 5.8 \times 10^6$
$3.7 \times 10^{-5} = 0.000037$ **d**	**d**	$0.000052 = 5.2 \times 10^{-5}$

d To write a number shown in scientific notation as a number in expanded form, look at the power of 10. The exponent tells how many places to move the decimal point—right for positive, left for negative. To write a number in scientific notation, place the decimal point directly after the ones digit. Next, count the number of places you need to move. Then drop the zeros at the end.

TEST-TAKING TECH

The TI-30XS MultiView™ online calculator features a setting, using the SCI numeric notation mode, which allows calculations to be performed using scientific notation.

1. The distance between the sun and Mercury is about 58,000,000 km. What is this distance written in scientific notation?

   A. 5.8×10^6
   B. 5.8×10^7
   C. 58×10^6
   D. 58×10^7

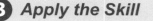

DIRECTIONS: Read each question, and choose the **best** answer.

2. There are 25,400,000 nanometers in an inch. What is this number written in scientific notation?

   A. 2.54×10^6
   B. 2.54×10^7
   C. 2.54×10^8
   D. 2.54×10^9

3. The width of a rectangle is 2^6, and the length is 2^5. What is the area of the rectangle?

   A. 2^1
   B. 2^{11}
   C. 2^{30}
   D. 4^{11}

4. The width of a certain strand of human hair is about 1.5×10^{-3} cm. What is the width of 2×10^5 of these hairs placed next to each other?

   A. 3.5×10^8 cm
   B. 3×10^{-2} cm
   C. 3×10^8 cm
   D. 3×10^2 cm

5. Which has the same value as $5^1 + 4^0$?

   A. 9
   B. 8
   C. 6
   D. 5

6. Which of the following expressions is equivalent to $5(7^2 7^2) + 5(7^4 7^{-4}) - (7^8 7^{-4})$?

   A. $4(7^4) + 5$
   B. $6(7^8) + 1$
   C. $10(7^4) - (7^{-2})$
   D. $10(7^4) - (7^2)$

7. For what value of x is the expression $(x^2 + 4)^2 (x^3 + 8)^{-3} (x^4 + 16)^4$ undefined?

   A. -8
   B. -4
   C. -2
   D. 2

DIRECTIONS: Read each question, and choose the **best** answer.

8. Which has the same value as $6(2^{-3}) + (5)(2^{-4}) + (4)(2^{-5})$?

   A. $\dfrac{15}{2}$
   B. $\dfrac{19}{8}$
   C. $\dfrac{19}{16}$
   D. -256

9. What is the answer to the equation $(3x^2 + 3x + 2) + 2(x^2 - 5x - 2)$?

   A. $(5x^2 - 2x)$
   B. $(5x^2 - 13x - 6)$
   C. $(5x^2 + 13x + 6)$
   D. $(5x^2 - 7x - 2)$

10. What is the answer to the equation $(3x^2 + 3x + 2) - 2(x^2 - 5x - 2)$?

    A. $(x^2 + 13x + 6)$
    B. $(x^2 - 7x - 2)$
    C. $(x^2 + 8x + 4)$
    D. $(x^2 - 2x)$

11. What is the answer to the equation $\dfrac{[(6x^2 + 4) - 2(2 - 3x^2)]}{4x}$?

    A. $\dfrac{x}{2} + \dfrac{5}{2x}$
    B. $3x$
    C. $\dfrac{2}{x}$
    D. $3x^2$

12. Max says that x^2 is always greater than x^{-2}. Which value of x shows that Max is incorrect?

    A. $\dfrac{1}{3}$
    B. $\sqrt{3}$
    C. 3
    D. 30

Patterns and Functions

MATH CONTENT TOPICS: Q.2.a, Q.2.b, Q.2.e, Q.3.d, Q.6.c, A.1.b, A.1.e, A.1.i, A.7.a, A.7.b
MATH PRACTICES: MP.1.a, MP.1.b, MP.1.e, MP.2.a, MP.2.c, MP.3.a, MP.4.a, MP.4.b, MP.5.c

1 Learn the Skill

A **mathematical pattern** is an arrangement of numbers and terms created by following a specific rule. You can identify the rule used to make a pattern, and apply it to find other terms in the pattern. An algebraic rule is often called a function. A **function** contains x- and y-values. There is only one y-value for each x-value. Think of a function as a machine. For each x-value you put into the machine, only one y-value will come out.

2 Practice the Skill

By practicing the skill of identifying and extending patterns, you will improve your study and test-taking abilities, especially as they relate to the GED® Mathematical Reasoning Test. Study the table and information below. Then answer the question that follows.

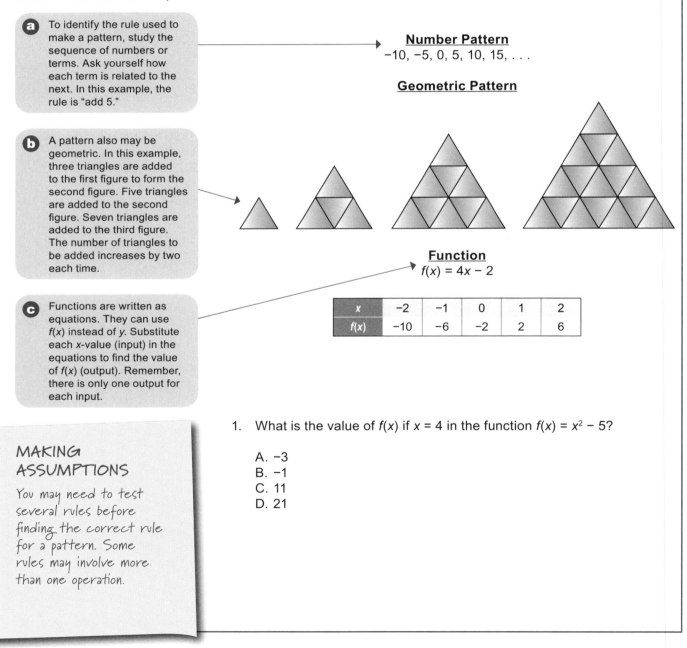

a To identify the rule used to make a pattern, study the sequence of numbers or terms. Ask yourself how each term is related to the next. In this example, the rule is "add 5."

Number Pattern
−10, −5, 0, 5, 10, 15, . . .

Geometric Pattern

b A pattern also may be geometric. In this example, three triangles are added to the first figure to form the second figure. Five triangles are added to the second figure. Seven triangles are added to the third figure. The number of triangles to be added increases by two each time.

Function
$f(x) = 4x − 2$

c Functions are written as equations. They can use $f(x)$ instead of y. Substitute each x-value (input) in the equations to find the value of $f(x)$ (output). Remember, there is only one output for each input.

x	−2	−1	0	1	2
f(x)	−10	−6	−2	2	6

MAKING ASSUMPTIONS

You may need to test several rules before finding the correct rule for a pattern. Some rules may involve more than one operation.

1. What is the value of $f(x)$ if $x = 4$ in the function $f(x) = x^2 − 5$?

A. −3
B. −1
C. 11
D. 21

3 Apply the Skill

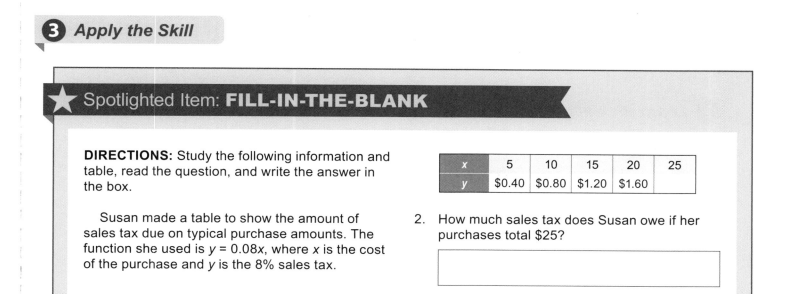

⭐ Spotlighted Item: **FILL-IN-THE-BLANK**

DIRECTIONS: Study the following information and table, read the question, and write the answer in the box.

x	5	10	15	20	25
y	$0.40	$0.80	$1.20	$1.60	

Susan made a table to show the amount of sales tax due on typical purchase amounts. The function she used is $y = 0.08x$, where x is the cost of the purchase and y is the 8% sales tax.

2. How much sales tax does Susan owe if her purchases total $25?

DIRECTIONS: Read each question, and choose the **best** answer.

3. For the function $f(x) = \frac{x}{5}$, which of the following x-values has a whole number output?

   A. 19
   B. 21
   C. 22
   D. 25

4. What is the rule for the following pattern?

   2; 4; 16; 256; 65,536; . . .

   A. multiply the previous term by 2
   B. add twice the previous term
   C. square the previous term
   D. multiply the previous term by 4

5. What is the sixth term in the sequence below?

   192, 96, 48, 24, . . .

   A. 15
   B. 12
   C. 6
   D. 3

6. If $f(x) = 2 - \frac{2}{3}x$, then what is x when $f(x) = 4$?

   A. −3
   B. $-\frac{4}{9}$
   C. $\frac{4}{9}$
   D. 3

DIRECTIONS: Study the following information and table, read the question, and choose the **best** answer.

7. The following table is supposed to correspond to the function $y = \frac{x + 1}{x^2 + 1}$.

x	−2	−1	0	1	2
y	−0.2	0	1	0.5	0.6

   All of the above y-values are correct **except** which one?

   A. −0.2
   B. 0
   C. 0.5
   D. 0.6

DIRECTIONS: Study the following information and table, read the question, and choose the **best** answer.

The following table contains data for the distance d an airplane travels in t hours. It is supposed to correspond to the function $d = vt$, where v is the speed of the airplane.

t	2	3	4	5	6	7
d	500	900	1,000	1,250	1,500	1,750

8. All of the above values of d fit the data **except** which one?

   A. 900
   B. 1,000
   C. 1,250
   D. 1,500

UNIT 3

One-Variable Linear Equations

MATH CONTENT TOPICS: Q.2.a, Q.2.e, Q.3.d, A.2.a, A.2.b, A.2.c
MATH PRACTICES: MP.1.a, MP.1.b, MP.1.e, MP.2.a, MP.3.a, MP.4.b, MP.5.a, MP.5.c

① Learn the Skill

A **one-variable linear equation** is an equation that consists of expressions involving only number values and products of constants and a variable, such as $2x + 6 = 12$. The solution of a one-variable linear equation is the value of the variable that makes the equation true.

To solve a one-variable linear equation, use inverse operations to group variable terms on one side of the equation and constant terms on the other side of the equation. In the above example, subtract 6 from each side of the equal (=) sign so that $2x = 6$.

Next, use **inverse operations** to isolate the variable. Inverse operations are operations that undo each other. Addition and subtraction are inverse operations, as are multiplication and division. In the example above, both $2x$ and 6 can be divided by 2, so that $x = 3$.

② Practice the Skill

By practicing the skill of solving one-variable linear equations, you will improve your study and test-taking abilities, especially as they relate to the GED® Mathematical Reasoning Test. Study the information below. Then answer the question that follows.

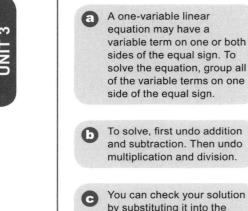

a A one-variable linear equation may have a variable term on one or both sides of the equal sign. To solve the equation, group all of the variable terms on one side of the equal sign.

b To solve, first undo addition and subtraction. Then undo multiplication and division.

c You can check your solution by substituting it into the original equation. If the solution makes the equation true, then it is correct.

Solve the equation

$$5x + 7 = 19 - 3x$$
$$5x + 3x + 7 = 19 - 3x + 3x \quad \leftarrow \quad \text{Add } 3x \text{ to both sides.}$$
$$8x + 7 = 19 \quad \leftarrow \quad \text{Group like terms.}$$
$$8x + 7 - 7 = 19 - 7 \quad \leftarrow \quad \text{Subtract 7 from both sides.}$$
$$8x = 12 \quad \leftarrow \quad \text{Group like terms.}$$
b $$\frac{8x}{8} = \frac{12}{8} \quad \leftarrow \quad \text{Divide both sides by 8.}$$
$$x = 1.5 \quad \leftarrow \quad \text{Simplify.}$$

Check:

$$5(1.5) + 7 \overset{?}{=} 19 - 3(1.5)$$

$$7.5 + 7 \overset{?}{=} 19 - 4.5$$

$$14.5 = 14.5$$

1. What value of x makes the equation $3x + 9 = 6$ true?

   A. −1
   B. −3
   C. 5
   D. 15

USING LOGIC

An equation states that two expressions are equal. When working with an equation, you must perform the same operations in the same order to both sides of the equation.

DIRECTIONS: Read each question, and choose the **best** answer.

2. Solve the equation for *x*.

   $0.5x - 4 = 12$

   A. 4
   B. 8
   C. 16
   D. 32

3. What value of *y* makes the equation true?

   $5y + 6 = 3y - 14$

   A. −1
   B. −2.5
   C. −4
   D. −10

4. Solve the equation for *t*.
   $$\frac{1}{2}t + 8 = \frac{5}{2}t - 10$$
   A. 9
   B. 3
   C. −1
   D. −6

5. Each month, Cameron earns $1,200 in salary plus an 8% commission on sales. The equation $T = 1,200 + 0.08s$ represents Cameron's total earnings each month. In July, Cameron earned a total, *T,* of $2,800. What was the value of Cameron's sales in July?

   A. $15,000
   B. $16,000
   C. $20,000
   D. $50,000

6. A rectangular yard is *x* feet wide. The yard is 4 feet longer than it is wide. The perimeter *P* of the yard is given by the equation $P = 4x + 8$. If the perimeter of the yard is 84 feet, how long is the yard?

   A. 19 feet
   B. 23 feet
   C. 24 feet
   D. 28 feet

DIRECTIONS: Read each question, and choose the **best** answer.

7. All of the following operations are used to solve for *x* in the equation below **except** one. Which is it?

   $9x - 2 = 4x + 8$

   A. addition
   B. division
   C. multiplication
   D. subtraction

8. Lucas solved the equation below and got an answer of *x* = 1.25.

   $3x = (8 - 0.25x) - (3 - 0.75x)$

   Which describes Lucas' solution?

   A. The solution is correct because *x* = 1.25 makes the equation true.
   B. The solution is incorrect because Lucas divided both sides of the equation by 2.5.
   C. The solution is incorrect because Lucas added 0.75*x* to both sides of the equation.
   D. The solution is incorrect because Lucas subtracted 0.5*x* from both sides of the equation.

9. Solve the equation for *x*.

   $-3x + 11 = x - 5$

   A. −1.5
   B. −4
   C. 2
   D. 4

10. Solve the equation for *y*.

    $0.6y + 1.2 = 0.3y - 0.9 + 0.8y$

    A. 1.6
    B. 2.4
    C. 2.6
    D. 4.2

11. Find the value of *n* that makes the equation true.
    $$\frac{n}{4} - \frac{1}{2} = \frac{3n}{2} + \frac{3}{4}$$
    A. −1
    B. 0
    C. 1
    D. 2

Two-Variable Linear Equations

MATH CONTENT TOPICS: Q.2.a, Q.2.e, A.2.a, A.2.b, A.2.d
MATH PRACTICES: MP.1.a, MP.1.b, MP.1.e, MP.2.a, MP.2.c, MP.4.a, MP.5.c

1 Learn the Skill

A **two-variable linear equation** is a mathematical sentence that equates two expressions, such as $4x + 2y = 14$, whose terms are made up of number values and products of constants and variables. Only one variable, such as x or y, but not both, may be present in a single term. A system of two-variable linear equations often may be solved using either:

- the **substitution** method, in which one of the equations is solved for one variable, and the value of that variable is substituted into the an original equation to solve for the second variable; or
- the **linear combination** method, or elimination, in which one or both equations are multiplied by a constant to produce new coefficients that are opposites, so that one variable may be cancelled out and the resulting equation may be solved for the other variable.

2 Practice the Skill

By practicing the skill of solving two-variable linear equations, you will improve your study and test-taking abilities, especially as they relate to the GED® Mathematical Reasoning Test. Study the information below. Then answer the question that follows.

a Either equation can be solved for either variable. It is easiest to solve for the variable with a coefficient of 1 or −1.

b This system also could be solved by multiplying the first equation by −2, adding it to the second equation, and solving the new equation for y.

c The value of the variable can be substituted into either of the original equations. You will get the same value for the second variable.

$4(2) - 2y = 2$
$8 - 2y = 2$
$-2y = -6$
$y = 3$

Solve the set of two-variable linear equations

$$\begin{cases} 2x + y = 7 \\ 4x - 2y = 2 \end{cases}$$

Substitution Method	Linear Combination Method
a Solve the first equation for y: $2x - 2x + y = 7 - 2x$ $y = 7 - 2x$ Substitute $7 - 2x$ for y; solve for x: $4x - 2(7 - 2x) = 2$ $4x - 14 + 4x = 2$ $8x - 14 + 14 = 2 + 14$ $8x = 16$ $x = 2$	**b** Multiply the first equation by 2: $4x + 2y = 14$ Add to the second equation: $\quad 4x + 2y = 14$ $\quad \underline{4x - 2y = \;\; 2}$ $\quad 8x + 0y = 16$ Solve the new equation for x: $8x = 16$ $x = 2$
c Substitute $x = 2$ and solve for y: $2(2) + y = 7$ $4 + y = 7$ $y = 3$ The solution is (2, 3).	**c** Substitute $x = 2$ and solve for y: $2(2) + y = 7$ $4 + y = 7$ $y = 3$ The solution is (2, 3).

1. Which ordered pair is the solution of the system of linear equations?

$$\begin{cases} x + 3y = 1 \\ 2x + 2y = 6 \end{cases}$$

A. (−2, 1)
B. (3, 1)
C. (4, −1)
D. (7, −2)

TEST-TAKING TIPS

The solution of a linear equation reflects the values of the variables that make both equations true. Check that your solution is correct by substituting ordered-pair values into the two original equations.

⭐ Spotlighted Item: **FILL-IN-THE-BLANK**

DIRECTIONS: Read each question. Then write your answers in the boxes below.

2. Solve the system of linear equations.

$$\begin{cases} 3x - y = 10 \\ 2x + y = 5 \end{cases}$$

$x =$ _____

$y =$ _____

3. Solve the system of linear equations.

$$\begin{cases} 4x - 3y = -1 \\ -2x + 5y = 11 \end{cases}$$

$x =$ _____

$y =$ _____

4. Solve the system of linear equations.

$$\begin{cases} 0.5x - 2y = 6 \\ 3x + 8y = 16 \end{cases}$$

$x =$ _____

$y =$ _____

5. Marta's age is 4 less than 2 times Gavin's age. The sum of their ages is 20. The system of equations below represents Marta's age m and Gavin's age g. How old are Marta and Gavin?

$$\begin{cases} m = 2g - 4 \\ m + g = 20 \end{cases}$$

Marta is _____ years old.

Gavin is _____ years old.

6. Solve the system of linear equations.

$$\begin{cases} 3x + 2y = 2 \\ 2x - 3y = -16 \end{cases}$$

$x =$ _____

$y =$ _____

DIRECTIONS: Read each question, and choose the **best** answer.

7. Solve the system of linear equations.

$$\begin{cases} x + y = 10 \\ 2x - y = 8 \end{cases}$$

A. $(-6, 16)$
B. $(-4, 12)$
C. $(4, 6)$
D. $(6, 4)$

8. Which system of equations can be solved by multiplying the first equation by 3 and then adding the second equation?

A. $\begin{cases} x - 3y = -5 \\ 2x - 2y = 4 \end{cases}$

B. $\begin{cases} 2x + y = 4 \\ 4x - 3y = -2 \end{cases}$

C. $\begin{cases} x + 3y = 7 \\ 5x + y = 7 \end{cases}$

D. $\begin{cases} 3x - 2y = -1 \\ x + 4y = 9 \end{cases}$

UNIT 3

Factoring

MATH CONTENT TOPICS: Q.1.b, Q.4.a, A.1.a, A.1.d, A.1.g, A.4.a, A.4.b
MATH PRACTICES: MP.1.a, MP.1.b. MP.1.e, MP.2.a, MP.2.c, MP.4.b

1 Learn the Skill

Factors are numbers or expressions that are multiplied together to form a product. Factors may have one term (for example, $4y$), two terms (for example, $4y + 5$), or more terms. Products of two factors with two terms each can be found using the FOIL method, in which you multiply the *F*irst, *O*uter, *I*nner, and *L*ast terms in that order.

Quadratic equations can be written as $ax^2 + bx + c = 0$, where a, b, and c are integers and a is not equal to zero. They can be solved by factoring the equations into two, two-term factors and setting each factor equal to zero. They also can be solved by substituting a, b, and c into the quadratic formula.

2 Practice the Skill

By practicing the skill of factoring and solving quadratic equations, you will improve your study and test-taking abilities, especially as they relate to the GED® Mathematical Reasoning Test. Read the example and strategies below. Then answer the question that follows.

a To solve a quadratic equation, rewrite the equation to set the quadratic expression equal to 0. Then factor and set each factor equal to 0. Then solve. Check both values by substituting them in the original equation.

b To solve a quadratic equation, you also may use the quadratic formula. Standard quadratic equations take the format
$$ax^2 + bx + c = 0$$
In this equation,
$$a = 1, b = 4, c = -12$$
Substitute values for a, b and c in the formula to find the value of x.

The FOIL Method
Multiply $(x + 2)(x - 4)$

*F*irst $x(x) = x^2$ *O*uter $x(-4) = -4x$ *I*nner $2(x) = 2x$ *L*ast $2(-4) = -8$

Factoring Quadratic Expressions
$$x^2 - 2x - 8$$
1. Factors of -8: $(1, -8), (-1, 8), (2, -4), (-2, 4)$
2. $-4 + 2 = -2$
3. $(x - 4)(x + 2)$
4. Check: $x^2 + 2x - 4x - 8 = x^2 - 2x - 8$

Solving Quadratic Equations

$x^2 + 4x = 12$

a $x^2 + 4x - 12 = 0$

$(x - 2)(x + 6) = 0$

If $x - 2 = 0$ and $x + 6 = 0$,
then $x = 2$ and $x = -6$

$x = \dfrac{-4 + 8}{2} = 2$ and

b $x = \dfrac{-b \pm \sqrt{b^2 - 4ac}}{2a}$

$x = \dfrac{-4 \pm \sqrt{16 - 4(1)(-12)}}{2(1)}$

$x = \dfrac{-4 \pm \sqrt{16 + 48}}{2}$

$x = \dfrac{-4 \pm \sqrt{64}}{2}$

$x = \dfrac{-4 \pm 8}{2}$

$x = \dfrac{-4 - 8}{2} = -6$

INSIDE THE ITEMS

Each term in an expression or equation belongs with the sign that precedes it. Remain mindful of these signs when solving equations.

1. Which of the following are factors of $x^2 + 5x - 6$?

   A. $(x + 2)(x - 3)$
   B. $(x - 2)(x - 3)$
   C. $(x + 6)(x - 1)$
   D. $(x + 2)(x + 3)$

DIRECTIONS: Read each question, and choose the **best** answer.

2. What is the product of $(x + 5)(x - 7)$?

   A. $x^2 - 2x - 12$
   B. $x^2 + 2x + 12$
   C. $x^2 + 2x + 35$
   D. $x^2 - 2x - 35$

3. Which of the following is equal to $(x - 3)(x - 3)$?

   A. $x^2 - 6x + 9$
   B. $x^2 + 6x - 9$
   C. $x^2 + 6x + 9$
   D. $x^2 - 9x - 6$

4. Which of the following is equal to $x^2 - 6x - 16$?

   A. $(x + 4)(x - 4)$
   B. $(x - 2)(x - 8)$
   C. $(x - 2)(x + 8)$
   D. $(x + 2)(x - 8)$

5. The dimensions of a rectangle are $2x - 5$ and $-4x + 1$. Which expression represents the area of the rectangle?

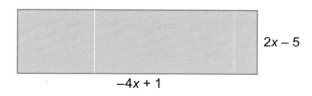

$2x - 5$

$-4x + 1$

   A. $-8x^2 + 22x - 5$
   B. $8x^2 + 22x - 5$
   C. $-8x^2 - 18x - 5$
   D. $8x^2 - 18x - 5$

6. If $4x + 1$ is one factor of $4x^2 + 13x + 3$, which of the following is the other factor?

   A. $x + 1$
   B. $x + 3$
   C. $x - 13$
   D. $x - 2$

DIRECTIONS: Read each question, and choose the **best** answer.

7. Which of the following can be a value of x in the equation $3x^2 - 10x + 5 = 0$?

   A. $\dfrac{10 \pm \sqrt{40}}{6}$
   B. $\dfrac{-4 \pm \sqrt{64}}{2}$
   C. 5
   D. 0

8. Miranda made a rectangular vegetable garden next to her house. She used the house as one side and fenced in most of the other three sides. She used 12 meters of fencing. The area of her garden is 32 square meters. To find a possible width of her garden, solve $w^2 - 12w = -32$. Which of the following is a possible width of her garden?

   A. 1 m
   B. 4 m
   C. 6 m
   D. 8 m

9. Solve: $2x^2 + x = \dfrac{1}{2}$

   A. $\dfrac{-1 \pm \sqrt{5}}{4}$
   B. $\dfrac{-4 \pm \sqrt{64}}{2}$
   C. 5
   D. 0

10. Which shows the solutions for the following equation?

    $2x^2 + 18x + 36 = 0$

    A. 3 and -6
    B. -3 and 6
    C. 3 and 6
    D. -3 and -6

11. Which expression has a product that has only two terms?

    A. $(x + 7)(x - 1)$
    B. $(x - 1)(x - 1)$
    C. $(x - 7)(x + 7)$
    D. $(x - 7)(x - 7)$

Rational Expressions and Equations

MATH CONTENT TOPICS: Q.1.b, Q.2.a, A.1.a, A.1.d, A.1.f, A.1.h, A.4.a
MATH PRACTICES: MP.1.a, MP.1.b, MP.1.e, MP.3.c, MP.4.b, MP.5.b

1 Learn the Skill

A **rational number** is a number that can be written in the form $\frac{a}{b}$, where a and b are integers and $b \neq 0$. A **rational expression** is a fraction whose numerator, denominator, or both are nonzero polynomials. A rational expression is undefined when the denominator is equal to 0. Rational expressions can be added, subtracted, multiplied, and divided.

A rational expression is in its simplified form if its numerator and denominator have no common factors other than 1. To simplify a rational expression, factor the numerator and denominator and divide out common factors.

A **rational equation** is an equation that contains rational expressions. A rational equation can be solved for the variable.

2 Practice the Skill

By practicing the skills of performing operations with rational expressions and solving rational equations, you will improve your study and test-taking abilities, especially as they relate to the GED® Mathematical Reasoning Test. Study the information below. Then answer the question that follows.

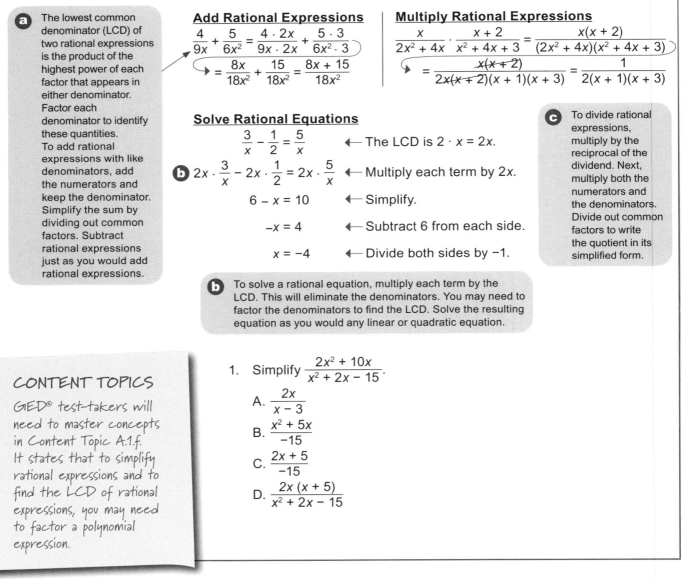

(a) The lowest common denominator (LCD) of two rational expressions is the product of the highest power of each factor that appears in either denominator. Factor each denominator to identify these quantities. To add rational expressions with like denominators, add the numerators and keep the denominator. Simplify the sum by dividing out common factors. Subtract rational expressions just as you would add rational expressions.

Add Rational Expressions

$$\frac{4}{9x} + \frac{5}{6x^2} = \frac{4 \cdot 2x}{9x \cdot 2x} + \frac{5 \cdot 3}{6x^2 \cdot 3}$$
$$= \frac{8x}{18x^2} + \frac{15}{18x^2} = \frac{8x + 15}{18x^2}$$

Multiply Rational Expressions

$$\frac{x}{2x^2 + 4x} \cdot \frac{x + 2}{x^2 + 4x + 3} = \frac{x(x + 2)}{(2x^2 + 4x)(x^2 + 4x + 3)}$$
$$= \frac{x(x + 2)}{2x(x + 2)(x + 1)(x + 3)} = \frac{1}{2(x + 1)(x + 3)}$$

Solve Rational Equations

$$\frac{3}{x} - \frac{1}{2} = \frac{5}{x}$$ ← The LCD is $2 \cdot x = 2x$.

(b) $2x \cdot \frac{3}{x} - 2x \cdot \frac{1}{2} = 2x \cdot \frac{5}{x}$ ← Multiply each term by $2x$.

$6 - x = 10$ ← Simplify.

$-x = 4$ ← Subtract 6 from each side.

$x = -4$ ← Divide both sides by -1.

(c) To divide rational expressions, multiply by the reciprocal of the dividend. Next, multiply both the numerators and the denominators. Divide out common factors to write the quotient in its simplified form.

(b) To solve a rational equation, multiply each term by the LCD. This will eliminate the denominators. You may need to factor the denominators to find the LCD. Solve the resulting equation as you would any linear or quadratic equation.

CONTENT TOPICS

GED® test-takers will need to master concepts in Content Topic A.1.f. It states that to simplify rational expressions and to find the LCD of rational expressions, you may need to factor a polynomial expression.

1. Simplify $\dfrac{2x^2 + 10x}{x^2 + 2x - 15}$.

A. $\dfrac{2x}{x - 3}$

B. $\dfrac{x^2 + 5x}{-15}$

C. $\dfrac{2x + 5}{-15}$

D. $\dfrac{2x \, (x + 5)}{x^2 + 2x - 15}$

⭐ Spotlighted Item: **DROP-DOWN**

DIRECTIONS: Read each question, and use the drop-down options to choose the **best** answer.

2. Solve $\frac{5}{2x} + \frac{1}{4} = \frac{3}{x}$.

   $x =$ | Drop-down |

   A. −4   B. −2   C. 2   D. 4

3. Solve $\frac{2}{x-1} = \frac{16}{x^2 + 3x - 4}$.

   $x =$ | Drop-down |

   A. −2   B. 1   C. 2   D. 4

4. Solve $\frac{5}{2x-6} - \frac{3}{x-3} = \frac{1}{2}$.

   $x =$ | Drop-down |

   A. −3   B. −1   C. 2   D. 3

5. Solve $\frac{4}{x+3} = \frac{x}{7}$.

   $x =$ | Drop-down 5.1 | or $x =$ | Drop-down 5.2 |

   Drop-Down Answer Options

5.1 A. −7	5.2 A. 1
B. −4	B. 2
C. −3	C. 4
D. −1	D. 7

DIRECTIONS: Read each question, and choose the **best** answer.

6. What is the lowest common denominator of the rational expression?

   $$\frac{x+2}{4x^2} + \frac{5}{6x}$$

   A. $24x^3$
   B. $12x^3$
   C. $12x^2$
   D. $6x^2$

7. Which expression can be simplified by dividing out the factor $(x + 4)$?

   A. $\frac{x+4}{x+8}$
   B. $\frac{x^2+4}{x^2-4}$
   C. $\frac{3x+12}{x^2-16}$
   D. $\frac{2x+8}{x^2-8x+16}$

DIRECTIONS: Read each question, and choose the **best** answer.

8. Simplify $\frac{5x}{x^2 + 6x + 9} \div \frac{10x^2 + 5x}{x+3}$.

   A. $\frac{1}{(x+3)(2x+1)}$
   B. $\frac{5x}{(x+3)(2x+1)}$
   C. $\frac{1}{3(3x+1)(x+3)}$
   D. $\frac{x+3}{(2x+1)(x^2+6x+9)}$

9. Jason says that if there is an x-term in the numerator and an x-term in the denominator, the expression can always be simplified. Which expression shows that Jason is incorrect?

   A. $\frac{x-5}{x+1}$
   B. $\frac{x-6}{6-x}$
   C. $\frac{3x}{3(x-2)}$
   D. $\frac{x^2-2x}{5x}$

Solving and Graphing Inequalities

MATH CONTENT TOPICS: Q.2.a, Q.2.e, Q.4.a, A.3.a, A.3.b, A.3.c, A.3.d
MATH PRACTICES: MP.1.a, MP.1.e, MP.2.a, MP.4.b, MP.4.c

❶ Learn the Skill

An **inequality** states that two algebraic expressions are not equal. Inequalities are written with less than (<) and greater than (>) symbols, as well as two additional symbols. The ≥ symbol means "is greater than or equal to" and the ≤ symbol means "is less than or equal to." A solution to an inequality can include an infinite amount of numbers. For example, solutions to $b < 5$ include $b = 4.5, 4, 3.99, 3, 2, 1, 0, -3, -10$, and so on. When each individual solution is plotted as a point on a number line, a solid line is formed, which represents the solution set.

❷ Practice the Skill

By practicing the skills of solving and graphing inequalities, you will improve your study and test-taking abilities, especially as they relate to the GED® Mathematical Reasoning Test. Study the information below. Then answer the question that follows.

ⓐ Solve inequalities as you do equations. If you multiply or divide an inequality by a negative number, you must reverse the sign of the inequality. For example, if the inequality shown was $16 \le -8x$, you would divide by -8 and reverse the sign, giving you $-2 \ge x$.

ⓑ For $x > 3$, every number to the right of 3 is in the solution set. Draw an open circle at 3 because 3 is not greater than 3 and therefore is not included in the solution set. Then draw a solid arrow to the right from 3.
For $x \le 3$, each number to the left of 3 *as well as* 3 is included in the solution set. Draw a closed circle at 3 to show that 3 is included. Then draw a solid arrow pointing to the left from 3.

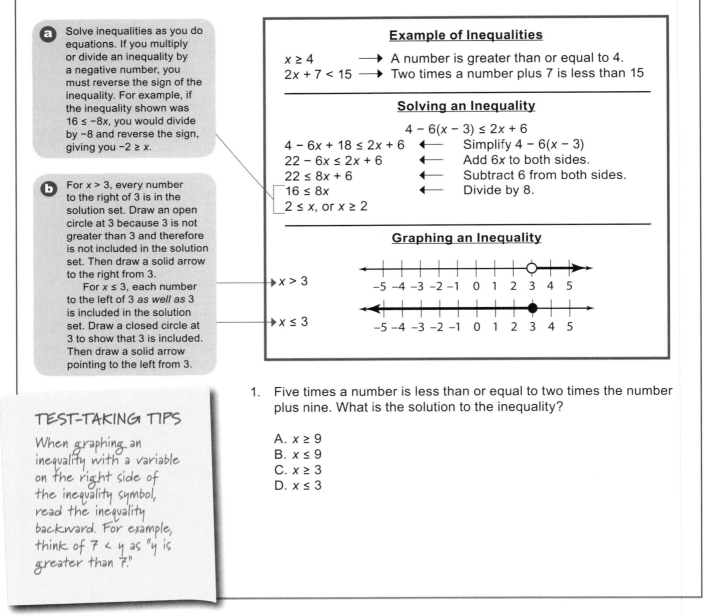

Example of Inequalities

$x \ge 4$ ⟶ A number is greater than or equal to 4.
$2x + 7 < 15$ ⟶ Two times a number plus 7 is less than 15

Solving an Inequality

$$4 - 6(x - 3) \le 2x + 6$$
$4 - 6x + 18 \le 2x + 6$ ⟵ Simplify $4 - 6(x - 3)$
$22 - 6x \le 2x + 6$ ⟵ Add $6x$ to both sides.
$22 \le 8x + 6$ ⟵ Subtract 6 from both sides.
$16 \le 8x$ ⟵ Divide by 8.
$2 \le x$, or $x \ge 2$

Graphing an Inequality

$x > 3$
$x \le 3$

TEST-TAKING TIPS

When graphing an inequality with a variable on the right side of the inequality symbol, read the inequality backward. For example, think of $7 < y$ as "y is greater than 7."

1. Five times a number is less than or equal to two times the number plus nine. What is the solution to the inequality?

A. $x \ge 9$
B. $x \le 9$
C. $x \ge 3$
D. $x \le 3$

DIRECTIONS: Read each question, and choose the **best** answer.

2. What is the solution to the inequality $x + 5 > 4$?

    A. $x > 1$
    B. $x < -1$
    C. $x < 1$
    D. $x > -1$

3. For what values of x is the inequality below true?

    $$2x + 6 \geq 8?$$

    A. $x \geq 1$
    B. $x \leq 1$
    C. $x \geq 7$
    D. $x \leq 7$

4. What inequality is shown on the number line?

    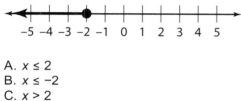

    A. $x \leq 2$
    B. $x \leq -2$
    C. $x > 2$
    D. $x > -2$

5. The product of a number and 5, increased by 3, is less than or equal to 13. What is the inequality?

    A. $5x + 2 \leq 13$
    B. $5x \leq 13 + 3$
    C. $5x + 3 < 13$
    D. $5x + 3 \leq 13$

6. The area of the following rectangle cannot be greater than 80 square centimeters. The length is 3 less than 3 times the width. Which inequality shows this relationship?

    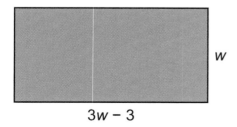

    $3w - 3$

    A. $80 \leq 2(w + 3w - 3)$
    B. $80 \geq 2(w + 3w - 3)$
    C. $80 \leq w(3w - 3)$
    D. $80 \geq w(3w - 3)$

7. Kara has $15 and Brett has $22. Together, they have less than the amount needed to buy a pair of concert tickets. Which inequality describes their situation?

    A. $37 < x$
    B. $x + 15 < 22$
    C. $x \leq 37$
    D. $x + 22 \leq 15$

8. A taxicab charges $2.00 as a base price and $0.50 for each mile. Josie needs to take a taxicab but only has $8. What is the greatest number of miles that Josie can ride in the cab?

    A. 6 miles
    B. 11 miles
    C. 12 miles
    D. 16 miles

9. The sum of a number and 12 is less than or equal to 5 times the number plus 3. Which inequality represents this situation?

    A. $x + 12 \geq 5(x - 3)$
    B. $x + 12 \leq 5x + 3$
    C. $x + 12 > 5x + 3$
    D. $5x + 3 > x + 12$

10. Which of the following shows the solution for the inequality $8 - 3x > 2x - 2$?

    A. $x > 2$
    B. $x < 2$
    C. $x > 6$
    D. $x < 6$

11. What is the solution to the following inequality?

    $$-x - 4x > 30 - 3(x + 8)?$$

    A. $-6\frac{3}{4} < x$
    B. $-3 < x$
    C. $-6\frac{3}{4} > x$
    D. $-3 > x$

12. The solution to which inequality is shown on the number line below?

    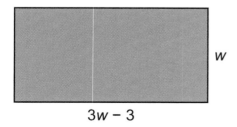

    A. $2x + 5 > 3x - 6$
    B. $3x - 2 \geq 4x - 1$
    C. $4x - 3 > 5x - 4$
    D. $5x + 1 \geq 4x + 2$

The Coordinate Grid

MATH CONTENT TOPICS: A.5.a
MATH PRACTICES: MP.1.e, MP.3.a

1 Learn the Skill

A **coordinate grid** is a visual representation of points, or ordered pairs. An **ordered pair** is a pair of values: an *x*-value and a *y*-value. The *x*-value is always shown first. The grid is made by the intersection of a horizontal line (*x*-axis) and a vertical line (*y*-axis). The point where the number lines meet is called the **origin**, which is (0, 0). The grid is divided into four **quadrants**, or sections.

The upper-right section of a grid is the first quadrant. Move counterclockwise to name the remaining quadrants. In an ordered pair, the first value (*x*-value) tells how many spaces to move (right for positive or left for negative). The *y*-value tells how many spaces to move (up for positive or down for negative).

2 Practice the Skill

By practicing the skills of locating and plotting points on the coordinate grid, you will improve your study and test-taking abilities, especially as they relate to the GED® Mathematical Reasoning Test. Study the grid and information below. Then answer the question that follows.

The coordinate grid below shows points *A, B, C,* and *D*. The coordinates for point *A* are (−1, 0). Point *B* is located at (−1, −5).

a To draw a line segment on the coordinate grid, plot the given points. Then draw a line to connect them.

b Changes to figures or points can be shown on a coordinate grid. A translation is one type of change. In a *translation*, a figure or point slides to a new position in a different quadrant.

c To plot a point whose *y*-coordinate is an expression, substitute the given value of *x* and solve for *y*. Then plot the point.

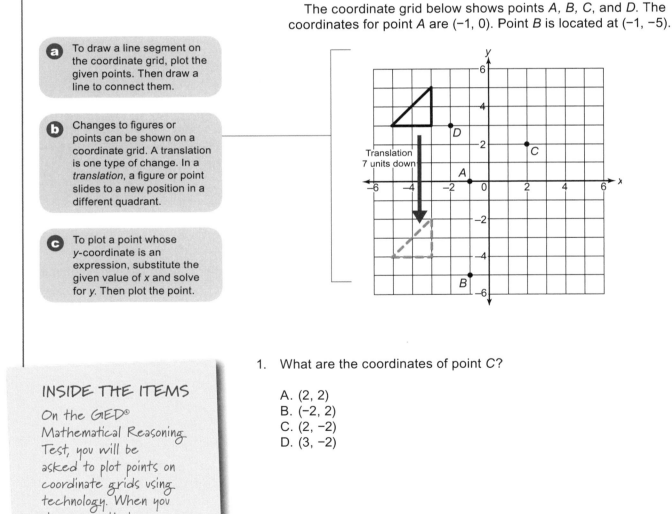

INSIDE THE ITEMS

On the GED®
Mathematical Reasoning
Test, you will be
asked to plot points on
coordinate grids using
technology. When you
do, ensure that you
click on the proper
coordinates.

1. What are the coordinates of point *C*?

A. (2, 2)
B. (−2, 2)
C. (2, −2)
D. (3, −2)

⭐ Spotlighted Item: **HOT SPOT**

DIRECTIONS: Read each question. Then mark your answer on the grid below.

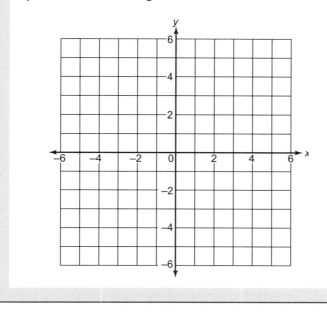

DIRECTIONS: Study the coordinate grid, read each question, and choose the **best** answer.

9. What are the coordinates of point *T*?

   A. (5, −4)
   B. (4, −4)
   C. (4, −5)
   D. (−4, 4)

2. Plot the point (5, −3).

3. Translate the point (5, −3) up 6 units.

4. Plot the point (4, 0).

5. Translate the point (4, 0) left 3 units.

6. Plot the point (x, x^2) for $x = 2$.

7. Plot the point $(x, 0.75x)$ for $x = -4$.

8. Plot the point (x, x^3) for $x = -1$.

10. Which of the following ordered pairs describes the location of point *S*?

    A. (1, 0)
    B. (−1, 0)
    C. (0, 1)
    D. (0, −1)

11. What are the coordinates of point *P*?

    A. (−5, −5)
    B. (−5, 5)
    C. (5, −5)
    D. (5, 5)

12. What characteristic do points *T* and *U* share?

    A. They have the same *y*-coordinate.
    B. They have the same *x*-coordinate.
    C. Both points have two negative *x*-coordinates.
    D. Both points have two positive *y*-coordinates.

UNIT 3

Graphing Linear Equations

MATH CONTENT TOPICS: A.1.b, A.5.a, A.5.d
MATH PRACTICES: MP.1.a, MP.1.e, MP.2.c, MP.4.b, MP.4.c

1 Learn the Skill

Some equations have two variables. In this case, the value of one variable depends on the other. You can show the possible solutions for an equation with two variables on a graph. A **linear equation** is one that forms a straight line when graphed. All of the solutions of the equation lie on a line. To draw a line, you must find at least two points on the line and connect them.

2 Practice the Skill

By practicing the skill of graphing linear equations, you will improve your study and test-taking abilities, especially as they relate to the GED® Mathematical Reasoning Test. Study the graph and information below. Then answer the question that follows.

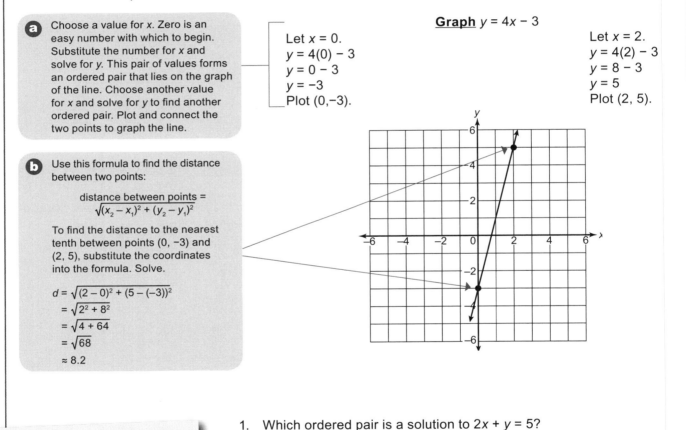

a Choose a value for *x*. Zero is an easy number with which to begin. Substitute the number for *x* and solve for *y*. This pair of values forms an ordered pair that lies on the graph of the line. Choose another value for *x* and solve for *y* to find another ordered pair. Plot and connect the two points to graph the line.

Let $x = 0$.
$y = 4(0) - 3$
$y = 0 - 3$
$y = -3$
Plot $(0, -3)$.

Graph $y = 4x - 3$

Let $x = 2$.
$y = 4(2) - 3$
$y = 8 - 3$
$y = 5$
Plot $(2, 5)$.

b Use this formula to find the distance between two points:

distance between points =
$$\sqrt{(x_2 - x_1)^2 + (y_2 - y_1)^2}$$

To find the distance to the nearest tenth between points $(0, -3)$ and $(2, 5)$, substitute the coordinates into the formula. Solve.

$d = \sqrt{(2 - 0)^2 + (5 - (-3))^2}$
$ = \sqrt{2^2 + 8^2}$
$ = \sqrt{4 + 64}$
$ = \sqrt{68}$
$ \approx 8.2$

1. Which ordered pair is a solution to $2x + y = 5$?

A. $(-1, 3)$
B. $(3, -1)$
C. $(0, -5)$
D. $(-2, 6)$

INSIDE THE ITEMS

If you think an ordered pair may be a solution to a linear equation, then the equation should be true for those values of *x* and *y*. Substitute the values of *x* and *y* from the ordered pair into the equation and simplify.

DIRECTIONS: Read each question, and choose the **best** answer.

2. Which of the following ordered pairs is a point on the line of the equation $x + 2y = 4$?

    A. $(-2, 0)$
    B. $(1, 3)$
    C. $(0, 2)$
    D. $(2, -4)$

3. Which ordered pair is a solution to $2x - y = 0$?

    A. $(0, 0)$
    B. $(1, -2)$
    C. $(-1, 2)$
    D. $(2, -2)$

4. What is the missing x-value if $(x, 3)$ is a solution to $y = 2x + 2$?

    A. -1

    B. $-\dfrac{1}{2}$

    C. $\dfrac{1}{2}$

    D. 1

5. A segment is drawn from the origin to $(-4, 3)$. What is the length of the segment?

    A. 1
    B. 5
    C. 7
    D. 12

6. Two points are located at $(2, 5)$ and $(4, 3)$. What is the distance between the points to the nearest hundredth?

    A. 1.41
    B. 2.45
    C. 2.65
    D. 2.83

DIRECTIONS: Read the information, and study the grid. Then choose the **best** answer to each question.

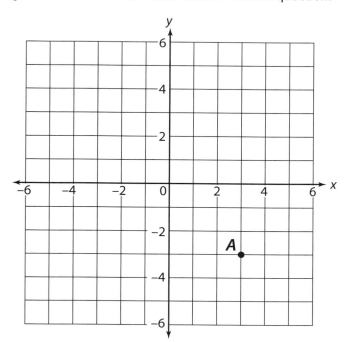

7. Point A lies on a line of the equation $x + 2y = -3$. Which of the following are other points on this line?

    A. $(0, -3)$
    B. $(-1, 2)$
    C. $(0, -2)$
    D. $(-5, 1)$

8. Marvin walks a straight line from $(-5, 2)$ to $(-3, 1)$ and stops. Then he walks a straight line from $(-3, 1)$ to $(-1, -4)$. What is the approximate distance Marvin traveled?

    A. 14.94
    B. 9.04
    C. 7.62
    D. 5.83

9. Point A lies on a circle that is centered at the origin. Given that all points on the circle are the same distance from the origin, which of the following represents the point on the circle on the positive y-axis?

    A. $(3\sqrt{2}, 0)$
    B. $(0, 3\sqrt{2})$
    C. $(3, 0)$
    D. $(0, 3)$

Slope

MATH CONTENT TOPICS: Q.2.a, Q.2.e, Q.6.c, A.5.b, A.6.a, A.6.b
MATH PRACTICES: MP.1.a, MP.1.b. MP.1.e, MP.3.a

1 Learn the Skill

Slope is a number that measures the steepness of a line. Slope can be positive, negative, or zero. Slope can be found by counting spaces on a graph or by using an algebraic formula. Finding slope from two points on a graph requires finding and dividing the **rise**, or the difference in y-values, by the **run**, or the difference in x-values.

The slope of a line can be used in combination with other information to find the formula of the line. The slope-intercept form can be used if the y-intercept is known: $y = mx + b$, where m is the slope and b is the y-intercept. The slope-point form can be used if one point is known: $y - y_1 = m(x - x_1)$ where m is the slope and (x_1, y_1) is the point.

2 Practice the Skill

By practicing the skill of finding the slope, you will improve your study and test-taking abilities, especially as they relate to the GED® Mathematical Reasoning Test. Study the information below. Then answer the question that follows.

a Use two points to find a slope. Start at the lower point. How many units must you climb to reach the other point? This is the rise, or numerator. How many units must you move left or right to reach the point? This is the run, or denominator. If you move left, the value is negative. There is also an algebraic formula you may use to find slope.

b To find the equation of a line, find the y-intercept (where the line crosses the y-axis). The line crosses the y-axis at −2. Next, find the slope. The slope of this line is −1. Substitute the values of m and b into the equation.

$y = mx + b$
$y = -1x + (-2)$
$y = -x - 2$

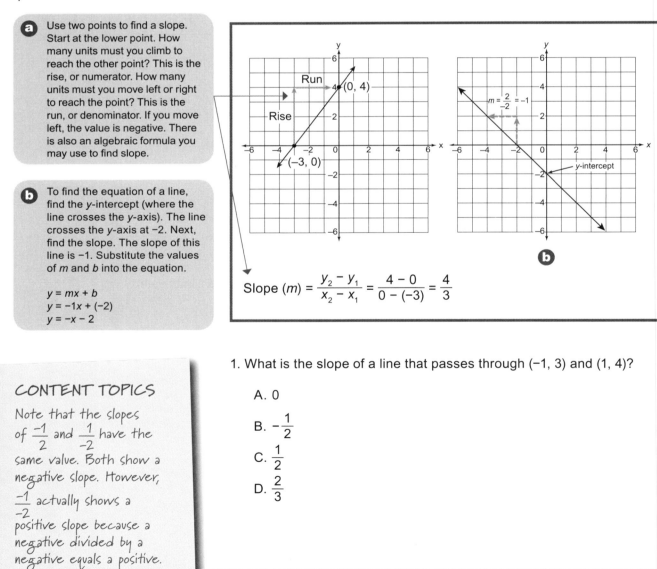

Slope $(m) = \dfrac{y_2 - y_1}{x_2 - x_1} = \dfrac{4 - 0}{0 - (-3)} = \dfrac{4}{3}$

CONTENT TOPICS

Note that the slopes of $\frac{-1}{2}$ and $\frac{1}{-2}$ have the same value. Both show a negative slope. However, $\frac{-1}{-2}$ actually shows a positive slope because a negative divided by a negative equals a positive.

1. What is the slope of a line that passes through (−1, 3) and (1, 4)?

A. 0
B. $-\dfrac{1}{2}$
C. $\dfrac{1}{2}$
D. $\dfrac{2}{3}$

DIRECTIONS: Study the grid, read the question, and choose the **best** answer.

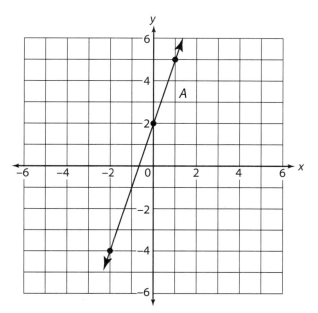

2. The following points lie on line A: (−2, −4), (0, 2), and (1, 5). What is the slope of line A?

    A. 3
    B. 9
    C. 10
    D. 12

DIRECTIONS: Study the information and diagram, read the question, and choose the **best** answer.

A ramp was built to allow wheelchair access to a front door. The ramp rises 2 feet, as shown in the diagram below.

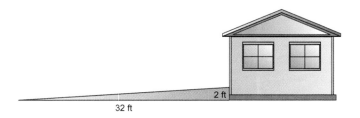

32 ft

3. What is the slope of the ramp?

    A. $\dfrac{1}{32}$

    B. $\dfrac{1}{18}$

    C. $\dfrac{1}{16}$

    D. $\dfrac{1}{8}$

DIRECTIONS: Read each question, and choose the **best** answer.

4. A linear function is represented by $f(x) = 2$. What is the slope of the line?

    A. −2
    B. −1
    C. 0
    D. 1

5. Identify which of the following equations are written in point-slope form.

    A. $3x + 3y = 18$
    B. $y = 2x + 3$
    C. $y + 3 = 6$
    D. $y + 3 = 3(x − 4)$

6. Write the point-slope equation of a line with slope 3 that passes through the point (−2, 5).

    A. $y = 3x + 2$
    B. $y = 3x + 6$
    C. $y − 5 = 3(x + 2)$
    D. $y = 3x + 11$

7. Write the point-slope equation of a line that goes through the points (−6, −1) and (9, −11).

    A. $y − 1 = -\dfrac{2(x + 6)}{3}$

    B. $y = 2x + 3$

    C. $y + 3 = (x − 0.5)$

    D. $y + 1 = -\dfrac{2}{3}(x + 6)$

8. Which of the following is equivalent to $(y − 2) = −5(x − 1)$?

    A. $y = −5x + 7$
    B. $y = −5x + 5$
    C. $y = −5x + 3$
    D. $y = −5x − 7$

9. Which equation shows a line parallel to $4 − y = 2x$?

    A. $2 + y = 2x$
    B. $y − 2 = \dfrac{1}{2}x$
    C. $−y = 2 − 2x$
    D. $y = −2x + 2$

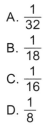

UNIT 3

Using Slope to Solve Geometric Problems

MATH CONTENT TOPICS: Q.2.a, Q.6.c, A.5.a, A.5.b, A.6.a, A.6.b, A.6.c
MATH PRACTICES: MP.1.a, MP.1.b, MP.1.c, MP.1.e, MP.2.c, MP.3.a, MP.4.b, MP.5.c

1 Learn the Skill

If two lines are **parallel** to each other, they have the same slope. If two lines are **perpendicular** to each other, their slopes are negative reciprocals of each other. For example, if the slope of one line is 2, the slope of a perpendicular line is $-\frac{1}{2}$.

These properties can help you to analyze geometric relationships between isolated lines and also between lines that describe 2-dimensional figures involving parallel and perpendicular lines. These include squares, rectangles, and triangles where one side is perpendicular to another.

2 Practice the Skill

By practicing the skill of using slope to solve geometric problems, you will improve your study and test-taking abilities, especially as they relate to the GED® Mathematical Reasoning Test. Study the information and grid below. Then answer the question that follows.

a The slope of a line, which may be given explicitly or appear in the equation of the line as the coefficient of *x*, determines the orientation of the line. The *y*-intercept of the line determines the line's overall placement. When assessing whether lines are parallel or perpendicular, it is the slope that is the key.

b The line whose equation is specified in the question will, in combination with the other three lines in the graph, form the boundary of a rectangle; opposite sides are parallel and adjacent sides are perpendicular. Here, Lines *A* and *B* are *parallel*. Lines *A* and *C* are *perpendicular*.

The graph below plots three lines:

- *A:* Slope of $\frac{3}{2}$ and *y*-intercept of 0
- *B:* Slope of $\frac{3}{2}$ and *y*-intercept of 4
- *C:* Slope of $-\frac{2}{3}$ and *y*-intercept of 2

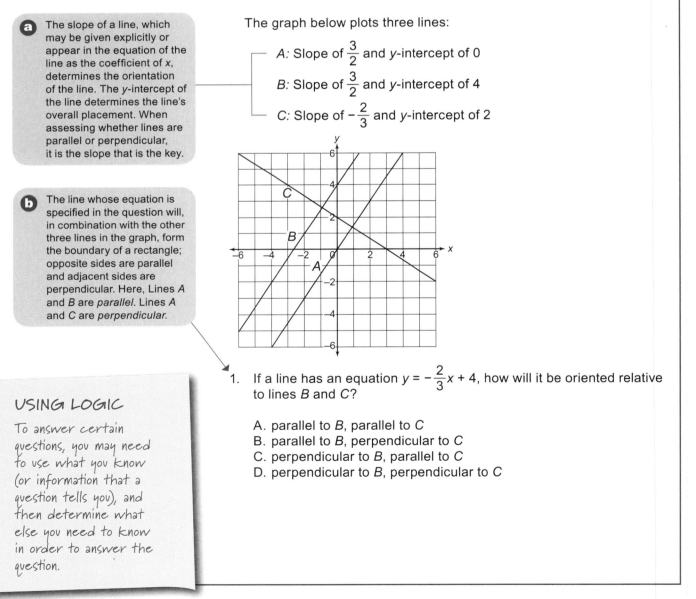

1. If a line has an equation $y = -\frac{2}{3}x + 4$, how will it be oriented relative to lines *B* and *C*?

   A. parallel to *B*, parallel to *C*
   B. parallel to *B*, perpendicular to *C*
   C. perpendicular to *B*, parallel to *C*
   D. perpendicular to *B*, perpendicular to *C*

USING LOGIC

To answer certain questions, you may need to use what you know (or information that a question tells you), and then determine what else you need to know in order to answer the question.

DIRECTIONS: Read each question, and choose the **best** answer.

2. What is the slope of a line parallel to $y = 4x + 3$?

   A. $-\dfrac{3}{4}$

   B. $-\dfrac{1}{4}$

   C. 3
   D. 4

3. What is the slope of a line perpendicular to $y = -3x + 2$?

   A. -3

   B. $-\dfrac{1}{3}$

   C. $\dfrac{1}{3}$

   D. 3

4. Which equation corresponds to a line perpendicular to $4 - y = 2x$?

   A. $2 + y = 2x$

   B. $y - 2 = \dfrac{1}{2}x$

   C. $-y = 2 - 2x$
   D. $y = -2x + 2$

5. Which equation corresponds to a line perpendicular to $y = -\dfrac{4}{3}x + 4$?

   A. $y = \dfrac{4}{3}x - 3$

   B. $y = \dfrac{3}{4}x - 1$

   C. $y = -\dfrac{3}{4}x + 1$

   D. $y = -\dfrac{4}{3}x + 3$

6. Which equation corresponds to a line perpendicular to $x = 5 - 3y$, that crosses the y-axis at $y = 3$?

   A. $\dfrac{1}{3}y = x + 1$

   B. $\dfrac{1}{3}y = x + 3$

   C. $y = -3x + 3$
   D. $y = 3x + 1$

DIRECTIONS: Study the following information and figure, read each question, and choose the **best** answer.

A rectangle is shown below, defined by points A, B, C, and D. Point A is at the origin, point C is at $(0, 8)$, and the line through points A and B has a slope of 3.

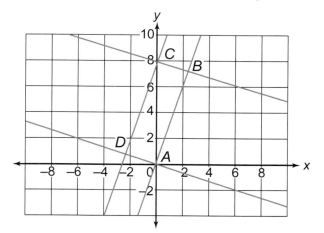

7. What is the equation of the line through points C and D?

   A. $y = \dfrac{1}{3}x + 8$

   B. $y = \dfrac{1}{3}x - 8$

   C. $y = 3x + 8$
   D. $y = 3x - 8$

8. What is the equation of the line through points B and C?

   A. $y = -\dfrac{1}{3}x - 8$

   B. $y = -\dfrac{1}{3}x + 8$

   C. $y = -3x - 8$
   D. $y = -3x + 8$

9. What are the coordinates of point B?

   A. (2.5, 7.2)
   B. (2.5, 7.5)
   C. (2.4, 7.2)
   D. (2.4, 7.5)

10. What are the coordinates of point D?

   A. (−2.7, 0.9)
   B. (−2.7, 0.8)
   C. (−2.4, 0.9)
   D. (−2.4, 0.8)

Graphing Quadratic Equations

MATH CONTENT TOPICS: Q.2.a, Q.6.c, A.5.a, A.5.e
MATH PRACTICES: MP.1.a, MP.1.b, MP.1.d, MP.2.c, MP.3.a, MP.4.a, MP.4.b, MP.5.c

1 Learn the Skill

Quadratic equations are equations set in the form $ax^2 + bx + c = 0$, where a does not equal 0. Quadratic equations exhibit various characteristics when shown graphically. These include zero, one or two points where the plot of such an equation crosses the x-axis, one point where it crosses the y-axis, either a maximum when $a < 0$ or a minimum when $a > 0$, and symmetry with respect to that maximum or minimum.

The coefficients in the equation—a, b, and c—can quantify these characteristics. For example, larger values of a will contract a curve, while smaller values of a will expand a curve. Negative values of a will turn it upside down. You also can use plotted data and knowledge of characteristics such as x- and y-intercepts to help determine the coefficients.

2 Practice the Skill

By practicing the skills associated with graphing quadratic equations, you will improve your study and test-taking abilities, especially as they relate to the GED® Mathematical Reasoning Test. Study the information and graph below. Then answer the question that follows.

a Curves cross the x-axis when $y = 0$; here $\frac{1}{3}x^2 + x - 4 = 0$. Values can be found by factoring, use of the quadratic formula, and so on.

b Curves cross the y-axis when $x = 0$; the constant term, in this case -4, is the y-intercept.

c Curves go through a minimum when $a > 0$, and a maximum when $a < 0$. Here, $a = \frac{1}{3} > 0$, so the curve has a minimum; y increases as one moves away from the minimum in either direction. Curves are symmetric about the maximum or minimum; for example, the two points where the curve crosses the x-axis are the same distance from the minimum.

The function $y = ax^2 + bx + c = \frac{1}{3}x^2 + x - 4$ is plotted in the following graph.

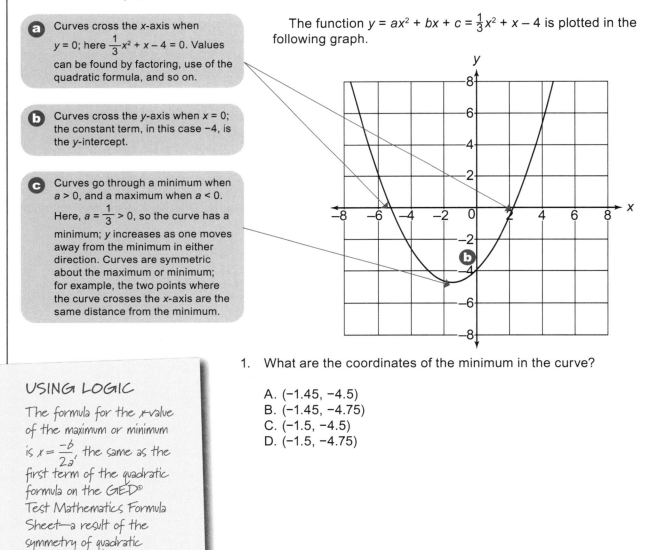

1. What are the coordinates of the minimum in the curve?

A. (−1.45, −4.5)
B. (−1.45, −4.75)
C. (−1.5, −4.5)
D. (−1.5, −4.75)

USING LOGIC

The formula for the x-value of the maximum or minimum is $x = \frac{-b}{2a}$, the same as the first term of the quadratic formula on the GED® Test Mathematics Formula Sheet—a result of the symmetry of quadratic functions.

UNIT 3

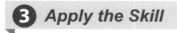
DIRECTIONS: Study the following quadratic equation, read each question, and choose the **best** answer.

$$y = x^2 + 2x - 8$$

2. Which of the following pairs of *x*-values represent where the curve crosses the *x*-axis?

    A. $x = -8$, $x = 8$
    B. $x = -4$, $x = 2$
    C. $x = -4$, $x = 4$
    D. $x = -2$, $x = 4$

3. Which of the following values of *y* represents where the curve crosses the *y*-axis?

    A. $y = -8$
    B. $y = -4$
    C. $y = 4$
    D. $y = 8$

4. Which of the following values of *x* represents where the curve goes through a minimum?

    A. $x = -2$
    B. $x = -1$
    C. $x = 1$
    D. $x = 2$

DIRECTIONS: Study the graph, read the question, and choose the **best** answer.

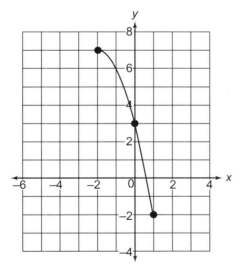

5. If the point at (−2, 7) is the maximum, what negative value of *x* corresponds to a *y*-value of −2?

    A. −3
    B. −4
    C. −5
    D. −6

DIRECTIONS: Study the following information and diagram, read each question, and choose the **best** answer.

The following graph features plots of five different quadratic equations of the form $y = ax^2 + bx + c$, identified by letters *A* through *E*.

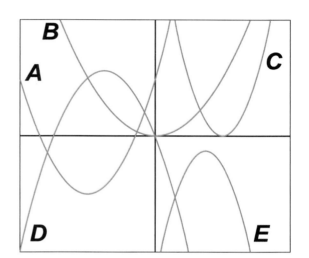

6. Which curves correspond to equations with $a < 0$?

    A. Curve *D* only
    B. Curves *A* and *D*
    C. Curves *C* and *E*
    D. Curves *D* and *E*

7. Which curves correspond to equations with $b = 0$?

    A. only Curve *B*
    B. only Curve *C*
    C. Curves *B* and *C*
    D. Curves *B* and *D*

8. Which curves correspond to equations with $\frac{b}{2a} < 0$?

    A. Curves *A* and *D*
    B. Curves *A* and *E*
    C. Curves *C* and *E*
    D. Curves *D* and *E*

9. Which curves correspond to equations with $c = 0$?

    A. Curve *B* only
    B. Curve *C* only
    C. Curves *B* and *C*
    D. Curves *B* and *D*

UNIT 3

Evaluation of Functions

MATH CONTENT TOPICS: Q.2.a, Q.6.c, A.5.e, A.7.b, A.7.c
MATH PRACTICES: MP.1.a, MP.1.b, MP.1.d, MP.1.e, MP.2.c, MP.3.a, MP.4.a, MP.5.c

UNIT 3

1 Learn the Skill

As you know, a **function** relates an input to an output. It always includes three parts: the input, the relationship, and the output. For example, an input of 1 and a relationship of $\times 2$ produces an output of 2 ($1 \times 2 = 2$). In the function $f(x) = x^2$, f is the function, x is the input, and x^2 is the output. The function $f(x) = x^2$ shows that the function f takes the x and squares it. So an input of 4 would result in an output of 16: $f(4) = 4^2$. Functions always have one output (y-value) for each input (x-value). Often, outputs are noted by the use of a y-value and inputs by the use of an x-value.

2 Practice the Skill

By practicing the skill of evaluating functions, you will improve your study and test-taking abilities, especially as they relate to the GED® Mathematical Reasoning Test. Study the information and graphs below. Then answer the question that follows.

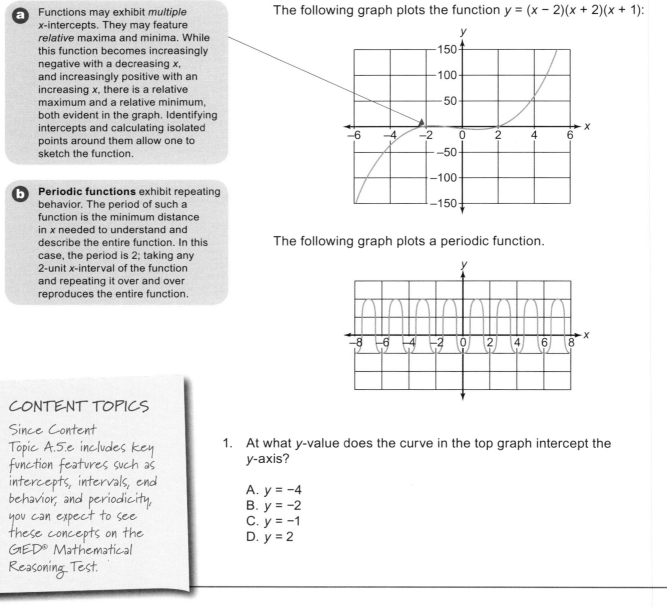

a Functions may exhibit *multiple* x-intercepts. They may feature *relative* maxima and minima. While this function becomes increasingly negative with a decreasing x, and increasingly positive with an increasing x, there is a relative maximum and a relative minimum, both evident in the graph. Identifying intercepts and calculating isolated points around them allow one to sketch the function.

b **Periodic functions** exhibit repeating behavior. The period of such a function is the minimum distance in x needed to understand and describe the entire function. In this case, the period is 2; taking any 2-unit x-interval of the function and repeating it over and over reproduces the entire function.

The following graph plots the function $y = (x - 2)(x + 2)(x + 1)$:

The following graph plots a periodic function.

CONTENT TOPICS

Since Content Topic A.5.e includes key function features such as intercepts, intervals, end behavior, and periodicity, you can expect to see these concepts on the GED® Mathematical Reasoning Test.

1. At what y-value does the curve in the top graph intercept the y-axis?

   A. $y = -4$
   B. $y = -2$
   C. $y = -1$
   D. $y = 2$

DIRECTIONS: Study the information and graph, read each question, and choose the **best** answer.

The following graph is a plot of the function $y = (x^2 + 1)(x - 4)$. Four x positions are labeled.

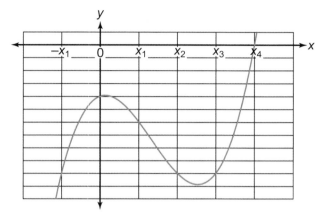

2. At which of the specified x-values is y increasing?

   A. x_1 only
   B. x_3 only
   C. x_4 only
   D. x_3 and x_4 only

3. At which of the specified x-values is y negative?

   A. x_1 only
   B. x_2 only
   C. x_1 and x_4 only
   D. x_1, x_2, and x_3 only

4. In what x interval does the curve go through a relative minimum?

   A. between x_1 and x_2
   B. between x_2 and x_3
   C. between x_3 and x_4
   D. to the right of x_4

5. At what y-value does the curve intercept the y-axis?

   A. $y = -5$
   B. $y = -4$
   C. $y = -3$
   D. $y = -1$

6. At which of the specified x-values does the curve intercept the x-axis?

   A. x_4
   B. x_3
   C. x_2
   D. x_1

DIRECTIONS: Read each question, and choose the **best** answer.

7. Which equation corresponds to the graph below?

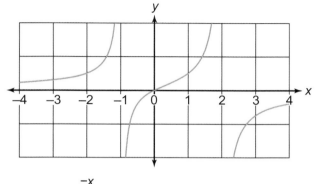

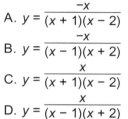

   A. $y = \dfrac{-x}{(x + 1)(x - 2)}$

   B. $y = \dfrac{-x}{(x - 1)(x + 2)}$

   C. $y = \dfrac{x}{(x + 1)(x - 2)}$

   D. $y = \dfrac{x}{(x - 1)(x + 2)}$

8. The following graph represents a periodic function. What is the period of the function?

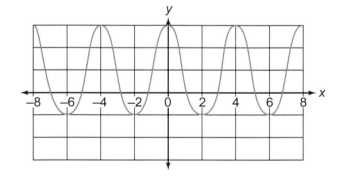

   A. 1
   B. 2
   C. 4
   D. 8

9. Which of the following sets of data points could correspond to a function?

   A. (−2, −2), (−1, −1), (0, 0), (−1, 1), (−2, 2)
   B. (2, −2), (1, −1), (0, 0), (1, 1), (2, 2)
   C. (−2, −2), (−1, −1), (0, 0), (1, −1), (2, −2)
   D. (−2, −2), (−1, −1), (0, 0), (−1, 1), (2, 2)

Comparison of Functions

MATH CONTENT TOPICS: Q.6.c, A.5.e, A.7.a, A.7.c, A.7.d
MATH PRACTICES: MP.1.a, MP.1.b, MP.1.e, MP.4.c

1 Learn the Skill

A **function** is a relation in which each input has exactly one output. Functions can be represented by sets of ordered pairs in tables, in graphs, algebraically, or by verbal descriptions. Two or more functions can be compared based on their slopes or rates of change, intercepts, the locations and values of minimums and maximums, and other features. You can compare two linear functions, two quadratic functions, or a linear function and a quadratic function.

When functions are compared, they may be presented in the same way or in different ways. For example, you may want to compare the rates of change of one function represented by a table of values and another function represented by an algebraic expression.

2 Practice the Skill

By practicing the skill of comparing functions, you will improve your study and test-taking abilities, especially as they relate to the GED® Mathematical Reasoning Test. Study the graph, table, and information below. Then answer the question that follows.

a The rate of change of a linear function is also known as its slope. In a graph, the rate of change is the ratio of the vertical change, or *rise*, to the horizontal change, or *run*. The function represented by this graph has a rate of change of $\frac{2}{3}$, meaning it rises 2 spots and runs 3 spots. Its intercepts are $y = -2$ and $x = 3$. In a table, the rate of change is the ratio of the change in y-value to the change in x-value. The function represented by this table has a rate of change of 2 and a y-intercept of 1.

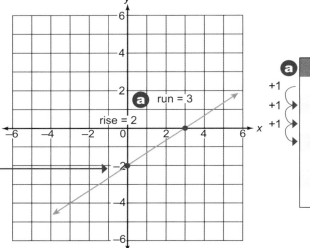

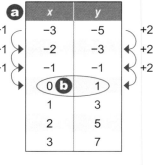

b The intercepts of a function are the values of one coordinate when the other coordinate is zero. In a graph, look for points that cross the axes. In a table, look at the rows in which one value is 0.

1. A function has a rate of change that is greater than the rate of change shown in the graph above and less than the rate of change shown in the table above. Which equation could represent the function?

    A. $f(x) = 3x + 2$

    B. $f(x) = \frac{1}{2}x - 1$

    C. $f(x) = x + 3$

    D. $f(x) = \frac{5}{2}x + 2$

DIRECTIONS: Study the graph, read each question, and choose the **best** answer.

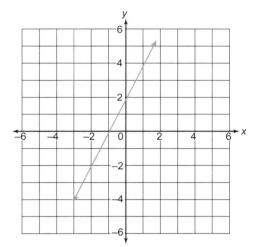

2. Which function has the same *y*-intercept as the function represented in the graph?

   A. $f(x) = x - 2$
   B. $f(x) = 2x + 3$
   C. $f(x) = -3x + 2$
   D. $f(x) = -6x - 1$

3. A function is represented by the set of ordered pairs below.

   {(−2, 2), (0, 6), (2, 10), (4, 14)}

   Which statement is true?

   A. The function has the same rate of change and *y*-intercept as the function represented in the graph.
   B. The function has the same rate of change and a different *y*-intercept from the function represented in the graph.
   C. The function has the same *y*-intercept and a different rate of change from the function represented in the graph.
   D. The function has a different rate of change and *y*-intercept from the function represented in the graph.

4. For *x* = −2, which function has the same value as the function represented in the graph?

   A. $f(x) = -x$
   B. $f(x) = \dfrac{x}{2} + 1$
   C. $f(x) = x + 4$
   D. $f(x) = 6x + 10$

DIRECTIONS: Study the table, read each question, and choose the **best** answer.

x	y
−3	−5
−2	0
−1	3
0	4
1	3
2	0
3	−5

5. Which function has the same *x*-intercepts as the function represented in the table?

   A. $f(x) = \dfrac{1}{2}x^2 - 2$
   B. $f(x) = \dfrac{1}{2}x^2 + 2$
   C. $f(x) = 2x^2 - 2$
   D. $f(x) = 2x^2 + 2$

6. For the function represented in the graph below, which is true?

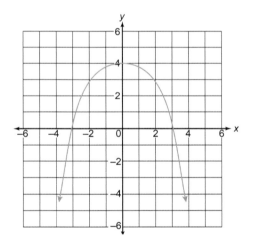

   A. The function represented in the graph has the same maximum value as the function represented in the table.
   B. The function represented in the graph has the same minimum value as the function represented in the table.
   C. The function represented in the graph has both the same minimum value and the same maximum value as the function represented in the table.
   D. The function represented in the graph has neither the same minimum value nor the same maximum value as the function represented in the table.

Unit 3 Review

DIRECTIONS: Read each question, and choose the **best** answer.

1. A painter charges $20 per hour for herself and $15 per hour for her assistant. In painting a living room, the assistant worked 5 hours more than the painter. The total charge for labor was $355.

   Let h be the number of hours that the painter worked. Which of the following equations can be used to find h?

   A. $20h + 15(h + 5) = 355$
   B. $20(h + 5) + 15h = 355$
   C. $20h + 15(h - 5) = 355$
   D. $20h - 15(h + 5) = 355$

2. If $x^2 = 36$, then $2(x + 5)$ could equal which of the following numbers?

   A. 6
   B. 11
   C. 12
   D. 22

3. Sara deposits $1,244 in her checking account each week. If she currently has $287 in her account, which equation represents her balance (B), at week w?

   A. $B = \$1,294 + \$287$
   B. $B = \$1,394$
   C. $B = \$1,244w + \$287$
   D. $B = \$1,531w$

4. What equation represents the sequence below?
   3, 2.5, 2, 1.5, 1, 0.5, 0, . . .

   A. $y = 3 - 0.5x$
   B. $y = 3 + 0.5x$
   C. $y = 3x - 0.5$
   D. $y = 3x + 0.5$

5. The number of men acting in a theater production is five more than half the number of women. Which of the following describes the number of men in the production?

   A. $2w + 5$
   B. $\frac{1}{2}w + 5$
   C. $2w - 5$
   D. $\frac{1}{2}w - 5$

DIRECTIONS: Read the question, and choose the **best** answer.

6. If $3x + 0.15 = 1.29$, what is the value of x?

   A. 0.38
   B. 1.14
   C. 1.29
   D. 1.34

DIRECTIONS: Read each question, study the grid, and choose the **best** answer.

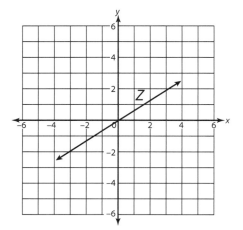

7. What is the slope of line Z?

   A. $-\frac{2}{3}$
   B. $\frac{2}{3}$
   C. $\frac{3}{2}$
   D. 2

8. What is the equation of line Z in slope-intercept form?

   A. $y = -\frac{2}{3}x$
   B. $y = \frac{2}{3}x$
   C. $y = -\frac{2}{3}x + 1$
   D. $y = \frac{2}{3}x - 1$

DIRECTIONS: Study the diagram, read each question, and choose the **best** answer.

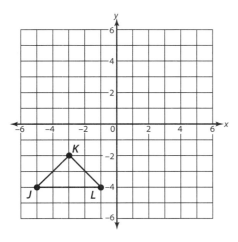

9. If triangle *JKL* is reflected across the *y*-axis, then what is the new location of point *K*? Mark your answer on the coordinate plane grid.

10. What is the slope of side *JL* in triangle *JKL*?

A. −2
B. −1
C. 0
D. 1

DIRECTIONS: Read each question, and choose the **best** answer.

11. The number of people voting in an election who were over 25 years old was 56 less than twice the number of those voting who were under 25 years old. Which expression represents the number of people who were over 25 years old who voted in the election?

A. 56x − 25
B. 2x − 56
C. x + 56
D. 56x + 25

12. The Earth is 149,600,000 kilometers from the sun. What is this distance written in scientific notation?

A. 1.496×10^{-7} km
B. 1.496×10^{-8} km
C. 1.496×10^{8} km
D. 1.496×10^{9} km

DIRECTIONS: Read the question, and choose the **best** answer.

13. Dahlia has a pass that allows her to get specialty health snacks without stopping to pay. The amount of the snack is automatically charged to her credit card. She pays a fee of $15 per month for this service. Each snack costs $1.25. She budgets $75 a month for her total snack bill. What is the maximum number of snacks she can buy each month and still stay within her budget?

A. 1.25
B. 15
C. 48
D. 60

DIRECTIONS: Study the information below, read each question, and choose the **best** answer.

The product of two consecutive integers is 19 less than their sum.

14. What equation represents the statement above?

A. $x + (x + 1) = 15 + x$
B. $x(x + 1) = x − 15$
C. $x + (x + 1) = 15x$
D. $x^2 − x + 18 = 0$

15. If the sum of the two numbers is 11, which pair below could be the two integers?

A. 0 and 2
B. 2 and 3
C. 4 and 5
D. 5 and 6

DIRECTIONS: Read the question and choose the **best** answer.

16. A scientist is studying a bacterium with a diameter of 1.8×10^{-6} meter and a virus with a diameter of 2.5×10^{-9}. About how many times greater is the diameter of the bacterium than the diameter of the virus?

A. 7 times
B. 70 times
C. 700 times
D. 7,000 times

DIRECTIONS: Read each question, and choose the **best** answer.

17. Francisco has a total of twenty $5 and $1 bills in his wallet. The total value of the bills is $52. How many $5 bills does Francisco have in his wallet?

    A. 0
    B. 4
    C. 8
    D. 12

18. If $f(x) = \dfrac{x^2 - 4}{4x}$, for which of the following values will the expression be undefined?

    A. $x - -1$
    B. $x = 0$
    C. $x = 1$
    D. $x - 2$

19. Each day for three days, Emmit withdrew $64 from his account. Which number shows the change in his account after the three days?

    A. −$192
    B. −$128
    C. −$64
    D. $192

20. Graph $y = x^2 + 2x - 8$ on the grid below.

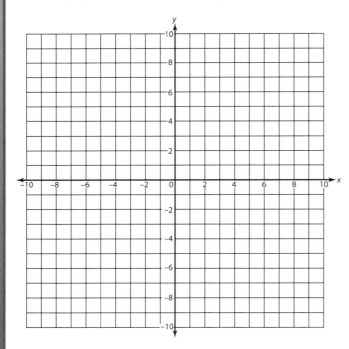

DIRECTIONS: Read each question, and choose the **best** answer.

21. A skier takes a chairlift 786 feet up the side of a mountain. He then skis down 137 feet and catches a different chairlift 542 feet up the mountain. What is his position when he gets off the chairlift relative to where he began on the first chairlift?

    A. −1,191 feet
    B. +679 feet
    C. 1,465 feet
    D. +1,191 feet

22. Which of the following inequalities is shown on the number line?

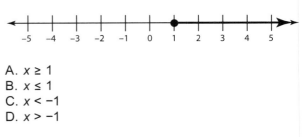

    A. $x \geq 1$
    B. $x \leq 1$
    C. $x < -1$
    D. $x > -1$

23. A summer family camp costs $230 for adults. The cost for a child is $30 less than one half the cost for adults. What is the cost for 3 children?

    A. $200
    B. $230
    C. $255
    D. $275

24. A square has an area of 4 square feet. What is the perimeter of the square, rounded to the nearest foot?

    A. 8
    B. 12.5
    C. 28
    D. 200

25. Which number is a solution of the inequality $2(1 - x) < 8$?

    A. −2
    B. −3
    C. −4
    D. −5

DIRECTIONS: Read each question, and choose the **best** answer.

26. For the function $f(x) = 3x - 6$ which of the following x-values has a positive whole number output?

  A. −1
  B. 0
  C. 2
  D. 3

27. Which of the following is equivalent to the equation $2x^2 + 18x + 36 = 0$?

  A. $2x(x + 6) + 6(x + 6) = 0$
  B. 6
  C. 3 and 6
  D. $2(x + 18) + 36 = 0$

28. The sum of a number and 20 is greater than or equal to 5 times the number plus 3. Which inequality represents this situation?

  A. $x + 20 \geq 5x + 3$
  B. $x + 20 \geq 5x - 3$
  C. $x + 20 \leq 5x + 3$
  D. $20 \geq 5x + 3$

DIRECTIONS: Study the grid, read each question, and choose the **best** answer.

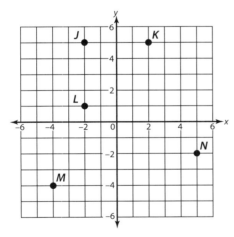

29. Points J, K, and L mark the corners of a rectangle. What is the location of the fourth corner needed to complete the rectangle? Mark your answer on the coordinate plane grid.

30. Which of the following is the equation of a line that passes through points L and K?

  A. $y = 3x + 6$
  B. $y = 2x + 3$
  C. $y = 1x + 3$
  D. $y = 1x + 2$

31. If the line that passes through L and K was extended, what would the y-value be at the point $x = 5$?

  A. 3
  B. 5
  C. 8
  D. 10

DIRECTIONS: Read each question, and choose the **best** answer.

32. The equation $h = 2t^2 - 3t + 1.125$ represents the height h of a ball above ground at time t seconds after being dropped. How many seconds does it take the ball to reach the ground?

  A. 1.125
  B. $\dfrac{1}{2}$
  C. $\dfrac{3 \pm \sqrt{18}}{4}$
  D. $\dfrac{3}{4}$

33. The weight of a mother elephant is 200 kg more than 4 times the weight of her newborn calf. Which of the following expressions represents the mother elephant's weight?

  A. $4n + 200$
  B. $4n - 2(200)$
  C. $(n - 200)$
  D. $4n - 200$

34. Nina purchased solar lights for her front walkway. The total amount she paid for 10 lights was $100, including $4.25 tax. What was the cost per light before tax?

  A. $7.92
  B. $8.18
  C. $8.65
  D. $9.58

35. Light travels at a speed of 299,792,458 m/s from the sun. What is this distance written in scientific notation?

    A. $2.99792458 \times 10^{-3}$ m/s
    B. 2.99792458×10^{8} m/s
    C. 2.99792458×10^{4} m/s
    D. 2.99792458×10^{5} m/s

36. The number of students at one university can be written as $2(8^4)$. How many students are at the university?

    A. 2,048
    B. 4,096
    C. 6,072
    D. 8,192

37. A ticket to a fair costs $20. Tokens are sold in packs of 10 for $15. Edward takes $100 to the fair. He has to buy his ticket, and he also wants to buy tokens to win prizes for his family. Which inequality represents the possible number of packs of tokens that he can buy?

    A. $100 - 20 \leq x$
    B. $20 \geq 100 - x$
    C. $20x - 15 < 80$
    D. $15x + 20 \leq 100$

38. What are the maximum packs of tokens that Edward can buy?

    A. 4
    B. 5
    C. 6
    D. 60

39. Jonathan's account balance decreases by $20 dollars per day. At the start of the week he has $2,000. How much does he have 3 days later?

    A. $60
    B. $1,500
    C. $1,900
    D. $1,940

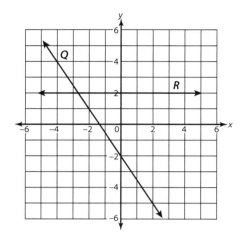

40. What are the coordinates of point Q?

    A. (4, 4)
    B. (−4, 4)
    C. (4, −6)
    D. (4, 6)

41. Which of the following is the equation of line R?

    A. $x = 2$
    B. $y = 2$
    C. $y = x + 2$
    D. $x = y + 2$

42. If the line R were shifted 2 units up the y-axis, what would the new equation of the line be?

    A. $y = 4$
    B. $y = 5$
    C. $y = 6$
    D. $y = 60$

43. Which function has the same slope as line Q?

    A. $2x - 3y = -5$
    B. $2x + 3y = 4$
    C. $3x - 2y = -5$
    D. $3x + 2y = 4$

The grid below includes the line $y = 2x + 3$.

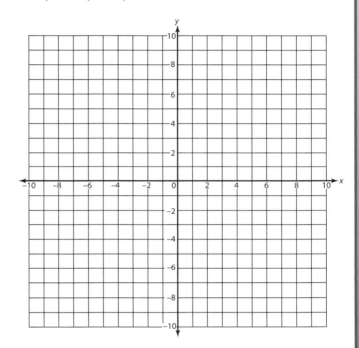

44. What is the slope of the line above?

45. What will the x-value be when y is equal to zero?

46. What will the y-value be when x is equal to zero?

47. What will the y-value be when x is equal to 30?

A. $y = 3$
B. $y = 13.5$
C. $y = 60$
D. $y = 63$

48. What will the x-value be if $y = 30$?

A. $x = 2$
B. $x = 3$
C. $x = 13.5$
D. $x = 30$

Time Elapsed (hr)	Height of Plant
1	2.5 cm
2	5 cm
3	7.5 cm
4	10 cm

49. Plot the information above on the graph below.

For example, 1 would be the x-value, and 2.5 cm would be the y-value, so that the first ordered pair is (1, 2.5).

50. What is the equation of the line above?

A. $y = 2.5x$
B. $y = 5x$
C. $y = 6x$
D. $y = 7x$

51. If the plant continues to grow at that rate, how tall will it be in 24 hours?

A. 4 cm
B. 50 cm
C. 60 cm
D. 120 cm

DIRECTIONS: Read each question, and choose the **best** answer.

52. If $10x + 3.15 = 58.15$, what is the value of x?

A. 4.5
B. 5.5
C. 6.5
D. 7.5

53. Kira bought eight T-shirts. After she redeemed a $10-dollar coupon, she paid a total of $50 for the T-shirts, before tax. What was the original price of each T-shirt?

A. $8.75
B. $8.00
C. $7.50
D. $5.00

54. If $2(y - 4) = 4 - 3y$, what is the value of y?

A. 2.4
B. 1.6
C. −8
D. −12

DIRECTIONS: Read the information and each question, and choose the **best** answer.

One printing press has a fixed daily cost of $50 and a variable cost of $1.50 for every 30 pages printed. A second second printing press has a fixed daily cost of $10 and a variable cost of $2 for every 30 pages produced.

55. Determine the number of pages for which the total daily costs will be the same.

A. 80
B. 1,500
C. 2,400
D. 4,500

56. What is the total daily cost for this number of items?

A. $2
B. $10
C. $50
D. $170

DIRECTIONS: Read each question, and choose the **best** answer.

$$a + b = 10$$
$$3a - 4b = 9$$

57. What is the value of b in the equations above?

A. 3
B. −4
C. 7
D. 9

58. Which of the following is equivalent to the value of a in the equations above?

A. $2^0 + 1$
B. $2^4 - 3^2$
C. 3^2
D. $3^2 + 2$

DIRECTIONS: Read each question, and choose the **best** answer.

59. Tickets to a fundraising concert cost $6 for adults and $2 for children. If 175 tickets were sold, totalling $750, which of the following represents the number of children's tickets sold?

A. $c = 175 - a$
B. $2a + 6c = 175$
C. $6a + 2c = 175$
D. $6a + 2c = 750$

60. Which expression is equivalent to the cube root of −27?

A. $(-1)^2 \cdot \sqrt{9}$
B. $\dfrac{9^2}{3}$
C. $(-1)^{-1}(3)$
D. $(-3)^9$

61. One-eighth a number is two more than one-fourth the number. What is the number?

A. −16
B. −4
C. 8
D. 16

DIRECTIONS: Read each question, and choose the **best** answer.

62. Which has the same value as $8^2 + 4^0$?

    A. 1
    B. 4
    C. 64
    D. 65

63. Mark multiplied a number by itself. He found a product of 30. What is the number, rounded to the nearest tenth?

    A. 5.5
    B. 15
    C. 30
    D. 60

64. If $f(x) = 2x - 3$, then what is x when $f(x) = 4$?

    A. 3
    B. 3.5
    C. 4
    D. 5.5

65. If $4x^2 = 121$, what is the value of x?

    A. 4.5
    B. 5
    C. 5.5
    D. 6

66. A warehouse in the shape of a cube has a volume of 6,859 cubic feet. What is the surface area measured in squared feet?

    A. 19
    B. 361
    C. 2,166
    D. 6,859

67. If $z = 6$, which of the following expressions is undefined?

    A. $\dfrac{4z - 3}{z - 3}$

    B. $\dfrac{3z - 18}{2z + 12}$

    C. $\dfrac{4z - 24}{6}$

    D. $\dfrac{3z}{2z - 12}$

68. A shape having the points A (−2, 1), B (−4, 1), and C (−3, −2) is reflected across the y-axis. Plot the new shape on the grid below.

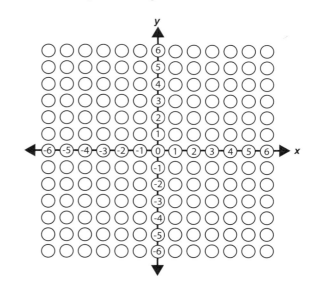

DIRECTIONS: Read the information and each question, then choose the **best** answer.

A student records the following numerical pattern: 100, 95, 90, 85

69. What is the next term in the sequence?

    A. 80
    B. 70
    C. 60
    D. 50

70. Which of the following equations can be used to represent the pattern above?

    A. $y = x$
    B. $y = 2$
    C. $y = x + 2$
    D. $y = 100 - 5x$

DIRECTIONS: Read the question, and choose the **best** answer.

71. Which of the following is equivalent to $(3x - 2y)(3x + 2y)$?

    A. $9x^2 + 4y^2$
    B. $9x^2 - 4y^2$
    C. $9x^2 + 6xy - 4y^2$
    D. $9x^2 - 6xy + 4y^2$

Huong McDoniel

Huong McDoniel's journey took her from Vietnam to the Philippines and Guam and on to Arizona and to her life today as a college faculty member in New Mexico.

Huong McDoniel left behind her books, but not her love of learning. As a teenager during the fall of Saigon, Huong McDoniel packed two suitcases: one with clothes, the other with science and math books. Before climbing to the top of the platform of the U.S. Embassy in Saigon, where helicopters were evacuating refugees, McDoniel was forced to leave her textbooks behind.

Flown to an aircraft carrier, McDoniel and 6,000 others then crowded onto a ship equipped for only 600 crew members. After living in refugee camps in the Philippines and Guam, McDoniel moved to Tucson, Arizona. At the time, she didn't yet speak English and first worked as a dishwasher. Her dream of becoming a teacher seemed as distant as her early life in Vietnam.

But then McDoniel moved to Albuquerque, New Mexico, where in 1989 she decided to pursue a GED® certificate while raising three children and also learning English. With help from tutors at Central New Mexico (CNM) Community College, McDoniel passed the GED® Test on her first try.

McDoniel continued her studies at CNM, earning an associate's degree in liberal arts and herself becoming a tutor. She then enrolled at the University of New Mexico, from which she earned an undergraduate degree in math and a master's degree in education. Today, McDoniel works as a full-time faculty member at CNM and speaks to GED® graduates about their achievements.

"The more you learn, the more your dream begins to expand. Then you start to believe you can do more. Slowly, I started thinking maybe I could become a teacher."

CAREER HIGHLIGHTS: *Huong McDoniel*

- Born in Vietnam and airlifted from Saigon during Operation Frequent Wind in 1975
- Married to Doug McDoniel, fellow faculty member at Central New Mexico Community College
- Raised three children while earning her associate's degree and working as a college tutor
- Achieved her dream of becoming a teacher

Geometry

Unit 4: Geometry

Look around your home, office, or town. Chances are, wherever you look—furniture, rooms, buildings, neighborhoods, or cities—you'll see a variety of geometric figures. Geometry enables us to solve many everyday problems using figures such as triangles, circles, and solids.

Geometry also appears frequently on the GED® Mathematical Reasoning Test. Among other concepts, in Unit 4 you will study triangles and quadrilaterals, polygons, circles, pyramids, cones, spheres, and composite plane figures and solids— all of which will help you prepare for the GED® Mathematical Reasoning Test.

Table of Contents

Whether at work or at home, people today use geometry to help solve a variety of real-world problems.

UNIT 4

Triangles and Quadrilaterals

MATH CONTENT TOPICS: Q.2.a, Q.2.e, Q.4.a, Q.4.c, A.2.a, A.2.b
MATH PRACTICES: MP.1.a, MP.1.b, MP.1.e, MP.2.a, MP.4.b

① Learn the Skill

A **triangle** is a closed three-sided figure with three angles. The sum of the three interior angles of any triangle is always 180°. A triangle can be classified according to its side lengths or angle measures. Triangles can be classified by their largest angle size: *right* (90°), *acute* (less than 90°), or *obtuse* (greater than 90°). They also can be classified by their sides: *equilateral* = three congruent sides; *isosceles* = at least two congruent sides; *scalene* = no congruent sides.

A **quadrilateral** is a closed four-sided figure with four angles. The sum of the four interior angles of any quadrilateral is always 360°. The sides of a quadrilateral may or may not be congruent or parallel. Parallelograms and rectangles have two sets of congruent, parallel sides. Rhombuses and squares have four congruent sides.

② Practice the Skill

By practicing the skill of computing the area and perimeter of triangles and quadrilaterals, you will improve your study and test-taking abilities, especially as they relate to the GED® Mathematical Reasoning Test. Study the information and figures below. Then answer the question that follows.

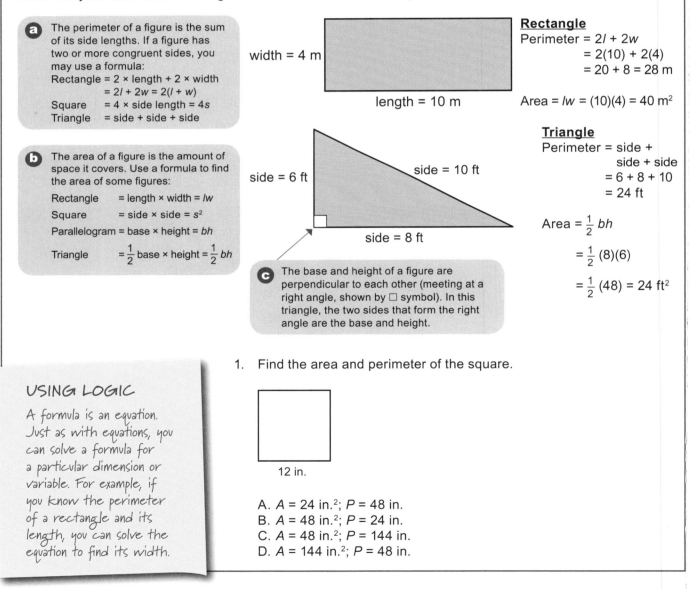

a The perimeter of a figure is the sum of its side lengths. If a figure has two or more congruent sides, you may use a formula:
Rectangle = 2 × length + 2 × width
$= 2l + 2w = 2(l + w)$
Square $= 4 × $ side length $= 4s$
Triangle $= $ side + side + side

b The area of a figure is the amount of space it covers. Use a formula to find the area of some figures:
Rectangle $= $ length × width $= lw$
Square $= $ side × side $= s^2$
Parallelogram $= $ base × height $= bh$
Triangle $= \frac{1}{2}$ base × height $= \frac{1}{2} bh$

c The base and height of a figure are perpendicular to each other (meeting at a right angle, shown by □ symbol). In this triangle, the two sides that form the right angle are the base and height.

width = 4 m

length = 10 m

side = 6 ft   side = 10 ft

side = 8 ft

Rectangle
Perimeter = 2l + 2w
$= 2(10) + 2(4)$
$= 20 + 8 = 28$ m

Area $= lw = (10)(4) = 40$ m²

Triangle
Perimeter = side + side + side
$= 6 + 8 + 10$
$= 24$ ft

Area $= \frac{1}{2} bh$
$= \frac{1}{2} (8)(6)$
$= \frac{1}{2} (48) = 24$ ft²

1. Find the area and perimeter of the square.

12 in.

A. $A = 24$ in.²; $P = 48$ in.
B. $A = 48$ in.²; $P = 24$ in.
C. $A = 48$ in.²; $P = 144$ in.
D. $A = 144$ in.²; $P = 48$ in.

USING LOGIC

A formula is an equation. Just as with equations, you can solve a formula for a particular dimension or variable. For example, if you know the perimeter of a rectangle and its length, you can solve the equation to find its width.

UNIT 4

DIRECTIONS: Study the figure, read each question, and choose the **best** answer.

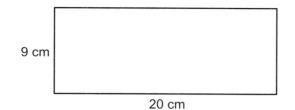

9 cm

20 cm

2. What is the area of the rectangle?

    A. 29 cm²
    B. 58 cm²
    C. 90 cm²
    D. 180 cm²

3. What is the perimeter of the rectangle?

    A. 29 cm
    B. 58 cm
    C. 90 cm
    D. 180 cm

DIRECTIONS: Study the figure, read each question, and choose the **best** answer.

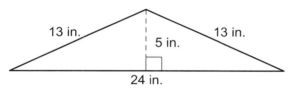

13 in.   13 in.
        5 in.
        24 in.

4. What is the area of the triangle?

    A. 60 in.²
    B. 65 in.²
    C. 120 in.²
    D. 156 in.²

5. What is the perimeter of the triangle?

    A. 29 in.
    B. 37 in.
    C. 50 in.
    D. 55 in.

DIRECTIONS: Study the figure, read each question, and choose the **best** answer.

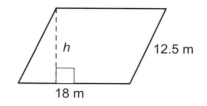

h   12.5 m

18 m

6. What is the perimeter of the parallelogram?

    A. 30.5 m
    B. 61 m
    C. 112.5 m
    D. 225 m

7. The area of the parallelogram is 450 m². What is the height?

    A. 25 m
    B. 36 m
    C. 50 m
    D. 72 m

DIRECTIONS: Read each question, and choose the **best** answer.

8. A triangle has an area of 20 in². The base of the triangle measures 4 in. What is its height?

    A. 5 in.
    B. 10 in.
    C. 40 in.
    D. 80 in.

9. The area of a square is equal to its perimeter. Which could be the side length of the square?

    A. 2 ft
    B. 4 ft
    C. 8 ft
    D. 16 ft

10. Leon is installing a fence around a rectangular vegetable garden with a perimeter of 60 feet. The garden is 12 feet wide. How long is the garden?

    A. 48 ft
    B. 24 ft
    C. 18 ft
    D. 5 ft

Pythagorean Theorem

MATH CONTENT TOPICS: Q.2.b, Q.4.e
MATH PRACTICES: MP.1.a, M.P.2.b, MP.3.a, MP.4.b

1 Learn the Skill

A **right triangle** is a triangle with a right (90°) angle. The legs (shorter sides) and **hypotenuse** (longest side) of a right triangle have a special relationship. This relationship, described by the **Pythagorean Theorem**, states that, in any right triangle, the sum of the squares of the lengths of the legs is equal to the square of the length of the hypotenuse.

In equation form, the Pythagorean Theorem is $a^2 + b^2 = c^2$. Through the use of the Pythagorean Theorem, you may solve for the missing length of one leg or the hypotenuse of a right triangle provided that you have the other two measurements.

2 Practice the Skill

By practicing the skill of using the Pythagorean Theorem to find the missing side of a right triangle, you will improve your study and test-taking abilities, especially as they relate to the GED® Mathematical Reasoning Test. Read the examples and strategies below. Then answer the question that follows.

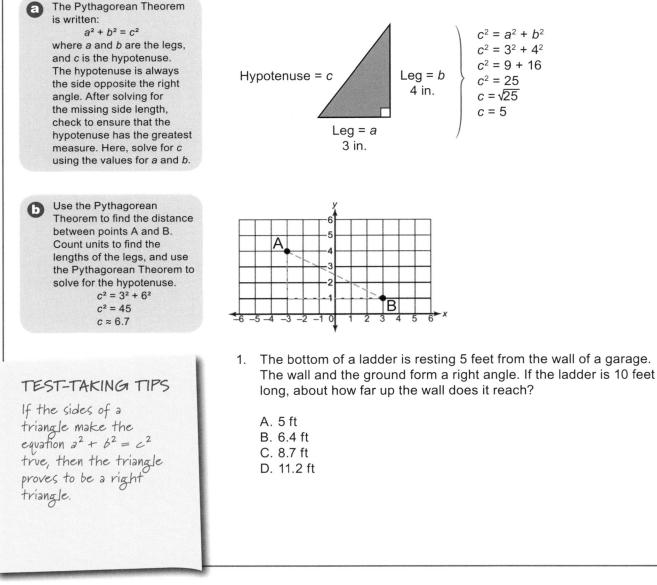

a The Pythagorean Theorem is written:
$$a^2 + b^2 = c^2$$
where a and b are the legs, and c is the hypotenuse. The hypotenuse is always the side opposite the right angle. After solving for the missing side length, check to ensure that the hypotenuse has the greatest measure. Here, solve for c using the values for a and b.

Hypotenuse = c Leg = b
4 in.

Leg = a
3 in.

$c^2 = a^2 + b^2$
$c^2 = 3^2 + 4^2$
$c^2 = 9 + 16$
$c^2 = 25$
$c = \sqrt{25}$
$c = 5$

b Use the Pythagorean Theorem to find the distance between points A and B. Count units to find the lengths of the legs, and use the Pythagorean Theorem to solve for the hypotenuse.
$c^2 = 3^2 + 6^2$
$c^2 = 45$
$c \approx 6.7$

TEST-TAKING TIPS

If the sides of a triangle make the equation $a^2 + b^2 = c^2$ true, then the triangle proves to be a right triangle.

1. The bottom of a ladder is resting 5 feet from the wall of a garage. The wall and the ground form a right angle. If the ladder is 10 feet long, about how far up the wall does it reach?

A. 5 ft
B. 6.4 ft
C. 8.7 ft
D. 11.2 ft

DIRECTIONS: Study the information and figure below. Then read each question, and choose the **best** answer.

A telephone pole is 30 feet tall. A cable attached to the top of the pole is anchored to the ground 15 feet away from the base of the pole.

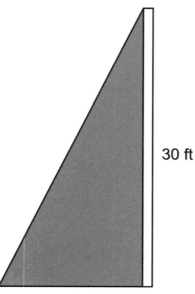

30 ft

15 ft

2. What is the length of the cable to the nearest tenth of a foot?

   A. 26
   B. 30.7
   C. 32.2
   D. 33.5

3. If a 35-foot cable were run from the top of the pole and anchored to the ground at a distance from the pole, about how far away from the pole would it be anchored?

   A. 16 feet
   B. 18 feet
   C. 30 feet
   D. 38 feet

4. If the telephone pole were 2 feet taller, and the cable was still anchored in 15 feet away from the pole, how would the change in pole height affect the length of the cable?

   A. The cable would be exactly 2 feet longer.
   B. The length of the cable would not change.
   C. The cable would be about 1.8 feet longer.
   D. The cable would be about 2.2 feet longer.

DIRECTIONS: Study the information and diagram, read each question, and choose the **best** answer.

The river is 120 meters wide. Sara starts out swimming across the river. The current pushes her, so she ends up 40 meters downriver from where she started.

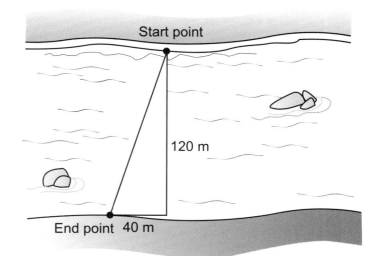

Start point

120 m

End point 40 m

5. To the nearest whole meter, how many meters did Sara actually swim?

   A. 113
   B. 105
   C. 126
   D. 160

6. If the current had not been so strong and had only swept Sara 20 meters downstream, about how many meters would she actually have swam? Round to the nearest whole number.

   A. 122
   B. 118
   C. 116
   D. 106

DIRECTIONS: Read the question, and choose the **best** answer.

7. What is the distance between points M (−4, 5) and N (4, 3)? Round to the nearest tenth.

   A. 6.3
   B. 6.5
   C. 7.3
   D. 8.2

UNIT 4

Polygons

MATH CONTENT TOPICS: Q.2.a, Q.2.e, Q.4.c
MATH PRACTICES: MP.1.a, MP.1.b, MP.1.e, MP.2.c, MP.3.a, MP.3.b, MP.4.a

1 Learn the Skill

A **polygon** is any closed figure with three or more sides. Triangles, squares, and rectangles are all examples of polygons. A polygon is named according to its number of sides; for example, a pentagon has five sides, a hexagon has six sides, and an octagon has eight sides.

A **regular polygon** has congruent sides and angles. An equilateral triangle and a square are examples of regular polygons. The perimeter of a regular polygon is the product of its side length and number of sides.

An **irregular polygon** has sides and angles that are **incongruent**, or unequal. An irregular polygon may have two or more sides that are congruent, such as a rectangle. The perimeter of an irregular polygon is the sum of its side lengths.

2 Practice the Skill

By practicing the skill of computing side length and perimeter of polygons, you will improve your study and test-taking abilities, especially as they relate to the GED® Mathematical Reasoning Test. Study the information below. Then answer the question that follows.

a This figure is a regular pentagon. Since all of the sides of a regular polygon are congruent, the perimeter of a regular polygon is the number of sides × the side length.

b This figure is an irregular pentagon. The perimeter of an irregular polygon is the sum of its side lengths.

Which figure has the greater perimeter?

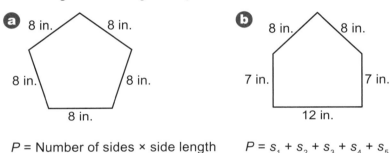

P = Number of sides × side length
P = 5(8)
P = 40 in.

$P = s_1 + s_2 + s_3 + s_4 + s_5$
P = 12 + 7 + 8 + 8 + 7
P = 42 in.

The perimeter of the irregular pentagon on the right is greater than the perimeter of the regular pentagon on the left.

USING LOGIC

The perimeter of a regular polygon is the product of the side length and the number of sides. If you know any two of those pieces of information (perimeter, side length, number of sides), you can find out the third.

1. A regular hexagon has a side length of 5 inches. What is the perimeter of the hexagon?

   A. 11 in.
   B. 25 in.
   C. 30 in.
   D. 36 in.

DIRECTIONS: Read each question, and choose the **best** answer.

2. A regular pentagon has a side length of 9.6 feet. What is the perimeter of the pentagon?

   A. 38.4 ft
   B. 48 ft
   C. 52 ft
   D. 57.6

3. An architect designs a home with a stained-glass window in the shape of a regular octagon. Each side of the widow measures 12 inches. What is the perimeter of the frame for the stained-glass window?

   A. 20 in.
   B. 72 in.
   C. 96 in.
   D. 108 in.

4. Sacha found the perimeter of a nine-sided polygon by multiplying the side length by the number of sides. What **must** be true of the figure Sacha drew?

   A. It has 9 congruent sides.
   B. It has 9 congruent angles.
   C. It has 9 congruent sides or 9 congruent angles.
   D. It has 9 congruent sides and 9 congruent angles.

DIRECTIONS: Study the diagram, read the question, and choose the **best** answer.

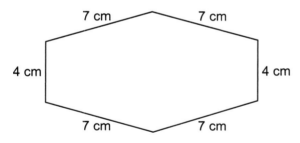

5. What is the perimeter of the figure?

   A. 18 cm
   B. 28 cm
   C. 36 cm
   D. 40 cm

DIRECTIONS: Read each question, and choose the **best** answer.

6. Find the perimeter of the figure below.

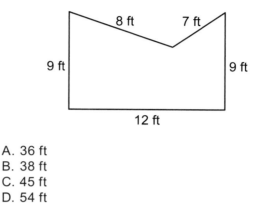

   A. 36 ft
   B. 38 ft
   C. 45 ft
   D. 54 ft

7. What is the perimeter of the trapezoid?

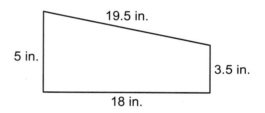

   A. 14 in.
   B. 20 in.
   C. 46 in.
   D. 72 in.

8. A regular polygon has a perimeter of 39 feet. Which could be the side length of the polygon?

   A. 7 feet
   B. 6.5 feet
   C. 5.5 feet
   D. 4 feet

9. The irregular pentagon below has a perimeter of 40 cm. What is the missing side length?

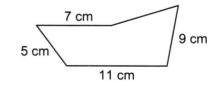

   A. 6 cm
   B. 7 cm
   C. 8 cm
   D. 9 cm

Circles

MATH CONTENT TOPICS: Q.2.a, Q.2.e, Q.4.a, Q.4.b
MATH PRACTICES: MP.1.a, MP.1.b, MP.1.e, MP.2.c, MP.4.a, MP.4.b

1 Learn the Skill

A **circle** is the set of points that are a fixed distance from a central point. The distance from the center of a circle to any point on the circle is called the **radius**. The **diameter** is the distance across a circle through its center. The diameter is always twice the radius.

Recall that the distance around a polygon is its perimeter. However, because circles lack sides, they are not polygons and therefore do not have perimeters. Instead, the distance around a circle is known as its **circumference**.

To use the formula for circumference ($C = \pi d$), you must know the diameter of a circle. To use the formula for the area of a circle ($A = \pi r^2$), you must know its radius. If you know the radius of a circle, you may double it to find the diameter. If you know the diameter of a circle, you may divide it by 2 to find the radius.

2 Practice the Skill

By practicing the skills of finding the circumference and area of a circle, you will improve your study and test-taking abilities, especially as they relate to the GED® Mathematical Reasoning Test. Read the example and strategies below. Then answer the question that follows.

a Identify the important information given in the paragraph and in the figure. The paragraph tells you that hotel workers decide to make the diameter of the fence *twice* that of the pool. The figure gives you the diameter of the pool. You need to know both pieces of information to answer the question.

b Using the formula for circumference requires that you know either the length of the **diameter** (a chord that passes through the center of a circle) or the **radius** (any line segment from the center of the circle to a point on the circle). The radius is always half the length of the diameter. This figure shows the diameter of the pool.

Workers at the Vista Hotel want to erect a circular fence around a circular swimming pool. They decide to make the diameter of the fence twice that of the pool. The workers need to know the circumference of the fence in order to buy the correct amount of metal fencing.

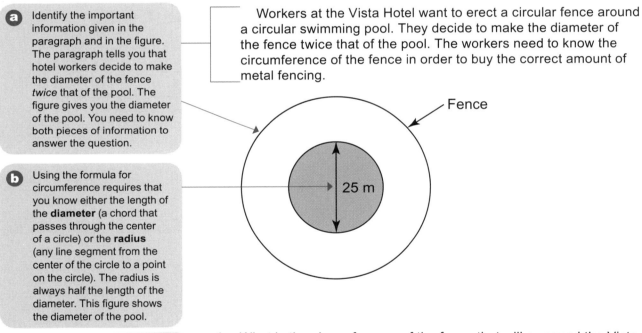

Fence

25 m

1. What is the circumference of the fence that will surround the Vista Hotel swimming pool?

A. 50 m
B. 78.5 m
C. 157 m
D. 785 m

TEST-TAKING TIPS

Use estimation to help choose a reasonable answer when multiplying by π. For example, to multiply 50 by 3.14, first round 3.14 to 3. Since 50 × 3 = 150, answer choice C seems to be the most reasonable one.

DIRECTIONS: Read each question, and choose the **best** answer.

2. The diameter of the smaller circle is equal to the radius of the larger circle, which is 7 inches.

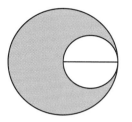

   What is the area of the larger circle?

   A. 21.98 in.²
   B. 38.46 in.²
   C. 131.88 in.²
   D. 153.86 in.²

3. Alisha is painting a perfectly round sun as part of a mural on the side of a building. If the diameter of her sun is 15 cm, what is its area to the nearest square centimeter?

   A. 5 cm²
   B. 56 cm²
   C. 177 cm²
   D. 707 cm²

4. A circle has a diameter of 25 inches. To the nearest inch, what is its circumference?

   A. 39 inches
   B. 79 inches
   C. 157 inches
   D. 491 inches

5. Jon and Gretchen are laying a circular brick patio in their backyard. The patio is shown in the diagram below.

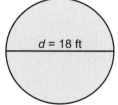

$d = 18$ ft

   If the pavers charge $1.59 per square foot, how much will the pavers charge for the whole patio?

   A. $89.87
   B. $254.34
   C. $404.40
   D. $1,617.60

6. A circle has a circumference of 47 inches. To the nearest inch, what is its diameter?

   A. 30 inches
   B. 15 inches
   C. 8 inches
   D. 7 inches

7. What is the radius of a circle with area 1,256 m²?

   A. 10 meters
   B. 20 meters
   C. 40 meters
   D. 200 meters

DIRECTIONS: Study the information and diagram, read each question, and choose the **best** answer.

Henry bought a circular rug as shown below.

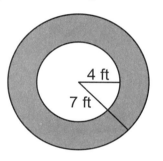

4 ft

7 ft

8. The rug is divided into a white interior and a gray border. What is the area of the interior of the rug in square feet? Round to the nearest tenth.

   A. 12.6
   B. 25.1
   C. 50.2
   D. 153.9

9. What is the area of the entire area rug to the nearest square foot?

   A. 50
   B. 104
   C. 154
   D. 204

10. Henry wants to add a fringed edge around the outside of the rug. About how many feet of edging should he buy to go around the outside edge of the rug?

   A. 44
   B. 28
   C. 25
   D. 13

MATH CONTENT TOPICS: Q.4.a, Q.4.b, Q.4.c, Q.4.d
MATH PRACTICES: MP.1.a, MP.1.b, MP.1.c, MP.1.e, MP.3.a

1 Learn the Skill

Composite plane figures are made up of two or more 2-dimensional, or 2-D, shapes. The perimeter of a composite plane figure is the distance around the entire figure. It can be calculated by adding the lengths of the exterior sides. In a composite plane figure, you sometimes must divide the figure into smaller sections, such as triangles, squares, and rectangles, to find the area.

2 Practice the Skill

By practicing the skills of recognizing composite plane figures and calculating their area and perimeter, you will improve your study and test-taking abilities, especially as they relate to the GED® Mathematical Reasoning Test. Study the information below. Then answer the question that follows.

a To find the area of an irregular figure, first divide the figure into simple shapes. This figure can be divided into three rectangles. The dimensions of the two outer rectangles are given. One side of the middle rectangle is given (6 cm). To find the other side, use measurements of sides you know. For example, the length of the entire figure is 15 cm. By subtracting 4 cm and then 6 cm, you can find the length of the middle rectangle (5 cm).

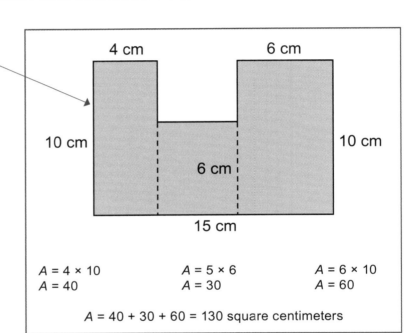

$A = 4 \times 10$ $A = 5 \times 6$ $A = 6 \times 10$
$A = 40$ $A = 30$ $A = 60$

$A = 40 + 30 + 60 = 130$ square centimeters

INSIDE THE ITEMS

To find the perimeter of a composite plane figure, add the length of each side. If no number is given for a side, you will need to figure it out by addition or by subtraction.

1. What is the perimeter of the figure above?

A. 130 cm
B. 116 cm
C. 58 cm
D. 45 cm

DIRECTIONS: Study the figure, read the question, and choose the **best** answer.

2. Kirsten sewed a tablecloth in the shape shown below. What is the area of her tablecloth in square feet?

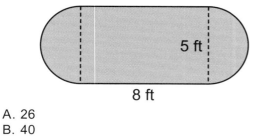

5 ft

8 ft

A. 26
B. 40
C. 47.9
D. 59.625

DIRECTIONS: Study the figure, read each question, and choose the **best** answer.

A kindergarten student designs the following shape using blocks on the carpet floor.

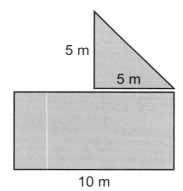

5 m

5 m

10 m

3. What is the area of the triangular portion of the figure?

A. 12.5 m²
B. 25 m²
C. 50 m²
D. 59.63 m²

4. If the width of the rectangle is 5 m, **what is the total area of the figure above?**

A. 5 m²
B. 12.5 m²
C. 50 m²
D. 62.5 m²

DIRECTIONS: Study the figure, read the question, and choose the **best** answer.

Karen and Bill poured cement to make the patio shown in the diagram.

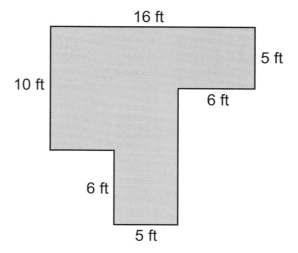

16 ft

5 ft

10 ft

6 ft

6 ft

5 ft

5. What is the area of Karen and Bill's patio in square feet?

A. 160
B. 100
C. 80
D. 30

DIRECTIONS: Study the figures, read the question, and choose the **best** answer.

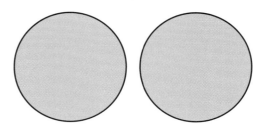

6. Two identical circular patterns were observed in the middle of a cornfield. If the radius of one circle is 5 m, what is the total area of both circles, measured to the nearest square meter?

A. 10
B. 31
C. 79
D. 157

Scale Drawings

MATH CONTENT TOPICS: Q.3.b, Q.3.c
MATH PRACTICES: MP.1.a, MP.1.b

1 Learn the Skill

When corresponding angles and corresponding sides of two figures are equal, the figures are exactly the same shape and size. These are known as **congruent figures**. When corresponding angles of two figures are equal but the lengths of their corresponding sides are proportional, the figures have the same shape but not the same size. These are known as **similar figures**.

Scale drawings, such as those involving maps and blueprints, are similar figures. A **scale factor** is the ratio of a dimension in a scale drawing to the corresponding dimension in an actual drawing or in reality. Ratios can be used to determine the scale factor of a drawing. Proportions can be used to determine an unknown dimension in an actual or scale drawing, given the scale factor and the corresponding dimension.

2 Practice the Skill

By practicing the skill of proportional reasoning, you will improve your study and test-taking abilities, especially as they relate to the GED® Mathematical Reasoning Test. Study the information and figures below. Then answer the question that follows.

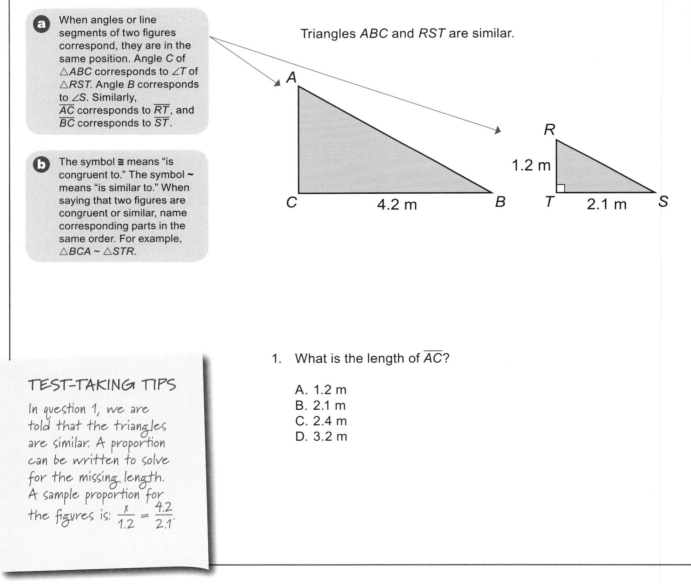

a When angles or line segments of two figures correspond, they are in the same position. Angle C of $\triangle ABC$ corresponds to $\angle T$ of $\triangle RST$. Angle B corresponds to $\angle S$. Similarly, $\overline{AC}$ corresponds to $\overline{RT}$, and $\overline{BC}$ corresponds to $\overline{ST}$.

b The symbol ≅ means "is congruent to." The symbol ~ means "is similar to." When saying that two figures are congruent or similar, name corresponding parts in the same order. For example, $\triangle BCA \sim \triangle STR$.

Triangles ABC and RST are similar.

TEST-TAKING TIPS

In question 1, we are told that the triangles are similar. A proportion can be written to solve for the missing length. A sample proportion for the figures is: $\dfrac{x}{1.2} = \dfrac{4.2}{2.1}$.

1. What is the length of $\overline{AC}$?

A. 1.2 m
B. 2.1 m
C. 2.4 m
D. 3.2 m

UNIT 4

③ *Apply the Skill*

DIRECTIONS: Study the figures, read each question, and write the answer in the box.

Triangle *ABC* and triangle *FGH* are similar figures.

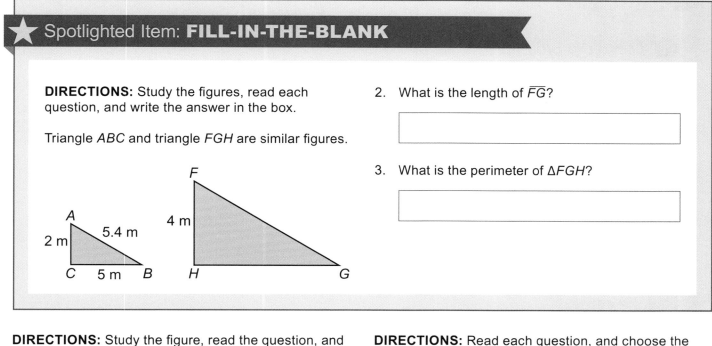

2. What is the length of $\overline{FG}$?

3. What is the perimeter of Δ*FGH*?

DIRECTIONS: Study the figure, read the question, and choose the **best** answer.

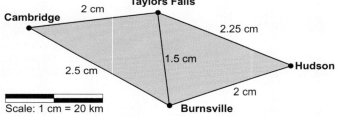

4. Jack drove from Cambridge to Burnsville. Pedro drove from Hudson to Burnsville. How much farther did Jack drive than Pedro?

   A. 0.5 km
   B. 10 km
   C. 40 km
   D. 50 km

DIRECTIONS: Read the question, and choose the **best** answer.

5. Erika drove from Plymouth to Manchester and back again. On a map, these two cities are 2.5 cm apart. If the map scale is 1 cm:6 km, how many kilometers did she drive?

   A. 2.4
   B. 8.5
   C. 15
   D. 30

DIRECTIONS: Read each question, and choose the **best** answer.

6. Triangles 1 and 2 shown below are congruent. The lengths of two sides of Triangle 1 are given.

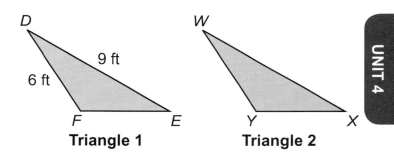

Triangle 1   **Triangle 2**

If the perimeter of Triangle 1 is 19 ft, what is the length of $\overline{XY}$?

   A. 4 ft
   B. 6 ft
   C. 9 ft
   D. 19 ft

7. A furniture maker made a model of a table design. The model of the table is 12 inches long and 4 inches wide. The actual table will be 60 inches long. What is the scale factor of the actual table?

   A. 5
   B. 6
   C. 15
   D. 16

UNIT 4

Prisms and Cylinders

MATH CONTENT TOPICS: Q.2.a, Q.2.e, Q.4.b, Q.5.a, Q.5.b, Q.5.c
MATH PRACTICES: MP.1.a, MP.1.b, MP.1.d, MP.1.e, MP.3.a, MP.3.b, MP.4.a, MP.4.b

1 Learn the Skill

A **solid figure** is a 3-dimensional figure. Solid figures include cubes, prisms, pyramids, cylinders, and cones. The **volume** of a solid figure is the amount of space it takes up, as measured in cubic units. The volume of a prism or cylinder is the product of the area of its base and its height. The **surface area** of a solid figure is the sum of the areas of its two bases and the area of its lateral surfaces.

If you know the volume of a cube or prism and either the area of its base or its height, you can calculate the other quantity. Similarly, if you know the volume of a cylinder and either its radius or height, you can solve for the other dimension.

2 Practice the Skill

By practicing the skills of computing the surface area and volume of prisms and cylinders, you will improve your study and test-taking abilities, especially as they relate to the GED® Mathematical Reasoning Test. Study the information below. Then answer the question that follows.

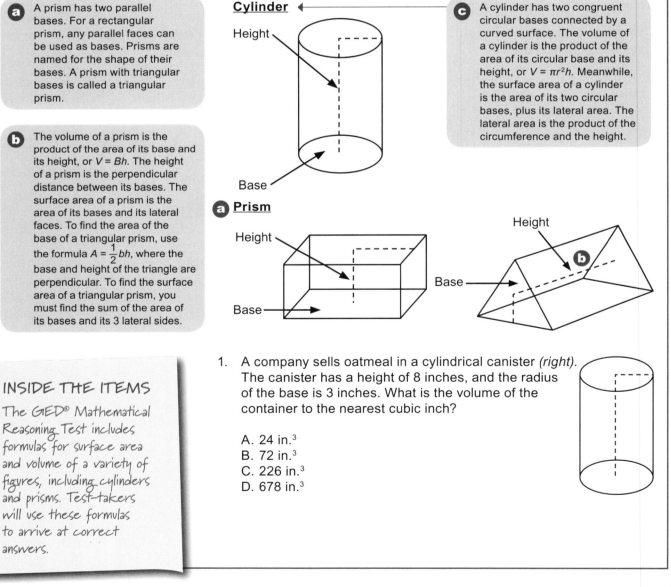

a A prism has two parallel bases. For a rectangular prism, any parallel faces can be used as bases. Prisms are named for the shape of their bases. A prism with triangular bases is called a triangular prism.

b The volume of a prism is the product of the area of its base and its height, or $V = Bh$. The height of a prism is the perpendicular distance between its bases. The surface area of a prism is the area of its bases and its lateral faces. To find the area of the base of a triangular prism, use the formula $A = \frac{1}{2}bh$, where the base and height of the triangle are perpendicular. To find the surface area of a triangular prism, you must find the sum of the area of its bases and its 3 lateral sides.

c A cylinder has two congruent circular bases connected by a curved surface. The volume of a cylinder is the product of the area of its circular base and its height, or $V = \pi r^2 h$. Meanwhile, the surface area of a cylinder is the area of its two circular bases, plus its lateral area. The lateral area is the product of the circumference and the height.

Cylinder

Height

Base

a Prism

Height

Base

Height

Base

b

INSIDE THE ITEMS

The GED® Mathematical Reasoning Test includes formulas for surface area and volume of a variety of figures, including cylinders and prisms. Test-takers will use these formulas to arrive at correct answers.

1. A company sells oatmeal in a cylindrical canister *(right)*. The canister has a height of 8 inches, and the radius of the base is 3 inches. What is the volume of the container to the nearest cubic inch?

   A. 24 in.³
   B. 72 in.³
   C. 226 in.³
   D. 678 in.³

DIRECTIONS: Read the question, and choose the **best** answer.

2. A rectangular bale of hay has the following dimensions: length = 40 inches, height = 20 inches, and width = 20 inches. Darla had 50 hay bales delivered to her farm. How many cubic inches of hay did she have delivered?

   A. 8,000 in.³
   B. 16,000 in.³
   C. 160,000 in.³
   D. 800,000 in.³

DIRECTIONS: Study the diagram, read each question, and choose the **best** answer.

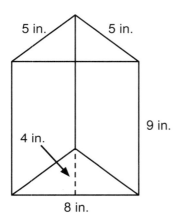

3. Which expression can be used to find the surface area of the triangular prism above?

   A. $(8 \times 4) + (9 \times 5) + (9 \times 8)$
   B. $(8 \times 4) + 2(9 \times 5) + (9 \times 8)$

   C. $\frac{1}{2}(8 \times 4) + (9 \times 5) + (9 \times 8)$

   D. $\frac{1}{2}(8 \times 4) + 2(9 \times 5) + (9 \times 8)$

4. A prism has a triangular base with an area of 24 square inches. The prism has the same volume as the triangular prism above. What is the height of the prism?

   A. 3 in.
   B. 6 in.
   C. 9 in.
   D. 12 in.

DIRECTIONS: Read each question, and choose the **best** answer.

5. A plastic display case is in the shape of a rectangular prism. The prism is 8 inches long, 6 inches wide, and 10 inches high. What area of plastic was used to make the display case?

   A. 188 in.²
   B. 256 in.²
   C. 376 in.²
   D. 480 in.²

6. The rain barrel shown below has a volume of 9,156.24 cubic centimeters.

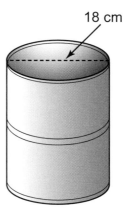

   What is the height of the rain barrel in centimeters?

   A. 2.25
   B. 9
   C. 36
   D. 113.04

7. Morgan needs to find the circumference of a cylindrical can. He knows the height and volume of the can. He divides the volume by the height and gets an answer of x square centimeters. Which describes the next steps Morgan should take to calculate the circumference?

   A. Divide x by 3.14, then take the square root to find the radius. Multiply the radius by 3.14 to find the circumference.
   B. Divide x by 3.14, then take the square root to find the radius. Multiply the radius by 6.28 to find the circumference.
   C. Take the square root of x to find the product of the radius and 3.14. Multiply by 2 to find the circumference.
   D. Take the square root of x to find the product of the radius and 6.28, which is equal to the circumference.

Pyramids, Cones, and Spheres

MATH CONTENT TOPICS: Q.2.a, Q.2.e, Q.5.d, Q.5.e
MATH PRACTICES: MP.1.a, MP.1.b, MP.1.e, MP.2.c, MP.4.a, MP.4.b

1 Learn the Skill

A **pyramid** is a 3-dimensional figure that has a polygon as its single base and triangular faces. A **cone** has one circular base. The volume of a pyramid is $V = \frac{1}{3}Bh$. The volume of a cone is $V = \frac{1}{3}\pi r^2 h$.

The **surface area** of a solid figure is the sum of the areas of surfaces. The surface area of a pyramid is the sum of the area of its base and its triangular faces. Use the slant height (height of the triangle) to find the areas of the faces. The formula for surface area of a pyramid is $SA = B + \frac{1}{2}Ps$, where B is the area of the base, P is the perimeter of the base, and s is the slant height. The surface area of a cone is the sum of its circular base and its curved surface. The formula for surface area is $SA = \pi r^2 + \pi rs$.

A **sphere** is shaped like a ball and has no bases or faces. The formula for volume of a sphere is $\frac{4}{3}\pi r^3$. The formula for surface area of a sphere is $4\pi r^2$.

2 Practice the Skill

By practicing the skills of computing the area and volume of pyramids, cones, and spheres, you will improve your study and test-taking abilities, especially as they relate to the GED® Mathematical Reasoning Test. Study the figures and information below. Then answer the question that follows.

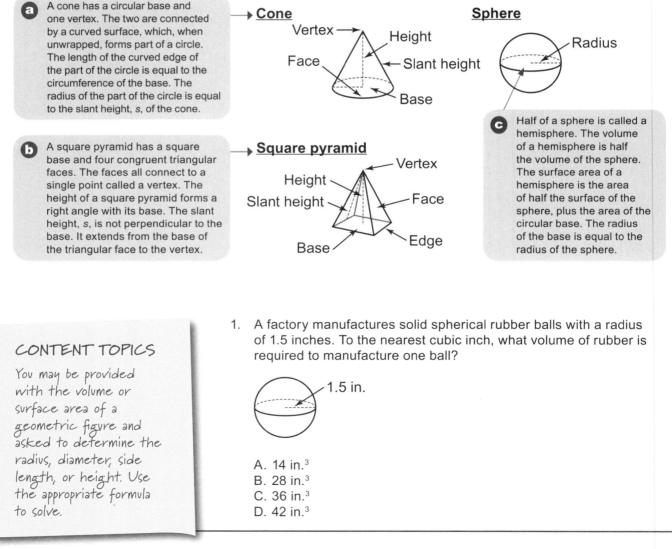

a A cone has a circular base and one vertex. The two are connected by a curved surface, which, when unwrapped, forms part of a circle. The length of the curved edge of the part of the circle is equal to the circumference of the base. The radius of the part of the circle is equal to the slant height, s, of the cone.

Cone
Vertex
Face
Height
Slant height
Base

Sphere
Radius

b A square pyramid has a square base and four congruent triangular faces. The faces all connect to a single point called a vertex. The height of a square pyramid forms a right angle with its base. The slant height, s, is not perpendicular to the base. It extends from the base of the triangular face to the vertex.

Square pyramid
Vertex
Height
Slant height
Face
Base
Edge

c Half of a sphere is called a hemisphere. The volume of a hemisphere is half the volume of the sphere. The surface area of a hemisphere is the area of half the surface of the sphere, plus the area of the circular base. The radius of the base is equal to the radius of the sphere.

CONTENT TOPICS

You may be provided with the volume or surface area of a geometric figure and asked to determine the radius, diameter, side length, or height. Use the appropriate formula to solve.

1. A factory manufactures solid spherical rubber balls with a radius of 1.5 inches. To the nearest cubic inch, what volume of rubber is required to manufacture one ball?

1.5 in.

A. 14 in.^{3}
B. 28 in.^{3}
C. 36 in.^{3}
D. 42 in.^{3}

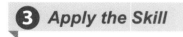

DIRECTIONS: Study the information and figure, read each question, and choose the **best** answer.

A paper cup has the shape of the cone below.

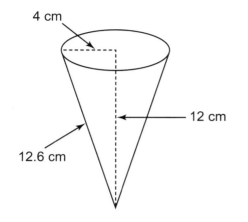

4 cm

12 cm

12.6 cm

2. To the nearest cubic centimeter, what volume of water can the cup hold?

A. 17 cm³
B. 201 cm³
C. 603 cm³
D. 1,809 cm³

3. To the nearest square centimeter, what area of paper is required to make the cone? Assume there is no overlap of paper.

A. 151 cm²
B. 158 cm²
C. 201 cm²
D. 208 cm²

DIRECTIONS: Read each question, and choose the **best** answer.

4. What is the surface area of a sphere with radius 9 centimeters? Round your answer to the nearest square centimeter.

A. 254 cm²
B. 339 cm²
C. 1,017 cm²
D. 3,052 cm²

5. A cone and a hemisphere each have a radius of 6 inches. What is the height of the cone if the two figures have the same volume?

A. 4 in.
B. 12 in.
C. 24 in.
D. 72 in.

DIRECTIONS: Study the information and figures, read each question, and choose the **best** answer.

A chocolate shop makes specialty shapes and sizes of chocolate. Lia ordered the two chocolate figures shown below.

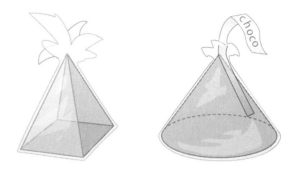

6. The chocolate in the shape of a pyramid has a square base with a side length of 2 cm and height of 3 cm. What is the volume of the chocolate to the nearest tenth?

A. 12 cm³
B. 6 cm³
C. 4 cm³
D. 2 cm³

7. The chocolate in the shape of a cone has the same height as and twice the volume of the chocolate in the shape of a pyramid. What is the radius of the cone to the nearest tenth?

A. 2.6 cm
B. 1.6 cm
C. 1.3 cm
D. 1.1 cm

DIRECTIONS: Read the question, and choose the **best** answer.

8. A tent has the shape of the square pyramid shown below.

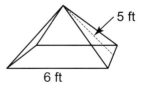

5 ft

6 ft

What area of fabric is needed to make the tent? Assume no overlap.

A. 51 square feet
B. 60 square feet
C. 66 square feet
D. 96 square feet

UNIT 4

Composite Solids

MATH CONTENT TOPICS: Q.2.a, Q.2.e, Q.5.a, Q.5.b, Q.5.c, Q.5.d, Q.5.f
MATH PRACTICES: MP.1.a, MP.1.b, MP.1.c, MP.1.e, MP.2.c, MP.3.a, MP.4.a, MP.4.b, MP.5.c

1 Learn the Skill

Many real-world objects, such as prisms, cylinders, pyramids, cones, and spheres are composed of simpler geometric solids. By breaking down **composite solids** into simpler figures, you may find larger and more complex dimensions, such as surface area and volume.

2 Practice the Skill

By practicing the skill of calculating surface areas and volumes of composite solids, you will improve your study and test-taking abilities, especially as they relate to the GED® Mathematical Reasoning Test. Study the information and diagram below. Then answer the question that follows.

a Dimensions of various elements in a composite figure may not always appear explicitly but can be inferred from the geometry. For example, the 80-meter side length of the square is also equal to the diameter of the semicircles in the figure.

b There often are multiple ways to break up a composite solid problem. In question 1, one can calculate volumes of the square prism at the center and the associated semi-cylinders separately, and then add them. Alternately, one can find the area of the figure, and then multiply that by the height of the skyscraper to get the total volume.

The following shows a horizontal cross-section of a skyscraper. It consists of a square core, with semicircular sections along each side of the square. The skyscraper is 150 meters high.

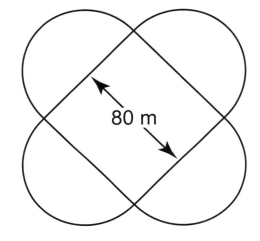

80 m

USING LOGIC

In some cases, it may be useful to view a complex solid as a simple solid with portions of that solid removed. Examples would include a rectangular block with cylindrical holes or a cone with the tip removed.

1. To the nearest 1,000 cubic meters, what is the volume occupied by the skyscraper?

A. 1,714,000 m³
B. 2,467,000 m³
C. 3,221,000 m³
D. 3,974,000 m³

★ Spotlighted Item: **FILL-IN-THE-BLANK**

DIRECTIONS: Study the diagram, read each question, and then write your answer in the box.

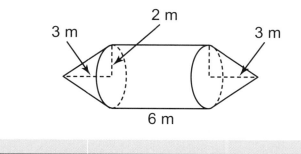

2 m

3 m   3 m

6 m

2. What is the combined volume, to the nearest cubic meter, of the cones in the figure?

3. What is the volume of the figure to the nearest cubic meter?

DIRECTIONS: Read each question, and choose the **best** answer.

4. Karen and Bill had cement poured to make the patio shown in the diagram below. If they have the cement for the patio poured 3 inches deep, how many cubic feet of cement will they use?

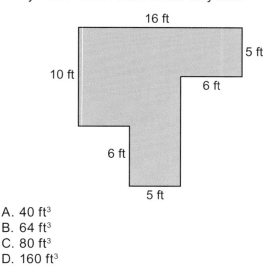

16 ft

5 ft

10 ft

6 ft

6 ft

5 ft

A. 40 ft³
B. 64 ft³
C. 80 ft³
D. 160 ft³

5. A closed, cylindrical container has an external radius R, and an external length H. If the thickness of material making up the container is t, what is the volume of material making up the container?

A. $V = \pi\left[R^2H - (R - t)^2(H - 2t)\right]$
B. $V = \pi\left[R^2H - (R - t)^2(H - t)\right]$
C. $V = \pi\left[(R + t)^2(H + t) - R^2H\right]$
D. $V = \pi\left[(R + t)^2(H + 2t) - R^2H\right]$

DIRECTIONS: Study the information and diagram, read each question, and choose the **best** answer.

The following sketch represents a funnel, with the inside dimensions of the funnel shown.

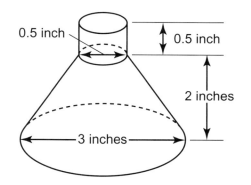

0.5 inch   0.5 inch

2 inches

3 inches

6. To the nearest tenth of a square inch, what is the inside surface area of the bottom portion of the funnel?

A. 9.4
B. 11.8
C. 13
D. 13.3

7. What is the total inside surface area of the funnel, to the nearest tenth of a square inch?

A. 11.8
B. 13
C. 13.4
D. 13.8

UNIT 4

DIRECTIONS: Read each question, and choose the **best** answer.

1. A square has an area of 64 square meters. What is the side length of the square?

   A. 4 meters
   B. 8 meters
   C. 16 meters
   D. 32 meters

2. Kelly is using ribbon to trim two identical placemats, each in the shape of a regular hexagon. The ribbon is 80 inches long. After trimming the placemats she has 8 inches of ribbon left over. What is the side length of each placemat?

   A. 4.5 inches
   B. 6 inches
   C. 9 inches
   D. 12 inches

DIRECTIONS: Study the information and diagram, read each question, and choose the **best** answer.

A ramp is 12 feet long and rises 2 feet from the ground, as shown below.

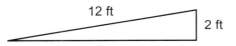

12 ft 2 ft

3. To the nearest tenth of a foot, what is the horizontal length of the ramp?

   A. 10 feet
   B. 10.6 feet
   C. 11.8 feet
   D. 11.9 feet

4. The design of the ramp is changed so that its horizontal length increases to 15 feet. To the nearest tenth of a foot, by about how much does the length of the ramp increase?

   A. 3 feet
   B. 3.1 feet
   C. 3.2 feet
   D. 3.3 feet

DIRECTIONS: Study the diagram and information, read each question, and write your answer in the box below.

A square is inscribed in a circle with its vertices as points on the circle.

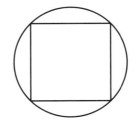

The area of the square is 25 square feet.

5. What is the length of one side of the square?

   feet

6. To the nearest tenth, what is the diameter of the circle?

   feet

7. To the nearest tenth, what is the area of the circle?

   square feet

8. To the nearest tenth, what is the circumference of the circle?

   feet

DIRECTIONS: Study the diagram and information, read the question, and choose the **best** answer(s).

9. The figures below are regular polygons.

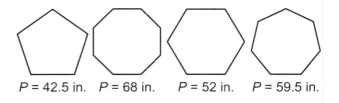

   $P = 42.5$ in. $P = 68$ in. $P = 52$ in. $P = 59.5$ in.

   Circle the figures whose side lengths measure 8.5 inches.

UNIT 4

DIRECTIONS: Read each question, and choose the **best** answer.

10. A rectangular dining table is 8 feet long and 4.5 feet wide. What area of wood was used to create the table top?

    A. 18 square feet
    B. 25 square feet
    C. 32 square feet
    D. 36 square feet

11. To the nearest tenth, what is the diameter of a circle with area of 254 square centimeters?

    A. 9 cm
    B. 18 cm
    C. 40.5 cm
    D. 80.1 cm

12. The parallelogram and square have the same area.

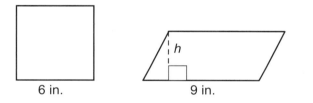

    6 in.   9 in.

    What is the height of the parallelogram?

    A. 3 in.
    B. 4 in.
    C. 6 in.
    D. 9 in.

13. Instead of following the sidewalk around the outside of a park to her car, Wanda cut through the park as shown.

Wanda

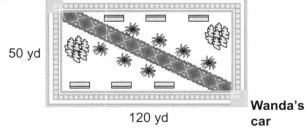

50 yd

120 yd   **Wanda's car**

    How many fewer yards did Wanda walk than if she had taken the sidewalk back to her car?

    A. 130
    B. 80
    C. 40
    D. 10

DIRECTIONS: Study the diagram and information, read each question, and choose the **best** answer.

The scale of the drawing below is 1 inch : 3 feet.

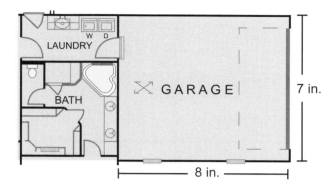

14. What are the actual dimensions of the garage?

    A. 7 feet by 8 feet
    B. 14 feet by 16 feet
    C. 21 feet by 24 feet
    D. 24 feet by 25 feet

15. The actual width of the laundry room is 5.4 feet. How wide is the laundry room in the scale drawing?

    A. 0.6 inch
    B. 1.8 inches
    C. 4.6 inches
    D. 7.2 inches

DIRECTIONS: Study the diagram and information, read each question, and choose the **best** answer.

The trapezoid below has a perimeter of 58 feet.

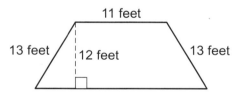

11 feet

13 feet   12 feet   13 feet

16. What is the missing side length of the trapezoid?

    A. 9 feet
    B. 12 feet
    C. 21 feet
    D. 22 feet

17. What is the area of the trapezoid?

    A. 132 square feet
    B. 192 square feet
    C. 208 square feet
    D. 252 square feet

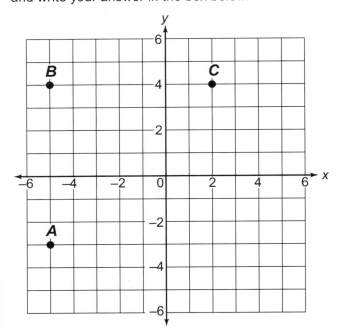

18. What is the distance between points *A* and *C*? Round your answer to the nearest tenth.

DIRECTIONS: Study the diagram and information, read the question, and choose the **best** answer.

A contractor poured concrete to form the set of steps shown below. Each step rises 8 inches and is 10 inches deep.

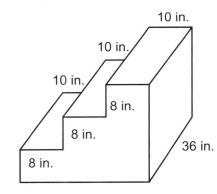

19. What volume of concrete did the contractor use?

A. 8,640 cubic inches
B. 17,280 cubic inches
C. 18,432 cubic inches
D. 25,920 cubic inches

DIRECTIONS: Read each question, and choose the **best** answer.

20. A circular piece of a stained-glass window has an area of 113 square inches. The piece is surrounded by a strip of lead to connect it to the rest of the design. About how long is the strip of lead rounded to the nearest tenth?

A. 6 in.
B. 18.96 in.
C. 36 in.
D. 37.7 in.

21. A right triangle has an area of 216 cm². One of the sides that forms the right angle is 24 cm long. What is the perimeter of the triangle?

A. 30 cm
B. 42 cm
C. 72 cm
D. 85 cm

22. Evan says that the area of a circle is always greater than its circumference. Which length radius demonstrates that Evan is not correct?

A. 1.5 cm
B. 2.5 cm
C. 4 cm
D. 10 cm

DIRECTIONS: Study the diagram and information, read the question, and choose the **best** answer.

A backyard pool is shown in the diagram.

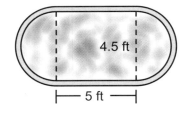

23. What is the perimeter of the pool?

A. 28.26 ft
B. 24.13 ft
C. 19.13 ft
D. 14.13 ft

DIRECTIONS: Study the figures and information, and read the question. Then use the drag-and-drop option to complete the diagrams.

24. The four figures below have the same perimeter.

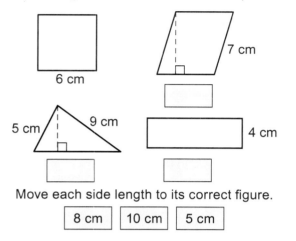

Move each side length to its correct figure.

| 8 cm | 10 cm | 5 cm |

DIRECTIONS: Read the question, and choose the **best** answer.

25. Tony and Katherine are ordering carpeting for their living room, shown below. They need to determine the number of square feet of carpeting to order.

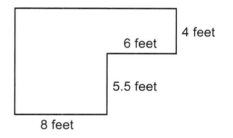

Tony and Katherine can use each of the following methods to determine the area of the living room floor **except** which one?

A. Add the area of one rectangle that measures 8 feet by 9.5 feet to the area of another rectangle that measures 6 feet by 4 feet.
B. Add the area of one rectangle that measures 14 feet by 4 feet to the area of another rectangle that measures 8 feet by 5.5 feet.
C. Subtract the area of one rectangle that measures 6 feet by 4 feet from the area of another rectangle that measures 10 feet by 13.5 feet.
D. Subtract the area of one rectangle that measures 5.5 feet by 6 feet from the area of another rectangle that measures 14 feet by 9.5 feet.

DIRECTIONS: Read each question, and choose the **best** answer.

26. Brendan bent a piece of wire into the irregular figure shown below.

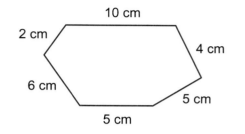

Brendan could bend the same piece of wire into each of the following regular polygons **except** which one?

A. octagon with side length 4 cm
B. pentagon with side length 6.4 cm
C. hexagon with side length 5.4 cm
D. quadrilateral with side length 8 cm

27. Maggie is baking a pie in a dish with a 9-inch. diameter. She needs to roll the pie crust so that it extends 1 inch beyond the dish. Rounded to the nearest tenth, what area of pie crust does she need?

A. 95 in.^{2}
B. 78.5 in.^{2}
C. 64.6 in.^{2}
D. 38.5 in.^{2}

DIRECTIONS: Study the diagram, read the question, and choose the **best** answer.

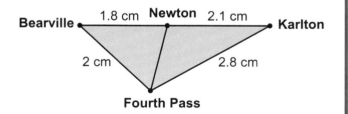

28. If the actual distance between Karlton and Fourth Pass is 98 km, what is the scale of the map?

A. 1 cm:49 km
B. 1 cm:47 km
C. 1 cm:35 km
D. 1 cm:27 km

DIRECTIONS: Study the diagram and information, read each question, and choose the **best** answer.

A star-shaped mirror has five congruent triangular sections and one pentagonal section.

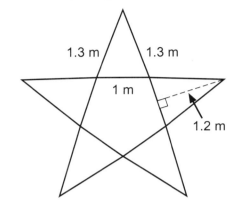

29. A wood frame is built to fit the outside of the mirror. What length of wood is needed to build the frame?

    A. 18 m
    B. 13 m
    C. 6.5 m
    D. 3 m

30. The area of the pentagonal section is 1.72 square meters. What is the total area of the mirror?

    A. 3 m²
    B. 3.97 m²
    C. 4.72 m²
    D. 5.16 m²

DIRECTIONS: Study the diagram and information, read the question, and choose the **best** answer.

31. The pyramid and cone below have the same volume.

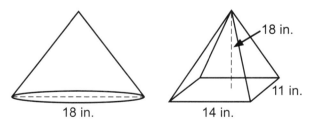

    To the nearest tenth, what is the height of the cone?

    A. 10.9 in.
    B. 11.4 in.
    C. 13.2 in.
    D. 18 in.

DIRECTIONS: Read each question, and choose the **best** answer.

32. Darren places an 18-foot ladder so that it reaches 14 feet above the ground. What is the distance between the wall and the base of the ladder?

    A. 4 feet
    B. 11.3 feet
    C. 12.8 feet
    D. 22.8 feet

33. A tree that is 24 feet tall casts a shadow that is 3.6 feet long. At the same time of day, a second tree casts a shadow that is 4.5 feet long. How tall is the second tree?

    A. 30 feet
    B. 19.2 feet
    C. 67.5 feet
    D. 15 feet

34. The two triangles below are similar.

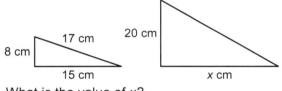

    What is the value of x?

    A. 42.5 cm
    B. 37.5 cm
    C. 27 cm
    D. 10.7 cm

35. A chocolate company sells its specialty hot cocoa in cylindrical canisters. The canister holds 3,740 cubic centimeters of cocoa.

    If the canister is 17.5 cm high, what is the diameter of the canister in centimeters?

    A. 8.25
    B. 16.5
    C. 38.89
    D. 68

DIRECTIONS: Read the question, and choose the **best** answer.

36. The irregular polygon below has a perimeter of 42 meters.

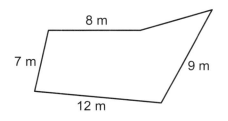

What is the missing side length?

A. 6 m
B. 7 m
C. 14 m
D. 18 m

DIRECTIONS: Study the diagram, read each question, and choose the **best** answer

The two pyramids in the figure have the same volume.

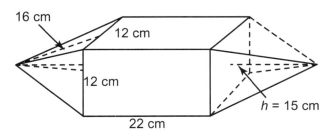

37. What is the volume of the figure?

A. 1,440 cubic centimeters
B. 1,704 cubic centimeters
C. 3,288 cubic centimeters
D. 4,608 cubic centimeters

38. What is the surface area of the figure?

A. 1,440 cubic centimeters
B. 1,776 cubic centimeters
C. 1,824 cubic centimeters
D. 2,112 cubic centimeters

DIRECTIONS: Read the question, and choose the **best** answer from the drop-down list.

39. Emma built the gingerbread house shown below.

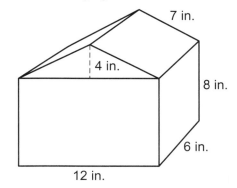

How many square inches of gingerbread, including the bottom of the house, did Emma use?

Emma used [Drop-down] square inches of gingerbread.

A. 418   B. 420   C. 492   D. 540

DIRECTIONS: Study the diagram and information, and read each question. Then write your answer in the box below.

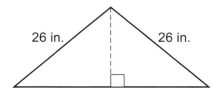

The perimeter of the triangle is 100 in.
The area of the triangle is 240 in².

40. What is the base of the triangle?

in.

41. What is the height of the triangle?

in.

DIRECTIONS: Study the diagram and information, read each question, and choose the **best** answer.

The pool of a fountain in a park is shaped like a crescent moon, as shown in the green part of the diagram.

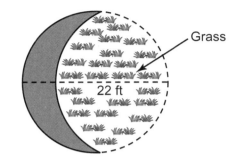
Grass
22 ft

42. If the grass covers 253.3 square feet, what is the area of the fountain pool?

   A. 126.64 square feet
   B. 379.94 square feet
   C. 633.24 square feet
   D. 1,266.46 square feet

43. A circular fence is to be built around the grass and pool area. There needs to be a distance of 5 feet between the fence and the pool and grass. How many feet of fencing will be needed?

   A. 69.08
   B. 74.08
   C. 84.78
   D. 100.48

DIRECTIONS: Read the question, and choose the **best** answer.

44. The diameter of Circle A is equal to the radius of Circle B. The area of Circle A is 314 cm². To the nearest tenth, what is the circumference of Circle B?

   A. 125.6 cm
   B. 62.8 cm
   C. 40 cm
   D. 31.4 cm

DIRECTIONS: Study the diagram and information, read each question, and write your answer in the box below.

The figure below is composed of a square and a semicircle. The perimeter of the figure is 36.56 feet.

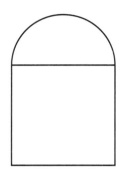

45. What is the side length of the square?

   feet

46. To the nearest tenth, what is the area of the figure?

   square feet

DIRECTIONS: Read each question, and choose the **best** answer.

47. What is the surface area of a sphere with a radius of 3.5 inches? Round your answer to the nearest square inch.

   A. 44 in²
   B. 88 in²
   C. 154 in²
   D. 539 in²

48. A rectangular prism has the same volume as a cube with an edge length of 12 feet. Which could be the dimensions of the prism?

   A. 4 feet by 6 feet by 10 feet
   B. 4 feet by 16 feet by 27 feet
   C. 6 feet by 9 feet by 16 feet
   D. 6 feet by 12 feet by 18 feet

DIRECTIONS: Study the diagram and information, read each question, and select the **best** answer.

Carlos sewed the round picnic blanket shown in the diagram.

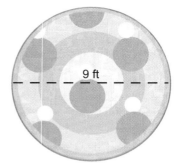

9 ft

49. To the nearest hundredth, what is the area of the blanket in square feet?

   A. 28.26
   B. 63.59
   C. 127.17
   D. 254.34

50. What is the circumference of the blanket in inches?

   A. 63.59
   B. 169.56
   C. 339.12
   D. 763.02

DIRECTIONS: Study the diagram and information, read each question, and write your answer in the boxes below.

Carmen is making a decorative pillow in the shape of the cylinder below.

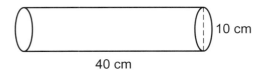

10 cm

40 cm

51. To the nearest square centimeter, what area of fabric will she need to make the pillow? Assume no overlap of the fabric.

   [ ] cm²

52. To the nearest cubic centimeter, what volume of stuffing will she need for the pillow?

   [ ] cm³

DIRECTIONS: Study the diagram and information, read each question, and choose the **best** answer from the drop-down list.

An architect used a hemisphere and a rectangular prism to build a model of a new planetarium below.

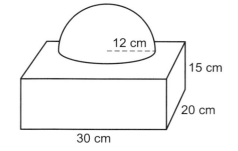

12 cm
15 cm
20 cm
30 cm

53. The total volume of the model is about
   [Drop-down] cubic centimeters.

   A. 4,500   B. 9,000   C. 12,600   D. 16,200

54. The actual diameter of the planetarium dome will be 30 meters. The scale of the model is
   [Drop-down].

   A. 1 cm = 1.25 m
   B. 1 cm = 2.5 m
   C. 1 cm = 3 m
   D. 1 cm = 3.5 m

DIRECTIONS: Read the question, and choose the **best** answer.

55. A corporate farm is considering buying two large plots of farmland. The smaller of the two plots is 5.6 miles long and 3.8 miles wide. The larger plot of land is exactly 2 times the width and 4 times the area of the smaller plot of land.

PLOTS OF FARMLAND

5.6 mi
Plot 1   3.8 mi
Plot 2

What is the length of the larger plot of farmland?

   A. 11.2 mi
   B. 15.2 mi
   C. 22.4 mi
   D. 37.6 mi

Answer Key

UNIT 1 NUMBER SENSE AND OPERATIONS

LESSON 1, pp. 2–3
1. **D**; **DOK Level:** 1; **Content Topic:** Q.1.d; **Practices:** MP.1.a, MP.1.e
$56,832 rounded to the thousands place is $57,000, since the 8 in the hundreds place rounds the 6 thousands to 7 thousands. It is not $56,000, since that would involve an incorrect application of rounding (rounding "down" rather than rounding "up"). It also is neither $56,800 nor $56,900, since that would involve rounding to the hundreds place, rather than the thousands place.

2. **B**; **DOK Level:** 1; **Content Topic:** Q.1.d; **Practices:** MP.1.a, MP.1.e
One hundred eighty-two is the proper way to write 182 in words. *One hundred eight-two* and *one hundred and eighteen-two* write out the numbers 8 and 18, respectively, rather than the number 80. *One-hundred eighty and two* includes an unnecessary and incorrect hyphen between *one* and *hundred*, while also including the unnecessary word *and* between *eighty* and *two*.

3. **C**; **DOK Level:** 1; **Content Topic:** Q.1.d; **Practices:** MP.1.a, MP.1.e
Jonathan's test score of 86 rounded to the tens place is 90. The answer option of 80 is incorrect because it involves rounding in the wrong direction. The answer option of 100 also is incorrect because it would involve rounding to the hundreds place, rather than the tens place. Finally, the answer option of 86 is incorrect because it does not involve rounding at all.

4. **A**; **DOK Level:** 1; **Content Topic:** Q.1.d; **Practices:** MP.1.a, MP.1.e, MP.5.c
1384 is greater than 1337 and less than 1420, so the book would be found on shelf I. The other three shelves have ranges of book numbers higher than 1384.

5. **C**; **DOK Level:** 2; **Content Topic:** Q.1.d; **Practices:** MP.1.a, MP.1.e
Since all three yardage numbers of 2,250; 2,450; and 2,700 have equivalent values of 2 in the thousands place, you next must look at the hundreds place to properly sequence them. The proper sequence involves *2,250* with *2 hundreds*, *2,450* with *4 hundreds*, and *2,700* with *7 hundreds*. The answer options of A, B, and D involve improper sequencing at the hundreds place.

6. **B**; **DOK Level:** 2; **Content Topic:** Q.1.d; **Practices:** MP.1.a, MP.1.e
As in the previous problem, all four numbers have equivalent values of 2 in the thousands place, so one must again look at the hundreds place. Doing so, one finds that Tuesday's swim yardage (2,700 yards) is the greatest. Thursday's yardage (2,500 yards) is the next greatest. Monday's (2,450 yards) is next, followed by Wednesday (2,250 yards). Hence, listing the days in order of yardage, from greatest to least, one gets Tuesday, Thursday, Monday, and Wednesday (choice B).

7. **A**; **DOK Level:** 2; **Content Topic:** Q.1.d; **Practices:** MP.1.a, MP.1.b, MP.1.e, MP.2.c, MP.5.c
By comparing the thousands places of the three annual mileages, one finds that the fewest miles were bicycled in 2006 and the most in 2007. That eliminates B, C, and D as possible answers.

8. **A**; **DOK Level:** 2; **Content Topics:** Q.1.d, Q.6.c; **Practices:** MP.1.a, MP.1.e
All six numbers have 1 hundred thousand, so you next must compare at the ten thousands place. Because the sales figures for January and February both include 5 ten thousands, you next must compare at the thousands place. At the thousands place, January has 5 thousands and February has none, so A is the correct answer.

9. **A**; **DOK Level:** 2; **Content Topics:** Q.1.d, Q.6.c; **Practices:** MP.1.a, MP.1.e
The month with the lowest sales is March since, comparing the digits in the ten-thousands places, it is the one with the lowest value, 3. One way to increase the number of items sold is to reduce prices, and so it might make sense to have a special sale with reduced prices in the month with the lowest sales: March (choice A).

10. **B**; **DOK Level:** 2; Content Topics: Q.1.d, Q.6.c; **Practices:** MP.1.a, MP.1.e, MP.5.c
This question asks to identify a trend, which involves a more critical examination of all the sales data. According to the table, two winter months, January and February, have the highest sales totals, so B is the correct answer and A and D are therefore incorrect. Sales totals changed each month from January through June, so answer option C also is incorrect.

LESSON 2, pp. 4–5
1. **B**; **DOK Level:** 1; **Content Topics:** Q.2.a, Q.2.e; **Practices:** MP.1.a, MP.4.a
Phrases such as *how much is left* indicate subtraction. Working from right to left, first subtracting the numbers in the ones column, (6 − 0), gives 6. Subtracting the numbers in the tens column, (5 − 4), gives 1. When subtracting the numbers in the hundreds column (2 − 3), note that the bottom number is greater than the top number, so regroup, (12 − 3), giving 9. The result is 916.

2. **1,050**; **DOK Level:** 1; **Content Topics:** Q.2.a, Q.2.e; **Practices:** MP.1.a, MP.4.a
Adding the two numbers, beginning with the ones column, (7 + 3), gives a 10, so regroup by moving the 1 to the tens column. In the tens column, you have as a result (1 + 6 + 8), giving 15. Again, regroup by moving the 1 to the hundreds column, so that you have (1 + 4 + 5), giving 10. The final result is, then, 1,050 miles.

3. **288**; **DOK Level:** 1; **Content Topics:** Q.2.a, Q.2.e; **Practices:** MP.1.a, MP.4.a
The answer is the difference between the two numbers. In the ones place, the top number (7) is less than the bottom number (9), so regroup; (17 − 9) gives 8. The regrouping left a 2 in the hundreds column, and a 9 in the tens column, so for the tens column you have (9 − 1), or 8. Nothing is subtracted from the remaining 2 in the hundreds column, so the final result is 288.

4. **$360**; **DOK Level:** 1; **Content Topics:** Q.2.a, Q.2.e; **Practices:** MP.1.a, MP.4.a
To get the answer, multiply 40 by 9. In the ones column, multiply 0 by 9 to get 0. In the tens column, multiply 4 by 9, giving 36, for a partial product. Next, include the zero placeholder of 360. The result, then, is $360.

5. **$540**; **DOK Level:** 1; **Content Topics:** Q.2.a, Q.2.e;
Practices: MP.1.a, MP.1.b, MP.4.a, MP.5.c
To solve, the monthly payment must be multiplied by the number of months in one year: 12. To multiply 45 by 12, start with multiplying 45 by the 2 in the ones column, giving a partial product of 90. Multiplying the 45 by the 1 in the tens column and adding a zero placeholder gives a partial product of 450. Adding the partial products (450 + 90) gives $540.

6. **$16**; **DOK Level:** 1; **Content Topics:** Q.2.a, Q.2.e;
Practices: MP.1.a, MP.4.a
Since the four friends split the $64 cost *equally*, divide 64 by 4. Dividing the first digit of the dividend (6) by the divisor (4) gives a 1 as the tens digit of the quotient. Multiplying *4* by 1, writing the product (4) under 6 in the dividend, and subtracting gives a 2. Next, after you carry down the ones digit in the dividend (4), divide 24 by the divisor (4), getting 6 as the ones digit in the quotient. There is no remainder, so the answer is $16.

7. **10**; **DOK Level:** 3; **Content Topics:** Q.1.b, Q.2.a, Q.2.e;
Practices: MP.1.a, MP.1.b, MP.2.c, MP.3.a, MP.5.c
Since 60 is an even number, 2 is the smallest factor; dividing 60 by 2 gives 30, which is the largest factor. The remaining factors can be found by looking for numbers between 2 and 30 that divide evenly into 60. The number 3 is the next such number; that fact also identifies 20 as a factor. Continuing, the numbers 4 and 15 are identified next, followed by 5 and 12, and then 6 and 10. There are no other factors between 6 and 10, so all factors have been determined. The complete list is: 2, 3, 4, 5, 6, 10, 12, 15, 20, and 30. Excluding 1 and 60, that makes 10 factors in all.

8. **$11,340**; **DOK Level:** 1; **Content Topics:** Q.2.a, Q.2.e;
Practices: MP.1.a, MP.4.a
The solution requires multiplying 630 by 18. First multiplying 630 by 8 gives a partial product of 5,040. Then, multiplying 630 by 1 and including the zero placeholder gives a partial product of 6,300. Adding the partial products, 5,040 and 6,300, gives an answer of $11,340.

9. **241**; **DOK Level:** 3; **Content Topics:** Q.2.a, Q.2.e, Q.7.a;
Practices: MP.1.a, MP.1.b, MP.3.a, MP.4.a, MP.5.c
This problem first requires recognition of the fact that the quarterback needs to pass for enough yards during the final two games to make up the difference between 3,518 yards and 4,000 yards. Subtracting 3,518 from 4,000 gives 482 yards. Since the question asks for the *average* needed for the last two games, divide 482 yards by 2, giving 241 yards as a result.

10. **4**; **DOK Level:** 3; **Content Topics:** Q.1.b, Q.2.a, Q.2.e;
Practices: MP.1.a, MP.1.b, MP.2.c, MP.3.a, MP.5.c
The first step involves finding the list of all whole numbers that divide into 36 with no remainder: 1, 2, 3, 4, 6, 9, 12, 18, and 36. The list of numbers that divide into 20 with no remainder includes: 1, 2, 4, 5, 10, and 20. There are two numbers in common between the two lists (2 and 4) with 4 being the largest common factor.

11. **18**; **DOK Level:** 3; **Content Topics:** Q.1.b, Q.2.a, Q.2.e;
Practices: MP.1.a, MP.1.b, MP.2.c, MP.3.a, MP.5.c
The number 6, expressed as the product of its smallest factors, is 2 × 3, while 9 can be written as 3 × 3. The two numbers have in common one factor of 3. By multiplying 3 by the remaining factors—2 from 6 and 3 from 9—you get a result divisible by both: 2 × 3 × 3 = 18, which is the smallest whole number divisible by both.

12. **42**; **DOK Level:** 1; **Content Topics:** Q.2.a, Q.2.e;
Practices: MP.1.a, MP.4.a
To find the answer, divide 504 by 12. Dividing 50 by 12 gives 4 as the tens digit of the quotient, with a remainder of 2. Form the next partial dividend by writing the remainder of 2 and bringing down the 4. Dividing the 24 by 12 gives a 2 for the ones digit of the quotient. The resulting answer is 42.

LESSON 3, *pp. 6–7*

1. **D**; **DOK Level:** 1; **Content Topics:** Q.2.a, Q.2.e;
Practices: MP.1.a, MP.4.a
The change in temperature is found by subtracting the final temperature from the starting temperature: (12°F) − (−3°F). Subtracting an integer is the same as adding its opposite, so the expression can be rewritten as (12°F) + (3°F) = 15°F. Since the temperature increased during the day, the change is positive, eliminating A and B as possibilities. The magnitude of the change must be more than 12°F, since the temperature started below zero; that eliminates C as a choice, confirming D and the correct answer.

2. **$114**; **DOK Level:** 1; **Content Topics:** Q.2.a, Q.2.e;
Practices: MP.1.a, MP.4.a
Recognizing that a withdrawal represents a negative change in Uyen's balance, the new balance can be found by addition: ($154) + (−$40) = $114.

3. **+7 spaces**; **DOK Level:** 2; **Content Topics:** Q.2.a, Q.2.e; **Practices:** MP.1.a, MP.4.a
To find the change after the first two moves, add (+3 spaces) + (−4 spaces) to get −1 space. Take that result and add (+8 spaces) to get a final result of +7 spaces.

4. **3,368**; **DOK Level:** 2; **Content Topics:** Q.2.a, Q.2.e;
Practices: MP.1.a, MP.4.a
Recognizing that graduation represents a decrease in enrollment, to find the number of students following graduation, add +3,342 students and (−587 students) to get +2,755 students. Add that result to (−32 students) to get 2,723 students enrolled at the end of summer. Finally, add those +2,723 students to the +645 new students to get a final enrollment of 3,368 students.

5. **+26**; **DOK Level:** 2; **Content Topics:** Q.2.a, Q.2.e;
Practices: MP.1.a, MP.1.b, MP.1.c, MP.2.c, MP.3.a, MP.4.a
The simplest way to find this change in the number of students is to recognize that it is the difference between the final enrollment in the fall (3,368 students, as determined in the previous question), and the initial enrollment (3,342 students). That difference is (3,368 students) + (−3,342 students) = 26 students. One could also work through the three addition problems separately.

6. **A**; **DOK Level:** 1; **Content Topics:** Q.2.a, Q.2.e;
Practices: MP.1.a, MP.4.a
The change in position can be found by subtracting the initial position (212 feet) from the final position (−80 feet). Recognizing that subtracting a number is the same as adding its opposite, the expression is: (−80 feet) + (−212 feet) = −292 feet (A). Answer choice B incorrectly switches the sign of the final position, and answer choice C incorrectly switches the sign of the initial position. Answer choice D switches the sign of both positions.

Answer Key

UNIT 1 (continued)

7. D; DOK Level: 2; **Content Topics:** Q.1.d, Q.2.a, Q.2.e; **Practices:** MP.1.a, MP.1.b, MP.1.c, MP.2.c, MP.3.a, MP.4.a
One can start at point *A* and count the number of spaces needed to get to point *B*, or start at point *B* and count the number of spaces needed to get to point *A*. Either way, the result is 11. Note that while subtracting $(-4) - (+7) = -11$, and $(+7) - (-4) = +11$, the *absolute value* of the difference of the two numbers is always greater than or equal to zero, never negative.

8. D; DOK Level: 2; **Content Topics:** Q.2.a, Q.2.e, Q.6.c; **Practices:** MP.1.a MP.1.b, MP.1.c, MP.3.a, MP.4.a
One can solve this problem by first adding all of the positive scores, $8 + 3 + 4 = 15$, and then all of the negative scores, $(-6) + (-4) = -10$. Melanie's final score is the sum of the two results: $(+15) + (-10) = +5$. Alternately, one can add the results from Rounds 1 and 2, then add that result to the score from Round 3, and so forth. Answer choice A is the sum of the absolute values of all the scores, and so doesn't recognize that a negative score decreases the total. Answer choice B is the sum of all the positive scores. Answer choice C is the sum of the scores of the last two rounds.

9. B; DOK Level: 2; **Content Topics:** Q.2.a, Q.2.e, Q.6.c; **Practices:** MP.1.a, MP.1.b, MP.1.c, MP.3.a, MP.4.a
To find Melanie's new overall score, add her most recent score (-8 points) to her score at the end of Round 5 (5 points). 5 points + -8 points = $5 - 8$ points, or -3 points. Other answers result from incorrect computation or use of sign.

LESSON 4, pp. 8–9

1. C; DOK Level: 1; **Content Topics:** Q.1.b, Q.2.a, Q.2.e; **Practices:** MP.1.a, MP.4.a
To add the two fractions, the lowest common denominator must be found; in this case it is 20. Expressing the fractions in terms of the common denominator gives the sum $\frac{12}{20} + \frac{15}{20} = \frac{27}{20} = 1\frac{7}{20}$.

2. Team 2, Team 5, Team 3, Team 1, and Team 4; DOK Level: 3; **Content Topics:** Q.1.a, Q.1.b, Q.2.e, Q.6.c; **Practices:** MP.1.a, MP.1.b, MP.4.a
One could solve this problem by expressing all the fractions in terms of the lowest common denominator (30). Alternately, one can reason through the problem by first noting that Team 2 was the team that filled its bowl, since their numerator equals the denominator. One also can note that Team 4 is the only team with less than half its bowl filled, so was in last place, behind Team 1. The remaining two teams are in second and third places—their bowls were filled more than halfway—and since they have the same denominator, comparison is direct. The resulting list, then, is Team 2, Team 5, Team 3, Team 1, and Team 4.

3. $\frac{1}{3} + \frac{1}{2} = \frac{5}{6}$; DOK Level: 1; **Content Topics:** Q.1.b, Q.2.a, Q.2.e, Q.6.c; **Practices:** MP.1.a, MP.2.c, MP.4.a
By identifying the fractions corresponding to the two teams and adding them together, one gets: $\frac{1}{3} + \frac{1}{2} = \frac{2}{6} + \frac{3}{6} = \frac{5}{6}$. Because the denominators are different, you must find the lowest common denominator, in this case 6. From there, you divide the original denominators, 2 and 3, into the new denominator, 6, to get the new numerators. Then you add the renamed fractions together to solve.

4. $\frac{22}{8}, \frac{13}{8}$; DOK Level: 1; **Content Topics:** Q.1.b, Q.2.a; **Practices:** MP.1.a, MP.4.a
The problem requires you to first find the lowest common denominator. Since 4 divides into 8 with no remainder, 8 is the lowest common denominator. Taking the first number and expressing it as required: $2\frac{3}{4} = \frac{11}{4} = \frac{22}{8}$, where the number has first been converted into an improper fraction with 4 as the denominator, and then converted to have 8 as the denominator by multiplying both the numerator and denominator by 2. Expressing the second number as required: $1\frac{5}{8} = \frac{13}{8}$.

5. $\frac{5}{2} \times \frac{2}{1} = 5$; DOK Level: 1; **Content Topics:** Q.2.a, Q.2.e; **Practices:** MP.1.a, MP.4.a
As prompted, this problem involves division of two fractions. The first fraction must be expressed as an improper fraction: $2\frac{1}{2} = \frac{5}{2}$. Since division is involved, the expression can be rewritten as a multiplication problem using the reciprocal of the second fraction: $\frac{5}{2} \times \frac{2}{1} = 5$.

6. $\frac{1}{20}, \frac{1}{5}, \frac{3}{10}, \frac{1}{2}, \frac{3}{4}$; DOK Level: 2; **Content Topics:** Q.1.a, Q.1.b, Q.1.d; **Practices:** MP.1.a, MP.1.b, MP.4.a
Each interval on the number line represents a step of $\frac{1}{20}$. Point A is one step from 0, so has a fractional value of $\frac{1}{20}$. Point B is four steps from 0, so has a fractional value of $\frac{4}{20}$, which reduces to $\frac{1}{5}$. Point C is six steps from 0, so has a fractional value of $\frac{6}{20}$, which reduces to $\frac{3}{10}$. Continuing in the same way, points D and E represent $\frac{1}{2}$ and $\frac{3}{4}$, respectively.

LESSON 5, pp. 10-11

1. C; DOK Level: 2; **Content Topics:** Q.2.a, Q.2.e, Q.3.c; **Practices:** MP.1.a, MP.1.b, MP.1.e, MP.2.c, MP.4.a
The proportion $\frac{3}{12} = \frac{4}{x}$ represents the situation. The top number in each ratio represents the number of gallons and the bottom number represents the cost. The cross product is 48. Dividing the cross product by 3 gives a quotient of 16, so the cost of 4 gallons is $16.

2. **B**; **DOK Level:** 2; **Content Topics:** Q.3.a, Q.3.c; **Practices:** MP.1.a, MP.2.a
The unit rate is the ratio of miles per hour. The top number in each ratio is the number of miles and the bottom number in each ratio is the number of hours. Multiply to find a cross product of 260 and then divide the cross product, by the third number, 65, to find the answer of 4 hours.

3. **A**; **DOK Level:** 2; **Content Topic:** Q.3.c; **Practices:** MP.1.a, MP.2.a
The ratio of wins to losses is 5:1. The top number in each ratio is the number of wins and the bottom number in each ratio is the number of losses. Multiply to find a cross product of 25 and divide the cross product by the third number, 5, to find the number of losses by the Jammers, 5.

4. **A**; **DOK Level:** 2; **Content Topics:** Q.2.a, Q.2.e, Q.3.c; **Practices:** MP.1.a, MP.1.e
The ratio of the number of pants sold to the number of shirts sold is 92:64. This ratio can be simplified to 23:16 by dividing each number in the ratio by 4. It is important to write the numbers in the ratio in the same order as described.

5. **C**; **DOK Level:** 1; **Content Topics:** Q.2.a, Q.2.e, Q.3.a; **Practices:** MP.1.a, MP.1.e, MP.2.a, MP.4.a
A unit rate is a ratio with a denominator of 1. To find the unit rate, divide each term by 9: 558 ÷ 9 = 62.

6. **A**; **DOK Level:** 2; **Content Topics:** Q.2.a, Q.2.e, Q.3.c; **Practices:** MP.1.a, MP.1.e
The ratio of sugar to water is $\frac{2}{10}$, which simplifies to $\frac{1}{5}$. It is important to write the numbers in the ratio in the same order as described.

7. **B**; **DOK Level:** 2; **Content Topic:** Q.3.c; **Practices:** MP.1.a, MP.2.a
The ratio of teachers to students is 1:12. The top number in each ratio is the number of teachers and the bottom number in each ratio is the number of students. The number of teachers is unknown. The cross product is 36. Dividing by 12 gives a quotient of 3.

8. **C**; **DOK Level:** 2; **Content Topics:** Q.2.a, Q.2.e, Q.3.a, Q.3.c; **Practices:** MP.1.a, MP.1.b, MP.1.e, MP.2.c, MP.4.a
The proportion $\frac{20}{4} = \frac{120}{x}$ represents the situation. The top number in each ratio is the number of minutes and the bottom number is the number of miles. The cross product is 480. Dividing the cross product by 20 gives a quotient of 24.

9. **D**; **DOK Level:** 2; **Content Topics:** Q.2.a, Q.2.e, Q.3.c; **Practices:** MP.1.a, MP.1.b, MP.1.e, MP.2.c, MP.4.a
The proportion $\frac{2}{7} = \frac{14}{x}$ represents the situation. The top number in each ratio is the number of adults and the bottom number is the number of children. The cross product is 98. Dividing the cross product by 2 gives a quotient of 49.

10. **D**; **DOK Level:** 2; **Content Topics:** Q.2.a, Q.2.e, Q.3.c; **Practices:** MP.1.a, MP.1.b, MP.1.e, MP.2.c, MP.4.a
The proportion $\frac{3}{2} = \frac{144}{x}$ represents the situation. The top number in each ratio is the number of cars and the bottom number is the number of trucks. The cross product is 288. Dividing the cross product by 3 gives a quotient of 96.

11. **B**; **DOK Level:** 2; **Content Topics:** Q.2.a, Q.2.e, Q.3.c; **Practices:** MP.1.a, MP.1.e
The ratio of touchdowns to interceptions thrown is 32:12. This ratio can be simplified to 8:3 by dividing each number in the ratio by 4.

LESSON 6, *pp. 12–13*
1. **A**; **DOK Level:** 2; **Content Topics:** Q.2.a, Q.2.e; **Practices:** MP.1.a, MP.1.b, MP.1.e, MP.2.c, MP.4.a
Change received is the difference between the total owed and the amount paid. Add to find the total owed: $2.95 + $1.29 = $4.24. Subtract from $5.00 to find the difference: $5.00 − $4.24 = $0.76.

2. **D**; **DOK Level:** 2; **Content Topics:** Q.2.a, Q.2.e, Q.6.c; **Practices:** MP.1.a, MP.1.b, MP.1.e, MP.2.c, MP.4.a
To find the total amount that Coach Steve will spend on uniforms and soccer balls, multiply the cost of each piece of equipment by its quantity. The cost of the uniforms is 12 × $17 = $204.00. The cost of the soccer balls is 6 × $12.95 = $77.70. The total cost is the sum of those two amounts $204.00 + $77.70 = $281.70. It is important to pay close attention to both the cost and the quantity of each piece of equipment.

3. **B**; **DOK Level:** 2; **Content Topics:** Q.2.a, Q.2.e, Q.6.c; **Practices:** MP.1.a, MP.1.b, MP.1.e, MP.2.c, MP.4.a
Find the difference between the total cost of the shin guards and the total cost of the knee pads. The cost of the knee pads is 12 × $8.95 = $107.40. The cost of the shin guards is 12 × $10.95 = $131.40. Subtract: $131.40 − $107.40 = $28.00. Alternately, the difference between the cost of one pair of shin guards and one pair of knee pads is $10.95 − $8.95 = $2.00, and 12 × $2.00 = $24.00.

4. **A**; **DOK Level:** 1; **Content Topics:** Q.1.a, Q.6.c; **Content Practice:** MP.1.a
Compare the numbers place by place from left to right. Since 1 is less than 2, eliminate turkey (answer option B) and roast beef (answer option D). To compare weights of the chicken and ham, look at the first decimal place, tenths. Since 5 is less than 7, the package of chicken weighed the least.

5. **D**; **DOK Level:** 1; **Content Topics:** Q.1.a, Q.6.c: **Content Practice:** MP.1.a
Compare each weight to 2.25. Since 1 is less than 2, the packages of both chicken and ham weighed less than 2.25 pounds. Next, look at the tenths place of the weights for the turkey and roast beef. Since 0 and 1 are less than 2, the packages of both turkey and roast beef also weighed less than 2.25. So, all four packages weighed less than 2.25 pounds.

6. **B**; **DOK Level:** 2; **Content Topics:** Q.2.a, Q.2.e; **Practices:** MP.1.a, MP.1.b, MP.1.e, MP.2.c, MP.4.a
At Paper Plus, 15 reams of paper cost 15 × $5.25 = $78.75. At Discount Paper, 15 reams of paper cost 15 × $3.99 = $59.85. The amount saved is the difference between these two amounts: $78.75 − $59.85 = $18.90. Alternately, the savings on each ream of paper is $5.25 − $3.99 = $1.26, so the savings on 15 reams of paper is 15 × $1.26 = $18.90.

7. **D**; **DOK Level:** 3; **Content Topics:** Q.1.a, Q.6.c; **Practices:** MP.1.e, MP.3.c, MP.5.a
To compare decimals, begin with the left-most place and move to the right. Marti's batting average has the greatest digit in the ten-thousandths place, so it is likely that she compared the digits in the wrong order.

Answer Key

UNIT 1 *(continued)*

8. C; **DOK Level:** 1; **Content Topics:** Q.1.a, Q.6.c; **Content Practice:** MP.1.a
To compare decimals, start with the left-most place. All of the batting averages have the same digit in the tenths place. Looking at the hundredths place, 3 is greater than 2, so Krysten had the highest batting average.

LESSON 7, pp. 14–15
1. C; **DOK Level:** 2; **Content Topics:** Q.2.a, Q.2.e, Q.3.d; **Practices:** MP.1.a, MP.1.e, MP.2.c, MP.4.a
Since 27 out of 45 children in the neighborhood are in elementary school, the fraction of children who are in elementary school is $\frac{27}{45}$. Dividing numerator by denominator gives a decimal of 0.6. Multiply the decimal by 100 and write the percent sign: 0.6 × 100 = 60. So, 60% of the children are in elementary school. Alternately, write a proportion with a part of 27, a base of 45, and an unknown rate, and solve for the unknown rate.

2. A; **DOK Level:** 1; **Content Topics:** Q.2.a, Q.2.e, Q.3.c, Q.3.d; **Practices:** MP.1.a, MP.1.e
To write a percent as a fraction, drop the percent sign and write the percent as a fraction with the denominator 100. Simplify. $\frac{25 \div 25}{100 \div 25} = \frac{1}{4}$.

3. C; **DOK Level:** 2; **Content Topics:** Q.2.a, Q.2.e, Q.3.d; **Practices:** MP.1.a, MP.1.e, MP.4.a
To write a fraction as a percent, divide the numerator by the denominator. Then multiply the decimal by 100 and write a percent sign. $\frac{1}{8}$ = 0.125 × 100 = 12.5 → 12.5%.

4. B; **DOK Level:** 2; **Content Topics:** Q.2.a, Q.2.e, Q.3.d; **Practices:** MP.1.a, MP.1.e, MP.2.c, MP.4.a
If 0.22 of the respondents answered "Yes," then 1 − 0.22 = 0.78 of the respondents who answered "No." To write a decimal as a fraction, write the decimal digits, 78, over the place value of the last decimal digit, hundredths. Then simplify. $\frac{78 \div 2}{100 \div 2} = \frac{39}{50}$.

5. C; **DOK Level:** 2; **Content Topics:** Q.2.a, Q.2.e, Q.3.c, Q.3.d; **Practices:** MP.1.a, MP.1.e, MP.2.c, MP.4.a
Since the Strikers won 9 out of 13 games, the fraction of games the Strikers won is $\frac{9}{13}$. Dividing numerator by denominator gives a decimal of 0.692. Multiply the decimal by 100 and write the percent sign: 0.692 × 100 = 69.2. So, the team won approximately 69.2% of its games. Alternately, write a proportion with a part of 9, a base of 13, and an unknown rate, and solve for the unknown rate.

6. D; **DOK Level:** 2; **Content Topics:** Q.2.a, Q.2.e, Q.3.c, Q.3.d; **Practices:** MP.1.a, MP.1.b, MP.1.e, MP.2.c, MP.4.a
Use the equation **base × rate = part**, where the base is 300, the rate is 75% or 0.75, and the part is unknown. Multiply: 0.75 × 300 = 225. Alternately, set up and solve the proportion $\frac{part}{300} = \frac{75}{100}$.

7. C; **DOK Level:** 2; **Content Topics:** Q.2.a, Q.2.e, Q.3.c, Q.3.d; **Practices:** MP.1.a, MP.1.e, MP.2.c, MP.4.a
Use the equation **base × rate = part**, where the base is 552, the rate is 12% or 0.12, and the part is unknown. Multiply: 0.12 × 552 = 66.24. Alternately, set up and solve the proportion $\frac{part}{552} = \frac{12}{100}$.

8. B; **DOK Level:** 2; **Content Topics:** Q.2.a, Q.2.e, Q.3.d; **Practices:** MP.1.a, MP.1.e, MP.2.c, MP.4.a
To find the percent increase, first find the amount of the increase by subtracting the original salary from the new salary: $25,317.40 − $24,580 = $737.40. Divide the amount of change by the original salary and write the decimal as a percent. $737.40 ÷ $24,580.00 = 0.03 = 3%.

9. C; **DOK Level:** 2; **Content Topics:** Q.2.a, Q.2.e, Q.3.c, Q.3.d; **Practices:** MP.1.a, MP.1.e, MP.2.c, MP.4.a
To find the amount of tax paid, use the equation **base × rate = part**, where the base is 425, the rate is 6% or 0.06, and the part is unknown. Multiply: 0.06 × 425 = 25.50. Alternately, set up and solve the proportion $\frac{part}{425} = \frac{6}{100}$. Then add the amount of the tax to the price of the bicycle: $425 + $25.50 = $450.50.

10. B; **DOK Level:** 2; **Content Topics:** Q.2.a, Q.2.e, Q.3.c, Q.3.d; **Practices:** MP.1.a, MP.1.e, MP.2.c, MP.4.a
To find the amount of the discount, use the equation **base × rate = part**, where the base is 659, the rate is 20% or 0.2, and the part is unknown. Multiply: 0.20 × 659 = 131.80. Alternately, set up and solve the proportion $\frac{part}{659} = \frac{20}{100}$. Subtract the amount of the discount from the original price to find the sale price: $659 − $131.80 = $527.20.

11. B; **DOK Level:** 2; **Content Topics:** Q.2.a, Q.2.e, Q.3.c, Q.3.d; **Practices:** MP.1.a, MP.1.e, MP.2.c, MP.4.a
To find the number of calls, use the equation **base × rate = part**, where the base is 420, the rate is 45% or 0.45, and the part is unknown. Multiply: 0.45 × 420 = 189. Alternately, set up and solve the proportion $\frac{part}{420} = \frac{45}{100}$.

12. D; **DOK Level:** 2; **Content Topics:** Q.2.a, Q.2.e, Q.3.d; **Practices:** MP.1.a, MP.1.e, MP.2.c, MP.4.a
Use the equation $I = prt$, where I is the amount of interest earned. In this case, p is the amount of the investment, $5,000; r is the interest rate, 5% or 0.05; and t the time, 9 months, or 0.75 year. I = 5,000 × 0.05 × 0.75 = 187.50.

UNIT 1 REVIEW, pp. 16–23
1. D; **DOK Level:** 1; **Content Topics:** Q.2.a, Q.2.e; **Practices:** MP.1.a, MP.4.a
One-third of 24 is the same as 24 divided by 3, or 8. Two-thirds is twice that number, or 16 (choice D). Choices A, B, and C are evenly spaced integers leading up to the correct answer.

2. C; **DOK Level:** 2; **Content Topics:** Q.2.a, Q.2.e; **Practices:** MP.1.a, MP.4.a
The cost of the four chairs is 4 times $65.30, or $261.20. Adding that to the cost of the table, $764.50, gives a total of $1,025.70 (choice C). Choice A is the sum of the cost of the table and the cost of *one* chair. Choice B is the sum of the cost of the table and the cost of *two* chairs. Choice D is the sum of the cost of the table and *five* chairs.

3. **A**; **DOK Level:** 1; **Content Topics:** Q.2.a, Q.2.e; **Practices:** MP.1.a, MP.4.a

The difference between the miles driven the first day and the second day is found by subtracting 135.8 from 210.5, giving 74.7 (choice A). Choice B is twice the correct answer. Choice C is twice the distance driven the second day. Choice D is the sum of the miles driven the first and second days.

4. **C**; **DOK Level:** 2; **Content Topics:** Q.2.a, Q.2.e; **Practices:** MP1.a, MP.4.a

The solution is found by dividing $4\frac{1}{2}$ by $1\frac{1}{2}$ or, by rewriting the numbers as improper fractions, dividing $\frac{9}{2}$ by $\frac{3}{2}$. Dividing by $\frac{3}{2}$ is the same as multiplying by $\frac{2}{3}$, so the solution is $\frac{9}{2} \times \frac{2}{3} = \frac{9}{3} = 3$ (choice C). Choices A, B, and D are evenly spaced integers surrounding the correct answer.

5. **C**; **DOK Level:** 3; **Content Topics:** Q.1.b, Q.2.a; **Practices:** MP.1.a, MP.1.b, MP.1.e, MP.5.c

Multiples of 6 include 12, 18, 24, 30, 36, 42, and 48. Multiples of 8 include 16, 24, 32, 40, and 48. The lowest number common to both lists is 24 (choice C). Choice A is the sum of the two numbers. Choice B is a multiple of 6 but not of 8. Choice D is the product of 6 and 8, and so has both as factors, but is not the smallest such number.

6. **B**; **DOK Level:** 1; **Content Topic:** Q.1.a; **Practice:** MP.1.a

The two numbers before the first comma represent millions, and so are written *twenty-one million*. The next three numbers represent thousands, and so are written *three hundred forty-three thousand*. The final three numbers are written *eight hundred forty-five*. Combining them gives choice B. Choice A has an unnecessary "and" in the thousands portion. Meanwhile, choice C incorrectly omits the word "hundred" in the thousands portion. Choice D lists the last three digits, rather than rendering them in the accepted form.

7. **C**; **DOK Level:** 3; **Content Topics:** Q.1.b, Q.2.a; **Practices:** MP.1.a, MP.1.b, MP.1.e, MP.5.c

The list of numbers that divide evenly into 24, excluding 1 and 24, include 2, 3, 4, 6, 8, and 12. That is a total of 6 numbers (choice C). The remaining choices are integers distributed around the correct answer.

8. **C**; **DOK Level:** 2; **Content Topics:** Q.2.a, Q.2.e, Q.6.c; **Practices:** MP.1.a, MP.1.d, MP.2.c, MP.4.a

The total number of students listed is 864. The number of students that walk home is 54, giving a fraction of $\frac{54}{864}$. The number 864 divided by 54 equals 16 with no remainder, so the fraction can be reduced to $\frac{1}{16}$. One also can arrive at the solution by dividing the numerator and denominator by factors of 2 or 3 until no further reduction is possible. Other options involve multiplication or division of an extraneous factor of 2 or 3.

9. **D**; **DOK Level:** 2; **Content Topics:** Q.2.a, Q.2.e, Q.6.c; **Practices:** MP.1.a, MP.2.c, MP.4.a

The total number of students is 864. The number of them that take the bus or stay after school is the sum of 468 and 224, or 692. The fraction that take the bus or stay after school is, then, $\frac{692}{864}$ which, since both numerator and denominator are divisible by 4, reduces to $\frac{173}{216}$.

10. **D**; **DOK Level:** 2; **Content Topics:** Q.2.a, Q.2.e, Q.3.d; **Practices:** MP.1.a, MP.1.b, MP.4.a

The period Kara's friend takes to pay back her investment plus interest is 36 months, or 3 years. She pays 6% interest, or (0.06) ($1,250) = $75, each year. For three years, the interest will be (3)($75), or $225. The interest combined with the original investment that Kara gets after 3 years is ($225) + ($1,250) = $1,475 (choice D). Choice A represents the interest alone. Choice B is the original investment *minus* the interest. Choice C is the investment plus *one* year's worth of interest.

11. **B**; **DOK Level:** 2; **Content Topics:** Q.1.b, Q.2.a, Q.2.e; **Practices:** MP.1.a, MP.4.a

The answer is the difference between the two numbers. Rewriting the difference using improper fractions with a common denominator gives $\frac{16}{3} - \frac{19}{4} = \frac{64 - 57}{12} = \frac{7}{12}$ (choice B). The remaining choices are $\frac{6}{12}, \frac{8}{12}$, and $\frac{9}{12}$, each reduced appropriately, representing possible errors in conversion or subtraction.

12. **A**; **DOK Level:** 1; **Content Topic:** Q.1.a; **Practice:** MP.1.a

The digit following the hundreds place is 4, which is less than 5. As a result, the digit in the hundreds place, 5, remains the same and subsequent digits in the number are replaced with zeros (choice A). Choice B is the number rounded to the nearest ten. Choice C is the number rounded up to the next higher hundred. Choice D is the number rounded to the nearest thousand.

13. **C**; **DOK Level:** 1; **Content Topic:** Q.1.a; **Practice:** MP.1.a

One hundred three is written as 103, and goes in the thousands place just before the comma. *Seven hundred fifty* is written as 750. Combining the two gives $103,750 (choice C). Choice A confuses *fifty* with 5. Choice B confuses *fifty* with 15. Choice D confuses *one hundred three* with 130.

14. **A**; **DOK Level:** 2; **Content Topics:** Q.2.a, Q.2.e; **Practices:** MP.1.a, MP.4.a

The cost of two pretzels is (2)($1.95) = $3.90. The cost of two soft drinks is (2)($0.99) = $1.98. Adding the two gives a total cost of $5.88. The change received from a $10 bill would be ($10.00 − $5.88) = $4.12 (choice A). Choice B is the change one would get back after buying two pretzels and *one* drink. Choice C is the cost of the food, not the change. Choice D is the change one would get back after buying *one* pretzel and *one* drink.

15. **C**; **DOK Level:** 2; **Content Topic:** Q.1.a; **Practices:** MP.1.a, MP.1.b

Since numerators for all the fractions listed are 1, the fraction with the smallest denominator will represent the largest number. The smallest denominator is 3, in the fraction $\frac{1}{3}$, corresponding to soccer.

UNIT 1 *(continued)*

16. B; **DOK Level:** 2; **Content Topics:** Q.1.b, Q.2.a, Q.2.e; **Practices:** MP.1.a, MP.2.c, MP.4.a
The answer is the sum of the two fractions representing lacrosse and basketball. Rewriting them with common denominators gives $\frac{1}{4} + \frac{1}{6} = \frac{3}{12} + \frac{2}{12} = \frac{5}{12}$. Option A is the result of erroneously adding the two numerators (1 + 1 = 2) and the denominators (4 + 6) to get the resulting fraction. Option C is the result of incorrectly converting $\frac{1}{4}$ to $\frac{4}{12}$. Option D results from erroneously summing 3 and 2 and getting 4.

17. D; **DOK Level:** 2; **Content Topics:** Q.1.b, Q.2.a, Q.2.e, Q.3.d, Q.6.c; **Practices:** MP.1.a, MP.2.c, MP.4.a
The fraction for volleyball $\left(\frac{1}{20}\right)$ can be converted to percent by dividing the numerator by the denominator (getting 0.05) and multiplying by 100 (getting 5%). The fraction for frisbee $\left(\frac{1}{5}\right)$ is equal to 0.20, or 20%. Adding the two gives (5 + 20) = 25%.

18. 67; **DOK Level:** 1; **Content Topics:** Q.2.a, Q.2.e, Q.3.a; **Practices:** MP.1.a, MP.4.a
The rate is the distance (301.5 miles) divided by the time (4.5 hours), or 67 miles per hour.

19. $180; **DOK Level:** 2; **Content Topics:** Q.2.a, Q.2.e; **Practices:** MP.1.a, MP.4.a
The change in share price is ($52 − $43) = $9 per share. The total profit from Scarlett's investment is that change times the number of shares: $9 × 20 = $180.

20. 7; **DOK Level:** 2; **Content Topics:** Q.2.a, Q.2.e; **Practices:** MP.1.a, MP.2.c, MP.4.a
Dividing the total number of people (426) by the number of people that can ride in one bus (65) gives 6 with a remainder of 36. Those left over will require a seventh bus, so the answer is 7.

21. −20; **DOK Level:** 2; **Content Topic:** Q.2.a; **Practices:** MP.1.a, MP.4.a
The product of −1 and 2 is −2. That result multiplied by −3 is +6. That result times 4 is 24, and the product of 24 and −5 is −120. Dividing −120 by 6 is −20.

22. 7; **DOK Level:** 2; **Content Topics:** Q.2.a, Q.2.e, Q.3.c; **Practices:** MP.1.a, MP.1.b, MP.2.c, MP.4.a
Dividing 45 by 7 gives 6 with a remainder of 3. To ensure that the proportion is no more than 7 to 1, a seventh chaperone must be included.

23. 5; **DOK Level:** 1; **Content Topics:** Q.2.a, Q.2.e, Q.3.a; **Practices:** MP.1.a, MP.4.a
The solution requires dividing the distance (135 miles) by the unit rate of speed (27 miles per hour). The result is $\left(\frac{135}{27}\right) = 5$ hours.

24. $28; **DOK Level:** 2; **Content Topics:** Q.2.a, Q.2.e, Q.3.a; **Practices:** MP.1.a, MP.4.a
If each pound costs $8, then $3\frac{1}{2}$ pounds will cost $3\frac{1}{2} \times 8 = \frac{7}{2} \times 8 = 7 \times 4 = \$28$, whereby the $3\frac{1}{2}$ has been converted to an improper fraction to simplify the calculation.

25. 6; **DOK Level:** 3; **Content Topic:** Q.1.b; **Practices:** MP.1.a, MP.1.b, MP.1.e, MP.5.c
Factors of 18 are 1, 2, 3, 6, 9, and 18. Neither 9 nor 18 divide evenly into 42. The number 6 does, however, making that the largest common factor of the two numbers.

26. B; **DOK Level:** 2; **Content Topic:** Q.1.a; **Practice:** MP.1.a
Comparing the first two items on the menu, one finds that the $9.65 for the elk sandwich is greater than the $5.89 for the walleye fillet. Comparison of the cost of the elk sandwich with the cost of each of the remaining items shows the elk sandwich to be the item with the highest price on the menu.

27. B; **DOK Level:** 2; **Content Topics:** Q.2.a, Q.2.e; **Practices:** MP.1.a, MP.2.c, MP.4.a
The cost of 3 kid's buffalo platters is (3)($3.50) = $10.50. Adding that to the cost of the wild boar barbecue ($9.19) and the walleye fillet ($5.89) gives a total of ($10.50 + $9.19 + $5.89) = $25.58. The money Kurt has remaining after paying is ($50.00 − $25.58) = $24.42 (choice B). Choice A is the cost with including only *one* kid's platter, rather than *three*. Choice C is the *cost* of the items listed in the question, not the change back from $50. Choice D is the change one would get if only *one* kid's platter were purchased.

28. C; **DOK Level:** 2; **Content Topics:** Q.2.a, Q.2.e; **Practices:** MP.1.a, MP.2.c, MP.4.a
The cost of two elk sandwiches is (2)($9.65) = $19.30. The cost of three kid's platters is (3)($3.50) = $10.50. The difference is ($19.30 − $10.50) = $8.80 (choice C). Choice A is the cost of *one* elk sandwich minus the cost of *one* kid's platter. Choice B is the cost of two *boar barbecues* minus the cost of three kid's platters. Choice D is the cost of two elk sandwiches minus the cost of *one* kid's platter.

29. D; **DOK Level:** 1; **Content Topic:** Q.1.a; **Practice:** MP.1.a
Fifty-six thousand is written as *56,000*. *Two hundred, twenty-eight* is written as *228*. Combining the two gives 56,228 which, when written as a string of digits, is choice D.

30. B; **DOK Level:** 2; **Content Topics:** Q.2.a, Q.2.e; **Practices:** MP.1.a, MP.4.a
The balance of the account after depositing the $246 is ($198 + $246) = $444. The two checks remove ($54 + $92) = $146 from the account. The ending balance is, then, ($444 − $146) = $298 (choice B). Choice A is the result of *subtracting* the deposit amount from the account balance and *adding* the check amounts. Choice C is the result of adding the $92 check rather than subtracting. Choice D is the result of adding the deposit amount *and* the check amounts to the balance.

31. C; **DOK Level:** 2; **Content Topics:** Q.2.a, Q.2.e, Q.3.c; **Practices:** MP.1.a, MP.4.a
If the ratio of men to women is 2:3, that means that $\frac{\text{Number of men}}{\text{Number of women}} = \frac{2}{3} = \frac{\text{Number of men}}{180}$. By cross multiplying, one finds that the number of men is $\frac{2}{3}$ of 180, or 120 (choice C).

32. A; **DOK Level:** 2; **Content Topics:** Q.2.a, Q.2.e, Q.3.a; **Practices:** MP.1.a, MP.4.a
The rate is 1 scarf per $1\frac{2}{3}$ hours. The proportion. $\frac{1}{1\frac{2}{3}} = \frac{x}{4}$, where the top numbers represent scarves and the bottom numbers represent hours, can be used to solve the problem. Cross multiply: $(1 \times 4) \div 1\frac{2}{3} = 4 \div \frac{5}{3} = \frac{4}{1} \times \frac{3}{5} = \frac{12}{5} = 2\frac{2}{5}$. Since $x = 2\frac{2}{5}$, the answer is $2\frac{2}{5}$ scarves (Choice A).

33. D; DOK Level: 2; Content Topics: Q.2.a, Q.2.e, Q.3.d; **Practices:** MP.1.a, MP.4.a
The decimal equivalent of 84% is 0.84. Multiplying 175 students by 0.84 gives the number who attended the meeting, 147 athletes (choice D). Choice A is the number of students who did *not* attend. Choice B confuses percent with number. Choice C is the number not attending plus 100.

34. A; DOK Level: 2; Content Topics: Q.2.a, Q.2.e, Q.3.d; **Practices:** MP.1.a, MP.4.a
The number of people in favor of the new road can be found by multiplying the number of people surveyed (1,200) by the decimal equivalent of 35% (0.35). The result is 420 residents. The number who objected to the new road is (1,200 − 420) = 780 residents (choice A). Choice B is the number of residents in favor of the new road. Choice C is the result of assuming 70% were in favor of it. Choice D is the result of confusing percent with number.

35. D; DOK Level: 2; Content Topics: Q.2.a, Q.2.e; **Practices:** MP.1.a, MP.1.d, MP.2.c, MP.4.a
The amount Tom makes during the year is $200 per week times 52 weeks per year, or $10,400. The amount he pays for rent in a year is $300 per month times 12 months per year, or $3,600. The money he has left is $10,400 − $3,600 = $6,800 (choice D). Choice A is the result of taking the difference between $300 and $200 and multiplying by 12. Choice B is the result of taking the difference between $300 and $200 and multiplying by 52. Choice C is the result of assuming there are 4 weeks in a month, finding his income to be $800 per month, subtracting $300 to get $500 left over per month, and multiplying that result by 12.

36. B; DOK Level: 2; Content Topics: Q.2.a, Q.4.a; **Practices:** MP.1.a, MP.2.c, MP.4.a
The decimal equivalent of Ben's mileage is 25.80 miles. Subtracting that from Stefan's gives 32.95 miles − 25.80 miles = 7.15 miles (choice B). The remaining choices represent numbers equal to 32 − 25 = 7, plus decimals or fractions that fall near the correct answer.

37. C; DOK Level: 2; Content Topics: Q.2.a, Q.3.d, Q.4.a; **Practices:** MP.1.a, MP.2.c, MP.4.a
The difference between the mileage for Stefan and Jackson is 32.95 miles − 26.375 miles = 6.575 miles. Dividing that result by Jackson's mileage (26.375 miles) gives 0.2493 which, converted to the nearest whole percent, is 25% (choice C). The remaining choices are regularly spaced whole number percentages around the correct answer.

38. A; DOK Level: 2; Content Topics: Q.2.a, Q.2.e; **Practices:** MP.1.a, MP.2.c
The ratio of Green Party supporters to Libertarian Party supporters is 10:2, which can be reduced to 5:1 (choice A). Choice B inverts the ratio. Choice C has reduced the Libertarian Party number from 2 to 1, but fails to reduce the Green Party number from 10 to 5. Choice D is the same as choice B, but without reduction of the ratio.

39. B; DOK Level: 2; Content Topics: Q.2.a, Q.2.e; **Practices:** MP.1.a, MP.2.c, MP.4.a
If there were 78 Democrats among a sample of 200 people surveyed, the best guess at the number of Democrats in a sample twice that size (2 × 200 = 400) would be (2)(78) = 156 (choice B). Choice A assumes all of the additional people surveyed would identify as Democrats. Choice C assumes the number remains the same regardless of the sample size. Choice D is the result of *dividing* 78 by 2, rather than *multiplying* by 2.

40. D; DOK Level: 2; Content Topics: Q.2.a, Q.2.e, Q.3.d, Q.6.c; **Practices:** MP.1.a, MP.1.b, MP.2.c, MP.4.a
The number of people in the survey that was neither Democrat nor Republican was (46 + 10 + 2) = 58. Dividing 58 by the number of people surveyed gives $\left(\frac{58}{200}\right)$ = 0.29, which, when converted to percent, is 29% (choice D). Choice A is the percent that were Democrat or Republican. Choice C is the percent equivalent of the ratio of those who were neither Democrat nor Republican (58) to the number that were Democrat or Republican (142): $\left(\frac{58}{142}\right)$ = 0.41. Choice B is the result of subtracting choice C from 100%.

41. C; DOK Level: 2; Content Topics: Q.2.a, Q.2.e, Q.3.d; **Practices:** MP.1.a, MP.2.c, MP.4.a
The difference between the population at the end and the beginning of the 5-year period is (45,687 − 43,209) = 2,478. Dividing that by the beginning population (43,209) gives $\left(\frac{2,478}{43,209}\right)$ = 0.0573. Converting that to percent is (100)(0.0573) = 5.73%; rounding to the nearest whole percent is 6% (choice C). The remaining choices are evenly spaced whole-number percentages around the correct answer.

42. A; DOK Level: 1; Content Topics: Q.2.a, Q.2.e, Q.3.d; **Practices:** MP.1.a, MP.4.a
The fractional equivalent of 54% is $\frac{54}{100}$. Both the numerator and denominator can be divided by 2 to give $\frac{27}{50}$ (choice A). Other choices are fractions close to 54 percent, but are either more or less than it.

43. C; DOK Level: 1; Content Topics: Q.2.a, Q.2.e; **Practices:** MP.1.a, MP.2.c, MP.4.a
The number of months in one year is 12, so the amount paid in one year is $165.40 per month times 12 months, giving $1,984.80 (choice C). Choices A, B, and D are the amounts paid in 6 months, 10 months, and 24 months, respectively.

44. B; DOK Level: 2; Content Topics: Q.2.a, Q.2.e; **Practices:** MP.1.a, MP.4.a
The solution requires multiplying $1\frac{3}{8}$ by 3. Converting $1\frac{3}{8}$ to an improper fraction gives $\frac{11}{8}$, multiplying by 3 gives $\frac{33}{8}$, and rewriting as a proper fraction gives $4\frac{1}{8}$ (choice B). Alternately, one could view the problem as $(3)\left(1\frac{3}{8}\right) = (3)\left(1 + \frac{3}{8}\right) = \left(3 + \frac{(3)(3)}{8}\right) = \left(3 + \frac{9}{8}\right) = \left(3 + 1 + \frac{1}{8}\right) = 4\frac{1}{8}$. Choice A is the result of neglecting to add the 1 from the reduction of $\frac{9}{8}$. Choices C and D are the result of miscalculating the result by $+\frac{1}{8}$ and $+\frac{1}{4}$, respectively.

Answer Key

UNIT 1 (continued)

45. D; DOK Level: 2; Content Topics: Q.2.a, Q.2.e, Q.3.a; Practices: MP.1.a, MP.4.a
The total cost is $8.99 per pound times 1.76 pounds, or $15.8224; rounding to the nearest penny gives $15.82 (choice D). Choice A is the result of dividing by 1.76 rather than multiplying. Choice B is the result of erroneously using 1.6 as the number of pounds of cheese. Choice C is the result of rounding the cost to the nearest dime.

46. A; DOK Level: 2; Content Topics: Q.2.a, Q.2.e; Practices: MP.1.a, MP.2.c, MP.4.a
The total number of months is 15 years times 12 months per year, or 180 months. Dividing the total cost over the life of the mortgage by the total number of months is $\left(\frac{\$324,000}{180}\right)$ = $1,800 (choice A).

47. A; DOK Level: 2; Content Topic: Q.1.a; Practices: MP.1.a, MP.1.e
Scanning down the series of numbers and focusing on the digits to the left of the commas, one finds the largest number begins with 29 thousand (Saturday). The next largest begins with 25 thousand (Sunday), followed by 21 thousand (Friday), and then 16 thousand (Thursday). The next two largest numbers both begin with 14 thousand (Monday and Tuesday), so one needs to look at the hundreds digit. Monday's hundreds digit (9) is larger than Tuesday's (6), so Monday completes the list: Saturday, Sunday, Friday, Thursday, and Monday.

48. C; DOK Level: 2; Content Topic: Q.1.a; Practices: MP.1.a, MP.1.e
The digits to the left of the comma are lowest for Wednesday (corresponding to 13 thousand), making that the day with the lowest receipts. The remaining choices are other days with relatively low receipts, listed in chronological order.

49. B; DOK Level: 3; Content Topic: Q.1.a; Practices: MP.1.a, MP.1.c, MP.3.a, MP.5.c
The two days with the highest receipts are Saturday and Sunday, making the weekends the days where the greatest amount of food is sold (choice B). Choice A is incorrect since, although receipts do decrease during the first three days of the week, they increase again on Thursday and Friday. Choice C is incorrect since sales decrease from Saturday to Sunday. Choice D may or may not be true, but there is no way to tell from the data in the table; receipts may increase on weekends, not because of weekend specials, but because people are more available to visit restaurants on the weekend.

50. C; DOK Level: 2; Content Topics: Q.2.a, Q.2.e; Practices: MP.1.a, MP.4.a
The cost for the three meals was ($13 + $15 + $16) = $44. Adding the tip gives ($44 + $10) = $54. If Fred and Mary split the cost equally, they each pay $\left(\frac{\$54}{2}\right)$ = $27 (choice C). Choice A is the result if the bill and tip are split evenly *three* ways. Choice B is the result of splitting the bill *two* ways, without figuring in the tip. Choice D is the *total* cost, including the tip.

51. D; DOK Level: 2; Content Topic: Q.1.a; Practice: MP.1.a
The type of cookies with the lowest sales is sugar cookies (32). The next highest number (56) corresponds to coconut cookies, followed by oatmeal cookies (89), followed by chocolate cookies (125). So the list in that order would be sugar, coconut, oatmeal, and chocolate (choice D).

52. A; DOK Level: 2; Content Topics: Q.2.a, Q.2.e; Practices: MP.1.a, MP.2.c, MP.4.a
The amount withdrawn from Justina's checking account each month ($2,300) exceeds the amount deposited ($2,000) by $300. Over the course of one year, the balance as a result will decrease by (12)($300) = $3,600. Since the balance decreases, the change is −$3,600 (choice A). Choice B is the change in her balance each *month*. Choices C and D are the same as choices A and B, albeit with the absence of the negative sign.

53. A; DOK Level: 3; Content Topics: Q.2.a, Q.2.e; Practices: MP.1.a, MP.3.a, MP.4.a
The solution involves summing the drops (300 feet + 180 feet + 300 feet = 780 feet), and subtracting the sum from the rises (240 feet + 130 feet = 370 feet), giving (780 feet − 370 feet) = 410 feet. Since the current height is lower than the initial height, the answer is −410 feet (choice A). Choice D is the opposite of the correct choice. Choices B and C are the result of treating the initial 300-foot drop as an increase of 300 feet, with and without the negative sign.

54. C; DOK Level: 2; Content Topic: Q.2.a; Practices: MP.1.a, MP.1.b, MP.1.e, MP.3.a, MP.4.a
Subtracting −15 from a number is the same as adding +15 to the number. Getting a result of −12 from adding 15 to a number means that the number is −12 − 15 = −27 (choice A). Choice B is the result of subtracting 15 from +12. Choices C and D are the same as choices A and B, with the negative signs removed.

55. B; DOK Level: 2; Content Topics: Q.2.a, Q.2.e; Practices: MP.1.a, MP.4.a
The balance of the account after the $287 check is deposited is ($1,244 + $287) = $1,531. The balance decreases by $50 when Sara makes her withdrawal, giving a final balance of ($1,531 − $50) = $1,481 (choice B). Choice A is the result of only adding the $50 cash withdrawal to the initial balance. Choice C is the result of adding the deposit but neglecting to subtract the withdrawn cash. Choice D is the result of adding both the deposit and the cash to the initial balance.

56. C; DOK Level: 2; Content Topics: Q.2.a, Q.2.e; Practices: MP.1.a, MP.1.b, MP.3.a, MP.4.a
If Ellie budgets $65 for her total bill, and $5 of that goes to pay the fee each month, there is ($65 − $5) = $60 per month to pay the tolls. Since each toll is $1.25, the number of tolls that can be paid with $60 is $\frac{\$60}{\$1.25}$ = 48 tolls (choice C).

57. D; DOK Level: 3; Content Topics: Q.2.a, Q.2.e; Practices: MP.1.a, MP.4.a
The skier's position increases 786 feet, then decreases 137 feet, and then increases 542 feet. If you consider the skier's starting point as 0 ft, then the change in position is (786 − 137 + 542) feet = 1,191 feet (choice D).

58. A; DOK Level: 2; **Content Topics:** Q.2.a, Q.2.e; **Practices:** MP.1.a, MP.4.a
If the change in the account balance each day is $64, the change in three days will be (3)($64) = $192. Since the change represents withdrawals, the change in the balance will be negative: −$192 (choice A). Choice B is the change in the account balance after *two* days. Choices C and D are the negatives of choices B and A, respectively.

59. D; DOK Level: 1; **Content Topics:** Q.2.a, Q.2.e; **Practices:** MP.1.a, MP.2.c, MP.4.a
The total of the monthly expenses is the sum of all the numbers in the table, $45,600 (choice D). Choice A is the result of taking the salary number and subtracting the remaining entries in the table. Choice B is the highest number in the table. Choice C is the sum of all entries in the table, except the miscellaneous entry.

60. B; DOK Level: 1; **Content Topics:** Q.2.a, Q.2.e; **Practices:** MP.1.a, MP.2.c, MP.4.a
The sum of expenses excluding salaries, in dollars, is ($3,600 + $800 + $1,200 + $1,600) = $7,200 (choice B).

61. C; DOK Level: 2; **Content Topics:** Q.2.a, Q.2.e, Q.3.d; **Practices:** MP.1.a, MP.2.c, MP.4.a
The expenses for supplies and miscellaneous total $1,200 + $1,600 = $2,800. The corresponding percentage of the total expenses is the percent equivalent of the fraction $\frac{\$2,800}{\$45,600}$ = 0.0614 which, to the nearest tenth of a percent, is 6.1% (choice C). Choice A is the percentage representing *all* non-salary expenses. Choice B is the result of dividing the sum of supplies and miscellaneous expenses by the *salary* expenses, rather than by the *total* expenses. Choice D is the percent corresponding to supplies only.

62. D; DOK Level: 1; **Content Topics:** Q.2.a, Q.2.e; **Practices:** MP.1.a, MP.2.c, MP.4.a
The sum of Morgan's scores is equal to 1 + 3 + 1 − 1 + 1 − 1 + 1 = 5 (choice D). The remaining choices are the possible scores below Morgan's, including Tom's (4) and Dana's (2).

63. C; DOK Level: 2; **Content Topics:** Q.2.a, Q.2.e; **Practices:** MP.1.a, MP.2.c, MP.3.a, MP.4.a
Morgan's score is 5. Summing the scores for Tom and Dana give 4 and 2, respectively. The scores, in increasing order, are 2 (Dana), 4 (Tom), and 5 (Morgan).

64. 13°F; DOK Level: 2; **Content Topics:** Q.1.d, Q.2.a, Q.2.e; **Practices:** MP.1.a, MP.4.a
The temperature at 10 A.M. is four marker lines to the right of the 60°F line. Since there are 10 markers for every 10 degrees, the space between marker lines represents 1 degree. As a result, the temperature at 10 A.M. is 64°F. Similarly, the temperature at 6 P.M. is 77°F. The change in temperature between those two times is, as a result, (77°F − 64°F) = 13°F.

65. 6°F; DOK Level: 2; **Content Topics:** Q.1.d, Q.2.a, Q.2.e; **Practices:** MP.1.a, MP.4.a
There are six marker lines between the 6 P.M. and 2 P.M. temperatures, each representing 1 degree of difference; the magnitude of the total change is 6°F. Since the 6 P.M. temperature is lower than the 2 P.M. temperature, the change is positive: 6°F.

66. Any choice in top box, 3 in bottom; DOK Level: 3; **Content Topics:** Q.2.a, Q.2.d; **Practices:** MP.1.a, MP.1.b, MP.1.c, MP1.e, MP.2.c, MP.3.a, MP.4.a, MP.5.c
The requirement that the expression be undefined implies that the denominator be zero. To make the denominator zero means that twice the missing number in the denominator must equal 6. That number must, therefore, be 3. That is sufficient to make the expression undefined, regardless of the numerator, so any of the other choices may be substituted into the box in the numerator.

67. $\frac{1}{5}$, DOK Level: 2; **Content Topics:** Q.2.a, Q.2.e; **Practices:** MP.1.a, MP.4.a
The amount of whole milk stocked is 15 gallons. The total number of gallons stocked is (15 + 20 + 20 + 20) = 75. Dividing 15 by 75 gives a fraction of $\frac{1}{5}$. Equivalent fractions would include $\frac{2}{10}$ or $\frac{4}{20}$, but neither of those choice possibilities can be constructed from the numbers provided.

68. $\frac{2}{5}$, $\frac{7}{10}$, and $\frac{5}{4}$; DOK Level: 2; **Content Topics:** Q.1.a, Q.2.a; **Practices:** MP.1.a, MP.4.a
There are 10 marker lines for each 0.5 length of the number line, so adjacent marker lines are separated by $\frac{1}{20}$. Point A is eight marker lines above zero, and therefore corresponds to the value $\frac{8}{20}$. Reducing that result by dividing both the numerator and denominator by 4 gives $\frac{2}{5}$. Point B is four marker lines above the 0.5 division, and therefore corresponds to a value of $0.5 + \frac{4}{20} = \frac{5}{10} + \frac{2}{10} = \frac{7}{10}$. Point C is five marker lines above the 1 division, and therefore corresponds to a value of $1 + \frac{5}{20} = \frac{4}{4} + \frac{1}{4} = \frac{5}{4}$.

69. $\frac{11}{20}$; DOK Level: 2; **Content Topics:** Q.1.b, Q.2.a, Q.2.e; **Practices:** MP.1.a, MP.4.a
The difference can be written as $\frac{5}{4} - \frac{7}{10}$. Using 20 as a common denominator gives $\frac{25}{20} - \frac{14}{20} = \frac{11}{20}$.

70. $\frac{93}{100} = \frac{\text{\#circuits}}{4,000}$; DOK Level: 2; **Content Topics:** Q.3.c, Q.3.d; **Practices:** MP.1.a, MP.1.b
The ratio of circuits that passed is given as $\frac{93}{100}$. The ratio also can be written as $\frac{\text{\#circuits}}{4,000}$. The two ratios represent the same thing, and so are equal to each other. By multiplying 93 × 4,000 and then dividing the product by 100, you arrive at 3,720 circuits that passed testing.

UNIT 2 MEASUREMENT/DATA ANALYSIS

LESSON 1, *pp. 26–27*
1. A; DOK Level: 2; **Content Topics:** Q.2.a, Q.2.e; **Practices:** MP.1.a, MP.1.b, MP.1.d, MP.1.e, MP.2.c, MP.3.a
Convert all measurements to similar units. In this case, divide 30 mL by 10 to get 3 cL. Next, add 3 cL + 2 cL to get 5 cL.

UNIT 2 (continued)

2. **30 feet**; **DOK Level:** 2; **Content Topics:** Q.2.a, Q.2.e;
Practices: MP.1.a, MP.1.e
Since 1 yard = 3 feet, multiply by 3 to convert yards to feet.
Since 6 yards = 6 × 3 = 18 feet, the total wood required =
18 feet + 12 feet = 30 feet.

3. **640 g**; **DOK Level:** 2; **Content Topics:** Q.2.a, Q.2.e,
Q.3.c; **Practices:** MP.1.a, MP.1.b, MP.1.e, MP.2.c, MP.3.a,
MP.4.a
2 km × 1,000 = 2,000 m
$$\frac{Mass}{Length} = \frac{40\ g}{125\ m} = \frac{x}{2,000\ m}$$
$125x = 80,000$
$x = 640\ g$

4. **5,500 m**; **DOK Level:** 3; **Content Topics:** Q.2.a, Q.2.e,
Q.3.a, Q.3.c, Q.6.c; **Practices:** MP.1.a, MP.1.b, MP.1.d, MP.1.e,
MP.2.c, MP.3.a, MP.4.a
First, convert 2 km to m by multiplying by 1,000 so that 2 km =
2,000 m. From there, calculate the total distance run: 2,000 m
+ 2(1,500 m) + 5(100 m) = 5,500 m.

5. **0.0966 s**; **DOK Level:** 2; **Content Topics:** Q.2.a, Q.2.e;
Practices: MP.1.a, MP.1.b, MP.1.d, MP.1.e, MP.2.c, MP.3.a,
MP.4.a
Set up a proportion to help find the unknown variable:
$$\frac{distance}{time} = \frac{200\ m}{19.32\ s} = \frac{1\ m}{x}$$
$200x = 19.32$
$x = 0.0966\ s$

6. **D**; **DOK Level:** 2; **Content Topics:** Q.2.a, Q.2.e;
Practices: MP.1.a, MP.1.e
Two feeders hold 6 × 2 = 12 fluid ounces. Meanwhile, 1
large feeder = 1 cup of liquid (8 fluid ounces).
The largest feeder = 1 pint (2 cups). Since 1 cup = 8 fluid
ounces, 2 cups = 16 fluid ounces.
Total feed required = 12 + 8 + 16 = 36 fluid ounces.

7. **C**; **DOK Level:** 2; **Content Topics:** Q.2.a, Q.2.e;
Practices: MP.1.a, MP.1.b, MP.1.d, MP.1.e, MP.2.c, MP.3.a,
MP.4.a
Set up an equation to find the unknown. Let x = the total
amount of plastic that flowed out of the printer.
$$\frac{Plastic}{Time} = \frac{10\ mL}{1\ second} = \frac{x}{3,600\ seconds}$$
$x = 36,000\ mL$
Next, convert mL to L so that 36,000 ÷ 1,000 = 36 L.

8. **A**; **DOK Level:** 2; **Content Topics:** Q.2.a, Q.2.e;
Practices: MP.1.a, MP.1.b, MP.1.d, MP.1.e, MP.2.c, MP.3.a
For spill A, convert kL to L multiplying by 1,000. For spill C,
convert minutes to hours (30 minutes − 0.5 hour). Set up an
equation to help find the spill rate for each disaster:

Spill A
$$\frac{Quantity\ of\ oil\ spilled}{Time} = \frac{287,000,000\ L}{5\ h} = \frac{x}{1h}$$
$x = 57,400,000\ L/h$

Spill B
$$\frac{Quantity\ of\ oil\ spilled}{Time} = \frac{260,000\ L}{8\ h} = \frac{x}{1h}$$
$x = 32,500\ L/h$

Spill C
$$\frac{Quantity\ of\ oil\ spilled}{Time} = \frac{292,000\ L}{0.5\ h} = \frac{x}{1h}$$
$x = 584,000\ L/h$

Spill A has the highest spill rate.

9. **D**; **DOK Level:** 2; **Content Topics:** Q.2.a, Q.2.e;
Practices: MP.1.a, MP.1.b, MP.1.d, MP.1.e, MP.2.c, MP.3.a
Note that the spill with the highest spill rate (as shown in
previous question) will leak the most oil into the sea at the
end of 30 minutes. The spill rates in the previous question
are in Liters per hour. To find the amount of oil leaked in
30 minutes, divide the rates by 2.

Spill A
57,400,000 ÷ 2 = 28,700,000 L. To convert to kL, divide by
1,000: 28,700,000 ÷ 1,000 = 28,700 kL.

LESSON 2, pp. 28–29

1. **C**; **DOK Level:** 2; **Content Topics:** Q.2.a, Q.2.e, Q.4a;
Practices: MP.1.a, MP.1.b, MP.1.e
Since 1 cm on the blueprint represents 3 feet on the actual
structure, some conversion is required.

Actual width = 5 × 3 = 15 ft
Actual height = 4 × 3 = 12 ft
Actual length = 2 × 3 = 6 ft
Actual volume = $l × w × h$ = 15 ft × 12 ft × 6 ft = 1,080 ft³.

2. **D**; **DOK Level:** 2; **Content Topics:** Q.2.a, Q.2.e, Q.4.c,
Q.4.d, Q.5.a; **Practices:** MP.1.a, MP.1.b, MP.1.e, MP.2.c,
MP.3.a, MP.4.a
Figure A has 2 portions (square and rectangle).
Area of rectangle = $l × w$
= 250m × 30m
= 7,500 m²
Area of square = $S²$
= 50m × 50m
= 2,500 m²
Area of Figure A = Area of rectangle + Area of square
= 7,500 m² + 2,500 m²
= 10,000 m² (10,000 square meters)

3. **D**; **DOK Level:** 2; **Content Topics:** Q.2.a, Q.2.e, Q.4.a, Q.4.c, Q.4.d; **Practices:** MP.1.a, MP.1.b, MP.1.e, MP.2.c, MP.3.a, MP.4.a

Perimeter is the distance around the entire figure. This figure has 6 sides.

P = 250 m + 80 m + 50 m + 50 m + 200 m + 30 m

P = 660 m

Note that the side measuring 80 m is a combination of the width of the rectangle and the width of the square (30 m + 50 m). Likewise, the side measuring 200 m is the length of the rectangle, minus the part length of the square (250 m − 50 m).

4. **B**; **DOK Level:** 2; **Content Topics:** Q.2.a, Q.2.e, Q.4.c, Q.4.d, Q.5.a; **Practices:** MP.1.a, MP.1.b, MP.1.e, MP.2.c, MP.3.a, MP.4.a

Figure B is composed of 2 rectangles that are measured in ft.

Area of horizontal rectangle = $l \times w$

= 50 ft × 15 ft

= 750 ft^2

Area of vertical rectangle = 20 ft × 10 ft

= 200 ft^2

Area of Figure B = Sum of both rectangles

= 750 ft^2 + 200 ft^2

= 950 ft^2 (950 sq ft)

5. **A**; **DOK Level:** 3; **Content Topics:** Q.2.a, Q.2.e, Q.4.a, Q.4.c, Q.4.d; **Practices:** MP.1.a, MP.1.b, MP.1.e, MP.2.c, MP.3.a, MP.4.a

Perimeter of Figure A = 660 m

If 1 m = 3.28 ft, we can set up an equation to find the cross product:

$$\frac{1 \text{ m}}{3.28 \text{ ft}} = \frac{660 \text{ m}}{x}$$

x = 660 × 3.28

x = 2,164.8 ft

Perimeter of Figure B = 50 ft + 15 ft + 15 ft + 20 ft + 10 ft + 20 ft + 20 ft + 20 ft = 170 ft

The difference between Figure A and B is: 2,164.8 − 170 = 1,994.8 ft.

6. **D**; **DOK Level:** 2; **Content Topics:** Q.2.a, Q.2.e, Q.5.a, Q.5.f; **Practices:** MP.1.a, MP.1.b, MP.1.e, MP.2.c

Volume of a container = area of base × height

Area of Figure B = 950 ft^2

Volume = 950 ft^2 × 30 ft = 28,500 ft^3 (28,500 cubic feet)

7. **B**; **DOK Level:** 2; **Content Topics:** Q.2.a, Q.2.e, Q.5.a; **Practices:** MP.1.a, MP.1.b, MP.1.c, MP.1.e, MP.2.c, MP.3.a, MP.4.a

Volume of prism = area of base × height

= $l \times w \times h$

600 ft^3 = 20 ft × 15 ft × h

600 ft^3 = 300 ft^2 × h

600 ft^3 ÷ 300 ft^2 = h

2 ft = h

8. **D**; **DOK Level:** 2; **Content Topics:** Q.2.a, Q.2.e, Q.5.a; **Practices:** MP.1.a, MP.1.b, MP.1.c, MP.1.e, MP.2.c, MP.3.a, MP.4.a

Perimeter of a Rectangle = $l + l + w + w$

56 in. = 2l + 4 in. + 4 in.

56 in. = 2l + 8 in.

56 in. − 8 in. = 2l

48 in. = 2l

1l = 24 in.

9. **C**; **DOK Level:** 2; **Content Topics:** Q.2.a, Q.2.e, Q.5.a; **Practices:** MP.1.a, MP.1.b, MP.1.c, MP.1.e, MP.2.c, MP.3.a, MP.4.a

Volume of a cube = s^3

27 ft^3 = 3 ft × 3 ft × 3 ft

Length of base = 3 ft.

10. **B**; **DOK Level:** 2; **Content Topics:** Q.2.a, Q.2.e, Q.5.a; **Practices:** MP.1.a, MP.1.b, MP.1.c, MP.1.e, MP.2.c, MP.3.a, MP.4.a

Recall that the volume of a prism is the area of the base × height. Let h represent the height of the distribution center.

Volume = area of base × height, so

1 cubic km = 2 square km × h.

1 = 2 h, so $h = \frac{1}{2}$

h = 0.5 km

LESSON 3, *pp. 30–31*

1. **C**; **DOK Level:** 2; **Content Topics:** Q.2.a, Q.2.e, Q.6.c; **Practices:** MP.1.a, MP.1.b, MP.1.c, MP.1.e, MP.2.c, MP.3.a

When these data entries are ordered from least to greatest, the two middle numbers are 65 and 67. Adding these numbers, then diving them by two gives 66. Other responses result from choosing numbers that are not middle numbers.

2. **B**; **DOK Level:** 2; **Content Topics:** Q.2.a, Q.2.e, Q.6.c; **Practices:** MP.1.a, MP.1.b, MP.1.c, MP.1.e, MP.2.c, MP.3.a

To find the range of a data set, one needs to arrange all data points from least to greatest, then subtract the smallest number from the greatest number. In this case, it would be 17.2 seconds − 11.8 seconds = 5.4 seconds.

3. **C**; **DOK Level:** 2; **Content Topics:** Q.2.a, Q.2.e, Q.6.c; **Practices:** MP.1.a, MP.1.b, MP.1.c, MP.1.e, MP.2.c, MP.3.a

To find the median in a data set, one needs to ensure data points are ordered from least to greatest. In this arrangement, the middle number will be the median. The two middle numbers are 12.8 and 13.5. Adding these numbers and then dividing them by two gives a median of 13.15 s. The other answer choices result from choosing different middle values, or from not arranging the data set in increasing order.

4. **B**; **DOK Level:** 2; **Content Topics:** Q.2.a, Q.2.e, Q.6.c, Q.7.a; **Practices:** MP.1.a, MP.1.b, MP.1.c, MP.1.e, MP.2.c, MP.3.a

Add all data points (this gives 111.2 s), then divide by the number of data entries (8) to give a mean of 111.2 ÷ 8 = 13.9. The difference between Sarah's time and the mean time of the other runners is: 13.9 − 12.1 = 1.8 s.

5. **A**; **DOK Level:** 2; **Content Topics:** Q.2.a, Q.2.e, Q.6.c, Q.7.a; **Practices:** MP.1.a, MP.1.b, MP.1.c, MP.1.e, MP.2.c, MP.3.a

Add all data points (this gives 111.2 s), then divide by the number of data entries (8) to give a mean of 111.2 ÷ 8 = 13.9. To find the median, locate the two middle numbers, 12.8 and 13.5. Adding these numbers, then dividing them by two gives a median of 13.15 s. The mean of 13.9 was slightly greater than the median of 13.15.

Answer Key

UNIT 2 *(continued)*

6. C; DOK Level: 2; **Content Topics:** Q.2.a, Q.2.e, Q.6.c, Q.7.a; **Practices:** MP.1.a, MP.1.b, MP.1.c, MP.1.e, MP.2.c, MP.3.a
Since this data set includes an outlier (85), the median would give a better description of ice cream sold on a typical day. Arranging numbers from smallest to largest leaves 22 and 24 in the middle. The number in the middle of these two values is 23. Other answer choices result from calculation of mean instead of median, or from selecting the incorrect median.

7. B; DOK Level: 2; **Content Topics:** Q.2.a, Q.2.e, Q.6.c, Q.7.a; **Practices:** MP.1.a, MP.1.b, MP.1.c, MP.1.e, MP.2.c, MP.3.a
The formula for calculating the mean is as follows:
$$Mean = \frac{Sum\ of\ all\ data}{Number\ of\ data\ entries}$$
Rearranging the equation above gives:
Sum of all data = Mean × Number of data entries
Therefore, $4,443 × 6 = $26,658. Since the total from Monday through Friday is $21,757, the sales made on Saturday are: $26,658 − $21,757 = $4,901.

8. A; DOK Level: 2; **Content Topics:** Q.2.a, Q.2.e, Q.6.c; **Practices:** MP.1.a, MP.1.b, MP.1.c, MP.1.e, MP.2.c, MP.3.a
Mean score = Sum of all entries divided by the number of entries
Mean = 317 ÷ 4 = 79.25%
Answer choice B represents the median score, choice C represents the maximum score, and choice D represents the sum of all entries.

LESSON 4, *pp. 32–33*
1. B; DOK Level: 2; **Content Topics:** Q.1.b, Q.8.b; **Practices:** MP.1.a, MP.1.b, MP.1.e, MP.2.c, MP.3.a
By the fifth event, there are 4 striped + 2 black = 6 marbles remaining in the bag. The probability of selecting a black marble is 2:6, which can reduced to 1:3.

2. A; DOK Level: 1; **Content Topic:** Q.8.b; **Practices:** MP.1.a, MP.1.b
There are a total of 8 sections on the spinner. One of the sections is labeled with the number 6. Therefore, there is a 1 in 8 chance that the spinner will land on the number 6.

3. C; DOK Level: 2; **Content Topics:** Q.1.b, Q.8.b; **Practices:** MP.1.a, MP.1.b, MP.3.a
There are two sections of the spinner labeled with either a 4 or an 8. Since there are 8 total sections of the spinner, there is a $\frac{2}{8}$ chance of landing on either a 4 or an 8. The ratio of $\frac{2}{8}$ can be reduced to $\frac{1}{4}$, or 0.25.

4. A; DOK Level: 1; **Content Topic:** Q.8.b; **Practices:** MP.1.a, MP.1.b
This question is asking about experimental probability, so we must go by only the data that Maude has obtained. In her two spins, Maude failed to land on an odd number either time. Therefore, based on Maude's experiment, she has a $\frac{0}{2}$ chance of spinning an odd number.

5. B; DOK Level: 3; **Content Topic:** Q.8.b; **Practices:** MP.1.a, MP.1.b, MP.1.e, MP.2.c
This problem involves compound probability. The probability that Maude lands on an odd number is $\frac{1}{2}$. The probability that she lands on the number 2 is $\frac{1}{8}$. The probability that she lands on the odd number first, followed by the number 2 is found by multiplying—not by adding. We want the probability of both, not one or the other. Therefore the answer is $\frac{1}{2} × \frac{1}{8} = \frac{1}{16}$, which converts to 0.0625.

6. A; DOK Level: 2; **Content Topics:** Q.2.a, Q.2.e, Q.8.b; **Practices:** MP.1.a, MP.1.b
The number of total complaints on this particular day has been 15. Of those 15, 3 have concerned the clothing department, making up 20% of the complaint calls for the day.

7. D; DOK Level: 2; **Content Topics:** Q.2.a, Q.2.e, Q.8.b; **Practices:** MP.1.a, MP.1.b
A total of 6 complaints were received for the electronics department and 4 for the housewares department, making a total of 10 calls for the two departments. There have been a total of 15 calls so far. The probability of the next call concerning the electronics or the housewares department is $\frac{10}{15}$, or $\frac{2}{3}$.

8. C; DOK Level: 2; **Content Topics:** Q.2.a, Q.2.e, Q.8.b; **Practices:** MP.1.a, MP.1.b
First, add the number of complaints that involved departments other than electronics = 4 + 2 + 3 = 9. Therefore, the probability of complaints involving departments other than electronics is $\frac{9}{15}$, or 0.6.

9. C; DOK Level: 1; **Content Topics:** Q.2.a, Q.2.e; **Practices:** MP.1.a, MP.1.b
The probability it will not rain tomorrow is $\frac{60}{100} = \frac{3}{5}$.

LESSON 5, *pp. 34–35*
1. B; DOK Level: 2; **Content Topics:** Q.6.a, Q.6.c; **Practices:** MP.1.a, MP.3.a, MP.4.c
The difference between the amount of rainfall in the two parks was the greatest in April, where there was a four-inch difference.

2. The bar for Contestant A should be circled.
DOK Level: 2; **Topics:** Q.6.a, Q.6.c; **Practices:** MP.1.a, MP.3.a, MP.4.c
Contestant D won the contest with a 20-foot jump. Contestant A jumped half that distance, at 10 feet.

3. The distance of 15 feet should be circled.
DOK Level: 2; **Content Topics:** Q.6.a, Q.6.c; **Practices:** MP.1.a, MP.3.a, MP.4.c
The only two contestants who jumped the same distance were contestants B and E. They both jumped 15 feet.

4. An X should be placed in the bar for Contestant D.
DOK Level: 2; **Content Topics:** Q.6.a, Q.6.c; **Practices:** MP.1.a, MP.3.a, MP.4.c, MP.5.a
Contestant D jumped 20 feet, which is further than 18 feet, therefore disproving the statement.

5. **The bar for Contestant C should be extended to a distance of 15 feet on the graph.**
DOK Level: 2; **Content Topics:** Q.6.a, Q.6.c; **Practices:** MP.1.a, MP.3.a, MP.4.c
Contestant C initially jumped 5 feet, so tripling it would give 15 feet.

6. **17; DOK Level:** 1; **Content Topic:** Q.6.c; **Practices:** MP.1.a, MP.2.c
The line should be drawn on Contestant D's bar at the 17-foot mark.

7. **Both 8 and 10 hours should be circled, since the scatter plot shows a frequency of scores 80% and higher in that range of study time.**
DOK Level: 2; **Content Topics:** Q.6.a, Q.6.c; **Practices:** MP.1.a, MP.3.a, MP.4.c
The other study times yield test scores either entirely below 80% or partly below (and some at or above) 80%, as with 6 hours of study.

8. **Students should circle 5 levels: associate's degree, bachelor's degree, master's degree, professional degree, and doctoral degree.**
DOK Level: 2; **Content Topics:** Q.6.a, Q.6.c; **Practices:** MP.1.a, MP.3.a, MP.4.c
In 2012, 5 levels of education resulted in lower unemployment than the national average of 6.8%. Those included associate's degree (6.2%), bachelor's degree (4.5%), master's degree (3.5%), professional degree (2.1%), and doctoral degree (2.5%).

LESSON 6, *pp. 36–37*
1. **C; DOK Level:** 2; **Content Topic:** Q.6.a; **Practice:** MP.2.c
Food represents more than one-quarter of the whole, or 25%. So, the answer must be greater than 25%. That eliminates answer options A and B. Look at the remaining answer choices: 30% is between one-quarter and one-third, while 45% is almost one-half. The sector of the graph that represents food is slightly larger than one-quarter, so 30% is the best estimate.

2.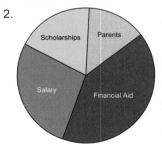
DOK Level: 2; **Content Topic:** Q.6.a; **Practices:** MP.1.b, MP.2.c, MP.4.c
Financial Aid represents 45%, which is slightly less than 50%, or half. *Salary* and *Scholarships* are both about 25%, or one-quarter, but *Salary* represents slightly more than one-quarter and *Scholarships* represents slightly less than one-quarter. *Parents* represent 15%, which is the smallest percent. Therefore it's the smallest part of the circle.

3. **D; DOK Level:** 2; **Content Topic:** Q.6.a; **Practice:** MP.2.c
People who drive a car to work represent slightly more than half of the circle graph, so you can rule out the other three answer choices in favor of option D, or 60%.

4. **A; DOK Level:** 2; **Content Topic:** Q.6.a; **Practices:** MP.1.a, MP.1.b, MP.2.c, MP.3.a
The librarian could make the best argument to order this August those categories of books that are most popular last September. The most popular categories are represented by the largest parts of the circle. The largest parts of the circle are for nonfiction and mystery, so the librarian could make the best argument to order nonfiction and mystery books this August.

LESSON 7, *pp. 38–39*
1. **B; DOK Level:** 3; **Content Topics:** Q.6.b, Q.7.a; **Practices:** MP.1.e, MP.2.c, MP.3.a, MP.4.c
There are 16 points in each half of the data set, and so the lower quartile point will be between the 8th and 9th data values. Counting in from the left, the 8th data point is at value 6, and the 9th data point is at value 7. The quartile point is halfway between the two values, or 6.5.

2. **C; DOK Level:** 3; **Content Topics:** Q.6.b, Q.7.a; **Practices:** MP.1.e, MP.2.c, MP.3.a, MP.4.c
Since there is an even number of data points (40), the median value will be halfway between two points (the 20th and 21st points). Counting in from the left, one finds that the 20th point has a value of 7, and the 21st point has a value of 8. So, the median is 7.5 hours. Note that you get the same answer if you count in from the right. Choices B and D are values you get by counting in 20 points from either end but not correctly figuring the median. Choice A provides an incorrect median.

3. **B; DOK Level:** 1; **Content Topics:** Q.6.b, Q.7.a; **Practices:** MP.2.c, MP.4.c
The mode is the value that occurs most frequently in a data set. When analyzing dot plots, it is the value with the most dots. In this case, the value with the most dots is 7 hours. The other choices are drawn from the previous item, to check for possible confusion between median and mode.

4. **D; DOK Level:** 1; **Content Topics:** Q.6.b, Q.7.a; **Practices:** MP.2.c, MP.4.c
The range represents the difference between the largest and smallest values. In this case, the maximum hours of sleep is 12 hours, and the minimum is 4 hours. Option D represents the difference between these two values.

5. **A; DOK Level:** 1; **Content Topics:** Q.6.b, Q.7.a; **Practices:** MP.2.c, MP.4.c
Each dot represents a subject. Count the number of dots in the column representing 9 hours to determine the amount of subjects in that column. Option A represents this number.

Answer Key

UNIT 2 (continued)

6. **C**; **DOK Level**: 3; **Content Topics**: Q.2.a, Q.2.e, Q.6.b, Q.7.a; **Practices**: MP.1.a, MP.1.b, MP.1.e, MP.2.c, MP.3.a, MP.4.a, MP.4.c
According to the histogram, the show enjoyed high ratings among teens and adults under the age of 50. It was fairly popular among young viewers and adults ages 35 to 49. It was not, however, equally popular among all age groups—the show evidenced weaker ratings among adults ages 50 to 64 and 65 and over.

7. **A**; **DOK Level**: 1; **Content Topics**: Q.2.a, Q.2.e, Q.6.b, Q.7.a; **Practices**: MP.2.c, MP.4.c
The range is the difference between the greatest and the lowest values in a data set. In this case, the values range from 15 to 18, so the range is $18 - 15 = 3$. Answer option B is the number of different values in the data set. Answer option C is the number of dots (or data values) corresponding to the mode. Answer option D is the mean.

UNIT 2 REVIEW, pp. 40–47

1. **B**; **DOK Level**: 1; **Content Topics**: Q.2.a, Q.2.e; **Practices**: MP.1.a, MP.1.d, MP.2.c, MP.4.a
To determine the number of yards that the artist actually wants to use, the number of feet (840) must be divided by the number of feet in a yard (3). That gives $\frac{(840)}{(3)} = 280$ yards (choice B). Choice A is the result of dividing 840 feet by 12 (the number of inches in a foot), rather than by 3. Choice C is the number of yards the artist will have to *buy*, since the company only sells it in rolls of 100 yards. Choice D is the result of *multiplying* 840 feet by 3, rather than *dividing* by 3.

2. **D**; **DOK Level**: 2; **Content Topics**: Q.2.a, Q.2.e; **Practices**: MP.1.a, MP.1.d, MP.2.c, MP.4.a
Since the problem asks about two textbooks, the mass of the textbooks is twice the mass of one book: (2)(1 kg) = 2 kg. To convert that to grams, the 2 kg must be multiplied by 1,000 grams per kilogram, giving 2,000 grams. Since each shoelace has a mass of 1 gram, it takes 2,000 shoelaces to come up with a combined mass equal to the mass of two textbooks.

3. **D**; **DOK Level**: 2; **Content Topics**: Q.2.a, Q.2.e, Q.4.a; **Practices**: MP.1.a, MP.1.b, MP.1.d, MP.2.c, MP.4.a
Since the two triangles are identical, the length of the side of the left triangle that is not explicitly specified is 15.5 m. The perimeter of the left triangle, then, is the sum of the lengths of the three sides, or (15.5 m + 28 m + 28 m) = 71.5 m. Since there are two such triangles, the total perimeter is (2)(71.5 m) = 143 m.

4. **C**; **DOK Level**: 2; **Content Topics**: Q.2.a, Q.2.e, Q.4.a; **Practices**: MP.1.a, MP.1.b, MP.1.d, MP.2.c, MP.4.a
When the three pieces fit together, they form a rectangle with length 10.5 ft + 12 ft = 22.5 ft and height 15 ft. The area of the rectangle will be the product of the length and width, or (22.5 ft)(15 ft) = 337.5 ft² (choice C).

5. **A**; **DOK Level**: 2; **Content Topics**: Q.2.a, Q.2.e; **Practices**: MP.1.a, MP.4.a
The sum of the masses of the four kinds of powder is (250 + 250 + 300 + 375) grams = 1,175 grams. Converting that to kilograms requires dividing the 1,175 grams by 1,000 grams, giving 1.175 kg (choice A). Choices B and C involve conversion errors of 10 and 100, respectively. Choice D is the number of *grams* of powder, rather than *kilograms*.

6. **A**; **DOK Level**: 2; **Content Topics**: Q.2.a, Q.2.e; **Practices**: MP.1.a, MP.1.b, MP.4.a
The time it takes the airliner to travel from Boston to Chicago is found by dividing the distance (850 miles) by the average speed (500 mph), giving 1.7 hours. That is the same as 1 hour and (0.7 hours) $\left(\frac{60\ \text{minutes}}{\text{hour}}\right)$ = 1 hour and 42 minutes. When the plane leaves Boston at 11:30 A.M., it is 10:30 A.M. in Chicago. When the plane arrives in Chicago, 1 hour and 42 minutes later, it is 11:30 A.M. plus 42 minutes, or 12:12 P.M. in Chicago (choice A). Choice B is the time in Boston when the plane lands in Chicago. The 1:42 in choice C is the flight time. Choice D is result of *adding* the hour time difference to Boston time, rather than *subtracting*, to get Chicago time.

7. **D**; **DOK Level**: 2; **Content Topics**: Q.2.a, Q.2.e, Q.4.a; **Practices**: MP.1.a, MP.1.b, MP.4.a
The width of the fenced area is twice the width of a tennis court (2 × 60 ft = 120 ft), plus twice the 10-foot margin (2 × 10 = 20 ft), giving 140 ft. The length of the fenced area is the length of a tennis court (120 ft), plus twice the 15-foot margin (2 × 15 = 30 ft), giving 150 ft. The amount of fencing needed is the perimeter, which is twice the sum of the width and length, or 2(140 ft + 150 ft) = 2(290 ft) = 580 ft.

8. **C**; **DOK Level**: 2; **Content Topics**: Q.2.a, Q.2.e, Q.5.a; **Practices**: MP.1.a, MP.1.d, MP.2.c, MP.4.a
Since Container A is a cube, all the sides have lengths of 8 cm. The volume, then, is 8 cm × 8 cm × 8 cm = 512 cm³ (choice C). Choice A is three times the side length, rather than the cube of the side length. Choice B is the square of the side length. Choice D is the surface area.

9. **A**; **DOK Level**: 2; **Content Topics**: Q.2.a, Q.2.e, Q.5.a; **Practices**: MP.1.a, MP.4.a
The volume of Container B is the product of the lengths of the three sides: 12 cm × 8 cm × 10 cm = 960 cm³. The amount of water needed to fill the two containers is the sum of their volumes, or 512 cm³ + 960 cm³ = 1,472 cm³ (choice A).

10. **B**; **DOK Level**: 2; **Content Topics**: Q.2.a, Q.2.e, Q.6.c, Q.7.a; **Practices**: MP.1.a, MP.4.a
To find the mean, add the numbers of hours watched to get a total (213 hours), and divide by the 8 weeks to get 26.625 hours. Rounding that number to the nearest tenth gives 26.6 hours (choice B).

11. **A**; **DOK Level**: 2; **Content Topics**: Q.1.a, Q.2.a, Q.2.e, Q.6.c, Q.7.a; **Practices**: MP.1.a, MP.1.b, MP.1.d, MP.2.c, MP.4.a
The median value is 27.5, half-way between the fourth and fifth data points when the numbers are listed in numerical order. The mean is 26.6 hours. So the median is slightly greater than the mean (choice A).

12. **C**; **DOK Level:** 2; **Content Topics:** Q.1.a, Q.2.a, Q.2.e, Q.7.a; **Practices:** MP.1.a, MP.1.b, MP.1.d, MP.2.c, MP.4.a
The maximum number of hours is 35 hours watched during week 8. The minimum number of hours is 15.5 hours watched during week 3. The difference, 35 hours − 15.5 hours = 19.5 hours, is the range (choice C).

13. **C**; **DOK Level:** 2; **Content Topics:** Q.2.a, Q.2.e, Q.8.a, Q.8.b; **Practices:** MP.1.a, MP.1.b, MP.1.c, MP.1.d, MP.2.c, MP.3.a, MP.4.a
There are a total of six sides. Three of the sides have even numbers. The probability of rolling an even number is, then, $\frac{3}{6}$ = 0.5, which is 50% (choice C).

14. **B**; **DOK Level:** 2; **Content Topics:** Q.2.a, Q.2.e, Q.8.a, Q.8.b; **Practices:** MP.1.a, MP.1.b, MP.1.c, MP.1.d, MP.2.c, MP.3.a, MP.4.a
There are a total of six sides, of which two sides have either a 2 or a 4. The probability of rolling a 2 or a 4 is then $\frac{2}{6}$ = 0.333, which is 33% (choice B).

15. **B**; **DOK Level:** 3; **Content Topics:** Q.2.a, Q.2.e, Q.8.a, Q.8.b; **Practices:** MP.1.a, MP.1.b, MP.1.c, MP.1.d, MP.1.e, MP.2.c, MP.3.a, MP.4.a, MP.5.c
For each of the six sides of one die, there are six possible results for the other die. The total number of possible combinations is (6 × 6) = 36 combinations. There is only one way of rolling a sum of a 2; both dice must come up with a 1. There are three ways of both rolling a sum of 4: both dice coming up 2, the first coming up 1 and the other 3, or the first coming up 3 and the other 1. So, out of the 36 possible rolls, there are 4 that could produce totals of either 2 or 4. That gives a probability, expressed as a fraction, of $\frac{4}{36} = \frac{1}{9}$.

16. **D**; **DOK Level:** 2; **Content Topics:** Q.2.a, Q.2.e; **Practices:** MP.1.a, MP.4.a
The time spent traveling is 45 minutes, or 45 minutes ÷ 60 minutes/hour = 0.75 hours. If Devaughn drives at 45 miles per hour for 0.75 hours, the distance he can travel is 45 × 0.75 = 33.75 miles.

17. **C**; **DOK Level:** 2; **Content Topics:** Q.2.a, Q.2.e, Q.3.a; **Practices:** MP.1.a, MP.4.a
If Mrs. Jackson walks for 25 minutes, that is a period of $\frac{25\ \text{minutes}}{60\ \text{minutes per hour}} = \frac{5}{12}$ hours. 1.25 miles = $1\frac{1}{4}$ miles = $\frac{5}{4}$ miles Dividing the distance by the time gives $\left(\frac{5}{4}\ \text{miles} \div \frac{5}{12}\ \text{hours}\right) = \left(\frac{5}{4} \times \frac{12}{5}\right)$ mph = 3 mph.

18. **A**; **DOK Level:** 2; **Content Topics:** Q.2.a, Q.2.e; **Practices:** MP.1.a, MP.1.b, MP.1.d, MP.4.a
From 11:50 A.M. until noon, 10 minutes go by. From noon until 2:10 P.M., 2 hours and 10 minutes go by. Adding the two gives 2 hours and 20 minutes of elapsed time during the trip.

19. **B**; **DOK Level:** 2; **Content Topics:** Q.1.a, Q.6.c; **Practices:** MP.1.a, MP.1.d, MP.2.c, MP.5.c
There are only two years where the amount of bonuses increased—from 2003–2004 and from 2004-2005. The increase between 2004–2005 was greater, as can be evidenced by the steeper line on the graph.

20. **D**; **DOK Level:** 2; **Content Topic:** Q.6.c; **Practices:** MP.1.a, MP.1.b, MP.2.c
The only year in which the data point is clearly below $5,000 is 2008, where the amount is between $4,000 and $5,000.

21. **Negative**; **DOK Level:** 2; **Content Topic:** Q.6.c; **Practice:** MP.1.a
While the correlation isn't perfect, there is a clear trend in the data showing that the number of shots made generally decreases with increasing distance. That represents a negative correlation.

22. **20**; **DOK Level:** 2; **Content Topics:** Q.2.a, Q.2.e, Q.6.c; **Practices:** MP.1.a, MP.2.c, MP.4.a
The spread in performance can be found for each distance. For 5 feet, it is 10 − 8 = 2 shots made. For 10 feet, it is 10 − 7 = 3 shots made. For 15 feet, it is 9 − 5 = 4 shots made. For 20 feet, it is 7 − 2 = 5 shots made. For 25 feet it is 3 − 0 = 3 shots made. For 30 feet, it is 1 − 0 = 1 shot made. The largest spread is, therefore, at 20 feet.

23. **A**; **DOK Level:** 2; **Content Topics:** Q.2.a, Q.2.e, Q.5.a; **Practices:** MP.1.a, MP.1.b, MP.4.a
If the length, width, and height are each doubled, the new dimensions of the box are 30 ft × 6 ft × 16 ft. The volume is the product of the three dimensions, or 2,880 ft³. The new volume also can be found by taking the volume of the original box, (15 ft × 3 ft × 8 ft) = 360 ft³, and multiplying it by 2 × 2 × 2 = 8.

24. **D**; **DOK Level:** 3; **Content Topics:** Q.2.a, Q.2.e, Q.8.a, Q.8.b; **Practices:** MP.1.a, MP.1.b, MP.1.c, MP.1.d, MP.1.e, MP.2.c, MP.3.a, MP.4.a
The probability of coming up with a three on the die is $\frac{1}{6}$. The probability of getting a head when flipping a coin is $\frac{1}{2}$. The probability of all three events happening is $\frac{1}{6} \times \frac{1}{2} \times \frac{1}{2} = \frac{1}{24}$.

25. **B**; **DOK Level:** 3; **Content Topic:** Q.8.a; **Practices:** MP.1.a, MP.1.b, MP.1.c, MP.1.d, MP.1.e, MP.2.c, MP.3.a, MP.5.c
There are 4 × 3 × 2 × 1 = 24 possible ways of arranging four distinct boxes in a row. In this case, half are duplicates because, in each case, the two green boxes can be switched without making any identifiable change. Half of the remaining 12 arrangements are duplicates because, in each case, the two red boxes can be switched without making any identifiable changes. That leaves 6 unique arrangements (choice B). The solution also can be determined by systematically identifying the arrangements. (For example, if the first box is green, the remaining three can be ordered green/red/red, red/green/red, and red/red/green. If the first box is red, the remaining three can be ordered green/green/red, green/red/green, and red/green/green—for a total of six unique arrangements.)

26. **C**; **DOK Level:** 3; **Content Topics:** Q.2.a, Q.2.e, Q.8.a, Q.8.b; **Practices:** MP.1.a, MP.1.b, MP.1.c, MP.1.d, MP.1.e, MP.2.c, MP.3.a, MP.5.c
When rolling three six-sided dice, there are (6)³ = 216 possible results. Of those 216 possibilities, there are 6 where all three dice have the same number. That corresponds to a probability of $\frac{6}{216} = \frac{1}{36}$.

UNIT 2 *(continued)*

27. D; DOK Level: 3; **Content Topics:** Q.2.a, Q.2.e, Q.8.a, Q.8.b; **Practices:** MP.1.a, MP.1.b, MP.1.c, MP.1.d, MP.1.e, MP.2.c, MP.3.a, MP.4.a, MP.5.c
The probability of two heads coming up on a given toss is independent of what has happened in previous tosses. There remain four possible results of the toss, with only one of the four being a pair of heads. So the probability is still 25%.

28. A; DOK Level: 2; **Content Topics:** Q.2.a, Q.2.e, Q.8.b; **Practices:** MP.1.a, MP.1.b, MP.2.c, MP.4.a
There are eight sections on the wheel. Four are prize sections and four are "Sorry" sections, meaning no prize is awarded. So the probability of winning a prize is four out of eight, or 0.5.

29. C; DOK Level: 3; **Content Topics:** Q.2.a, Q.2.e, Q.8.a, Q.8.b; **Practices:** MP.1.a, MP.1.b, MP.1.d, MP.2.c, MP.3.a, MP.4.a, MP.5.c
Again, there are eight possible results on the wheel. If the spin comes up "Cake," the player winds a cake. If the spin comes up "Your choice," the player gets to choose his prize—in this case, a cake. That means there are two results that allow the player to win a cake. So the probability of winning a cake is two out of eight, or 25%.

30. B; DOK Level: 2; **Content Topics:** Q.2.a, Q.2.e, Q.6.c, Q.7a; **Practices:** MP.1.a, MP.2.c, MP.4.a
The greatest daily amount raised is $7,600. The least daily amount raised is $4,400. The difference, $7,600 − $4,400 = $3,200, is the range (choice B). Choice A is half the correct answer. Choice C is the minimum, and choice D is the maximum.

31. C; DOK Level: 1; **Content Topics:** Q.2.a, Q.2.e, Q.6.c, Q.7a; **Practices:** MP.1.a, MP.2.c, MP.4.a
The sum of the results for the five days is $28,500. Dividing that by five days gives the daily mean: $\frac{\$28,500}{5} = \$5,700$.

32. C; DOK Level: 1; **Content Topics:** Q.2.a, Q.2.e, Q.2.c; **Practices:** MP.1.a, MP.2.c, MP.4.a
The median is the middle figure in an odd-numbered data set. In this case, it is $5,400.

33. B; DOK Level: 2; **Content Topics:** Q.2.a, Q.2.e, Q.6.c, Q.7a; **Practices:** MP.1.a, MP.1.d, MP.2.c, MP.3.a, MP.4.a
If the goal for the seven-day total is $45,000, and they have raised $28,500 during the first five days, they must raise $45,000 − $28,500 = $16,500 during the final two days. That is a mean of $16,500 ÷ 2 = $8,250 for each of the two final days.

34. 0.4; DOK Level: 2; **Content Topics:** Q.2.a, Q.2.e, Q.6.c, Q.7a; **Practices:** MP.1.a, MP.1.b, MP.4.a
The total of all numbers in the chart is 11. Since there are 27 numbers in the chart, divide 11 by 27 to find the mean: 11 ÷ 27 = 0.407 or, rounded to the nearest tenth, 0.4.

35. 1; DOK Level: 2; **Content Topics:** Q.1.a, Q.6.c, Q.7a; **Practices:** MP.1.a, MP.1.b, MP.1.d, MP.2.c
The score of 1 appears 8 times in the table, more than any other score. That means that 1 is the mode.

36.

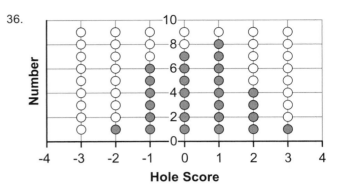

DOK Level: 2; **Content Topic:** Q.6.b; **Practices:** MP.1.a, MP.1.d, MP.2.c
The score of −2 appears once. The score of −1 appears 6 times. The score of 0 appears 7 times. The score of 1 appears 8 times. The score of 2 appears 4 times. The score of 3 appears once.

37.

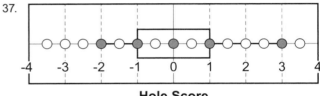

DOK Level: 2; **Content Topics:** Q.1.a, Q.6.b; **Practices:** MP.1.a, MP.1.b, MP.1.d, MP.2.c
There are 27 points, so the median value will be the 14th, counting in from either direction. There are 13 points in each half of the distribution, so the quartiles will be at the 7th points, counting in from their respective ends. The 1st quartile point is −1, and the 3rd quartile point is 1. The minimum value is −2, and the maximum value is 3. Using those points produces the correct box plot.

38. 17.6; DOK Level: 2; **Content Topics:** Q.2.a, Q.2.e; **Practices:** MP.1.a, MP.4.a
The length of the football field is $\left(100 \text{ yards} \times \frac{3 \text{ feet}}{\text{yard}}\right) =$ 300 feet. The number of feet in a mile is 5,280. So to find the number of football-field lengths in one mile, divide 5,280 feet by 300 feet, giving 17.6 lengths.

39. 5.7; DOK Level: 2; **Content Topics:** Q.2.a, Q.2.e, Q.4.a; **Practices:** MP.1.a, MP.4.a
The perimeter of the football field is the twice the length (2 × 300 feet) plus twice the width (2 × 160 feet), or 600 feet + 320 feet = 920 feet. Dividing 5,280 by 920 feet gives 5.739 times around the football field perimeter to go one mile. Rounding to the nearest tenth gives 5.7.

40. D; DOK Level: 3; **Content Topics:** Q.8.a, Q.8.b; **Practices:** MP.1.a, MP.1.b, MP.1.c, MP.1.d, MP.1.e, MP.2.c, MP.3.a, MP.5.c
There are 4 × 3 × 2 × 1 = 24 possible outcomes of dealing the four cards. There is only one way to get 1/2/3/4. The probability that 1/2/3/4 will be the result is, then, $\frac{1}{24}$.

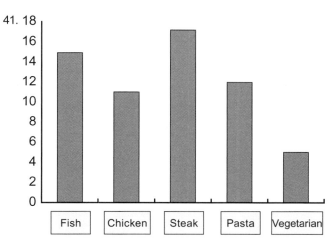

41.

DOK Level: 2; **Content Topics:** Q.1.a, Q.6.a, Q.6.c.; **Practices:** MP.1.a, MP.1.b, MP.2.b
The bar heights, as indicated on the vertical axis, must correspond to the number of meals for each kind provided. The first bar is 15 high, corresponding to the number of fish meals provided; the word *Fish* must be dragged to the appropriate spot below that bar. Continue in similar fashion to complete the bar graph.

42.

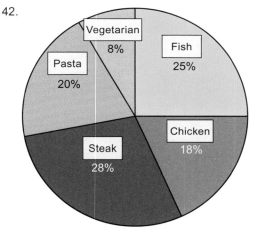

DOK Level: 2; **Content Topics:** Q.1.a, Q.6.a, Q.6.c; **Practices:** MP.1.a, MP.1.b, MP.2.b
The process is similar to the one used for the bar graph. The percentages of each kind of meal, relative to the total of 60, can be estimated or calculated exactly to enable proper placement of meal type on the circle graph. Alternately, one can note that, for example, steaks accounted for the largest number of meals and so "Steak" can be written in the appropriate spot in the largest sector of the circle graph. Continue in that fashion to complete the graph.

43. **Bar / Circle; DOK Level:** 2; **Content Topics:** Q.6.a, Q.6.c; **Practices:** MP.1.a, MP.2.b
A bar graph is best for comparing the number of meals ordered with each other, since the heights of the bars are proportional to the number ordered, and the vertical scale gives quantitative information. A circle graph is best for comparing the number of meals of a given type with the total number of meals, since one can visually assess how much of the whole circle is made up by any part.

44. **C; DOK Level:** 2; **Content Topics:** Q.1.d, Q.6.c; **Practices:** MP.1.a, MP.1.b
While the ordering of the names in the legend correspond to choice A, and that is the correct ordering at age 20, at age 10 Kris is the tallest, then Mike, then Peter, so the correct answer is C.

45. **B; DOK Level:** 2; **Content Topic:** Q.6.c; **Practices:** MP.1.a, MP.1.b
The sharpest rise of any of the lines occurs for Mike in the year following his 11th birthday (choice B). Peter shows a marked increase in the steepness of his line in the year following his 13th birthday (choice A), but the increase over that year is not as great as the one experienced by Mike. While Kris is the tallest for the first 12 years, her line does not feature any major increases in slope.

46. **B; DOK Level:** 2; **Content Topic:** Q.6.a; **Practices:** MP.1.a, MP.2.b
West Park High is the left-hand circle graph. White students account for more than half of the students there. The next largest part is for Asian students, who occupy more than one-quarter of the total circle. That makes them the second largest group at that school.

47. **A; DOK Level:** 2; **Content Topics:** Q.3.c, Q.6.a; **Practices:** MP.1.a, MP.2.b
The relative area of the part representing Hispanic students is smaller for West Park than for North Hill, which eliminates choices C and D. Using a fingertip as a ruler, one also can estimate that the width of the Hispanic sector for West Park is about half that for North Hill, making the correct choice 1:2 (choice A).

48.

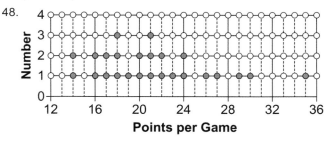

DOK Level: 1; **Content Topic:** Q.6.b; **Practice:** MP.1.a
The data points are listed in order, so one need only count up the number of instances for each score and mark the corresponding points on the graph.

Answer Key

UNIT 2 *(continued)*

49.

Points per Game

DOK Level: 2; **Content Topic:** Q.6.b; **Practices:** MP.1.a, MP.1.b, MP.2.c

The first interval of the histogram ranges from 12 to 15. There are two points at 14. In the 16–19 range, there are 8 points. Continuing in this manner, one completes the histogram.

50. **C; DOK Level:** 2; **Content Topics:** Q.2.a, Q.2.e, Q.6.b, Q.7.a; **Practices:** MP.1.a, MP.1.b, MP.2.c

The nominal value of the bolt diameter, expressed in decimal form, is 0.125 inch. Finding that value on the vertical axis and scanning across the line, and noting the median values for each box (the lines in the middle of each box), one finds that the median value for Batch 3 lies on the line marked 0.125 inch.

51. **A; DOK Level:** 3; **Content Topics:** Q.1.a, Q.6.b, Q.7.a; **Practices:** MP.1.a, MP.1.b, MP.1.c, MP.1.d, MP.2.c, MP.3.a, MP.5.c

Batch 1 is within the required range except for the values above the upper quartile. The other 3 batches include values below upper quartile, so more of the nuts are rejected.

UNIT 3 ALGEBRA, FUNCTIONS, AND PATTERNS

LESSON 1, *pp. 50–51*

1. **A; DOK Level:** 1; **Content Topic:** A.1.c; **Practices:** MP.1.a, MP.2.a

If x is the current age of Gabe's sister, then 3 times that age is $3x$ (choice A). Choice B *divides* the sister's age, rather than *multiplies*. Choices C and D *subtract* and *add* 3 to the sister's age, respectively, rather than *multiply*.

2. **$55x - 20$; DOK Level:** 1; **Content Topics:** Q.2.a, Q.2.e; **Practices:** MP.1.a, MP.4.a

The expression of $55x$ tells you that the plumber's earnings of $55 per hour must be multiplied by the number of hours he worked, or x. To find net earnings, subtract money spent on gas from the plumber's gross earnings, $55x - 20$.

3. **$w + 30$; DOK Level:** 1; **Content Topics:** Q.2.a, Q.2.e; **Practices:** MP.1.a, MP.4.a

The length is 30 yards more than the width w, so the correct expression is $w + 30$.

4. **$15x^2 - 30x$; DOK Level:** 1; **Content Topics:** Q.2.a, Q.2.e; **Practices:** MP.1.a, MP.4.a

The product of 5 and x multiplied by 6 less than the product of 3 and x is $5x(3x - 6)$, which, when simplified, is $15x^2 - 30x$.

5. **The algebraic expression is $-x^2 - 6x + 6$; DOK Level:** 1; **Content Topics:** Q.2.a, Q.2.e; **Practices:** MP.1.a, MP.4.a

A number times itself is x^2, and x^2 added to the product of 5 and x is $x^2 + 5x$. From there, $x^2 + 5x$ subtracted from the difference of 6 and x is $(6 - x) - (x^2 + 5x)$. Simplified, the expression is $6 - x - x^2 - 5x$, which further simplifies to $-x^2 - 6x + 6$.

6. **D; DOK Level:** 2; **Content Topics:** A.1.a, A.1.c; **Practices:** MP.1.a, MP.1.b, MP.2.a, MP.4.b

The perimeter of a rectangle is the sum of the lengths of its four sides. In this case, there are two sides of length $2w - 3$, and two sides of length w. Adding them together gives $2w - 3 + w + 2w - 3 + w$. This expression can be simplified by combining the like terms involving w, which sum to $6w$, and the like terms involving integers, which sum to -6. The final result is, then, $6w - 6$ (choice D). Choice A is the sum of the lengths only of the *two* sides given dimensions in the figure. Choice B is the product of the lengths of the two sides, which gives the area, not the perimeter. Choice C is the sum of the lengths of the two long sides plus only one of the short sides.

7. **B**; **DOK Level:** 1; **Content Topic:** A.1.g; **Practices:** MP.1.a, MP.2.a

The area of a rectangle is the product of the lengths of the sides. In this case, that is $w(2w - 3)$ (choice B). Choice A is the sum of those two sides. Choice C is the product of the two short sides. Choice D is the sum of the lengths of the four sides, or the perimeter.

8. **C**; **DOK Level:** 1; **Content Topic:** A.1.c; **Practices:** MP.1.a, MP.2.a

If g represents the width of the garage, then twice the width is $2g$, and twice the width increased by 10 feet is $2g + 10$ (choice C). Choice A is the product of $2g$ and 10, rather than the sum. Choice B is $2g$ divided by 10. Choice D is $2g$ *reduced* by 10 feet, rather than *increased*.

9. **A**; **DOK Level:** 1; **Content Topic:** A.1.c; **Practices:** MP.1.a, MP.2.a

If s is Michael's score on the science quiz, then one-half that score is $\frac{s}{2}$, and 8 more than one-half the score is $\frac{s}{2} + 8$ (choice A). Choice B switches the 2 and the 8. Choice C is 8 *less* than one-half his science quiz score, rather than 8 *more*. Choice D switches the s and the 8.

LESSON 2, pp. 52–53

1. **D**; **DOK Level:** 2; **Content Topics:** A.1.c, A.2.c; **Practices:** MP.1.a, MP.1.b, MP.1.e, MP.2.a, MP.2.c, MP.4.a

Since the goal is to find the amount of the first bill, let x represent the amount of the first bill. The second bill was $5 more than twice the amount of the first bill. The expression $2x$ represents twice x, and the expression $2x + 5$ represents 5 more than twice x. The two bills total $157, so the sum of the first bill, x, and the second bill, $2x + 5$, is 157. Therefore, $x + (2x + 5) = 157$.

2. **B**; **DOK Level:** 2; **Content Topics:** Q.2.a, A.1.c, A.2.c; **Practices:** MP.1.a, MP.1.b, MP.1.e, MP.2.a, MP.2.c, MP.4.a

Since the goal is to find the first number, let x represent the first of the two consecutive integers. Since the integers are consecutive, the second integer is 1 greater than the first integer, so the expression $x + 1$ represents the second integer. The sum of the two integers is 15, so $x + (x + 1) = 15$. Simplify the equation by grouping like terms: $2x + 1 = 15$.

3. **C**; **DOK Level:** 1; **Content Topics:** Q.2.a, A.1.b, A.1.c, A.2.a, A.2.c; **Practices:** MP.1.a, MP.1.b, MP.2.a, MP.2.c, MP.4.a

Start by representing the situation as an equation: $a = 2c - 4$. Next, substitute 20 for a and solve:
$20 = 2c - 4$
Add 4 to both sides so that: $24 = 2c$
Next, isolate the variable by dividing both sides of the equation by 2, so that $12 = c$.
Check your answer by plugging 12 into the original equation: $20 = 2(12) - 4$. Since 12 satisfies the equation, it is the correct response

4. **B**; **DOK Level:** 2; **Content Topics:** Q.2.a, Q.2.e, A.1.b, A.1.c, A.2.a, A.2.c; **Practices:** MP.1.a, MP.1.b, MP.2.a, MP.2.c, MP.4.a

Let x represent Stephanie's age. Stephanie's age, x, is 3 years greater than half of her sister's current age, 24. Half of Stephanie's sister's age is $\frac{1}{2}(24)$, so 3 years greater than that is $\frac{1}{2}(24) + 3$. Therefore, $x = \frac{1}{2}(24) + 3 = 12 + 3 = 15$.

5. **D**; **DOK Level:** 2; **Content Topics:** Q.2.a, Q.2.e, A.1.b, A.1.c, A.2.a, A.2.c; **Practices:** MP.1.a, MP.1.b, MP.2.a, MP.2.c, MP.4.a

Let x represent the number of cellos. The number of cellos is 2 more than one-third of the number of violins. One-third of the number of violins is $\frac{1}{3}(24)$, so 2 more than that is $\frac{1}{3}(24) + 2$. Therefore, $x = \frac{1}{3}(24) + 2 = 8 + 2 = 10$.

6. **A**; **DOK Level:** 2; **Content Topics:** A.1.b, A.1.c, A.2.a, A.2.c; **Practices:** MP.1.a, MP.1.b, MP.2.a, MP.2.c, MP.4.a

Let x = the number of aerobics classes and $2x$ = the number of yoga classes. Then, $x + 2x = 3$, which is the same as $3x = 3$.

7. **A**; **DOK Level:** 2; **Content Topics:** A.1.b, A.1.c, A.2.a, A.2.c; **Practices:** MP.1.a, MP.1.b, MP.2.a, MP.2.c, MP.4.a

The perimeter of a triangle is the sum of the lengths of its sides. Since the perimeter is 16.5 feet, $a + 2a + 2a - 1 = 16.5$. Simplify the equation by grouping like terms, so that $a(1 + 2 + 2) - 1 = 16.5$; $5a - 1 = 16.5$.

8. **B**; **DOK Level:** 2; **Content Topics:** Q.2.a, A.1.c, A.2.a, A.2.c; **Practices:** MP.1.a, MP.1.b, MP.1.e, MP.2.a, MP.2.c, MP.4.a

Since the goal is to find the number, let x represent the number. Four times the number is equal to $4x$. Four less than two times the number is four less than $2x$, or $2x - 4$. Equate the two expressions: $4x = 2x - 4$. Subtract $2x$ from both sides of the equation to group like terms: $4x - 2x = -4$. Simplify: $2x = -4$, so $x = -2$.

9. **B**; **DOK Level:** 2; **Content Topics:** Q.2.a, A.1.c, A.2.a, A.2.c; **Practices:** MP.1.a, MP.1.b, MP.1.e, MP.2.a, MP.2.c, MP.4.a

Since the goal is to find the number of Republican Party pins, let x represent the number of Republican Party pins. The number of Democratic Party pins is 14 less than three times x, or $3x - 14$. The sum of the number of Republican Party pins, x, and the number of Democratic Party pins, $3x - 14$, is 98, so $x + (3x - 14) = 98$. Group like terms: $4x - 14 = 98$. Simplify: $4x = 112$, so $x = 28$.

10. **B**; **DOK Level:** 2; **Content Topics:** Q.2.a, A.1.b, A.2.a; **Practices:** MP.1.a, MP.1.b, MP.1.e, MP.4.a

Simplify the equation by expanding the expressions using the distributive property: $10y - 4y - 8 + 3x = 15 - 5x$. Group like terms: $6y - 8 + 3x = 15 - 5x$. Simplify: $6y - 8 - 15 = -5x - 3x$, so $6y - 23 = -8x$. Next, substitute 2.5 for y and simplify: $6(2.5) - 23 = -8x$, so $15 - 23 = -8x$, and $-8 = -8x$. Dividing both sides by -1 gives $x = 1$.

LESSON 3, pp. 54–55

1. **C**; **DOK Level:** 1; **Content Topics:** Q.2.a, Q.2.b; **Practices:** MP.1.a, MP.4.a

If the area is 81 m², then the square root of the area is the square root of 81. This can be found using a calculator, or by noting the number 9, when multiplied by itself equals 81.

Answer Key

UNIT 3 (continued)

2. $x^2 > 0$, $x^3 < 0$, $\sqrt{x}$ **is undefined;** $\sqrt[3]{x} < 0$; **DOK Level: 1;**
Content Topics: Q.2.b, Q.2.c, Q.2.d, A.1.e;
Practices: MP.1.a, MP.1.b
The number in question is negative (e.g., −1). The square of a negative number (the first case) is positive and therefore greater than zero. The cube of a negative number (the second case) is negative 1 and therefore less than zero. The square root of a negative number (the third case) is undefined since there is no real number, negative or positive, that will, when multiplied by itself, result in a negative number. The cube root of a negative number (the fourth case), on the other hand, does exist and is negative.

3. 8; **DOK Level: 2; Content Topics:** Q.2.a, Q.2.c;
Practices: MP.1.a, MP.4.a
The cube root of 512, using a calculator if necessary, is 8. Since the problem involves the cube root, rather than the square root, −8 is not a correct answer, leaving 8 as the only possible correct answer.

4. D; DOK Level: 1; Content Topics: Q.2.a, Q.2.c, Q.2.e, A.1.e; **Practices:** MP.1.a, MP.4.a
The cube of the number 5 (5^3) is the same as $5 \times 5 \times 5 = 125$ (choice D). Choice A is 2 times 5, while choice B is 3 times 5. Choice C is the square of 5.

5. A; DOK Level: 1; Content Topics: Q.2.a, Q.2.c;
Practices: MP.1.a, MP.4.a
The length of a side of a cube is the cube root of the cube's volume which is, in this case, 64 cm³. The number that, when multiplied by itself, and then by itself again yields 64, is 4. So choice A, 4 cm, is the correct answer. Choice B is the square root of the volume. Choice C is one-fourth of the volume, and choice D is one-half of the volume.

6. A; DOK Level: 2; Content Topics: Q.2.a, Q.2.b, Q.2.e;
Practices: MP.1.a, MP.4.a
First, one must take the square root of 64, which is 8. (Note: $8 \times 8 = 64$, confirming the result.) Then, dividing the resulting 8 by 4, one gets 2 (choice A). Choice B is the result if one incorrectly assumes the square root of 64 is 16. Choice C is the square root of 64. Choice D is 64 divided by 4—the result if one forgets to take the square root.

7. C; DOK Level: 2; Content Topics: Q.2.a, Q.2.b;
Practices: MP.1.a, MP.4.a
Using a calculator to take the square root of 30, one finds the result to be 5.477 which, rounding to the nearest tenth, gives 5.5 (choice C). Choice B is the square root of 30 rounded *down*. Choice D is one-half of 30.

8. B; DOK Level: 2; Content Topics: Q.2.a, Q.2.b;
Practices: MP.1.a, MP.4.a
The side of a square of area 50 square feet, is the square root of 50 or, using the calculator, 7.07 ft. The perimeter is four times that result, or 28.28. Rounding to the nearest foot gives 28 ft (choice B). The answers are far enough apart that one also could have estimated, noting that 50 is very close to 7^2, indicating a side length close to 7 and a perimeter close to 4 × 7. Choice A is the approximate side length. Choice C is 7^2. Choice D is twice the area.

9. C; DOK Level: 3; Content Topics: Q.2.a, Q.2.b, Q.2.e;
Practices: MP.1.a, MP.1.b, MP.1.e, MP.2.c, MP.3.a, MP.4.a, MP.4.b, MP.5.a, MP.5.b, MP.5.c
One way to find the answer is to use logical reasoning and to remember that the $\sqrt{64}$ can be either +8 or −8. Think: If $(8 - x)^2 = 64$, then $8 - x = \sqrt{64}$. So $8 - x = -8$, and $x = 16$, or $8 - x = 8$, and x = 0. Because the student said the car is moving, its speed is 16 mph. That makes choice C the best answer.

10. B; DOK Level: 2; Content Topics: Q.2.a, Q.2.c, Q.2.e;
Practices: MP.1.a, MP.4.a
Using the calculator to find the cube root of 231, one finds a side length of 6.135 inches. Rounding that result to the nearest tenth of an inch gives the answer of 6.1 inches (choice B). Choice A is the result of rounding down to the nearest inch. Choice C is the result of rounding up to the nearest tenth of an inch. Choice D is the next step in the resulting progression.

LESSON 4, pp. 56–57

1. B; DOK Level: 1; Content Topics: Q.1.c, Q.2.e;
Practice: MP.1.a
Work backward to correctly answer the question. To get from 58,000,000 to 5.8, the decimal point must move seven places to the right. As a result, the number, expressed in scientific notation, is 5.8×10^7 (choice B). The 10 is raised to a *positive* power because the decimal point (in 58,000,000.00) was moved to the *left*. Choice A results from miscounting the number of places the decimal point is moved. Choice C is mathematically equivalent to the correct answer (B), but proper writing of numbers using scientific notation requires that the decimal point be located just to the right of the first digit. Choice D also violates that rule, as well as miscounts the number of places the decimal point must move.

2. B; DOK Level: 1; Content Topics: Q.1.c, Q.2.e;
Practice: MP.1.a
The decimal point in 25,400,000 moved left seven places from its original place to a point just to the right of the first digit in the number (2). As a result, the number, expressed in scientific notation, is 2.54×10^7 (choice B). The 10 is raised to a *positive* power because the decimal point moved *left*.

3. B; DOK Level: 2; Content Topics: Q.1.c, Q.2.a, Q.4.a;
Practices: MP.1.a, MP.4.a
The area of a rectangle is the product of the width and length: $(2^6)(2^5)$. According to the rules for the multiplication of numbers with exponents, since the bases are the same, one simply keeps the base and adds the exponents: $2^{(6+5)} = 2^{11}$ (choice B). Choice A subtracts the exponents, rather than adds them. Choice C multiplies the exponents. Choice D correctly sums the exponents, but incorrectly multiplies or adds the bases.

4. D; DOK Level: 2; **Content Topics:** Q.1.c, Q.2.a, Q.2.e; **Practices:** MP.1.a, MP.4.a

The width of a large number of hairs placed next to each other is the number of hairs multiplied by the width of each hair. In this case that is $(2 \times 10^5)(1.5 \times 10^{-3})$ cm. Rearranging, one gets $(2 \times 1.5)(10^5 \times 10^{-3})$ cm. The first term is simple multiplication resulting in a value of 3 and, since the powers of 10 have the same base, one simply adds the exponents for the second term $(5 - 3 = 2)$. The result is 3×10^2 cm (choice D). Choice A adds the bases of the two numbers, rather than multiplies, and incorrectly sums the exponents. Choices B and C correctly multiply the bases of the two numbers, but incorrectly sum the exponents—switching the signs in B and ignoring the negative sign in C.

5. C; DOK Level: 2; **Content Topic:** Q.2.a; **Practices:** MP.1.a, MP.4.a

The first term is a nonzero number raised to the first power, and so is simply the number 5. The second term is a non-zero number raised to the power of zero, which is always 1. So the sum can be rewritten as $5 + 1 = 6$ (choice C). Choice A is the sum of 5 and 4, neglecting the power of zero in the second term. Choice B sums 5 and 4, and then subtracts the powers of 1 and 0. Choice D incorrectly assumes 4^0 is zero.

6. A; DOK Level: 2; **Content Topics:** Q.1.c, Q.2.a, Q.2.b; **Practices:** MP.1.a, MP.4.a

Since the numbers with exponents all have the same base, the first term can be simplified to read $5(7^4)$. Similarly, the second term is $5(7^0) = 5$, and the final term is $-(7^4)$. Since the first and third terms involve a base to the same power, they can be combined, giving $(5 - 1)7^4 = 4(7^4)$. Adding in the second term gives the final result, $4(7^4) + 5$ (choice A).

7. C; DOK Level: 3; **Content Topics:** Q.2.d, A.1.e; **Practices:** MP.1.a, MP.1.b, MP.1.e, MP.2.c, MP.3.a, MP.4.b, MP.5.c

The expression does not include an opportunity for square roots of negative numbers, and the first and third terms are always positive and do not allow for division by zero. The middle term, however, has a −3 as an exponent, and so represents division by $(x^3 + 8)^3$. That expression will be zero if $x^3 = -8$, which is the case if $x = -2$ (choice C).

8. C; DOK Level: 2; **Content Topics:** Q.1.c, Q.2.a, Q.2.c; **Practices:** MP.1.a, MP.4.a

Because the exponents are negative, treat them as fractions, so that $2^{-3} = \frac{1}{8}$. With that in mind the first term is the same as $6\left(\frac{1}{8}\right) = \frac{6}{8}$. The second term is the same as $5\left(\frac{1}{16}\right) = \frac{5}{16}$. The final term is the same as $4\left(\frac{1}{32}\right) = \frac{4}{32}$. Noting that the lowest common denominator is 16, the sum becomes $\frac{(12 + 5 + 2)}{16} = \frac{19}{16}$ (choice C).

9. D; DOK Level: 2; **Content Topics:** Q.2.a, A.1.d; **Practices:** MP.1.a, MP.4.b

Multiplying the leading factor of 2 in the second term gives $(2x^2 - 10x - 4)$. Summing that with the first term, $(3x^2 + 3x + 2)$, and combining like terms, gives $(5x^2 - 7x - 2)$, which is the same as answer choice D.

10. A; DOK Level: 2; **Content Topics:** Q.2.a, A.1.d; **Practices:** MP.1.a, MP.4.b

Multiplying the leading factor of −2 in the second term gives $(-2x^2 + 10x + 4)$. Subtracting that from the first term $(3x^2 + 3x + 2)$, and combining like terms, gives $(x^2 + 13x + 6)$, option A. (The subtraction of the second term from the first result in positive $13x$ and 6 because they involved subtraction of negative values, which convert to addition of positive values.)

11. B; DOK Level: 3; **Content Topics:** Q.2.a, A.1.d, A.1.f; **Practices:** MP.1.a, MP.1.b, MP.4.b

Focusing first on the second term of the numerator, multiplying through by the leading factor of −2 gives $(-4 + 6x^2)$. Adding that to the first term of the numerator, $(6x^2 + 4)$, gives $12x^2$. Dividing that result by the denominator, $4x$, gives the final result of $3x$, which is option B.

12. A; DOK Level: 2; **Content Topics:** Q.2.a, Q.2.b; **Practices:** MP.1.a, MP.1.b, MP.1.d, MP.3.c, MP.5.c

Since $x^{-2} = \frac{1}{x^2}$, x^{-2} will be greater than x^2 for numbers less than 1 in magnitude. Only Choice A fits this criterion. For all other answer choices, $x^2 > x^{-2}$.

LESSON 5, pp. 58–59

1. C; DOK Level: 1; **Content Topics:** Q.2.a, Q.2.b, A.1.e, A.7.a, A.7.b; **Practices:** MP.1.a, MP.4.a

Substituting 4 into the equation gives $f(4) = (4)^2 - 5 = 16 - 5 = 11$. Choice A is the answer one gets if one takes the square root of 4, rather than the square of 4. Choice B is the result of ignoring the square completely. Choice D results if you add 5 to 4^2, rather than subtract 5 from 4^2.

2. \$2.00; DOK Level: 1; **Content Topics:** Q.2.a, Q.2.e, Q.3.d, Q.6.c, A.1.b, A.7.b; **Practices:** MP.1.a, MP.2.a, MP.4.a

If the total purchases, x, equals \$25, then the sales tax is $y = 0.08x = (0.08)(\$25) = \$2.00$.

3. D; DOK Level: 2; **Content Topics:** Q.2.a, A.1.b; **Practices:** MP.1.a, MP.1.b, MP.4.a

The correct answer must be a multiple of 5 (5, 10, 15, 20, 25, etc.), and the only choice that meets that requirement is 25 (choice D). The other choices are a mix of numbers that are not evenly divisible by 5.

4. C; DOK Level: 3; **Content Topics:** Q.2.a, Q.2.b; **Practices:** MP.1.a, MP.1.b, MP.1.e, MP.3.a, MP.4.a

Checking first the four basic operations, one sees that 4 is two more than and twice 2. But the next number in the sequence (16), is neither two more than 4 nor twice 4. (That eliminates choice A). It is readily apparent, however, that 4 is the square of 2 and, checking the next number in the sequence, 16 the square of 4. Checking the remaining numbers in the pattern, all follow that rule: they are all the square of the previous term (choice C). Choices B and D are both eliminated as possibilities by the first two numbers in the pattern.

Answer Key

UNIT 3 *(continued)*

5. C; DOK Level: 3; Content Topic: Q.2.a; **Practices:** MP.1.a, MP.1.b, MP.1.e, MP.3.a, MP.4.a
The first two numbers (192 and 96) differ by 96, but 96 and the next number in the pattern (48) do not differ by 96, so the rule is not a simple matter of subtraction. The second number is half the first number $\left(\frac{192}{96} = 2\right)$ and, checking the next number in the sequence $\left(\frac{96}{48} = 2\right)$, the rule holds. It also holds for the final number in the pattern, establishing the rule for this pattern as each term being half the previous term. The fifth term then will be half of 24, or 12. The sixth term will be half of 12, or 6 (choice C). Choice A does not fit the rule at all, and choices B and D are the fifth and seventh terms in the pattern, respectively.

6. A; DOK Level: 3; Content Topic: Q.2.a; **Practices:** MP.1.a, MP.1.b, MP.2.c, MP.4.b
A key to this problem is recognizing that it is asking for the value of x (input) that produces a value of $f(x) = 4$ (output). Setting the expression equal to 4: $2 - \frac{2}{3}x = 4$. Rearranging the equation, one gets $\frac{2}{3}x = -2$; multiplying both sides by $\frac{3}{2}$ gives $x = -3$ (choice A). Choice D is the result of a sign error. Choices B and C are the results of multiplying by $\frac{2}{3}$, rather than by $\frac{3}{2}$, without and with the sign error, in the final step.

7. C; DOK Level: 2; Content Topics: Q.2.a, Q.2.b, Q.6.c, A.1.b, A.1.e, A.1.i, A.7.a, A.7.b; **Practices:** MP.1.a, MP.1.b, MP.4.a
Substituting the various values of x into the expression for y, one finds all the corresponding values for y in the table, except for the value at $x = 1$. That value of y should be $\frac{(1 + 1)}{(1^2 + 1)} = \frac{(2)}{(2)} = 1$.

8. A; DOK Level: 3; Content Topics: Q.2.a, Q.2.e, Q.6.c, A.7.a, A.7.b; **Practices:** MP.1.a, MP.1.b, MP.1.e, MP.2.a, MP.2.c, MP.3.a, MP.4.a, MP.5.c
If one uses the equation to determine the value of v for the various data points, one finds that $v = 250$ for all the points except for the value at $t = 3$. For that value of t, the calculated value of v is 300, which differs from the result for all other data points.

LESSON 6, *pp. 60–61*
1. A; DOK Level: 1; Content Topics: Q.2.a, A.2.a; **Practices:** MP.1.a, MP.1.b, MP.1.e, MP.4.b
To find the value of x that makes the equation true, solve the equation for x. First, subtract 9 from both sides of the equation: $3x + 9 - 9 = 6 - 9$. Simplify: $3x = -3$. Next, undo the multiplication by dividing both sides of the equation by 3: $\frac{3x}{3} = \frac{-3}{3}$. Simplify: $x = -1$. Other responses result from use of incorrect operations (failure to divide by 3, adding rather than subtracting).

2. D; DOK Level: 1; Content Topics: Q.2.a, A.2.a; **Practices:** MP.1.a, MP.1.b, MP.1.e, MP.4.b
To solve the equation for x, isolate the variable on one side of the equation. First, add 4 to both sides of the equation: $0.5x - 4 + 4 = 12 + 4$. Simplify: $0.5x = 16$. Divide both sides of the equation by 0.5: $\frac{0.5x}{0.5} = \frac{16}{0.5}$. Alternately, multiply both sides of the equation by 2: $2(0.5x) = 2(16)$. Simplify: $x = 32$. Other responses result from use of incorrect operations or incorrect use of order of operations.

3. D; DOK Level: 1; Content Topics: Q.2.a, A.2.a; **Practices:** MP.1.a, MP.1.b, MP.1.e, MP.4.b, MP.5.c
To solve the equation for y, begin by grouping variable terms on one side of the equation and constant terms on the other side. Subtract $3y$ from both sides of the equation: $5y - 3y + 6 = 3y - 3y - 14$. Group like terms: $2y + 6 = -14$. Next, subtract 6 from both sides of the equation: $2y + 6 - 6 = -14 - 6$. Group like terms: $2y = -20$. Finally, divide both sides of the equation by 2: $\frac{2y}{2} = \frac{-20}{2}$. Simplify: $y = -10$. Other responses result from use of incorrect operations.

4. A; DOK Level: 1; Content Topics: Q.2.a, A.2.a; **Practices:** MP.1.a, MP.1.b, MP.1.e, MP.4.b
To solve the equation for t, begin by grouping variable terms on one side of the equation and constant terms on the other side. One way to do this is to subtract $\frac{1}{2}t$ from both sides: $\frac{1}{2}t + 8 - \frac{1}{2}t = \frac{5}{2}t - 10 - \frac{1}{2}t$. Next, simplify by grouping like terms and simplifying the fraction: $8 = 2t - 10$. Add 10 to both sides of the equation: $8 + 10 = 2t - 10 + 10$. Simplify $18 = 2t$. Finally, divide both sides of the equation by 2: $t = 9$. Other responses result from use of incorrect operations.

5. C; DOK Level: 2; Content Topics: Q.2.a, Q.2.e, Q.3.d, A.2.a, A.2.b, A.2.c; **Practices:** MP.1.a, MP.1.b, MP.1.e, MP.2.a, MP.4.b, MP.5.c
Since Cameron earned a total of \$2,800, $1,200 + 0.08s = 2,800$. Solve the equation for s. First, subtract 1,200 from both sides of the equation: $1,200 - 1,200 + 0.08s = 2,800 - 1,200$. Simplify: $0.08s = 1,600$. Divide both sides of the equation by 0.08: $\frac{0.08s}{0.08} = \frac{1600}{0.08}$, so $s = 20,000$. The answer of \$15,000 results from dividing 1,200 by 0.8. The answer of \$16,000 results from dividing 1,600 by 0.1. The answer of \$50,000 results from adding 1,200 to each side of the equation.

6. B; DOK Level: 2; Content Topics: Q.2.a, Q.2.e, A.2.a, A.2.b, A.2.c; **Practices:** MP.1.a, MP.1.b, MP.1.e, MP.2.a, MP.5.c
Since the perimeter of the yard is 84 feet, $4x + 8 = 84$. Solve the equation for x. First, subtract 8 from both sides of the equation: $4x + 8 - 8 = 84 - 8$. Simplify: $4x = 76$. Next, divide both sides of the equation by 4: $\frac{4x}{4} = \frac{76}{4}$. Simplify: $x = 19$. Since x represents the width of the yard, add 4 feet to find the length of the yard. The yard is 23 feet long.

7. **C**; **DOK Level:** 3; **Content Topics:** Q.2.a, A.2.a; **Practice:** MP.3.a

Solve the equation for x and then determine which operations were and were not used. Begin by grouping the variable terms on one side of the equation and the constant terms on the other side of the equation. **Subtract** $4x$ from both sides of the equation: $9x - 4x - 2 = 4x - 4x + 8$. Simplify: $5x - 2 = 8$. **Add** 2 to both sides of the equation: $5x - 2 + 2 = 8 + 2$. Simplify: $5x = 10$. **Divide** both sides of the equation by 5: $\frac{5x}{5} = \frac{10}{5}$. So, subtraction, addition, and division are used to solve for x.

8. **C**; **DOK Level:** 3; **Content Topics:** Q.2.a, A.2.a; **Practices:** MP.5.a, MP.5.c

Solve the equation. Then, compare each answer choice to the steps taken in your solution. First, eliminate the parentheses: $3x = 8 - 0.25x - 3 + 0.75x$. Group like terms: $3x = 5 + 0.5x$. Subtract $0.5x$ from both sides of the equation: $3x - 0.5x = 5 + 0.5x - 0.5x$. Simplify: $2.5x = 5$. Divide both sides of the equation by 2.5: $\frac{2.5x}{2.5} = \frac{5}{2.5}$. Simplify: $x = 2$. So, Lucas' solution is incorrect. Dividing both sides of the equation by 2.5 is a correct step in the solution. Adding $0.75x$ to both sides of the equation would result in an incorrect answer because $0.75x$ is already added to the right-hand side of the equation. Subtracting $0.5x$ from both sides of the equation is a correct step in the solution.

9. **D**; **DOK Level:** 1; **Content Topics:** Q.2.a, A.2.a; **Practices:** MP.1.a, MP.1.b, MP.1.e, MP.4.b

To solve the equation, group variable terms on one side of the equation and constant terms on the other side of the equation. Begin by both sides of the equation: $-3x + 11 + 3x = x - 5 + 3x$. Simply: $11 = 4x - 5$. Add 5 to both sides of the equation: $11 + 5 = 4x - 5 + 5$. Simplify: $16 = 4x$. Divide both sides by 4 to get $x = 4$. So, $x = 4$.

10. **D**; **DOK Level:** 1; **Content Topics:** Q.2.a, A.2.a; **Practices:** MP.1.a, MP.1.b, MP.1.e, MP.4.b

To solve the equation, group variable terms on one side of the equation and constant terms on the other side of the equation. Begin by grouping the y terms on the right side of the equation: $0.6y + 1.2 = 1.1y - 0.9$. Next, subtract $0.6y$ from both sides of the equation: $0.6y + 1.2 - 0.6y = 1.1y - 0.9 - 0.6y$. Simplify: $1.2 = 0.5y - 0.9$. Add 0.9 to both sides of the equation: $1.2 + 0.9 = 0.5y - 0.9 + 0.9$. Simplify: $2.1 = 0.5y$. Divide both sides of the equation by 0.5 to get $y = 4.2$.

11. **A**; **DOK Level:** 1; **Content Topics:** Q.2.a, A.2.a; **Practices:** MP.1.a, MP.1.b, MP.1.e, MP.4.b

To solve the equation, group variable terms on one side of the equation and constant terms on the other side of the equation. Begin by subtracting $\frac{3n}{2}$ from both sides of the equation: $\frac{n}{4} - \frac{3n}{2} - \frac{1}{2} = \frac{3n}{2} - \frac{3n}{2} + \frac{3}{4}$. Simplify: $\frac{n}{4} - \frac{3n}{2} - \frac{1}{2} = \frac{3}{4}$. Next, add $\frac{1}{2}$ to both sides of the equation: $\frac{n}{4} - \frac{3n}{2} - \frac{1}{2} + \frac{1}{2} = \frac{3}{4} + \frac{1}{2}$. Simplify: $\frac{n}{4} - \frac{3n}{2} = \frac{3}{4} + \frac{1}{2}$. To add or subtract fractions, the fractions must have like denominators. The least common multiple of 4 and 2 is 4, so write each fraction with a denominator of 4: $\frac{n}{4} - \frac{6n}{4} = \frac{3}{4} + \frac{2}{4}$. Simplify: $-\frac{5n}{4} = \frac{5}{4}$. Multiply both sides of the equation by $-\frac{4}{5}$: $\left(-\frac{4}{5}\right)\left(-\frac{5n}{4}\right) = \left(-\frac{4}{5}\right)\left(\frac{5}{4}\right)$. Simplify: $n = -1$. Answer choice C results from an incorrect sign, and answer choices B and D are other integers evenly spaced near the correct answer.

LESSON 7, pp. 62–63

1. **C**; **DOK Level:** 2; **Content Topics:** Q.2.a, A.2.a, A.2.d; **Practices:** MP.1.a, MP.1.b, MP.1.e, MP.2.c, MP.4.a

To solve this system by substitution, solve the first equation for x and then substitute that value into the second equation and solve for y. $x = 1 - 3y$, so $2(1 - 3y) + 2y = 6$. Expand the parentheses: $2(1) - 2(3y) + 2y = 6$. Simplify: $2 - 6y + 2y = 6$. Group like terms: $2 - 4y = 6$. Subtract 2 from each side of the equation: $-4y = 4$. Divide both sides of the equation by -4: $y = -1$. Substitute $y = -1$ into the first equation and solve for x: $x + 3(-1) = 1$. Simplify: $x - 3 = 1$. Add 3 to both sides of the equation: $x = 4$. So, the ordered pair is $(4, -1)$. To solve this equation by linear combination, multiply the first equation by -2: $-2x - 6y = -2$. Add this equation to the second equation and solve the resulting equation for y. Then substitute $y = -1$ into an original equation to solve for x.

2. **3**; **−1**; **DOK Level:** 2; **Content Topics:** Q.2.a, A.2.a, A.2.d; **Practices:** MP.1.a, MP.1.b, MP.1.e, MP.2.c, MP.4.a

To solve the system by linear combination, add the two equations: $5x + 0y = 15$. Divide both sides of the equation by 5: $x = 3$. Substitute 3 for x in either of the original equations: $3(3) - y = 10$. Solve: $9 - y = 10$; $y = -1$. To solve the system by substitution, solve either equation for y: $y = 5 - 2x$. Substitute $(5 - 2x)$ for y in the other equation: $3x - (5 - 2x) = 10$. Simplify: $3x - 5 + 2x = 10$. Group like terms: $5x - 5 = 10$. Solve: $5x = 15$, so $x = 3$. Substitute $x = 3$ into either equation to solve for y.

3. **2**; **3**; **DOK Level:** 2; **Content Topics:** Q.2.a, A.2.a, A.2.d; **Practices:** MP.1.a, MP.1.b, MP.1.e, MP.2.c, MP.4.a

Although this system can be solved by substitution, it is more easily solved by linear combination. Multiply the second equation by 2: $-4x + 10y = 22$. Add the new equation to the first equation so that $7y = 21$. Divide both sides of the equation by 7: $y = 3$. Substitute 3 for y in either of the original equations: $4x - 3(3) = -1$. Multiply: $4x - 9 = -1$. Add 9 to both sides of the equation: $4x = 8$. Divide both sides of the equation by 4: $x = 2$.

Answer Key

4. 8; **−1**; **DOK Level:** 2; **Content Topics:** Q.2.a, A.2.a, A.2.d; **Practices:** MP.1.a, MP.1.b, MP.1.e, MP.2.c, MP.4.a
Although this system can be solved by substitution, it is more easily solved by linear combination. Multiply the first equation by 4 so that the y-coefficients are opposites: $2x - 8y = 24$. Add this equation to the second equation: $5x + 0y = 40$. Divide both sides of the equation by 5: $x = 8$. Substitute 8 for x in either of the original equations: $3(8) + 8y = 16$. Multiply: $24 + 8y = 16$. Subtract 24 from both sides of the equation: $8y = -8$. Divide both sides of the equation by 8: $y = -1$. Alternately, multiply the first equation by -6 so that the x-coefficients are opposites. Combine the equations and solve for y, then substitute the value for y into one of the original equations to solve for x.

5. 12; **8**; **DOK Level:** 2; **Content Topics:** Q.2.a, Q.2.e, A.2.a, A.2.b, A.2.d; **Practices:** MP.1.a, MP.1.b, MP.1.e, MP.2.a, MP.2.c, MP.4.a
Since the first equation is already written in terms of m, substitute $2g - 4$ for m in the second equation: $2g - 4 + g = 20$. Group like terms: $3g - 4 = 20$. Add 4 to both sides of the equation: $3g = 24$. Divide both sides of the equation by 3: $g = 8$. Substitute 8 for g in either equation: $m = 2(8) - 4$; $m = 12$. To solve this system by linear combination, begin by rewriting the first equation: $m - 2g = -4$. Multiply this equation by -1: $-m + 2g = 4$. Add this equation to the second equation: $3g = 24$. Then solve for m.

6. −2; **4**; **DOK Level:** 2; **Content Topics:** Q.2.a, A.2.a, A.2.d; **Practices:** MP.1.a, MP.1.b, MP.1.e, MP.2.c, MP.4.a
In this system of equations, neither equation is easily solved for a variable and neither variable has coefficients that are multiples of each other. To solve this system, find the least common multiple of the coefficients of one of the variables. The least common multiple of 2 and 3 is 6. In order to eliminate the y terms, multiply the first equation by 3, and multiply the second equation by 2. Then add these two new equations together:

$$3(3x + 2y = 2) \longrightarrow 9x + 6y = 6$$
$$2(2x - 3y = -16) \longrightarrow \underline{4x - 6y = -32}$$
$$13x = -26$$
$$x = -2$$

Substitute -2 for x in either of the original equations: $3(-2) + 2y = 2$. Multiply: $-6 + 2y = 2$. Add 6 to both sides of the equation: $2y = 8$. Divide both sides of the equation by 2: $y = 4$. Alternately, multiply the first equation by 2 and the second equation by -3 and then add the new equations to eliminate the x terms. Then solve for y and substitute this value into one of the original equations to solve for x.

7. D; **DOK Level:** 2; **Content Topics:** Q.2.a, A.2.a, A.2.d; **Practices:** MP.1.a, MP.1.b, MP.1.e, MP.2.c, MP.4.a
To solve this system by linear combination, add the two equations together. The resulting equation is $3x + 0y = 18$. Simplify: $3x = 18$. Divide both sides of the equation by 3: $x = 6$. Substitute $x = 6$ into the first equation: $6 + y = 10$. Subtract 6 from both sides of the equation: $y = 4$. So, the solution to the system is $(6, 4)$. To solve this system by substitution, solve either equation for y. The first equation gives $y = 10 - x$. The substitute $10 - x$ for y in the second equation: $2x - (10 - x) = 8$. Simplify: $2x - 10 + x = 8$. Group like terms: $3x - 10 = 8$. Add 10 to both sides of the equation: $3x = 18$. So, $x = 6$. Substitute $x = 6$ into an original equation and solve for y, so that $y = 4$.

8. B; **DOK Level:** 2; **Content Topic:** A.2.d; **Practices:** MP.1.a, MP.1.b, MP.1.e, MP.4.a, MP.5.c
The goal of the linear combination method is to multiply one or both equations so that the coefficients of one variable are opposites of each other and cancel one another out, leaving one variable for which to solve. In answer choices A and C, the signs in the equations are the same (in option A, both x and $2x$ are positive and $-3y$ and $-y$ are negative; in option C, signs again are the same: both x and $5x$ are positive, as are $3y$ and y). In answer choice D, the signs are the same for x, but different for y. However, 3 times either $-2y$ or $4y$ doesn't allow for cancelling out of the y variable. However, answer choice B allows for linear combination when y is multiplied by 3. Then $3y$ may be added to $-3y$, cancelling out the y variable and leaving only x for which to solve.

LESSON 8, *pp. 64–65*
1. C; **DOK Level:** 2; **Content Topics:** A.1.a, A.1.d, A.1.g, A.4.a, A.4.b; **Practices:** MP.1.a, MP.1.b, MP.1.e, MP.2.a, MP.2.c
Factors of -6: 6 and -1, -6 and 1, 3 and -2, -3 and 2.
$x^2 + 5x - 6 = 0$
$x^2 + 6x - 1x - 6 = 0$
$(x^2 + 6x) + (-1x - 6) = 0$
$x(x + 6) - 1(x + 6) = 0$
$(x + 6)(x - 1) = 0$
$(x + 6) = 0$, or $(x - 1) = 0$
$x = -6$, or $x = 1$
Incorrect answer choices A, B, and D have not accurately factored the expression. Expand the brackets to get the original expression and check for accuracy.

2. D; **DOK Level:** 2; **Content Topics:** Q.1.b, A.1.a, A.1.d, A.1.g, A.4.a, A.4.b; **Practices:** MP.1.a, MP.1.b, MP.1.e, MP.2.a, MP.2.c
First: $x(x) = x^2$
Outer: $x(-7) = -7x$
Inner: $5(x) = 5x$
Last: $5(-7) = -35$
Quadratic Expression: $x^2 - 7x + 5x - 35 = x^2 - 2x - 35$
Note that incorrect answer choices fail to include appropriate signs (choices B and C) or did not accurately complete the FOIL process (all other choices).

3. **A**; **DOK Level:** 2; **Content Topics:** Q.1.b, A.1.a, A.1.d, A.1.g, A.4.a, A.4.b; **Practices:** MP.1.a, MP.1.b, MP.1.e, MP.2.a, MP.2.c

First: $x(x) = x^2$
Outer: $x(-3) = -3x$
Inner: $-3(x) = -3x$
Last: $-3(-3) = 9$
Quadratic Expression: $x^2 - 3x - 3x + 9 = x^2 - 6x + 9$

4. **D**; **DOK Level:** 2; **Content Topic:** Q.1.b; **Practices:** MP.1.a, MP.1.b, MP.1.e, MP.2.a, MP.2.c

First, find factors of -16: -16 and 1, 1 and -16, 2 and -8, -2 and 8, 4 and -4, -4 and 4.
Next, find the two factors of the third term (-16) that have a sum equal to the coefficient of the middle term (-6). Those factors are 2 and -8. Next, use the variable x as the first term in each factor and the integers as the second terms so that:
$x^2 - 6x - 16$
$x^2 - 8x + 2x - 16$
$(x^2 - 8x) + (2x - 16)$
$x(x - 8) + 2(x - 8)$
$(x + 2)(x - 8)$

5. **A**; **DOK Level:** 2; **Content Topics:** Q.1.b, Q.4a, A.1.a, A.1.g, A.4.a, A.4.b; **Practices:** MP.1.a, MP.1.b, MP.1.e, MP.2.a, MP.2.c

Area of rectangle $= l \times w$, so if
$l = 2x - 5$
$w = -4x + 1$, then area $= (2x - 5)(-4x + 1)$.
First: $2x(-4x) = -8x^2$
Outer: $2x(1) = 2x$
Inner: $-5(-4x) = 20x$
Last: $5(1) = -5$
Quadratic Expression: $-8x^2 + 22x - 5$
Answer choices B and D have incorrect a values and answer choices C and D have incorrect b values.

6. **B**; **DOK Level:** 2; **Content Topic:** Q.1.b; **Practices:** MP.1.a, MP.1.b, MP.1.e, MP.2.a, MP.2.c

By removing the factor $4x + 1$ from $4x^2 + 13x + 3$, you can determine the other factor by substitution. The factor $x + 3$ fulfills the expression $4x^2 + 13x + 3$. An alternative method would be to multiply $4x + 1$ by each answer choice to see which one results in the given quadratic expression.

7. **A**; **DOK Level:** 2; **Content Topics:** A.1.a, A.1.d, A.1.g, A.4.a, A.4.b, A.4.a; **Practices:** MP.1.a, MP.1.b, MP.1.e, MP.2.a, MP.2.c

First, substitute the values from answer choices C and D to see whether they solve the equation. Neither does. Next, try to solve the equation using answer choice B. Values from choice B are either 2 or 6, neither of which solves the equation. Lastly, use the quadratic formula to solve for answer choice A.
Begin with the formula:
$x = \dfrac{-b \pm \sqrt{b^2 - 4ac}}{2a}$
Next, substitute values so that:
$a = 3$
$b = -10$
$c = 5$
From there, plug values into the formula so that:
$x = \dfrac{-(-10) \pm \sqrt{(100 - 60)}}{6}$

Next, simplify so that:
$x = \dfrac{10 \pm \sqrt{40}}{6}$

8. **B**; **DOK Level:** 2; **Content Topics:** Q.4a, A.1.a, A.1.g, A.4.a, A.4.b; **Practices:** MP.1.a, MP.1.b, MP.1.e, MP.2.a, MP.2.c, MP.4.b

Rearrange the equation so that it equals zero. This equation represents the area of the garden. Factor the quadratic equation to find a possible width of the garden.
$w^2 - 12w + 32 = 0$
$w^2 - 8w - 4w + 32 = 0$
$(w^2 - 8w) + (-4w + 32) = 0$
$w(w - 8) - 4(w - 8)$
$(w - 4)(w - 8) = 0$
$(w - 4) = 0$, or $(w - 8) = 0$
$w = 4$, or $w = 8$
Since she only used 12m of fencing, w cannot be 8 since the shape is a rectangle.

9. **A**; **DOK Level:** 3; **Content Topics:** A.1.a, A.1.d, A.1.g, A.4.a, A.4.b; **Practices:** MP.1.a, MP.1.b, MP.1.e, MP.2.c, MP.4.b

First, substitute the values from answer choices C and D to see whether they solve the equation. Neither does. Next, try to solve the equation using answer choice B. Values from choice B are either 2 or -6, neither of which solves the equation. Lastly, use the quadratic formula to get answer choice A, after rewriting the equation to equal zero.
$2x^2 + x - 0.5 = 0$
Begin with the formula:
$x = \dfrac{-b \pm \sqrt{b^2 - 4ac}}{2a}$
Next, substitute values so that:
$a = 2$
$b = 1$
$c = -.5$
From there, plug values into the formula so that:
$\dfrac{-1 \pm \sqrt{1^2 - 4(2)(-0.5)}}{2(2)} = \dfrac{-1 \pm \sqrt{1 - (-4)}}{4} = \dfrac{-1 \pm \sqrt{5}}{4}$

10. **D**; **DOK Level:** 2; **Content Topic:** Q.1.b; **Practices:** MP.1.a, MP.1.b, MP.1.e, MP.2.a, MP.2.c

Since each term is divisible by 2, divide the terms so that: $x^2 + 9x + 18 = 0$. Next, find the two factors of the third term (18) that have a sum equal to the coefficient of the middle term (9). Those factors are 6 and 3. Next, use the variable x as the first term in each factor and the integers as the second terms so that: $(x + 3)(x + 6)$. Since $x + 3 = 0$, $x = -3$. Likewise, since $x + 6 = 0$, $x = -6$.

11. **C**; **DOK Level:** 2; **Content Topic:** Q.1.b; **Practices:** MP.1.a, MP.1.b, MP.1.e, MP.2.a, MP.2.c

To find a product with only two terms, look for factors with opposite signs. Both answer choices B and D use the same signs and thus will have three terms, so you can eliminate them as choices. Answer choice A has factors with opposite signs, but when you use the FOIL method you get $x^2 + 6x - 7$. Finally, answer choice C, which results in $x^2 - 49$, produces two terms.

Answer Key

UNIT 3 *(continued)*

LESSON 9, *pp. 66–67*

1. A; DOK Level: 2; **Content Topics:** Q.2.a, A.1.d, A.1.f;
Practices: MP.1.a, MP.1.b, MP.1.e, MP.4.b
To simplify the expression, begin by factoring the numerator and the denominator. The terms in the numerator have a common factor of $2x$, so $2x^2 + 10x = 2x(x + 5)$. The denominator is a quadratic expression in the form $Ax^2 + Bx + C$, and it can be factored. Since $(-3)(5) = -15$ and $-3 + 5 = 2$, $x^2 + 2x - 15 = (x - 3)(x + 5)$. Cancel out the common factor of $(x + 5)$. So, the simplified expression is $\frac{2x}{x - 3}$. The answer of $\frac{x^2 + 5x}{-15}$ is the result of separately simplifying the x^2 terms, the x terms, and the constant terms. The answer of $\frac{2x + 5}{-15}$ is the result of subtracting the x^2 and the x terms in the denominator from the corresponding terms in the numerator. The answer of $\frac{2x(x + 5)}{x^2 + 2x - 15}$ is the result of not factoring the denominator.

2. C; DOK Level: 2; **Content Topics:** Q.2.a, A.1.a, A.1.h;
Practices: MP.1.a, MP.1.b, MP.1.e, MP.4.b
To solve the rational equation, begin by identifying the lowest common denominator of the three expressions: $2x = 2 \cdot x$; $4 = 2^2$. So, the lowest common denominator is $2^2 \cdot x$, or $4x$. Multiply each term by $4x$: $4x \cdot \frac{5}{2x} + 4x \cdot \frac{1}{4} = 4x \cdot \frac{3}{x}$. Simplify: $10 + x = 12$. Subtract 10 from each side: $x = 2$.

3. D; DOK Level: 2; **Content Topics:** Q.2.a, A.1.a, A.1.d, A.1.f, A.1.h; **Practices:** MP.1.a, MP.1.b, MP.1.e, MP.4.b
Begin by factoring the denominators of the expression to find the lowest common denominator. The denominator $x^2 + 3x - 4$ factors as $(x + 4)(x - 1)$, so the lowest common denominator is $(x + 4)(x - 1)$. $(x + 4)(x - 1) \times \frac{2}{x - 1} = (x + 4)(x - 1) \times \frac{16}{(x + 4)(x - 1)}$. Simplify: $2(x + 4) = 16$. Multiply: $2x + 8 = 16$. Subtract 8 from both sides: $2x = 8$. So, $x = 4$.

4. C; DOK Level: 2; **Content Topics:** Q.2.a, A.1.a, A.1.d, A.1.f, A.1.h; **Practices:** MP.1.a, MP.1.b, MP.1.e, MP.4.b
Begin by factoring the denominators of the expression to find the lowest common denominator. The denominator $2x - 6$ factors as $2(x - 3)$, so the lowest common denominator is $2(x - 3)$.
$2(x - 3) \cdot \frac{5}{2(x - 3)} - 2(x - 3) \times \frac{3}{x - 3} = 2(x - 3) \times \frac{1}{2}$.
Simplify: $5 - 2(3) = x - 3$. Multiply: $5 - 6 = x - 3$. Subtract: $-1 = x - 3$. Add 3 to both sides: $x = 2$.

5. A; C; DOK Level: 2; **Content Topics:** Q.2.a, A.1.a, A.1.d, A.1.f, A.1.h; **Practices:** MP.1.a, MP.1.b, MP.1.e, MP.4.b
The denominators of the expressions are completely factored and there are no common factors, so the lowest common denominator is the product of the two denominators: $7(x + 3) \cdot \frac{4}{x + 3} = 7(x + 3) \cdot \frac{x}{7}$. Simplify: $7 \cdot 4 = x(x + 3)$. Multiply: $28 = x^2 + 3x$. Subtract 28 from both sides of the equation: $x^2 + 3x - 28 = 0$. Since $(7)(-4) = -28$ and $7 + (-4) = 3$, $x^2 + 3x - 28 = (x + 7)(x - 4)$. Therefore, $(x + 7)(x - 4) = 0$ and $x = -7$ or $x = 4$.

6. C; DOK Level: 2; **Content Topics:** Q.1.b, Q.2.a, A.1.a, A.1.d, A.1.f, A.1.h; **Practices:** MP.1.a, MP.1.b, MP.1.e, MP.4.b
To find the lowest common denominator of rational expressions, begin by factoring the denominators: $4x^2 = 2^2 \cdot x^2$; $6x = 2 \cdot 3 \cdot x$. The lowest common denominator contains the highest power of each factor that appears in either denominator, so the lowest common denominator is $2^2 \cdot 3 \cdot x^2$, or $12x^2$.

7. C; DOK Level: 1; **Content Topics:** Q.1.b, Q.2.a, A.1.d, A.1.f, A.4.a; **Practices:** MP.1.a, MP.1.b, MP.1.e, MP.4.b
To find the expression that can be simplified by dividing out the factor $(x + 4)$, completely factor the numerator and denominator of each expression. If the factor $(x + 4)$ appears in both numerator and denominator, then it can be divided out. In answer choice A, the numerator and denominator are completely factored; the factor $(x + 4)$ does not appear in the denominator. In answer choice B, the factored expression is $\frac{x^2 + 4}{(x + 2)(x - 2)}$, and the factor $(x + 4)$ does not appear in either the numerator or denominator. In answer choice C, the factored expression is $\frac{3(x + 4)}{(x + 4)(x - 4)}$ and the factor $(x + 4)$ appears in both the numerator and the denominator. So, the expression can be simplified by dividing out the factor $(x + 4)$. In answer choice D, the factored expression is $\frac{2(x + 4)}{(x - 4)(x - 4)}$. The factor $(x + 4)$ appears in the numerator but not the denominator.

8. A; DOK Level: 2; **Content Topics:** Q.2.a, A.1.a, A.1.d, A.1.f, A.1.h, A.4.a; **Practices:** MP.1.a, MP.1.b, MP.1.e, MP.4.b
To divide rational expressions, multiply by the reciprocal of the divisor:
$\frac{5x}{x^2 + 6x + 9} \div \frac{10x^2 + 5x}{x + 3} = \frac{5x}{x^2 + 6x + 9} \cdot \frac{x + 3}{10x^2 + 5x}$.
Multiply numerators and denominators:
$\frac{5x}{x^2 + 6x + 9} \times \frac{x + 3}{10x^2 + 5x} = \frac{5x(x + 3)}{(x^2 + 6x + 9)(10x^2 + 5x)}$.
Factor, and divide out common factors:
$\frac{5x(x + 3)}{(x^2 + 6x + 9)(10x^2 + 5x)} = \frac{5x(x + 3)}{(x + 3)(x + 3)(5x)(2x + 1)}$.
So, $\frac{5x}{x^2 + 6x + 9} \div \frac{10x^2 + 5x}{x + 3} = \frac{1}{(x + 3)(2x + 1)}$.

9. A; DOK Level: 2; **Content Topics:** Q.2.a, A.1.a, A.1.d, A.1.f, A.1.h; **Practices:** MP.1.a, MP.1.b, MP.1.e, MP.3.c, MP.4.b, MP.5.b
To find the expression that shows that Jason is incorrect, determine which expression cannot be simplified. In answer choice A, the numerator and denominator are completely factored and do not share any common factors. Therefore, although there is an x-term in both the numerator and the denominator, the expression cannot be simplified. In answer choice B, the numerator and the denominator are opposites. So, the numerator can be rewritten as $-1(6 - x)$, and the numerator and denominator have a common factor of $(6 - x)$. In answer choice C, the numerator and denominator have a common factor of 3. In answer choice D, the numerator can be rewritten as $x(x + 2)$, so the numerator and denominator have a common factor of x.

LESSON 10, *pp. 68–69*

1. **D; DOK Level:** 2; **Content Topics:** Q.2.a, A.3.a, A.3.d; **Practices:** MP.1.a, MP.1.e, MP.2.a, MP.4.b
Let x represent the number. Five times the number, $5x$, is less than or equal to two times the number, $2x$, plus 9. So, $5x \leq 2x + 9$. Subtract $2x$ from each side: $3x \leq 9$. Divide each side by 3: $x \leq 3$. Answer choice A is the result of writing the incorrect inequality symbol and failing to divide the constant by 3. Answer choice B is the result of failing to divide the constant by 3. Answer choice C is the result of writing the incorrect inequality symbol.

2. **D; DOK Level:** 1; **Content Topics:** Q.2.a, A.3.a; **Practices:** MP.1.a, MP.1.e, MP.4.b
Solve the inequality as you would solve an equation. Subtract 5 from each side: $x > 4 - 5$. Simplify: $x > -1$. Answer choice A is the result of a subtraction error. Answer choice B is the result of writing the incorrect inequality symbol. Answer choice C is the result of a subtraction error and writing the wrong inequality symbol.

3. **A; DOK Level:** 1; **Content Topics:** Q.2.a, A.3.a; **Practices:** MP.1.a, MP.1.e, MP.4.b
Solve the inequality as you would solve an equation. Subtract 6 from each side: $2x \geq 8 - 6$. Simplify: $2x \geq 2$. Divide each side by 2: $x \geq 1$. Answer choice B is the result of writing the inequality sign in the incorrect direction. Answer choice C is the result of adding 6 to each side rather than subtracting. Answer choice D is the result of adding 6 to each side rather than subtracting and writing the inequality in the wrong direction.

4. **B; DOK Level:** 1; **Content Topic:** A.3.b; **Practice:** MP.4.c
The closed circle on -2 indicates that -2 is part of the solution set. The arrow points to the left, so the graph shows the inequality $x \leq -2$. The graph of answer choice A would show a closed circle on 2 with an arrow pointing to the left. The graph of answer choice C would show an open circle on 2 with an arrow pointing to the right. The graph of answer choice D would show an open circle on -2 with an arrow pointing to the right.

5. **D; DOK Level:** 2; **Content Topics:** Q.2.a, A.3.a, A.3.d; **Practices:** MP.1.a, MP.1.e, MP.2.a, MP.4.b
Let x be the number. The product of the number and 5, $5x$, increased by 3 is less than or equal to 13. So, the inequality is $5x + 3 \leq 13$. Answer choice A represents "The product of a number and 5 increased by 2 is less than or equal to 13." Answer choice B represents "The product of a number and 5 is less than or equal to 13 increased by 3." Answer choice C uses the symbol for "less than," rather than the symbol for "less than or equal to."

6. **D; DOK Level:** 2; **Content Topics:** Q.2.a, Q.4.a, A.3.a, A.3.d; **Practices:** MP.1.a, MP.1.e, MP.2.a, MP.4.b
The area of a rectangle is the product of its length and its width, so the area of the rectangle is given by the expression $w(3w - 3)$. Because the area of the rectangle cannot be greater than 80 square centimeters, 80 is greater than or equal to the area. Therefore the inequality $80 \geq w(3w - 3)$ shows this relationship.

7. **A; DOK Level:** 2; **Content Topics:** Q.2.a, Q.2.e, Q.4.a, A.3.a, A.3.c, A.3.d; **Practices:** MP.1.a, MP.1.e, MP.2.a, MP.4.b
Let x be the amount needed to buy a pair of concert tickets. Together, Kara and Brett have $15 + 22 = \$37$. Since this is less than the amount needed to buy a pair of concert tickets, $37 < x$.

8. **C; DOK Level:** 2; **Content Topics:** Q.2.a, Q.2.e, Q.4.a, A.3.a, A.3.c, A.3.d; **Practices:** MP.1.a, MP.1.e, MP.2.a, MP.4.b
Let x be the number of miles traveled. The cost of the taxicab is $\$2.00$ plus $\$0.50$ per mile, or $2 + 0.5x$. Josie only has $\$8$, so the total cost must be less than or equal to $\$8$. This can be represented by the inequality $2 + 0.5x \leq 8$. Subtract 2 from each side: $0.5x \leq 6$. Multiply each side by 2: $x \leq 12$. Answer choice A is the result of subtracting $\$2$ from $\$8$. Answer choice B is the result of a computation error. Answer choice D is the result of dividing $\$8$ by $\$0.50$.

9. **B; DOK Level:** 2; **Content Topics:** Q.2.a, A.3.d; **Practices:** MP.1.a, MP.1.e, MP.2.a, MP.4.b
Let x be the number. The sum of a number and 12, or $x + 12$, is less than or equal to 5 times the number plus 3, or $5x + 3$. This situation can be represented by $x + 12 \leq 5x + 3$. Answer choice A shows that the first quantity is greater than or equal to the second quantity. Answer choice C shows that the first quantity is greater than the second quantity. Answer choice D shows that the second quantity is greater than the first quantity.

10. **B; DOK Level:** 2; **Content Topics:** Q.2.a, A.3.a, A.3.d; **Practices:** MP.1.a, MP.1.e, MP.2.a, MP.4.b
To solve the inequality, isolate the variable on one side of the inequality sign. To begin, subtract 8 from each side of the inequality so that $-3x > 2x - 10$. Next, subtract $2x$ from each side of the inequality so that $-5x > -10$. Divide each side by -5, and change the direction of the inequality sign because you are dividing by a negative number: $x < 2$.

11. **D; DOK Level:** 2; **Content Topics:** Q.2.a, A.3.a; **Practices:** MP.1.a, MP.1.e, MP.2.a, MP.4.b
To solve the inequality, begin by multiplying to eliminate the parentheses: $-x - 4x > 30 - 3x - 24$. Combine like terms: $-5x > 6 - 3x$. Add $3x$ to each side: $-2x > 6$. Divide each side by -2 and change the direction of the inequality sign because you are dividing by a negative number: $x < -3$, or $-3 > x$.

12. **C; DOK Level:** 2; **Content Topics:** Q.2.a, A.3.a, A.3.b; **Practices:** MP.1.a, MP.1.e, MP.2.a, MP.4.b
The number line represents the inequality $x < 1$. Solve each inequality to determine which has the solution $x < 1$. For answer choice A, $2x + 5 > 3x - 6$. Subtract $3x$ from each side: $-x + 5 > -6$. Subtract 5 from each side: $-x > -11$. Divide and change the direction of the inequality: $x < 11$. For answer choice C, $4x - 3 > 5x - 4$. Subtract $5x$ from each side: $-x - 3 > -4$. Add 3 to each side: $-x > -1$. Divide and change the direction of the inequality: $x < 1$. For answer choices B and D, the inequality sign indicates a closed circle, not an open one like in the graph.

Answer Key

LESSON 11, *pp. 70–71*
1. **A; DOK Level:** 1; **Content Topic:** A.5.a; **Practices:**
MP.1.e, MP.3.a
Point *C* is located 2 units to the right of the origin and 2 units
above the origin. Both of these directions are represented by
positive numbers, so point *C* is located at (2, 2). The ordered
pair (−2, 2) describes the location 2 units to the left of the origin
and 2 units above the origin. The ordered pair (2, −2) describes
the location 2 units to the right of the origin and 2 units below
the origin. The ordered pair (3, −2) describes the location
3 units to the right of the origin and 2 units below the origin.

2.

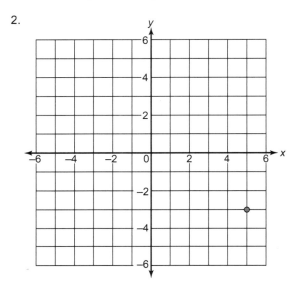

DOK Level: 1; **Content Topic:** A.5.a; **Practices:** MP.1.e,
MP.3.a
The point (5, −3) has a positive *x*-coordinate and a negative
y-coordinate. So, move 5 units to the right of the origin and
3 units below the origin to plot the point.

3.

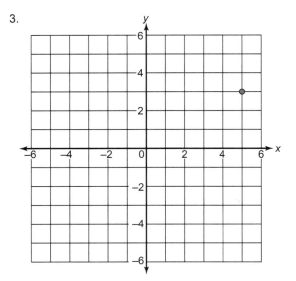

DOK Level: 2; **Content Topic:** A.5.a; **Practice:** MP.1.e
The point (5, −3) is 5 units to the right of the origin and
3 units below the origin. To translate the point up 6 units,
add 6 to the *y*-coordinate, which is −3. Since −3 + 6 = 3, plot
the point 5 units to the right of the origin and 3 units above
the origin.

4.

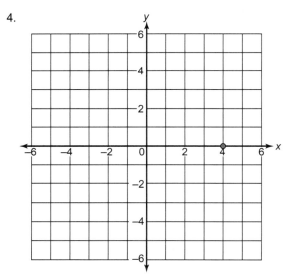

DOK Level: 1; **Content Topic:** A.5.a; **Practices:** MP.1.e,
MP.3.a
The point (4, 0) has a positive *x*-coordinate and a
y-coordinate of 0. So, move 4 units to the right of the origin
and 0 units above or below the origin to plot the point.

ANSWER KEY

5.

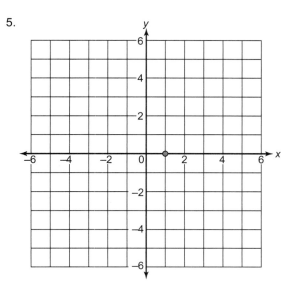

DOK Level: 2; **Content Topic:** A.5.a; **Practice:** MP.1.e
The point (4, 0) is 4 units to the right of the origin and 0 units above or below the origin. To translate the point left 3 units, subtract 3 from the *x*-coordinate, which is 4. Since 4 − 3 = 1, plot the point 1 unit to the right of the origin and 0 units above or below the origin.

6.

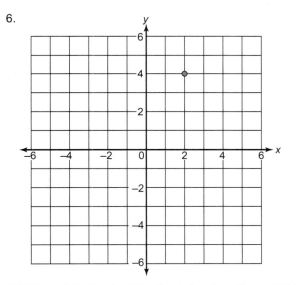

DOK Level: 2; **Content Topic:** A.5.a; **Practices:** MP.1.e
When *x* = 2, the *x*-coordinate is 2 and the *y*-coordinate is 2^2 = 4. So, plot the ordered pair (2, 4). Both numbers are positive, so move 2 units to the right of the origin and 4 units above the origin to plot the point.

7.

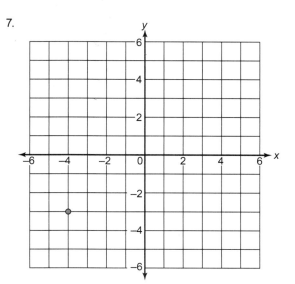

DOK Level: 2; **Content Topic:** A.5.a; **Practice:** MP.1.e
When *x* = −4, the *x*-coordinate is −4 and the *y*-coordinate is 0.75(−4) = −3. So, plot the ordered pair (−4, −3). Both numbers are negative, so move 4 units to the left of the origin and 3 units below the origin to plot the point.

8.

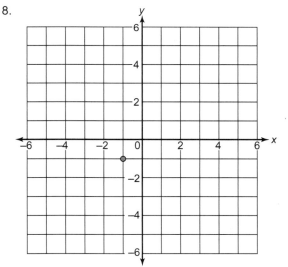

DOK Level: 2; **Content Topic:** A.5.a; **Practice:** MP.1.e
When *x* = −1, the *x*-coordinate is −1 and the *y*-coordinate is (−1)(−1)(−1) = −1. So, plot the ordered pair (−1, −1). Both numbers are negative, so move 1 unit to the left of the origin and 1 unit below the origin to plot the point.

Answer Key

UNIT 3 (continued)

9. B; DOK Level: 1; Content Topic: A.5.a; Practices: MP.1.e, MP.3.a

Point T is located 4 units to the right of the origin, which is represented by a positive number, and 4 units below the origin, which is represented by a negative number. So, point T is located at (4, −4). The ordered pair (5, −4) describes the location 5 units to the right of the origin and 4 units below the origin. The ordered pair (4, −5) describes the location 4 units to the right of the origin and 5 units below the origin. The ordered pair (−4, 4) describes the location 4 units to the left of the origin and 4 units above the origin.

10. A; DOK Level: 1; Content Topic: A.5.a; Practices: MP.1.e, MP.3.a

Point S is located 1 unit to the right of the origin, which is represented by a positive number, and 0 units above or below the origin. So, the ordered pair (1, 0) describes the location of point S. The ordered pair (−1, 0) describes the location 1 unit to the left of the origin. The ordered pair (0, 1) describes the location 1 unit above the origin. The ordered pair (0, −1) describes the location 1 unit below the origin.

11. A; DOK Level: 1; Content Topic: A.5.a; Practices: MP.1.e, MP.3.a

Point P is located 5 units to the left of the origin and 5 units below the origin. Both of these directions are represented by negative numbers, so point P is located at (−5, −5). The ordered pair (−5, 5) describes the location 5 units to the left of the origin and 5 units above the origin. The ordered pair (5, −5) describes the location 5 units to the right of the origin and 5 units below the origin. The ordered pair (5, 5) describes the location 5 units to the right of the origin and 5 units above the origin.

12. B; DOK Level: 1; Content Topic: A.5.a; Practices: MP.1.e, MP.3.a

The coordinates for points T and U are (4, 4) and (4, −4) respectively, so they have the same x-coordinate.

LESSON 12, pp. 72–73

1. B; DOK Level: 1; Content Topics: A.1.b, A.5.d; Practices: MP.1.a, MP.1.e, MP.4.b, MP.4.c

If an ordered pair is a solution to an equation, then it makes the equation true. Substitute the values for x and y for each ordered pair into the equation. For (−1, 3), $2x + y = 2(−1) + 3 = −2 + 3 = 1$. Since $1 \neq 5$, (−1, 3) is not a solution. For (0, −5), $2x + y = 2(0) + (−5) = 0 − 5 = −5$. Since $−5 \neq 5$, (0, −5) is not a solution. For (−2, 6), $2x + y = 2(−2) + 6 = −4 + 6 = 2$. Since $2 \neq 5$, (−2, 6) is not a solution. For (3, −1), $2x + y = 2(3) + (−1) = 6 − 1 = 5$. Since $5 = 5$, (3, −1) is a solution.

2. C; DOK Level: 1; Content Topics: A.1.b, A.5.d; Practices: MP.1.a, MP.1.e, MP.4.b, MP.4.c

If an ordered pair is a point on the line, then it makes the equation true. Substitute the values for x and y for each ordered pair into the equation. For (−2, 0), $x + 2y = −2 + 2(0) = −2 + 0 = −2$. Since $−2 \neq 4$, (−2, 0) is not a solution. For (1, 3), $x + 2y = 1 + 2(3) = 1 + 6 = 7$. Since $7 \neq 4$, (1, 3) is not a solution. For (2, −4), $x + 2y = 2 + 2(−4) = 2 − 8 = −6$. Since $−6 \neq 4$, (2, −4) is not a solution. For (0, 2), $x + 2y = 0 + 2(2) = 0 + 4 = 4$. Since $4 = 4$, (0, 2) is a solution.

3. A; DOK Level: 1; Content Topics: A.1.b, A.5.d; Practices: MP.1.a, MP.1.e, MP.4.b, MP.4.c

If an ordered pair is a solution to an equation, then it makes the equation true. Substitute the values for x and y for each ordered pair into the equation. For (1, −2), $2x − y = 2(1) − (−2) = 2 + 2 = 4$. Since $4 \neq 0$, (1, −2) is not a solution. For (−1, 2), $2x − y = 2(−1) − 2 = −2 − 2 = −4$. Since $−4 \neq 0$, (1, −2) is not a solution. For (2, −2), $2x − y = 2(2) − (−2) = 4 + 2 = 6$. Since $6 \neq 0$, (2, −2) is not a solution. For (0, 0), $2x − y = 2(0) − 0 = 0 − 0 = 0$. Since $0 = 0$, (0, 0) is a solution.

4. C; DOK Level: 2; Content Topics: A.1.b, A.5.d; Practices: MP.1.a, MP.1.e, MP.2.c, MP.4.c

Since $(x, 3)$ is a solution to $y = 2x + 2$, substitute 3 for y and then solve for x: $3 = 2x + 2$. To solve for x, begin by subtracting 2 from both sides of the equation: $3 − 2 = 2x$, so $1 = 2x$. Next, divide both sides of the equation by 2: $\frac{1}{2} = x$.

5. B; DOK Level: 2; Content Topics: A.1.b, A.5.d; Practices: MP.1.a, MP.1.e, MP.4.c

Use the equation $d = \sqrt{(x_2 − x_1)^2 + (y_2 − y_1)^2}$, where $x_2 = −4$, $x_1 = 0$, $y_2 = 3$, and $y_1 = 0$. Substitute the values and solve.

$d = \sqrt{(−4 − 0)^2 + (3 − 0)^2}$
$d = \sqrt{(−4)^2 + (3)^2}$
$d = \sqrt{16 + 9}$
$d = \sqrt{25}$
$d = 5$

6. D; DOK Level: 2; Content Topics: A.1.b, A.5.d; Practices: MP.1.a, MP.1.e, MP.4.c

Use the equation $d = \sqrt{(x_2 − x_1)^2 + (y_2 − y_1)^2}$, where $x_2 = 4$, $x_1 = 2$, $y_2 = 3$, and $y_1 = 5$. Substitute the values and solve.

$d = \sqrt{(4 − 2)^2 + (3 − 5)^2}$
$d = \sqrt{(2)^2 + (−2)^2}$
$d = \sqrt{4 + 4}$
$d = \sqrt{8}$
$d \approx 2.83$

7. D; DOK Level: 1; Content Topics: A.1.b, A.5.a, A.5.d; Practices: MP.1.a, MP.1.e, MP.4.c

If an ordered pair is a solution to an equation, then it makes the equation true. Substitute the values for x and y for each ordered pair into the expression $x + 2y$. If the expression has a value of $−3$, the equation is true and the ordered pair is a solution. For (0, −3), $x + 2y = 0 + 2(−3) = 0 − 6 = −6$. Since $−6 \neq −3$, (0, −3) is not a solution. For (−1, 2), $x + 2y = −1 + 2(2) = −1 + 4 = 3$. Since $3 \neq −3$, (−1, 2) is not a solution. For (0, −2), $x + 2y = 0 + 2(−2) = 0 − 4 = −4$. Since $−4 \neq −3$, (0, −2) is not a solution. For (−5, 1), $x + 2y = −5 + 2(1) = −5 + 2 = −3$. Since $−3 = −3$, (−5, 1) is a solution.

8. **C**; **DOK Level:** 3; **Content Topics:** A.1.b, A.5.a, A.5.d; **Practices:** MP.1.a, MP.1.e, MP.4.c

Use the distance formula. Solve $d = \sqrt{(x_2 - x_1)^2 + (y_2 - y_1)^2}$, where $x_2 = -3$, $x_1 = -5$, $y_2 = 1$, and $y_1 = 2$. Substitute the values and solve. The distance from $(-5, 2)$ to $(-3, 1)$ is:

$d = \sqrt{(-3 - (-5))^2 + (1 - 2)^2}$

$d = \sqrt{(-3 + 5)^2 + (1 - 2)^2}$

$d = \sqrt{(2)^2 + (-1)^2}$

$d = \sqrt{5} \approx 2.236$

The distance from $(-3, 1)$ $(-1, -4)$ is:

$d = \sqrt{(-1 - (-3))^2 + (-4 - 1)^2}$

$d = \sqrt{(-1 + 3)^2 + (-4 - 1)^2}$

$d = \sqrt{(2)^2 + (-5)^2}$

$d = \sqrt{29} \approx 5.385$

Add 2.236 + 5.385 to get 7.62.

9. **B**; **DOK Level:** 2; **Content Topics:** A.1.b, A.5.d; **Practices:** MP.1.a, MP.1.e, MP.4.c

Use the equation $d = \sqrt{(x_2 - x_1)^2 + (y_2 - y_1)^2}$, where $x_2 = 3$, $x_1 = 0$, $y_2 = -3$ and $y_1 = 0$. The result is $d = \sqrt{(3 - 0)^2 + (-3 - 0)^2} = \sqrt{(3)^2 + (-3)^2} = \sqrt{18} = 3\sqrt{2}$. The point that is located at the same distance from the origin, located on the positive y-axis is $(0, 3\sqrt{2})$ (choice B).

LESSON 13, *pp. 74–75*

1. **C**; **DOK Level:** 2; **Content Topics:** Q.2.a, Q.2.e, Q.6.c, A.5.b, A.6.a, A.6.b; **Practices:** MP.1.a, MP.1.b. MP.1.e, MP.3.a

Use the formula for slope: $\frac{y_2 - y_1}{x_2 - x_1} = m = \frac{4 - 3}{1 - (-1)} = \frac{1}{2}$

2. **A**; **DOK Level:** 2; **Content Topics:** Q.2.a, Q.2.e, Q.6.c, A.5.b, A.6.a, A.6.b; **Practices:** MP.1.a, MP.1.b. MP.1.e, MP.3.a

To find the slope of line A, plug any two sets of points (of the three supplied) into the formula for slope. For example: $m = \frac{y_2 - y_1}{x_2 - x_1}$, using $(-2, -4)$ and $(1, 5)$:

$m = \frac{5 - (-4)}{1 - (-2)} = \frac{5 + 4}{1 + 2} = \frac{9}{3} = 3$

3. **C**; **DOK Level:** 2; **Content Topics:** Q.2.a, Q.2.e, Q.6.c, A.5.b, A.6.a; **Practices:** MP.1.a, MP.1.b. MP.1.e, MP.3.a

The slope is $\frac{\text{rise}}{\text{run}} = \frac{2}{32} = \frac{1}{16}$.

4. **C**; **DOK Level:** 2; **Content Topics:** Q.2.a, Q.2.e, Q.6.c, A.5.b, A.6.a, A.6.b; **Practices:** MP.1.a, MP.1.b. MP.1.e, MP.3.a

If $f(x) = 2$, then using form $y = mx + b$, $y = 0x + 2$, so the slope is 0. Additionally, whenever y is directly equal to a number with no variable, the slope of the line is always 0. Also, if the y-values are equal at any two points on the line, the difference between y_1 and y_2 will be 0, which also makes the slope 0.

5. **D**; **DOK Level:** 2; **Content Topics:** Q.2.a, Q.2.e, Q.6.c, A.6.a; **Practices:** MP.1.a, MP.1.b. MP.1.e, MP.3.a

Compare answers to point-slope format:

$y - y_1 = m(x - x_1)$

Only answer choice D matches this format, so other options may be eliminated.

6. **C**; **DOK Level:** 2; **Content Topics:** Q.2.a, Q.2.e, Q.6.c, A.6.a, A.6.b; **Practices:** MP.1.a, MP.1.b. MP.1.e, MP.3.a

First, recall the point-slope formula: $y - y_1 = m(x - x_1)$

Next, insert values from the question: $y - 5 = 3(x + 2)$

7. **D**; **DOK Level:** 2; **Content Topics:** Q.2.a, Q.2.e, Q.6.c, A.6.a, A.6.b; **Practices:** MP.1.a, MP.1.b. MP.1.e, MP.3.a

Find the slope: $m = \frac{-11 - (-1)}{9 - (-6)} = -\frac{10}{15} = -\frac{2}{3}$

Next, plug values $(-6, -1)$ into the point-slope formula to get:

$y - y_1 = m(x - x_1)$

$y + 1 = -\frac{2}{3}(x + 6)$

8. **A**; **DOK Level:** 2; **Content Topics:** Q.2.a, Q.2.e, Q.6.c, A.6.a, A.6.b; **Practices:** MP.1.a, MP.1.b. MP.1.e, MP.3.a

The given equation is in point-slope form. The answer choices are in slope-intercept form. To write the given equation in slope-intercept form, begin by adding 2 to each side of the equation: $y = -5(x - 1) + 2$. Next, multiply to eliminate the parentheses: $y = -5x + 5 + 2$. Finally, combine like terms: $y = -5x + 7$.

9. **D**; **DOK Level:** 3; **Content Topics:** Q.2.a, Q.2.e, Q.6.c, A.6.a, A.6.b; **Practices:** MP.1.a, MP.1.b. MP.1.e, MP.3.a

If two lines are parallel, they have the same slope. The slope of a line written in slope-intercept form is the x-coefficient. To write the given equation in slope-intercept form, solve the equation $4 - y = 2x$ for y. First, substract 4 from each side: $-y = 2x - 4$. Next, multiply each term by -1: $y = -2x + 4$. So, the slope of the line is -2. Both choices C and D have x-coefficients of -2; however, choice C is not written in slope-intercept form and the slope of the line is actually 2. Choice D is correct.

LESSON 14, *pp. 76–77*

1. **C**; **DOK Level:** 2; **Content Topics:** Q.2.a, Q.6.c, A.6.c; **Practices:** MP.1.a, MP.2.c

Whether lines are parallel or perpendicular is determined by their slopes. The equation of the line in the question is given in slope-intercept form, with a slope of $-\frac{2}{3}$. Lines parallel to the given line have the same slope, such as line C. Lines perpendicular to the given line have slopes that are the negative reciprocal of $-\frac{2}{3}$, or $\frac{3}{2}$, which is the same as the slope of line B. So the specified line is perpendicular to B and parallel to C (choice C).

2. **D**; **DOK Level:** 1; **Content Topics:** A.5.b, A.6.c; **Practices:** MP.1.a, MP.2.c

The equation of the line is given in slope-intercept form $y = mx + b$, and so the slope $m = 4$. Lines that are parallel will have the same slope of 4 (choice D). Choice A is the negative of the ratio of b and m. Choice B is the negative reciprocal of m, which is the slope of a line *perpendicular* to the given line. Choice C is the value of the y-intercept, b.

Answer Key

UNIT 3 *(continued)*

3. C; DOK Level: 1; Content Topics: A.5.b, A.6.c;
Practices: MP.1.a, MP.2.c
The slope of the line given by the equation is −3. The slope of lines perpendicular to the given line will be the negative reciprocal, or $\frac{1}{3}$ (choice C). Choice A is the slope of the given line. Choice B is the reciprocal of the slope of the given line. Choice D is the negative of the slope of the given line.

4. B; DOK Level: 2; Content Topics: A.5.b, A.6.c;
Practices: MP.1.a, MP.2.c
Rearranging the equation to slope-intercept form, $y = mx + b$, one has $y = -2x + 4$. The slope is, then, $m = -2$. Any lines perpendicular to the given line will also have a slope of $\frac{1}{2}$. Of the options given, only choice B meets that requirement. Choice A has a slope of +2. Choice C, after rearranging it to read $y = 2x − 2$, has a slope of +2. Choice D has a slope of −2.

5. B; DOK Level: 2; Content Topics: A.5.b, A.6.c;
Practices: MP.1.a, MP.2.c
The equation is already in slope-intercept form, with a slope $m = -\frac{4}{3}$. Lines perpendicular to the given line will have a slope that is the negative reciprocal of that value: $\frac{3}{4}$. Of the options given, only choice B meets that requirement. The slope of choice A is the negative of the slope of the given line, the slope of choice C is the reciprocal, and the slope of choice D is equal to the slope of the given line.

6. A; DOK Level: 3; Content Topics: A.5.b, A.6.c;
Practices: MP.1.a, MP.2.c
Rearranging the given equation into slope-intercept form, one gets $y = -\frac{1}{3}x + \frac{5}{3}$; the slope is $-\frac{1}{3}$. Lines perpendicular to the given line have a slope that is the negative reciprocal, 3. The question specifies a y-intercept of 3, so the equation of the line, in slope-intercept form, is $y = 3x + 3$. Dividing both sides of the equation by 3, one gets choice A as an equivalent, alternative form.

7. C; DOK Level: 3; Content Topics: Q.6.c, A.5.a, A.5.b, A.6.a, A.6.b, A.6.c; **Practices:** MP.1.a, MP.1.b, MP.2.c, MP.3.a
The line through points C and D is parallel to the line through points A and B, and so has the same slope of 3. It is specified in the problem that point C is located on the y-axis at $y = 8$; that is the y-intercept of the line through points C and D. Both slope and intercept are known, and the equation of the line is $y = 3x + 8$ (choice C). Choice A has the correct y-intercept, but the reciprocal of the correct slope. Choice B has the reciprocal of the correct slope and the negative of the correct y-intercept. Choice D has the correct slope, but the negative of the correct intercept.

8. B; DOK Level: 3; Content Topics: Q.6.c, A.5.a, A.5.b, A.6.a, A.6.b, A.6.c; **Practices:** MP.1.a, MP.1.b, MP.2.c, MP.3.a
The line through points B and C is perpendicular to the line through A and B. As a result, the slope of the line is the negative reciprocal of the slope of the line through A and B, or $-\frac{1}{3}$. The y-intercept of the line through points B and C is point C, so $y = 8$. That combination of slope and y-intercept identifies choice B as the correct choice. Choice A has the negative of the correct y-intercept. Choice C has the reciprocal of the correct slope and the negative of the correct y-intercept. Choice D has the reciprocal of the correct slope.

9. C; DOK Level: 3; Content Topics: Q.2.a, Q.6.c, A.5.a, A.5.b, A.6.a, A.6.c; **Practices:** MP.1.a, MP.1.b, MP.1.c, MP.1.e, M.2.c, MP.3.a, MP.4.b, MP.5.c
The equation of the line that passes through points A and B is $y = 3x$. The equation of the line that passes through points B and C is $y = -\frac{1}{3}x + 8$. At point B, where the two lines intersect, the two y-values are the same, and so the expressions in x can be set equal to each other: $3x = -\frac{1}{3}x + 8$. Rearranging the equation gives $\frac{10}{3}x = 8$, so $x = \frac{24}{10}$ (after multiplying each side by $\frac{3}{10}$ to simplify x) = 2.4. Substituting that value of x into the equation for the line through points A and B gives $y = 3x = 3(2.4) = 7.2$. (The equation through points B and C could also be used.) So the correct answer is (2.4, 7.2), or choice C. The remaining choices are nearby points scattered around the correct answer.

10. D; DOK Level: 3; Content Topics: Q.2.a, Q.6.c, A.5.a, A.5.b, A.6.a, A.6.c; **Practices:** MP.1.a, MP.1.b, MP.1.c, MP.1.e, M.2.c, MP.3.a, MP.4.b, MP.5.c
Because it is parallel to the line that passes through points B and C, the equation of the line that passes through points A and D is $y = -\frac{1}{3}x$. Meanwhile, we know from question 7 that the equation of the line that passes through points C and D is $y = 3x + 8$. Setting the two equal to each other, one gets: $-\frac{1}{3}x = 3x + 8$. Rearranging, one gets $\frac{10}{3}x = -8$, so $x = -2.4$. Substituting that value of x into the equation $y = -\frac{1}{3}x$, one finds that $y = 0.8$. So the correct answer is (−2.4, 0.8), choice D. The remaining choices are nearby points distributed around the correct answer.

LESSON 15, *pp. 78–79*
1. D; DOK Level: 2; Content Topics: Q.2.a, Q.6.c, A.5.a, A.5.e; **Practices:** MP.1.a, MP.1.b, MP.4.a, MP.5.c
The x-value of the minimum is given by $x = \frac{-b}{2a} = \frac{-1}{2\left(\frac{1}{3}\right)} = -\frac{3}{2} = -1.5$. Substituting x into the equation gives $\frac{1}{3}(-1.5)^2 + (-1.5) - 4 = 0.75 + -5.5$, so $y = -4.75$. So the coordinates of the minimum is (−1.5, −4.75). The remaining choices are evenly distributed, nearby points.

2. B; DOK Level: 2; Content Topics: Q.2.a, A.5.a, A.5.e; **Practices:** MP.1.a, MP.1.b, MP.1.d, MP.4.b
The curve crosses the x-axis when $y = 0$. Substituting, and factoring the expression in x gives $(x + 4)(x - 2) = 0$. There are two solutions: $x = -4$ and $x = 2$ (choice B). Choice A is the constant term in the equation (c) and the negative of that number. Choice C works for the first value, but not for the second. Choice D includes the opposites of the correct answers.

3. A; DOK Level: 1; Content Topics: A.5.a, A.5.e; **Practices:** MP.1.a, MP.2.c
The curve crosses the y-axis when $x = 0$. The y-intercept is the constant term from the equation, so the answer is −8 (choice A). Choices B and C are half of the correct answer, with and without the minus sign. Choice D is the opposite of the correct answer.

4. B; DOK Level: 2; **Content Topics:** Q.2.a, A.5.a, A.5.e; **Practices:** MP.1.a, MP.1.b, MP.4.a, MP.5.c

The minimum occurs at $x = \frac{-b}{2a}$, where $b = 2$ (the coefficient of x) and $a = 1$ (the coefficient of x^2). That gives an x-value of $\frac{-2}{2} = -1$ (choice B). Choice A is twice the correct answer, choice C is the opposite of the correct answer, and choice D is the opposite of twice the correct answer.

5. C; DOK Level: 3; **Content Topics:** Q.6.c, A.5.a, A.5.e; **Practices:** MP.1.a, MP.1.b, MP.2.c, MP.3.a, MP.5.c

The given point at $y = -2$ has an x-value of $+1$, which is three units to the right of the x-value of the maximum. A corresponding point on the curve will be located three units to the left of the maximum, so that $x = -2 - 3 = -5$ (choice C). The other choices are evenly distributed points around the correct answer.

6. D; DOK Level: 2; **Content Topics:** Q.6.c, A.5.e; **Practices:** MP.1.a, MP.1.b, MP.2.c, MP.5.c

Quadratic equations with negative values of a feature maxima, rather than minima; negative values of a turn a curve upside-down. Both Curves D and E are upside-down (negative) curves with maxima.

7. A; DOK Level: 2; **Content Topics:** Q.6.c, A.5.e; **Practices:** MP.1.a, MP.1.b, MP.2.c, MP.5.c

Quadratic equations with $b = 0$ feature maxima or minima centered on the y-axis. Curve B is the only curve centered on the y-axis (choice A).

8. C; DOK Level: 2; **Content Topics:** Q.6.c, A.5.e; **Practices:** MP.1.a, MP.1.b, MP.2.c, MP.5.c

Curves achieve maxima or minima at x-values equal to $\frac{-b}{2a}$. If $\frac{b}{2a}$ is negative, the x-value of the maximum or minimum must be positive on the graph. Curves C and E (choice C) both have a vertex with a positive x-value. Curves A, B, and D have vertices that are 0 or negative.

9. D; DOK Level: 2; **Content Topics:** Q.6.c, A.5.e; **Practices:** MP.1.a, MP.1.b, MP.2.c, MP.5.c

The value of c is the y-value at which curves cross the y-axis. The curves that cross the y-axis at $y = 0$ are curves B and D (choice D).

LESSON 16, pp. 80–81

1. A; DOK Level: 2; **Content Topics:** Q.2.a, Q.6.c, A.5.e, A.7.c; **Practices:** MP.1.a, MP.4.a

The curve intercepts the y-axis when x equals zero. Substituting $x = 0$ into the function gives $y = (0-2)(0 + 2)(0 + 1) = (-2)(2)(1) = -4$ (choice A). The remaining choices correspond to the x-values where the curve intercepts the x-axis.

2. D; DOK Level: 1; **Content Topics:** Q.6.c, A.5.e, A.7.c; **Practices:** MP.1.a, MP.2.c

The function is decreasing at x_1, increasing at x_3, and increasing at x_4. The correct answer is choice D, x_3 and x_4 only.

3. D; DOK Level: 2; **Content Topics:** Q.6.c, A.5.e, A.7.c; **Practices:** MP.1.a, MP.2.c

The function is negative at x_1, x_2, and x_3. At x_4 the function equals 0.

4. B; DOK Level: 2; **Content Topics:** Q.6.c, A.5.e, A.7.c; **Practices:** MP.1.a, MP.2.c

The slope is negative when $x = x_2$ and positive when $x = x_3$, which means the curve must go through a minimum at some point in between (choice B). (This is also evident by visual inspection of the graph.)

5. B; DOK Level: 3; **Content Topics:** Q.6.c, A.5.a, A.5.e, A.7.c; **Practices:** MP.1.a, MP.1.b, MP.1.d, MP.2.c, MP.3.a, MP.5.c

The curve intercepts the y-axis when $x = 0$. Substituting $x = 0$ into the equation gives $y = (0^2 + 1)(0 - 4)$, which simplifies to $(1)(-4) = -4$ (choice B).

6. A; DOK Level: 2; **Content Topics:** Q.6.c, A.5.e, A.7.c; **Practices:** MP.1.a, MP.1.b, MP.2.c, MP.5.c

The first term $(x^2 + 1)$ can never be zero, since x^2 can never be negative for real values of x. The second term, $(x - 4)$ goes to zero when $x = 4$ (choice A). The remaining choices are integers between the correct answer and zero.

7. A; DOK Level: 2; **Content Topics:** Q.6.c, A.5.e; **Practices:** MP.1.a, MP.1.b, MP.2.c, MP.5.c

Because the numerator of the various answer options is either $+x$ or $-x$, all choices go through 0, consistent with the graph. One can infer from the graph that the function is undefined at $x = -1$ and $x = +2$; this means the denominator goes to 0 at those values. That eliminates choices B and D as possibilities. Substituting $x = 1$ into choice A gives $y = \frac{1}{2}$. Substituting $x = 1$ into choice C gives $y = \frac{-1}{2}$. Since the graph is positive at $x = 1$, choice A is correct.

8. C; DOK Level: 2; **Content Topics:** Q.6.c, A.5.e; **Practices:** MP.1.a, MP.1.b, MP.2.c

The function is at a maximum at $x = 0$. It goes through the next maximum at $x = 4$ and the next one at $x = 8$. Both the subsequent interval of 4 and the previous two intervals of 4 (extending back to $x = -8$) feature curve segments that are identical to the one between $x = 0$ and $x = 4$. So the period is 4 (choice C). Choices A and B cover only a portion of a full cycle of the pattern. Choice D is twice the correct answer.

9. C; DOK Level: 3; **Content Topic:** A.7.b; **Practices:** MP.1.a, MP.1.b, MP.1.e, MP.2.c, MP.3.a, MP.5.c

The essential feature to look for is an absence of multiple y-values for a given x-value. For example, choice A features x-values of -2 and -1 that each appear twice, but do so with multiple and differing y-values (for example, -2 and 2, as well as -1 and 1), respectively. The same situation occurs with choices B and D. Only choice C has five distinct points with no duplicate x-values, making it the correct option.

Answer Key

UNIT 3 (continued)

LESSON 17, pp. 82–83

1. C; **DOK Level:** 2; **Content Topics:** Q.6.c, A.5.e, A.7.a, A.7.d; **Practices:** MP.1.a, MP.1.b, MP.1.e, MP.4.c
The rate of change of a function represented algebraically, in function notation is given by the x-coefficient. A function with a rate of change that is greater than $\frac{2}{3}$ and less than 2 will have an x-coefficient that is between those two values. In answer choice A, the x-coefficient is 3. Since 3 is greater than 2, the rate of change of the function given by $f(x) = 3x + 2$ has a greater rate of change than the function represented by the table. In answer choice B, the x-coefficient is $\frac{1}{2}$. Since $\frac{1}{2}$ is less than $\frac{2}{3}$, the rate of change of the function given by $f(x) = \frac{1}{2}x - 1$ is less than the rate of change of the function represented by the graph. In answer choice C, the x-coefficient is 1. Since 1 is greater than $\frac{2}{3}$ and less than 2, the rate of change of the function given by $f(x) = x + 3$ is greater than the rate of change shown in the graph and less than the rate of change shown in the table. In answer choice D, the x-coefficient is $\frac{5}{2}$. Since $\frac{5}{2}$ is greater than 2, the rate of change of the function given by $f(x) = \frac{5}{2}x + 2$ is greater than the rate of change of the function represented by the table.

2. C; **DOK Level:** 2; **Content Topics:** Q.6.c, A.5.e, A.7.a, A.7.d; **Practices:** MP.1.a, MP.1.b, MP.1.e, MP.4.c
The function represented in the graph crosses the y-axis at $y = 2$. In function notation, the y-intercept is represented by the constant term. In answer choice A, the y-intercept is -2, so the intercept has the wrong sign. In answer choice B, the rate of change of the function is the same as the rate of change shown in the graph, but the y-intercept, 3, is not the same as the y-intercept shown in the graph. In answer choice C, the y-intercept is 2, which is the same as the y-intercept shown in the graph. In answer choice D, the y-intercept is -1, which is the same as the x-intercept shown in the graph.

3. B; **DOK Level:** 2; **Content Topics:** Q.6.c, A.5.e, A.7.a, A.7.d; **Practices:** MP.1.a, MP.1.b, MP.1.e, MP.4.c
First, determine the rate of change and the y-intercept of the function shown in the graph. The slope of the graph is $\frac{\text{rise}}{\text{run}} = \frac{2}{1} = 2$. The graph crosses the y-axis at $(0, 2)$, so the y-intercept is 2. Next, determine the rate of change and the y-intercept of the function represented by the ordered pairs. The slope is $m = \frac{6 - 2}{0 - (-2)} = \frac{4}{2} = 2$. So, the rate of change of the two functions is the same. The ordered pair $(0, 6)$ shows that the y-intercept of the function is 6. So, the y-intercepts of the two functions are different.

4. D; **DOK Level:** 2; **Content Topics:** Q.6.c, A.5.e, A.7.a, A.7.c, A.7.d; **Practices:** MP.1.a, MP.1.b, MP.1.e, MP.4.c
Looking at the graph, when $x = -2$, $f(x) = -2$. Evaluate each function for $x = -2$ and compare. For answer choice A, $f(-2) = -(-2) = 2$. For answer choice B, $f(-2) = \frac{-2}{2}(-2) + 1 = 2 + 1 = 3$. For answer choice C, $f(-2) = -2 + 4 = 2$. For answer choice D, $f(-2) = 6(-2) + 10 = -12 + 10 = -2$.

5. A; **DOK Level:** 2; **Content Topics:** Q.6.c, A.5.e, A.7.c, A.7.d; **Practices:** MP.1.a, MP.1.b, MP.1.e, MP.4.c
Begin by identifying the x-intercepts of the function represented in the table. At the x-intercepts, $y = 0$. So, the x-intercepts are -2 and 2. Next, set $f(x) = 0$ for each function and solve for x. For answer choice A, $f(x) = \frac{1}{2}x^2 - 2$, so if $f(x) = 0$, $\frac{1}{2}x^2 - 2 = 0$ and $\frac{1}{2}x^2 = 2$. Multiply each side of the equation by 2: $x^2 = 4$, and $x = \pm 2$. So, $f(x) = \frac{1}{2}x^2 - 2$ has the same x-intercepts as the function represented in the table. For answer choices B and D, the x^2 coefficient is positive, so the parabola opens upward. Since the y-intercept is 2, which is located above the x-axis, the graph of the function does not cross the x-axis and the function has no x-intercepts. For answer choice C, $f(x) = 2x^2 - 2$, so if $f(x) = 0$, $2x^2 - 2 = 0$ and $2x^2 = 2$. Divide each side by 2: $x^2 = 1$. So, $x = \pm 1$. Alternately, evaluate each function for -2 and 2. If the value of the function is 0, then the function has the same x-intercepts as the function represented in the table.

6. A; **DOK Level:** 2; **Content Topics:** Q.6.c, A.5.e, A.7.d; **Practices:** MP.1.a, MP.1.b, MP.1.e, MP.4.c
A quadratic function whose graph opens upward has a minimum value. A quadratic function whose graph opens downward has a maximum value. Therefore, the quadratic function shown in the graph has a maximum value, but no minimum value. From the graph, the maximum value of the function is 4. The greatest value shown of function represented in the table is 4. Since the value of the function decreases symmetrically as the x-value changes, this is the maximum value of the function. So, the two functions have the same maximum values.

UNIT 3 REVIEW, pp. 84–91

1. A; **DOK Level:** 2; **Content Topics:** Q.2.e, A.1.c, A.1.j; **Practices:** MP.1.a, MP.1.b, MP.2.a, MP.2.c
Total pay for painter = $20 \times h$. Total pay for assistant = $15 \times h$. Since the assistant worked 5 hours more than the painter, this can be represented by $15 \times (h + 5)$. The total charge for labor is represented as $20h + 15(h + 5) = \$355$.

2. D; **DOK Level:** 2; **Content Topics:** Q.2.e, A.1.b, A.1.c, A.1.i; **Practices:** MP.1.a, MP.1.b, MP.2.c, MP.4.a, MP.4.b
$\sqrt{x^2} = \sqrt{36}$, $x = \pm 6$. Substituting the values for x into the second equation gives 22 and -2. Since -2 is not an answer choice, the correct answer is D.

3. C; **DOK Level:** 2; **Content Topics:** Q.2.e, A.1.c, A.1.j, A.2.b; **Practices:** MP.1.a, MP.1.b, MP.2.a, MP.2.c
Use variables to set up the equation. Let w = week, and B = balance. Since the only thing that changes is that $1,244$ is added each week, this is a variable amount. The equation then can be written as: $B = \$1,244w + \$287$.

4. A; **DOK Level:** 2; **Content Topics:** Q.2.e, A.1.c, A.1.j; **Practices:** MP.1.a, MP.1.b, MP.2.a, MP.2.c
Note that each term decreases by 0.5. If x represents the xth term, the equation can be represented by $y = 3 - 0.5x$.

5. B; **DOK Level:** 2; **Content Topics:** Q.2.a, Q.2.e, A.1.b, A.1.c, A.1.j; **Practices:** MP.1.a, MP.1.b, MP.1.c, MP.1.d, MP.2.a, MP.2.c, MP.3.a
Let the number of women taking part in the production be w. Since the number of men taking part is half the number of women plus 5, it can be represented by the following equation: Men $= \frac{1}{2}w + 5$.

6. A; **DOK Level:** 2; **Content Topics:** Q.2.a, Q.2.e, A.2.a; **Practices:** MP.1.a, MP.1.b, MP.1.c, MP.1.d, MP.2.c
Rearrange the equation to solve for x:
$3x + 0.15 = 1.29$
$3x = 1.29 - 0.15$
$3x = 1.14$
$x = 0.38$

7. B; **DOK Level:** 2; **Content Topic:** A.5.b; **Practices:** MP.1.a, MP.1.b, MP.1.e, MP.2.a, MP.2.c
The slope of a line is represented by the change in y-values divided by the change in x-values. To find the slope, we will use the points $(-3, -2)$ and $(3, 2)$.
$m = \frac{(2 - (-2))}{(3 - (-3))}$
$m = \frac{4}{6} = \frac{2}{3}$

8. B; **DOK Level:** 2; **Content Topic:** A.6.b; **Practices:** MP.1.a, MP.1.b, MP.1.e, MP.2.a, MP.2.c
In this case, since the b value (y-intercept) is zero, the equation is $y = \frac{2}{3}x$ (using the slope found in question 7).

9. See graph. DOK Level: 2; **Content Topic:** A.5.a; **Practices:** MP.1.a, MP.1.b, MP.1.d, MP.1.e, MP.2.a, MP.2.c
Reflecting across the y-axis will cause the x-value to change signs. The new location of point K will be $(3, -2)$.

10. C; **DOK Level:** 2; **Content Topic:** A.5.b; **Practices:** MP.1.a, MP.1.b, MP.1.e, MP.2.a, MP.2.c
Line JL has a slope of zero, as there is no change in y-value. Answer choices A and B reflect a negative slope. Answer choice D reflects a positive slope.

11. B; **DOK Level:** 2; **Content Topics:** Q.2.a, Q.2.e, A.1.c; **Practices:** MP.1.a, MP.1.b, MP.1.e, MP.2.a, MP.2.c
Set up an equation to represent the situation. Let $x =$ voters under 25 years. Voters over 25 years $= 2x - 56$. Answer choices A and D include a multiple greater than twice the number of voters under 25 (e.g., $56x$). Answer choice C fails to double the x-value, and subtract 56.

12. C; **DOK Level:** 2; **Content Topic:** Q.2.e; **Practices:** MP.1.a, MP.1.b
Moving the decimal eight spots to the right gives the original value. Option C is the only answer choice that represents this value.

13. C; **DOK Level:** 2; **Content Topics:** Q.2.a, Q.2.e, A.2.a, A.2.b, A.2.c; **Practices:** MP.1.a, MP.1.b, MP.1.c, MP.1.d, MP.2.a, MP.2.c, MP.3.a
Set up an equation to help determine snack cost (T):
$T = \$15 + \$1.25x$
$\$75 = \$15 + 1.25x$
$\$60 = 1.25x$; $x = 48$

14. D; **DOK Level:** 3; **Content Topic:** A.1.c; **Practices:** MP.1.a, MP.1.b, MP.1.c, MP.1.d, MP.2.a, MP.2.c, MP.3.a, MP.4.a
Let the first integer be x, and the second be $x + 1$. The sum of the integers $= x + x + 1 = 2x + 1$.
Product of integers $= x(x + 1) = x^2 + 1x$
The equation can be represented by: $x^2 + 1x = 2x + 1 - 19$; rearranging gives $x^2 - 1x + 18 = 0$.

15. D; **DOK Level:** 1; **Content Topics:** Q.2.a, Q.2.e; **Practices:** MP.1.a, MP.1.b, MP.1.c, MP.2.a
Note than only in answer choice D do the numbers sum to 11. Choices A, B, and C can be eliminated.

16. C; **DOK Level:** 2; **Content Topics:** Q.1.c, Q.2.a, Q.2.e. **Practices:** MP.1.a, MP.2.c, MP.4.a
To compare the diameters, divide the diameter of the bacterium by the diameter of the virus. Remember, to divide powers with the same base, subtract the exponent in the denominator from the exponent in the numerator.
$\frac{1.8 \times 10^{-6}}{2.5 \times 10^{-9}} \approx 0.7 \times 10^3 \approx 7 \times 10^2 \approx 700$
Alternately, write both diameters with the same power of 10 and divide:
$1.8 \times 10^{-6} = 1{,}800 \times 10^{-9}$
$\frac{1{,}800 \times 10^{-9}}{2.5 \times 10^{-9}} \approx 720$, which rounds to the nearest hundred as 700.

17. C; **DOK Level:** 3; **Content Topic:** A.2.d; **Practices:** MP.1.a, MP.2.a, MP.2.c, MP.3.a, MP.4.a, MP.4.b
Set up two simultaneous equations to help solve the problem. Let the number of 5 dollar bills be x, and the number of 1 dollar bills be y. Rearrange, solve for 1 variable, then substitute.
$5x + y = 52$; $x + y = 20$, so $y = 20 - x$
$5x + (20 - x) = 52$
$4x = 32$
$x = 8$

UNIT 3 (continued)

18. B; DOK Level: 1; Content Topic: Q.2.d; Practice: MP.4.b
An expression is undefined when the denominator has a value of zero. Only answer choice B makes the denominator zero [4(0) = 0].

19. A; DOK Level: 1; Content Topics: Q.2.a, Q.2.e; Practices: MP.1.a, MP.1.b, MP.1.c, MP.1.d, MP.2.a, MP.2.c, MP.3.a
Money withdrawn = $64 × 3 = $192.
Since this money was withdrawn, −$192 represents the change in account over 3 days.

20. DOK Level: 2; Content Topic: A.5.e; Practices: MP.1.e, MP.4.c
The curve crosses the x-axis when $y = 0$. Substituting, and factoring the expression in x gives $(x + 4)(x − 2) = 0$. The solutions are $x = −4$ and $x = 2$, so points $(−4, 0)$ and $(2, 0)$ are the x-intercepts. The curve crosses the y-axis when $x = 0$. The y-intercept is the constant term from the equation, so point $(0, −8)$ is the y-intercept. The minimum occurs at $x = -\frac{b}{2a}$, where $b = 2$ and $a = 1$. That gives an x-value of $-\frac{2}{2} = −1$. The y-value at $x = −1$ is $(−1)^2 + 2(−1) − 8 = −9$, so the point $(−1, −9)$ is the vertex. Plot the x-intercepts, y-intercept, and vertex. If needed, make a table of points using other x-values. Draw the graph.

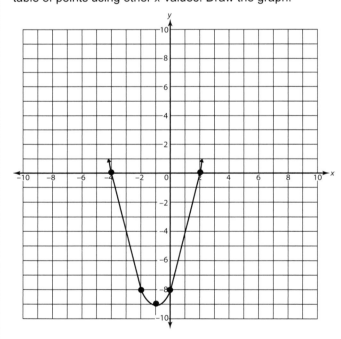

21. D; DOK Level: 2; Content Topics: Q.2.a, Q.2.e; Practices: MP.1.a, MP.1.b, MP.1.c, MP.1.d, MP.2.a, MP.2.c, MP.3.a
If we assume down is negative and up is positive, his position can be represented by the equation P below:
$P = 786 − 137 + 542 = 1{,}191$ ft. His position is 1,191 ft higher than where he began on the first chair lift.

22. A; DOK Level: 2; Content Topic: A.3.b; Practices: MP.1.a, MP.1.b, MP.1.c, MP.2.a, MP.2.c, MP.3.a
The value 1, as well as values greater than 1, is highlighted on the number line. It describes the inequality x as being greater than or equal to 1.

23. C; DOK Level: 2; Content Topics: A.2.a, A.2.b, A.2.c; Practices: MP.1.a, MP.1.b, MP.1.c, MP.2.a, MP.2.c, MP.3.a
Let the cost for an adult be x. Since the cost for a child is $30, less than half the adult price, it can be represented by:
$C = \frac{x}{2} − \$30$
Cost of 3 children = $3\left[\frac{230}{2} − 30\right]$
Cost of 3 children = $3 × 85 = \$255$.

24. C; DOK Level: 2; Content Topics: Q.2.b, Q.4.a; Practices: MP.1.a, MP.1.b, MP.1.c, MP.1.d, MP.2.a, MP.2.c, MP.3.a
Take the square root of 4 to find each side of the square. Multiply the length of one side by 4 to get a perimeter of 16 feet.

25. A; DOK Level: 2; Content Topics: Q.2.a, A.3.a; Practices: MP.1.a, MP.1.b, MP.1.e, MP.2.a, MP.4.b
To identify the value of x that is a solution of the inequality, solve the inequality. Begin by multiplying to eliminate the parentheses: $2 − 2x < 8$. Subtract 2 from each side and group like terms: $−2x < 6$. Divide each side by −2, and change the direction of the inequality: $x > −3$. Only choice A, −2, is greater than −3.

26. D; DOK Level: 2; Content Topics: Q.2.a, A.1.b; Practices: MP.1.a, MP.1.b, MP.1.c, MP.2.a, MP.2.c, MP.3.a, MP.4.a, MP.4.b
Set the equation to zero and solve for x. $f(x)$ has a value of zero when $x = 2$. Whole number values of x higher than 2 yield positive whole number y-values. Answer choice D is the only value of x higher than 2, so all other choices may be eliminated.

27. A; DOK Level: 3; Content Topics: Q.2.a, A.1.f, A.1.j, A.4.a; Practices: MP.1.a, MP.1.b, MP.1.c, MP.1.d, MP.2.a, MP.2.c, MP.3.a, MP.4.a, MP.4.b
The following equation may be solved using the quadratic formula, or by factoring.
$2x^2 + 18x + 36 = 0$
$(2x^2 + 12x) + (6x + 36) = 0$
$2x(x + 6) + 6(x + 6) = 0$
Only answer choice A reflects an equation equivalent to that of the original one. All other answer choices may be eliminated.

28. A; DOK Level: 2; Content Topic: A.3.a; Practices: MP.1.a, MP.1.b, MP.1.c, MP.2.a, MP.2.c, MP.3.a
Let the unknown number be x. The inequality can be represented by:
$x + 20 \geq 5x + 3$
Choice B uses an incorrect integer sign. Choice C uses an incorrect inequality sign. Choice D has incorrect values on the left side of the inequality.

29. See graph. DOK Level: 2; **Content Topic:** A.5.a;
Practices: MP.1.a, MP.1.b, MP.1.e, MP.2.a, MP.2.c.
In a rectangle, the lengths have equal measure, and the widths have equal measure. In this case, the rectangle is a square). The distance between *J* and *K* measures 4 units, the distance between *L* and the missing corner also measures 4 units. On the grid, only the point (2, 1) represents this value.

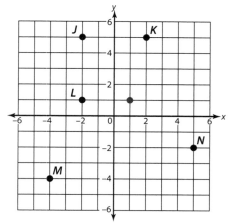

30. C; DOK Level: 2; **Content Topics:** Q.2.a, Q.2.e, Q.6.c, A.1.c, A.1.j, A.5.b; **Practices:** MP.1.a, MP.1.b, MP.1.d, MP.1.e, MP.2.a, MP.2.c
To calculate the slope, we will use the values for point *L* (−2, 1), and point *K* (2, 5). To find the slope, use the formula
$\frac{y_2 - y_1}{x_2 - x_1} = \frac{5 - 1}{2 - (-2)} = \frac{4}{4}$ = Slope of 1.
Next, plug the value for slope and the *y*-intercept of 3 (deduced from the point at which the line that passes through *L* and *K* crosses the *y*-axis) into the formula for slope: $y = mx + b$. As a result, $y = 1x + 3$.

31. C; DOK Level: 2; **Content Topics:** Q.2.a, Q.2.e, Q.6.c, A.1.c, A.1.j, A.5.b; **Practices:** MP.1.a, MP.1.b, MP.1.d, MP.1.e, MP.2.a, MP.2.c

The line that passes through points *L* and *K* has a slope of $\frac{4}{4}$ = 1 (from question 30). So, the line has the equation $y = x + b$. To find *b*, substitute the coordinates of point *K* (2, 5) for (*x*, *y*) and solve for *b*: $5 = 2 + b$, so $b = 3$. Therefore, the equation of the line is $y = x + 3$. To find the *y*-value when $x = 5$, substitute 5 for *x* and solve for *y*: $y = 5 + 3 = 8$.

32. D; DOK Level: 3; **Content Topics:** Q.2.a, Q.2.e, Q.5.a, A.4.a; **Practices:** MP.1.a, MP.1.b, MP.1.c, MP.1.d, MP.2.a, MP.2.c, MP.3.a, MP.4.a, MP.4.b
The ball hits the ground at $h = 0$. Set the equation equal to zero and solve the quadratic equation. $2t^2 - 3t + 1.125 = 0$. The quadratic formula can be used to solve this problem.
$a = 2$, $b = -3$, $c = 1.125$
$t = \frac{-b \pm \sqrt{b^2 - 4ac}}{2a}$
$t = \frac{[3 \pm \sqrt{(9 - 9)}]}{4}$
$t = \frac{3}{4}$

33. A; DOK Level: 2; **Content Topics:** Q.2.a, Q.2.e, A.1.c, A.1.j; **Practices:** MP.1.a, MP.1.b, MP.1.c, MP.2.a, MP.2.c, MP.3.a
Let the weight of the newborn calf be *n*. Then, the weight of the mother (*M*) can be represented by $M = (n \times 4) + 200$, or $4n + 200$.

34. D; DOK Level: 2; **Content Topics:** Q.2.a, Q.2.e, A.2.a, A.2.b, A.2.c; **Practices:** MP.1.a, MP.1.b, MP.1.c, MP.1.d, MP.2.a, MP.2.c, MP.3.a
Working backward is one strategy to use to find the cost per light before tax. The cost excluding tax = $100 − 4.25 = 95.75$, which represents the cost for 10 lights. Divide this value by 10 to find the cost of one light ($9.58).

35. B; DOK Level: 2; **Content Topics:** Q.2.a, Q.2.e; **Practice:** MP.4.a
Moving the decimal eight spots to the right gives the original value. Option B is the only answer choice that represents this value.

36. D; DOK Level: 2; **Content Topics:** Q.2.a, Q.2.e; **Practices:** MP.1.a, MP.1.b, MP.1.c, MP.2.a, MP.2.c, MP.3.a
Recall that $2(8^4) = 2(8 \times 8 \times 8 \times 8) = 2(4{,}096) = 8{,}192$.

37. D; DOK Level: 3; **Content Topics:** Q.2.a, Q.2.e, A.1.b, A.1.c, A.1.j, A.3.a, A.3.b; **Practices:** MP.1.a, MP.1.b, MP.1.c, MP.1.d, MP.2.a, MP.2.c, MP.3.a
Let *x* represent the packs of tokens bought. The total tokens bought plus the fair ticket must be less than or equal to $100. Only answer choice D ($15x + 20 \le 100$) represents this inequality.

38. B; DOK Level: 2; **Content Topics:** A.3.a, A.3.b; **Practices:** MP.1.a, MP.1.b, MP.1.c, MP.1.d, MP.2.a, MP.2.c, MP.3.a, MP.4.a
Set up an inequality. Let *x* represent the packs of tickets bought:
$15x + 20 \le 100$
$15x \le 100 - 20$
$15x \le 80$
$x \le 5.3$, which, since you cannot buy part of a pack, rounds downward to 5.

39. D; DOK Level: 2; **Content Topics:** A.1.b, A.1.c, A.1.j; **Practices:** MP.1.a, MP.1.b, MP.1.c, MP.1.d, MP.2.a, MP.2.c, MP.3.a
Let *x* represent each day. The equation can be represented as *Balance* = $2{,}000 - 20x$. After 3 days, his balance would be $1,940.

40. B; DOK Level: 1; **Content Topic:** A.5.a; **Practices:** MP.1.a, MP.1.b, MP.1.c, MP.2.a, MP.2.c, MP.3.a
Write the *x*-value (−4) first and the *y*-value (4) second. Answer choices A, C, and D all have incorrect *x*-values.

Answer Key

UNIT 3 *(continued)*

41. B; DOK Level: 2; Content Topic: A.6.b; Practices: MP.1.a, MP.1.b, MP.1.c, MP.1.d, MP.2.a, MP.2.c, MP.3.a
Note that since this is a completely horizontal line, the slope is zero. The line crosses the y-axis at $(0, 2)$, so the b-value is 2. Equation of a line is written as

$$y = mx + b.$$
$$y = 0x + 2$$
$$y = 2$$

Answer choices A and D may be eliminated as they are not written in this form. Answer choice C disregards the fact that the slope is zero.

42. A; DOK Level: 2; Content Topic: A.6.b; Practices: MP.1.a, MP.1.b, MP.1.c, MP.2.a, MP.2.c, MP.3.a
Note that, since this is a completely horizontal line, the slope is zero. The line will cross the y-axis at $(0, 4)$, so the b-value is 4. Equation of line would be $y = 4$.

43. D; DOK Level: 2; Content Topic: A.7.d; Practices: MP.1.a, MP.1.b, MP.1.d, MP.2.c, MP.4.b

To determine the slope of line Q, use the formula $\dfrac{y_2 - y_1}{x_2 - x_1}$, and plug in values from points on line Q. Both $(-4, 4)$ and $(-2, 1)$ are points on line Q, so insert those into the formula:

$$\frac{1 - 4}{-2 - (-4)} = -\frac{3}{2}.$$
$$m = -\frac{3}{2}$$

The slope of a line in $Ax + By = C$ format is $-\dfrac{A}{B}$. For choice D, A = 3 and B = 2, so $-\dfrac{A}{B} = -\dfrac{3}{2}$

44. 2; DOK Level: 2; Content Topic: A.5.b; Practices: MP.4.c
The slope of a line given in slope-intercept form is the x-coefficient of the equation. So, the slope of the line $y = 2x + 3$ is 2.

45. −1.5; DOK Level: 2; Content Topics: Q.2.a, Q.2.e; Practices: MP.1.a, MP.1.b, MP.1.c, MP.1.d, MP.2.a, MP.2.c, MP.3.a
This value can be found by examining the graph or by setting the y-value equal to 0:

$$0 = 2x + 3$$
$$2x = -3$$
$$x = -1.5$$

46. 3; DOK Level: 2; Content Topics: Q.2.a, Q.2.e; Practices: MP.1.a, MP.1.b, MP.1.c, MP.1.d, MP.2.a, MP.2.c, MP.3.a
This value can be found by examining the graph or by setting the x-value equal to zero:

$$y = 2(0) + 3$$
$$y = 3$$

47. D; DOK Level: 2; Content Topic: Q.2.a; Practices: MP.1.a, MP.1.b, MP.1.c, MP.2.a, MP.2.c, MP.3.a
This value can be found by plugging the value $x = 30$ into the equation of the line, so that:

$$y = 2(30) + 3$$
$$y = 63$$

48. C; DOK Level: 2; Content Topics: Q.2.a, A.1.b; Practices: MP.1.a, MP.1.b, MP.1.c, MP.1.d, MP.2.a, MP.2.c, MP.3.a
This value can be found by plugging the value $y = 30$ in the equation of the line, so that:

$$30 = 2(x) + 3$$
$$x = \frac{30 - 3}{2}$$
$$x = 13.5$$

49. DOK Level: 2; Content Topic: A.5.a; Practices: MP.1.a, MP.1.b, MP.1.c, MP.2.a, MP.2.c, MP.3.a
Time elapsed is to be plotted on the x-axis, and height of the plant on the y-axis.

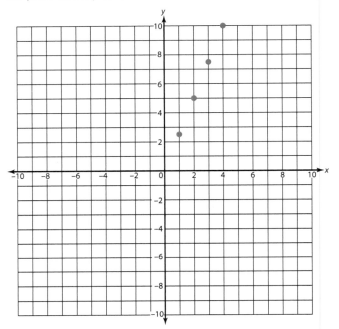

50. A; DOK Level: 2; Content Topic: A.6.b; Practices: MP.1.a, MP.1.b, MP.1.c, MP.2.a, MP.2.c, MP.3.a
We will use the first and last data entries to calculate the slope values Point *1* (1, 2.5), Point *2* (4, 10).

$$m = \frac{10 - 2.5}{4 - 1} = \frac{7.5}{3} = 2.5$$

By choosing a point on the line, such as (2,5), you can use the following formula:

$$y = mx + b$$
$$5 = 2.5(2) + b$$
$$5 = 5 + b$$
$$0 = b$$

Since the b-value is 0, and the equation of the line can be represented by $y = 2.5x$. Other choices do not represent the equation of the line.

51. C; DOK Level: 2; Content Topics: Q.2.a, Q.2.e, A.1.b, A.1.c, A.1.j; Practices: MP.1.a, MP.1.b, MP.1.c, MP.1.d, MP.2.c
Plug the value $x = 24$ in the equation of the line, so that $y = 2.5(24) = 60$ cm. After 24 hours, the plant will be 60 cm high.

52. B; DOK Level: 2; Content Topics: A.2.a, A.2.c; **Practices:** MP.1.a, MP.1.b, MP.1.c, MP.1.d, MP.2.c
Rearrange the equation to solve for x:
$10x + 3.15 = 58.15$
$\quad 10x = 58.15 - 3.15$
$\quad 10x = 55$
$\quad\quad x = 5.5$

53. C; DOK Level: 2; Content Topics: A.2.b, A.2.c; **Practices:** MP.1.a, MP.1.b, MP.1.c, MP.1.d, MP.2.a, MP.2.c, MP.3.a
Let x represent the price of each T-shirt. The total cost of the eight T-shirts is $8x$. After the coupon, the T-shirts cost $50, so $8x - 10 = 50$. To solve the equation, begin by adding 10 to each side: $8x = 60$. Divide each side by 8: $x = 7.50$. Choice A is the result of adding $20 to the price paid instead of $10. Choice B is the number of T-shirts. Choice D is the result of subtracting $10 from the price paid instead of adding.

54. A; DOK Level: 2; Content Topics: Q.2.a, Q.2.e, A.2.a; **Practices:** MP.1.a, MP.1.b, MP.1.c, MP.1.d, MP.2.c
To solve the equation, begin by multiplying to eliminate the parentheses: $2y - 8 = 4 - 3y$. Add $3y$ to both sides and group like terms: $5y - 8 = 4$. Add 8 to each side and group like terms: $5y = 12$. Divide each side by 5: $y = 2.4$.

55. C; DOK Level: 3; Content Topics: A.2.a, A.2.b, A.2.c; **Practices:** MP.1.a, MP.1.b, MP.1.c, MP.1.d, MP.2.c, MP.4.a, MP.4.b
Let x represent each set of 30 pages produced, and set up an equation for the total cost (T) on each printing press. First printing press: $T = 1.5x + 50$. Second printing press: $T = 2x + 10$. To find the quantity of pages for which both costs will be the same, set the equations equal to each other, and solve for x.
$1.5x + 50 = 2x + 10$
$-0.5x + 50 = 10$
$-0.5x = -40$
$x = 80$
Since x represents a set of 30 pages, multiply by 30 to get the total number of pages.
$30 \times 80 = 2{,}400$ pages

56. D; DOK Level: 2; Content Topics: Q.2.a, Q.2.e, A.1.b, A.1.c, A.1.j; **Practices:** MP.1.a, MP.1.b, MP.1.c, MP.1.d, MP.2.c, MP.4.a, MP.4.b
Plug the value $x = 80$ into either of the equations used in problem 55 to determine the total daily cost (T) for 80 sets of 30 pages.
$T = 1.5(80) + 50 = 170$ or $T = 2(80) + 10 = 170$.

57. A; DOK Level: 2; Content Topics: Q.2.a, Q.2.e, A.2.d; **Practices:** MP.1.a, MP.1.b, MP.1.c, MP.1.d, MP.2.c
Solve for one variable and then substitute it back into the other equation.
Solve for variable: $a = 10 - b$
Substitute value into the second equation:
$3(10 - b) - 4b = 9$
$30 - 3b - 4b = 9$
$30 - 7b = 9$
$-7b = -21$
$b = 3$

58. B; DOK Level: 3; Content Topic: A.2.d; **Practices:** MP.1.a, MP.1.b, MP.1.c, MP.1.d, MP.2.c
Substitute the value $b = 3$ (from question 57) into the first equation to solve for a.
$a + 3 = 10$, $a = 7$. Only answer choice B gives the value 7. Answer choice A is equal to 2. Answer choice C is equal to 9. Answer choice D is equal to 11.

59. A; DOK Level: 2; Content Topics: A.2.c, A.1.j; **Practices:** MP.1.a, MP.1.b, MP.1.c, MP.1.d, MP.2.c
Set up an equation to represent the situation. Let adult tickets be a, and children's tickets be c.
$a + c = 175$, so $c = 175 - a$

60. C; DOK Level: 2; Content Topics: Q.2.c, A.1.h; **Practices:** MP.1.a, MP.2.c, MP.4.a
The cube root of -27 is -3, because $(-3)^3 = -27$. Simplify each of the answer choices to determine whether it is equal to -3. Choice C is equal to $\frac{3}{-1}$, or -3, so choice C is correct. Since the square of a negative number is positive, choice A is equal to $1 \cdot \sqrt{9}$, or 3. Choice B is equal to $\frac{81}{3}$, or 27. Choice D is equal to the cube of -27.

61. A; DOK Level: 2; Content Topics: A.2.c, A.2.d; **Practices:** MP.1.a, MP.1.b, MP.2.c, MP.4.b.
Let x be the number. One-eight of the number is $\frac{x}{8}$. One-fourth of the number is $\frac{x}{4}$. Two more than one-fourth of the number is $\frac{x}{4} + 2$. So, $\frac{x}{8} = \frac{x}{4} + 2$. Multiply each term by 8 to eliminate the fractions: $x = 2x + 16$. Subtract $2x$ from each side and group like terms: $-x = 16$. So, $x = -16$.

62. D; DOK Level: 2; Content Topic: A.1.h; **Practices:** MP.1.a, MP.1.b, MP.1.c, MP.1.d, MP.2.c
$8^2 + 4^0 = 64 + 1 = 65$

63. A; DOK Level: 2; Content Topics: Q.2.b; **Practices:** MP.1.a, MP.1.b, MP.1.c, MP.1.d, MP.2.c.
Take the square root of the number to find the original number. So, $\sqrt{30} \approx 5.5$.

64. B; DOK Level: 2; Content Topics: A.1.b, A.1.j; **Practices:** MP.1.a, MP.1.b, MP.1.c, MP.1.d, MP.2.c
Put the value into the equation for $f(x)$ and solve for x:
$2x - 3 = 4$
$2x = 7$
$x = 3.5$

65. C; DOK Level: 3; Content Topics: A.1.b, A.1.j; **Practices:** MP.1.a, MP.1.b, MP.1.c, MP.1.d, MP.2.c
Solve for x so that $4x^2 = 121$. Divide both sides of the equation by 4 so that $x^2 = 30.25$ and $x \approx 5.5$.

66. C; DOK Level: 3; Content Topic: Q.5.a; **Practices:** MP.1.a, MP.1.b, MP.1.c, MP.2.c
Take the cube root of 6,859 to find the length of each side. $l = 19$ feet. Surface of each face = $19 \times 19 = 361$ square feet. Since a cube has six faces, the surface area is 6×361 square feet = 2,166 square feet.

67. D; DOK Level: 2; Content Topic: Q.2.d; **Practices:** MP.1.a, MP.1.b, MP.1.c, MP.1.d, MP.2.a, MP.2.c, MP.3.a
In an undefined expression, the denominator is equal to zero. Only answer choice D has an undefined denominator: $2(6) - 12 = 0$.

UNIT 3 *(continued)*

68. See graph. DOK Level: 2; **Content Topic:** A.5.a;
Practices: MP.1.d, MP.1.e
When a point is reflected across the *y*-axis, the sign of
its *x*-coordinate changes. To graph the reflected figure,
determine the coordinates of its vertices:
A (−2, 1) → (2, 1); B (−4, 1) → (4, 1);
C (−3, −2) → (3, −2).

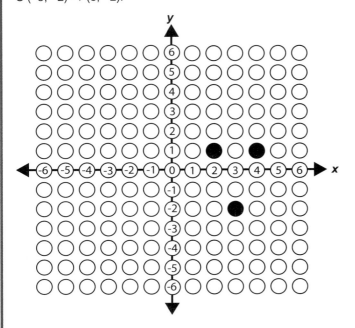

69. A; DOK Level: 2; **Content Topics:** Q.2.a, Q.2.e;
Practices: MP.1.a, MP.1.b, MP.1.c, MP.1.d, MP.2.a, MP.2.c,
MP.3.a
Note that each term decreases by 5, so the next term will
be 80. Answer choices B, C, and D represent terms in the
pattern, but not the next term.

70. D; DOK Level: 2; **Content Topics:** Q.2.a, Q.2.e, A.2.c;
Practices: MP.1.a, MP.1.b, MP.1.c, MP.1.d, MP.2.a, MP.2.c,
MP.3.a
The value 100 represents the starting point from which
multiples of 5 are subtracted each time. In the equation of
a line, 100 represents the *b* value, and *x* represents the
multiples of 5 being subtracted each time. This can be
represented in the equation as $y = 100 − 5x$.

71. B; DOK Level: 2; **Content Topics:** Q.2.a, Q.2.e, A.1.f;
Practices: MP.1.a, MP.1.b, MP.1.c, MP.1.d, MP.2.a, MP.2.c,
MP.3.a
To determine an expression equivalent to $(3x − 2y)(3x + 2y)$,
use the FOIL method, in which you multiply the *first*, then
outer, then *inner*, and finally *last* terms, so that you get
$9x^2 + 6xy − 6xy − 4y^2$. The $6xy$ terms cancel one another
out, leaving $9x^2 − 4y^2$ as the correct answer.

UNIT 4 GEOMETRY

LESSON 1, *pp. 94–95*
1. D; DOK Level: 1; **Content Topics:** Q.2.a, Q.4.a, Q.4.c;
Practices: MP.1.a, MP.1.e
To find the area of a square, multiply the side length by itself
or square the side length: $A = 12 × 12 = 12^2 = 144$ in². To
find the perimeter of a square, add the side length to itself
4 times or multiply the side length by 4: $P = 4 × 12 = 48$ in².
Answer choice A results from multiplying the side length
by 2 for the area and by 4 for the perimeter. Answer choice
B results from multiplying the side length by 4 for the area
and by 2 for the perimeter. Answer choice C results from
confusing the formulas for area and perimeter.

2. D; DOK Level: 1; **Content Topics:** Q.2.a, Q.4.a, Q.4.c;
Practices: MP.1.a, MP.1.e
To find the area of a rectangle, multiply the length by the
width: $A = 20 × 9 = 180$ cm². Answer choice A is the result
of adding the dimensions. Answer choice B is the perimeter
of the rectangle. Answer choice C is one-half the product of
the length and width.

3. B; DOK Level: 1; **Content Topics:** Q.2.a, Q.4.a, Q.4.c;
Practices: MP.1.a, MP.1.e
To find the perimeter of a rectangle, add the side lengths
or use a formula: $P = 2(l + w) = 2(20 + 9) = 2(29) = 58$ cm.
Answer choice A is the result of adding the dimensions
without doubling the sum. Answer choice C is one-half the
product of the length and width. Answer choice D is the
area of the rectangle.

4. A; DOK Level: 1; **Content Topics:** Q.2.a, Q.4.a, Q.4.c;
Practices: MP.1.a, MP.1.e
To find the area of a triangle, use the formula $A = \frac{1}{2} bh$,
where the base and height are perpendicular to each other.
The base of the triangle is 24 inches. The height of the
triangle is 5 inches. So, $A = \frac{1}{2} (24)(5) = 60$ in². Answer
choice B is the result of multiplying 13 × 5. Answer choice C
is the result of failing to multiply the product of the base and
the height by $\frac{1}{2}$. Answer choice D is the result of using
13 inches. as the height, rather than 5 inches.

5. C; DOK Level: 1; **Content Topics:** Q.2.a, Q.4.a, Q.4.c;
Practices: MP.1.a, MP.1.e
To find the perimeter of a triangle, add the side lengths
together: $P = 13 + 13 + 24 = 50$ inches. Answer choice A is
the sum of the base and the height. Answer choice B is the
result of failing to add 13 inches twice. Answer choice D is
the result of including the height of the triangle in the sum of
its side lengths.

6. B; DOK Level: 1; **Content Topics:** Q.2.a, Q.4.a, Q.4.c;
Practices: MP.1.a, MP.1.e
The perimeter of a parallelogram is the sum of its side
lengths. Since a parallelogram has two pairs of congruent
sides, the perimeter can also be found by using a formula:
$P = 2(18 + 12.5) = 2(30.5) = 61$ m. Answer choice A is the
result of simply adding the dimensions in the figure. Answer
choice C is the result of taking half of the product of the side
lengths. Answer choice D is the product of the side lengths.

7. **A**; **DOK Level:** 2; **Content Topics:** Q.2.a, Q.2.e, Q.4.a, Q.4.c, A.2.a, A.2.b; **Practices:** MP.1.a, MP.1.b, MP.1.e, MP.2.a, MP.4.b
The area of a parallelogram is given by the formula $A = bh$. Substitute 450 for A and 18 for b, then solve for h: $450 = 18h$. Divide both sides of the equation by 18: $h = 25$.

8. **B**; **DOK Level:** 2; **Content Topics:** Q.2.a, Q.2.e, Q.4.a, Q.4.c, A.2.a, A.2.b; **Practices:** MP.1.a, MP.1.b, MP.1.e, MP.2.a, MP.4.b
The area of a triangle is given by the formula $A = \frac{1}{2} bh$. Substitute 20 for A and 4 for b: $20 = \frac{1}{2} (4)h$. Multiply: $20 = 2h$. Divide both sides by 2: $h = 10$ inches.

9. **B**; **DOK Level:** 2; **Content Topics:** Q.2.a, Q.4.a, Q.4.c; **Practices:** MP.1.a, MP.1.b, MP.1.e
The area of a square is given by $A = s^2$. The perimeter of a square is given by $P = 4s$. Find the answer choice for which $A = P$. For answer choice A, $A = 2^2 = 4$ and $P = 4(2) = 8$. For answer choice B, $A = 4^2 = 16$ and $P = 4(4) = 16$. For answer choice C, $A = 8^2 = 64$ and $P = 4(8) = 32$. Answer choice D is the perimeter and area of the square that is described in the problem, not the side length.

10. **C**; **DOK Level:** 2; **Content Topics:** Q.2.a, Q.2.e, Q.4.a, Q.4.c, A.2.a, A.2.b; **Practices:** MP.1.a, MP.1.b, MP.1.e, MP.4.b
The perimeter of a rectangle is given by the formula $P = 2l + 2w$. Since Leon has 60 feet of fencing, the garden will have a perimeter of 60 feet. Substitute 60 for P and 12 for w and solve for l: $60 = 2l + 2(12)$. Multiply: $60 = 2l + 24$. Subtract 24 from each side: $36 = 2l$. Divide both sides by 2: $l = 18$ feet.

LESSON 2, pp. 96–97

1. **C**; **DOK Level:** 2; **Content Topics:** Q.2.b, Q.4.e; **Practices:** MP.1.a, MP.2.b, MP.4.b
Solve $10^2 - 5^2 = b^2$ to find that $100 - 25 = b^2$, $b^2 = 75$, and $b \approx 8.7$ (choice C). If a student selected option A, he or she simply found the difference of the lengths given. If a student selected option D, he or she added the squared side lengths ($100 + 25 = 125$, then taking the square root of 125) instead of subtracting.

2. **D**; **DOK Level:** 2; **Content Topics:** Q.2.b, Q.4.e; **Practices:** MP.1.a, MP.2.b, MP.4.b
Solve $a^2 + b^2 = c^2$ to find the hypotenuse so that $15^2 + 30^2 = c^2$. From there, $225 + 900 = c^2$, so $c^2 = 1{,}125$ and $c \approx 33.5$.

3. **B**; **DOK Level:** 2; **Content Topics:** Q.2.b, Q.4.e; **Practices:** MP.1.a, MP.2.b, MP.4.b
Solve $a^2 + b^2 = c^2$ so that $a^2 + 30^2 = 35^2$ and $a^2 + 900 = 1{,}225$. Subtract 900 from each side so that $a^2 = 325$ and $a \approx 18$ feet.

4. **C**; **DOK Level:** 3; **Content Topics:** Q.2.b, Q.4.e; **Practices:** MP.1.a, MP.2.b, MP.3.a, MP.4.b
Solve $a^2 + b^2 = c^2$ so that $15^2 + 32^2 = c^2 = 225 + 1{,}024 = 1{,}249$. The square root of 1,249 gives 35.3 feet and $35.3 - 33.5 = 1.8$. Since 33.5 is approximate, the cable is now about 1.8 inches longer.

5. **C**; **DOK Level:** 2; **Content Topics:** Q.2.b, Q.4.e; **Practices:** MP.1.a, MP.2.b, MP.4.b
Solve $a^2 + b^2 = c^2$ so that $40^2 + 120^2 = c^2$ for c to find that $c^2 = 16{,}000$. As a result, $c \approx 126.49$ m, which rounds to 126 m.

6. **A**; **DOK Level:** 2; **Content Topics:** Q.2.b, Q.4.e; **Practices:** MP.1.a, MP.2.b, MP.3.a, MP.4.b
Solve $a^2 + b^2 = c^2$ so that $20^2 + 120^2 = c^2$ for c to find that $c^2 = 14{,}800$. As a result, $c \approx 121.65$ m, which rounds to 122 m.

7. **D**; **DOK Level:** 2; **Content Topics:** Q.2.b, Q.4.e; **Practices:** MP.1.a, MP.2.b, MP.4.b
Plot the points on a grid; the distance between the points represents the hypotenuse; $d = \sqrt{(4 - (-4))^2 + (3 - 5)^2} = \sqrt{64 + 4} = \sqrt{68} \approx 8.246$, which rounds to 8.2.

LESSON 3, pp. 98–99

1. **C**; **DOK Level:** 1; **Content Topics:** Q.2.a, Q.4.c; **Practices:** MP.1.a, MP.1.e, MP.4.a
A regular hexagon has 6 congruent sides, so $P = 6s$. The side length is 5 inches, so $P = (6)(5) = 30$ inches. Answer choice A is the result of adding the number of sides to the side length. Answer choice B is the result of calculating the perimeter of a five-sided figure. Answer choice D is the result of calculating the perimeter of a figure with a side length of 6 inches.

2. **B**; **DOK Level:** 1; **Content Topics:** Q.2.a, Q.4.c; **Practices:** MP.1.a, MP.1.e, MP.4.a
A regular pentagon has all congruent sides. A pentagon has five sides, so the perimeter of a pentagon is $5s$. Multiply: $5 \times 9.6 = 48$. Answer choice A is the result of finding the perimeter of a four-sided figure. Answer choice C is the result of a computation error. Answer choice D is the result of finding the perimeter of a six-sided figure.

3. **C**; **DOK Level:** 1; **Content Topics:** Q.2.a, Q.2.e, Q.4.c; **Practices:** MP.1.a, MP.1.e, MP.4.a
The perimeter of the frame for the stained-glass window is the perimeter of a regular octagon with a side length of 12 inches. Multiply the number of sides in an octagon by the length of each side: $8 \times 12 = 96$ inches. Answer choice A is the result of adding $8 + 12$. Answer choice B is the result of finding the perimeter of a six-sided figure. Answer choice D is the result of finding the perimeter of a nine-sided figure.

4. **A**; **DOK Level:** 2; **Content Topic:** Q.4.c; **Practices:** MP.1.a, MP.1.b, MP.1.e, MP.3.b
For the perimeter of a figure to be equal to the side length multiplied by the number of sides, all of the side lengths of the figure must be the same; that is, the sides must be congruent. Although a regular polygon has congruent angles as well as congruent sides, congruent angles are unnecessary for perimeter to be equal to the product of the number of sides and the side length. For example, a rhombus is a figure whose sides are congruent but whose angles are not.

5. **C**; **DOK Level:** 1; **Content Topics:** Q.2.a, Q.4.c; **Practices:** MP.1.a, MP.1.e, MP.4.a
The perimeter of an irregular polygon is the sum of its side lengths. Add: $7 + 7 + 4 + 4 + 7 + 7 = 36$ cm. Answer choice A is the result of adding $4 + 7 + 7$. Answer choice B is the result of failing to include the side lengths that measure 4 cm. Answer choice D is the result of including an extra side with length 4 cm.

Answer Key

UNIT 4 (continued)

6. C; DOK Level: 1; Content Topics: Q.2.a, Q.4.c;
Practices: MP.1.a, MP.1.e, MP.4.a
The perimeter of the irregular polygon is the sum of its side lengths. Add: 12 + 9 + 8 + 7 + 9 = 45 ft. Answer choice A is the result of failing to include one of the sides that measures 9 feet. Answer choice B is the result of failing to include the side that measures 7 feet. Answer choice D is the result of including three sides that measure 9 feet.

7. C; DOK Level: 1; Content Topics: Q.2.a, Q.4.c;
Practices: MP.1.a, MP.1.e, MP.4.a
A trapezoid is an irregular quadrilateral, so the perimeter of the trapezoid is the sum of its side lengths. Add: 18 + 5 + 19.5 + 3.5 = 46 inches. Answer choice A is the result of multiplying 3.5 × 4. Answer choice B is the result of multiplying 5 × 4. Answer choice D is the result of multiplying 18 × 4.

8. B; DOK Level: 2; Content Topics: Q.2.a, Q.4.c;
Practices: MP.1.a, MP.1.e, MP.2.c, MP.3.a, MP.4.a
The perimeter of a regular polygon is the product of its side length and number of sides. The number of sides must be a whole number, so divide the perimeter by each answer choice to determine which could be the side length of the polygon. For answer choice A, if the side length is 7 feet, then the number of sides is 39 ÷ 7 ≈ 5.6, so the side length could not be 7 feet. For answer choice B, if the side length is 6.5 feet, then the number of sides is 39 ÷ 6.5 = 6, so the side length could be 6.5 feet. For answer choice C, if the side length is 5.5 feet, then the number of sides is 39 ÷ 5.5 ≈ 7.1, so the side length could not be 5.5 feet. For answer choice D, if the side length is 4 feet, then the number of sides is 39 ÷ 4 = 9.75, so the side length could not be 4 feet.

9. C; DOK Level: 2; Content Topics: Q.2.a, Q.4.c;
Practices: MP.1.a, MP.1.e, MP.2.c, MP.4.a
The perimeter of an irregular polygon is the sum of its side lengths. To find an unknown side length, subtract the known side lengths from the perimeter: 40 − (9 + 11 + 5 + 7) = 40 − 32 = 8. Other answer choices are the results of computation errors.

LESSON 4, pp. 100–101
1. C; DOK Level: 2; Content Topics: Q.2.a, Q.2.e, Q.4.b;
Practices: MP.1.a, MP.1.b, MP.1.e, MP.2.c, MP.4.a
The circumference of a circle is equal to πd. The diameter of the pool is 25 meters. Since the diameter of the fence is twice the diameter of the pool, the diameter of the fence is 2 × 25 = 50 meters. Substitute 50 for d and calculate the circumference: 50 × 3.14 = 157 meters. Answer choice A is the diameter of the fenced area. Answer choice B is the circumference of the pool. Answer choice D is the circumference of a circle with diameter 250.

2. D; DOK Level: 2; Content Topics: Q.2.a, Q.4.b;
Practices: MP.1.a, MP.1.b, MP.1.e, MP.2.c, MP.4.a
The area of a circle is equal to πr^2. The radius of the larger circle is 7 inches, so the area of the larger circle is 3.14 x 7² = 153.86 in². Answer choice A is the circumference of the smaller circle. Answer choice B is the area of the smaller circle. Answer choice C is the difference between the area of the larger circle and the circumference of the smaller circle.

3. C; DOK Level: 2; Content Topics: Q.2.a, Q.2.e, Q.4.a;
Practices: MP.1.a, MP.1.b, MP.1.e, MP.2.c, MP.4.a
The area of a circle is equal to πr^2. Since the diameter of the sun is 15 cm, the radius is 15 ÷ 2 = 7.5 cm. Substitute 7.5 for r and calculate the area: 3.14 × 7.5² = 176.63, which rounds to 177 cm.

4. B; DOK Level: 1; Content Topics: Q,2.a, Q.4.a;
Practices: MP.1.a, MP.1.b, MP.1.e, MP.2.c, MP.4.a
The circumference of a circle is equal to the product of its diameter and π. Solve $\pi d = C$ to find the circumference: 25 × 3.14 = 78.5, or about 79 inches. Answer choice A is the result of dividing the circumference by 2 and rounding downward. Answer choice C is the result of doubling the unrounded circumference. Answer choice D is the area of the circle, rounded to the nearest inch.

5. C; DOK Level: 2; Content Topics: Q.2.a, Q.2.e, Q.4.a;
Practices: MP.1.a, MP.1.b, MP.1.e, MP.2.c, MP.4.a
The area of a circle is equal to πr^2. Since the diameter of the circle is 18 feet, the radius is 18 ÷ 2 = 9 feet. Substitute 9 for r and calculate the area: 3.14 × 9² = 254.34. Then use the area to determine the cost for paving the patio by multiplying the cost per square foot by the number of square feet: 254.34 × $1.59 = $404.40.

6. B; DOK Level: 2; Content Topics: Q,2.a, Q.4.a;
Practices: MP.1.a, MP.1.b, MP.1.e, MP.2.c, MP.4.a, MP.4.b
The circumference of a circle is equal to the product of its diameter and π. Since the circumference is 47 inches, 47 = 3.14d. Divide each side by 3.14: d = 15 inches.

7. B; DOK Level: 2; Content Topics: Q,2.a, Q.4.a;
Practices: MP.1.a, MP.1.b, MP.1.e, MP.2.c, MP.4.a, MP.4.b
The area of a circle is equal to πr^2. Since the area is 1,256 square meters, 1,256 = 3.14r^2. Divide each side by 3.14: r^2 = 400 meters. Take the square root of each side: r = 20 meters. Answer choice A is the result of dividing the radius by 2. Answer choice C is the diameter of the circle. Answer choice D is the result of using the circumference formula and 1,256 meters to calculate the radius.

8. C; DOK Level: 2; Content Topics: Q.2.a, Q.2.e, Q.4.b;
Practices: MP.1.a, MP.1.b, MP.1.e, MP.2.c, MP.4.a
The area of a circle is equal to πr^2. The radius of the inner circle is 4 feet, so substitute 4 for r to compute the area: 3.14 × 4² = 50.2 square feet. Answer choice A is the result of failing to square the radius. Answer choice B is the circumference of the interior circle. Answer choice D is the area of the entire rug.

9. C; DOK Level: 1; Content Topics: Q.2.a, Q.2.e, Q.4.b;
Practices: MP.1.a, MP.1.b, MP.1.e, MP.2.c, MP.4.a
The area of a circle is equal to πr^2. The radius of the larger rug is 7, so substitute 7 for r to compute the area: 3.14 x 7² = 154 square feet.

10. A; DOK Level: 1; Content Topics: Q.2.a, Q.2.e, Q.4.b;
Practices: MP.1.a, MP.1.b, MP.1.e, MP.2.c, MP.4.a
The length of fringe that Henry needs is equal to the circumference of the rug, or πd. The fringe will go around the outside of the rug, so use d = 2(7) = 14 ft to find the circumference: 14 × 3.14 = 44 feet. Answer choice B is the product of the radius of the inner circle and the radius of the larger circle. Answer choice C is the circumference of the smaller, inner circle. Answer choice D is the result of using the radius of 4 as the diameter.

LESSON 5, pp. 102–103

1. C; DOK Level: 3; **Content Topics:** Q.4.a, Q.4.b, Q.4.c, Q.4.d; **Practices:** MP.1.a, MP.1.b, MP.1.c, MP.1.e, MP.3.a
Perimeter: 10 cm + 15 cm + 10 cm + 6 cm + 4 cm + 5 cm + 4 cm + 4 cm = 58 cm. The distance around the figure is 58 cm.

2. D; DOK Level: 3; **Content Topics:** Q.4.a, Q.4.c, Q.4.d; **Practices:** MP.1.a, MP.1.b, MP.1.c, MP.1.e, MP.3.a
Area of Rectangle = $l \times w$; 5 ft × 8 ft = 40 ft².
Area of Semicircle = $\frac{1}{2}\pi r^2$ so that $A = \frac{1}{2}(3.14)(2.5)^2 =$ 9.8125 ft². Since there are two semicircles, multiply this value by 2: 9.81 × 2 = 19.625 ft². Area of figure = 40 ft² + 19.625 ft² = 59.625 ft².

3. A; DOK Level: 3; **Content Topics:** Q.4.a, Q.4.c, Q.4.d; **Practices:** MP.1.a, MP.1.b, MP.1.c, MP.1.e, MP.3.a
Recall that area of a triangle = (base × height) ÷ 2, so that $A = (5\text{ m} \times 5\text{ m}) \div 2 = 12.5\text{ m}^2$.

4. D; DOK Level: 3; **Content Topics:** Q.4.a, Q.4.b, Q.4.c, Q.4.d; **Practices:** MP.1.a, MP.1.b, MP.1.c, MP.1.e, MP.3.a
Total area of composite figure = area of triangular portion + area of rectangular portion.
Area of rectangular portion = $l \times w$ = 10 m × 5 m = 50 m².
The total area, then, is 50 m² + 12.5 m² = 62.5 m²
Answer choice A represents the length of a side. Answer choice B represents the area of the triangular portion. Answer choice C represents the area of the rectangular portion.

5. A; DOK Level: 3; **Content Topics:** Q.4.a, Q.4.b, Q.4.c, Q.4.d; **Practices:** MP.1.a, MP.1.b, MP.1.c, MP.1.e, MP.3.a
To solve this problem, the large irregular shape must be divided into smaller regular shapes such as rectangles. To solve this problem, we have divided the shape horizontally into three rectangles.
Area of Rectangle 1
$A = l \times w$
A = 16 ft × 5 ft
A = 80 ft²
Area of Rectangle 2
A = 10 ft × 5 ft
A = 50 ft²
Area of Rectangle 3
A = 6 ft × 5 ft
A = 30 ft²
Total area of figure = 80 ft² + 50 ft² + 30 ft² = 160 ft².

6. D; DOK Level: 2; **Content Topics:** Q.4.a, Q.4.b, Q.4.d; **Practices:** MP.1.a, MP.1.b, MP.1.c, MP.1.e
Area of 2 circles = $2\pi r^2$ = 2(3.14)(25) = 157 square meters.

LESSON 6, pp. 104–105

1. C; DOK Level: 2; **Content Topics:** Q.3.b, Q.3.c; **Practices:** MP.1.a, MP.1.b
To find $\overline{AC}$, set up an equation.
$$\frac{\triangle ABC}{\triangle RST} = \frac{\overline{AC}}{\overline{RT}} = \frac{\overline{CB}}{\overline{TS}}$$
$$\frac{\overline{AC}}{1.2} = \frac{4.2}{2.1}$$
$$\overline{AC} = 2.4\text{ m}$$

Answer choices A and B represent given side lengths. Answer choice D is derived from improper calculation.

2. 10.8 m; DOK Level: 2; **Content Topics:** Q.3.b, Q.3.c; **Practices:** MP.1.a, MP.1.b
Since the triangles are similar, the length of side $\overline{FG}$ is proportional to the length of side $\overline{AB}$.
$$\frac{\overline{AC}}{\overline{FH}} = \frac{\overline{AB}}{\overline{FG}}$$
$$\frac{2\text{ m}}{4\text{ m}} = \frac{5.4}{\overline{FG}}$$
$$\overline{FG} = 10.8\text{ m}$$

3. 24.8 m; DOK Level: 2; **Content Topics:** Q.3.b, Q.3.c; **Practices:** MP.1.a, MP.1.b
To find the perimeter of ΔFGH, we can find the side $\overline{HG}$, then add all the sides. Alternately, one can find the perimeter of ΔABC, then multiply it by the scale factor. The perimeter of ΔABC = 5.4 m + 2 m + 5 m = 12.4 m. The scale factor is 2, since side $\overline{FH}$ is twice as large as side $\overline{AC}$. Therefore, the perimeter of ΔFGH = 2 × 12.4 m = 24.8 m.

4. B; DOK Level: 2; **Content Topics:** Q.3.b, Q.3.c; **Practices:** MP.1.a, MP.1.b
Set up an equation. Let J = the actual distance Jack travelled, and P = the distance Pedro travelled.
$$\frac{2.5\text{ cm}}{J} = \frac{1\text{ cm}}{20\text{ km}}$$
$$J = 50\text{ km}$$
$$\frac{2\text{ cm}}{P} = \frac{1\text{ cm}}{20\text{ km}}$$
$$P = 40\text{ km}$$
Jack travelled 10 km further than Pedro. Answer choice A is derived from improper calculation. Answer choices C and D represent the distance each person travelled, not the difference between them.

5. D; DOK Level: 2; **Content Topics:** Q.3.b, Q.3.c; **Practices:** MP.1.a, MP.1.b
Since these cities are 2.5 cm apart, Erika's distance is represented by 5 cm on the map. Set up an equation to represent the relationship. Let E represent the distance Erika travelled.
$$\frac{1\text{ cm}}{6\text{ km}} = \frac{5\text{ cm}}{E}$$
$$E = 30\text{ km}$$
Answer choices A and B result from incorrect calculations. Answer choice C results from failing to account for the return trip.

6. A; DOK Level: 3; **Content Topics:** Q.3.b, Q.3.c; **Practices:** MP.1.a, MP.1.b
Since the triangles are congruent, they are exactly the same size and shape, so Line $\overline{XY}$ = Line $\overline{EF}$. Since the perimeter of Triangle 1 is 19 ft:
Side $\overline{EF}$ = 19 − (9 ft + 6 ft)
= 19 ft − 15 ft
= 4 ft
Side $\overline{XY}$ = 4 ft

7. A; DOK Level: 3; **Content Topics:** Q.3.b, Q.3.c; **Practices:** MP.1.a, MP.1.b
Set up an equation to represent the relationship and find the scale factor.
$$\frac{\text{Actual}}{\text{Model}} = \frac{60}{12} = 5$$
The actual table is 5 times larger than the model. Answer choices B and D use incorrect computation. Answer choice C represents an incorrect equation.

Answer Key

LESSON 7, pp. 106–107

1. C; DOK Level: 1; Content Topics: Q.2.a, Q.5.b;
Practices: MP.1.a, MP.1.b, MP.1.d, MP.1.e, MP.4.a
The volume of a cylinder is the product of the area of its base and height, or $\pi r^2 h$. Substitute 3.14 for π, 3 for r and 8 for h: $3.14 \times 3^2 \times 8 = 3.14 \times 9 \times 8 = 226.08$ in³. So, to the nearest cubic inch, the volume of the canister is 226 cubic inches. Answer choice A is the product of the radius and the height. Answer choice B is the product of the radius squared and the height. Answer choice D is the result of multiplying by 3^3, instead of 3^2.

2. D; DOK Level: 2; Content Topics: Q.2.a, Q.2.e, Q.5.a;
Practices: MP.1.a, MP.1.b, MP.1.d, MP.1.e, MP.4.b
The volume of a rectangular prism is *lwh*. Multiply the length, width, and height of the bale of hay to find the volume of one bale: $40 \times 20 \times 20 = 16{,}000$ cubic inches. Next, multiply by 50 to find the volume of all 50 bales of hay: $50 \times 16{,}000 = 800{,}000$ cubic inches. Answer choice A is the result of writing an incorrect number of zeros in the product. Answer choice B is the volume of 1 bale of hay. Answer choice C is the result of a computation error.

3. B; DOK Level: 2; Content Topics: Q.2.a, Q.5.c;
Practices: MP.1.a, MP.1.b, MP.1.d, MP.1.e, MP.4.a
The surface area of a triangular prism is the sum of the areas of its bases and its 3 lateral sides. Each base has an area of $\frac{1}{2}bh = \frac{1}{2}(8)(4)$. Since there are two triangular bases, the total area of the bases is $2 \times \frac{1}{2}(8 \times 4) = 8 \times 4$. Meanwhile, each lateral face is a rectangle with length 9 inches. Two of the faces are 5 inches wide and one of the faces is 8 inches wide. So, the total lateral area of the prism is $(9 \times 5) + (9 \times 5) + (9 \times 8) = 2(9 \times 5) + (9 \times 8)$. Therefore, the total surface area is $(8 \times 4) + 2(9 \times 5) + (9 \times 8)$. Answer choice A only includes one of the lateral faces that measures 9 inches × 5 inches. Answer choice C includes only one base and only one of the lateral faces that measures 9 in. × 5 in. Answer choice D includes only one base.

4. B; DOK Level: 2; Content Topics: Q.2.a, Q.5.c;
Practices: MP.1.a, MP.1.b, MP.1.d, MP.1.e, MP.4.a, MP.4.b
The volume of a triangular prism is the product of the area of its base and its height. For the prism in problem 2, the area of the base of the prism is $\frac{1}{2}bh = \frac{1}{2}(8)(4) = 16$ in². The supplied height in the diagram is 9 inches. So, the volume is $16 \times 9 = 144$ in³. Since $V = Bh$, $h = V \div B$. To find the height of a triangular prism that has a volume of 144 in.³ and a base area of 24 in.², divide the volume by the base area: $144 \div 24 = 6$ in.

5. C; DOK Level: 2; Content Topics: Q.2.a, Q.2.e, Q.5.a;
Practices: MP.1.a, MP.1.b, MP.1.d, MP.1.e, MP.4.b
The surface area of a rectangular prism is the sum of the areas of its faces. The rectangular prism has two faces that measure 8 inches by 6 inches, two faces that measure 8 inches by 10 inches, and two faces that measures 6 inches by 10 inches. So, the surface area is $2(8 \times 6) + 2(8 \times 10) + 2(6 \times 10) = 96 + 160 + 120 = 376$ cubic inches.

6. C; DOK Level: 2; Content Topics: Q.2.a, Q.5.b;
Practices: MP.1.a, MP.1.b, MP.1.d, MP.1.e, MP.4.a, MP.4.b
The volume of a cylinder is given by $V = \pi r^2 h$. Substitute 9,156.24 for V, 3.14 for π, and $18 \div 2 = 9$ for r, since the diameter of a circle is twice its radius. Solve for h: $9{,}156.24 = 3.14 \times 9^2 \times h$. Multiply: $9{,}156.24 = 254.34h$. Divide: $h = 36$.

7. B; DOK Level: 3; Content Topics: Q.2.a, Q.4.b, Q.5.b;
Practices: MP.1.a, MP.1.b, MP.1.d, MP.1.e, MP.3.a, MP.3.b, MP.4.a, MP.4.b
The volume of a cylinder is given by $V = \pi r^2 h$. Morgan divides the volume by the height to get x, so $\frac{V}{h} = \frac{\pi r^2 h}{h} = \pi r^2 = x$. Morgan needs to find the circumference. Since $C = 2\pi r$, Morgan will need to find the radius of the cylinder. So, Morgan should divide x by π, or 3.14, to find r^2, and then take the square root to find r. Next, Morgan should multiply r by 2π, or 6.28, to find the circumference.

LESSON 8, pp. 108–109

1. A; DOK Level: 1; Content Topics: Q.2.a, Q.2.e, Q.5.e;
Practices: MP.1.a, MP.1.b, MP.1.e, MP.2.c, MP.4.a
The volume of a sphere is equal to $\frac{4}{3}\pi r^3$. Substitute 1.5 for r and calculate the volume: $V = \frac{4}{3} \times 3.14 \times 1.5^3 = \frac{4}{3} \times 3.14 \times 3.375 = 14.13$. So, to the nearest cubic inch the volume is 14 in³.

2. B; DOK Level: 1; Content Topics: Q.2.a, Q.2.e, Q.5.d;
Practices: MP.1.a, MP.1.b, MP.1.e, MP.2.c, MP.4.a
The volume of a cone is equal to $\frac{1}{3}\pi r^2 h$. Substitute 4 for r and 12 for h and calculate the volume: $V = \frac{1}{3}\pi r^2 h = \frac{1}{3} \times 3.14 \times 4^2 \times 12 = \frac{1}{3} \times 3.14 \times 16 \times 12 = 200.96$. So, to the nearest cubic centimeter, the volume is 201 cm³.

3. B; DOK Level: 2; Content Topics: Q.2.a, Q.2.e, Q.5.d;
Practices: MP.1.a, MP.1.b, MP.1.e, MP.2.c, MP.4.a
The cup does not have a circular base, so the area of paper is the surface area of the cone without the area of the base, or πrs. Substitute 4 for r and 12.6 for s and calculate the area: $3.14 \times 4 \times 12.6 = 158.26$, so, to the nearest square centimeter, the area of paper needed is 158 cm².

4. C; DOK Level: 1; Content Topics: Q.2.a, Q.5.d;
Practices: MP.1.a, MP.1.b, MP.1.e, MP.2.c, MP.4.a
The surface area of a sphere is $4\pi r^2$. Substitute 9 for r and calculate the surface area: $4 \times 3.14 \times 9^2 = 4 \times 3.14 \times 81 = 1{,}017.36$. So, to the nearest square centimeter, the surface area is 1,017 cm².

5. B; DOK Level: 3; Content Topics: Q.2.a, Q.5.d, Q.5.e; **Practices:** MP.1.a, MP.1.b, MP.1.e, MP.2.c, MP.4.a, MP.4.b
The only information provided is the radius of the figures, which is insufficient to find the volume of the cone.

However, you can use the radius to find the volume of the hemisphere. The volume of a sphere is $\frac{4}{3}\pi r^3$. The volume of a hemisphere is half the volume of a sphere, or $\frac{2}{3}\pi r^3$.

Substitute 6 for r and calculate the volume: $V = \frac{2}{3}\pi r^3 = \frac{2}{3}$ $\times 3.14 \times 6^3 = \frac{2}{3} \times 3.14 \times 216 = 452.16$. Next, substitute the volume and the radius into the formula for the volume of a cone and solve for the height: $V = \frac{1}{3}\pi r^2 h$, so $452.16 = \frac{1}{3} \times$ $3.14 \times 6^2 \times h$. Multiply: $452.16 = 37.68h$. Divide: $h = 12$.

6. C; DOK Level: 1; Content Topics: Q.2.a, Q.2.e, Q.5.d; **Practices:** MP.1.a, MP.1.b, MP.1.e, MP.2.c, MP.4.a
The volume of a pyramid is one-third the product of the area of its base and its height. Since the base is a square, the area of the base is $2^2 = 4$, and the volume of the pyramid is $\frac{1}{3}(4)(3) = 4$ cm³. Answer choice A is the result of failing to multiply by $\frac{1}{3}$. Answer choice B is the result of confusing the height and the side length. Answer choice D is the result of failing to square the side length.

7. B; DOK Level: 2; Content Topics: Q.2.a, Q.2.e, Q.5.d, Q.2.d; **Practices:** MP.1.a, MP.1.b, MP.1.e, MP.2.c, MP.4.a, MP.4.b
The volume of the cone (from question 6) is 4 cm³. Twice the volume then, is 8 cm³. The height of the cone is the same as the height of the pyramid, 3 cm. Substitute 8 for V and 3 for h in the formula for the volume of a cone: $8 = \frac{1}{3} \times$ $3.14 \times r^2 \times 3$. Multiply: $8 = 3.14r^2$. Divide: $r^2 = 2.5477$. Take the square root of each side: $r = 1.6$ cm.

8. D; DOK Level: 2; Content Topics: Q.2.a, Q.2.e, Q.5.d; **Practices:** MP.1.a, MP.1.b, MP.1.e, MP.2.c, MP.4.a
The amount of fabric is equal to the surface area of the pyramid. The pyramid has four triangular surfaces, each with base 6 feet and height 5 feet, and one square surface measuring 6 feet by 6 feet. So, the surface area is $6^2 + 4\left(\frac{1}{2}\right)$ $(6)(5) = 36 + 60 = 96$ square feet.

LESSON 9, *pp. 110–111*

1. B; DOK Level: 2; Content Topics: Q.2.a, Q.2.e, Q.5.a, Q.5.b, Q.5.c, Q.5.f; **Practices:** MP.1.a, MP.2.c, MP.4.a
The volume of the square core is $(80)(80)(150) = 960,000$ m³. The volume of the four semi-cylindrical sections are $(4)\left(\frac{1}{2}\right)\pi r^2 h$ (alternately, you may use the formula $2\pi r^2 h$), where $r = 40$ and $h = 150$. Substituting gives 1,507,200 m³. Adding gives $960,000 + 1,507,200 = 2,467,200 \approx 2,467,000$ m³ (choice B).

2. 25; DOK Level: 2; Content Topics: Q.2.a, Q.2.e, Q.5.d; **Practices:** MP.1.a, MP.2.c, MP.4.a
Each cone has a volume equal to $\frac{1}{3}\pi r^2 h$, where $r = 2$ and $h = 3$. Substitute so that $\frac{1}{3}\pi r^2 h = \frac{1}{3}\pi(2^2)3 =$ a volume of 12.56 cubic meters for each, or 25.12 cubic meters for the combined volume. The answer to the nearest cubic meter is 25.

3. 100; DOK Level: 2; Content Topics: Q.2.a, Q.2.e, Q.5.b, Q.5.f; **Practices:** MP.1.a, MP.2.c, MP.4.a
The volume of the cylindrical section is $\pi r^2 h$, where $r = 2$ and $h = 6$. Substitute so that $\pi r^2 h = \pi(2^2)6$, giving a volume of 75.36 cubic meters for the cylinder. Adding the volume of the two cones (25.12) gives 100.48 cubic meters or, rounded to the nearest cubic meter, 100 cubic meters.

4. A; DOK Level: 3; Content Topics: Q.2.a, Q.2.e, Q.5.c, Q.5.f; **Practices:** MP.1.a, MP.1.b, MP.2.c, MP.3.a, MP.4.a, MP.5.c
The volume of the cement is the area of the patio times its depth. To find the area, the patio must be divided into several rectangles. One way to do this is to break it into three rectangles positioned side by side—moving left to right, a 10 ft by 5 ft rectangle, a 16 ft by 5 ft rectangle, and a 5 ft by 6 ft rectangle. The areas of these rectangles are 50 sq ft, 80 sq ft, and 30 sq ft, respectively, for a total area of 160 sq ft. To find the volume, multiply the area by the depth in feet, 0.25 feet. That gives 40 cubic feet (choice A).

5. A; DOK Level: 3; Content Topics: Q.5.b, Q.5.f; **Practices:** MP.1.a, MP.1.b, MP.2.a, MP.2.c, MP.3.a, MP.4.b, MP.5.c
The volume occupied by the outside of the container is $\pi R^2 H$. The inside radius of the container is $(R - t)$, or the radius of the outside wall minus the thickness. The inside length of the space inside the container is $(H - 2t)$, since the quantity t must be subtracted from *both* ends. The inside volume is then $\pi(R - t)^2 (H - 2t)$. The volume of material making up the container is the difference between the two; factoring out a factor of π gives choice A.

6. C; DOK Level: 3; Content Topics: Q.2.a, Q.2.e, Q.5.d, Q.5.f; **Practices:** MP.1.a, MP.1.b, MP.1.c, MP.1.e, MP.2.c, MP.3.a, M.4.a, MP.5.c
The bottom portion of the funnel is not a complete cone, but instead is a cone with a part near the apex removed; see the figure below. The slope of the side can be found from the given dimensions. The rise (change in y) is 2 inches. The run (change in x) is the bottom radius $\left(\frac{3}{2} = 1.5 \text{ inches}\right)$ minus the top radius $\left(\frac{0.5}{2} = 0.25 \text{ inch}\right)$, or 1.25 inches. This gives a slope of $\frac{(2)}{(1.25)} = 1.6$. This slope is also equal to the height of the complete cone (x) divided by the bottom radius of 1.5, so that $x = 2.4$ inches. The corresponding slant height, from the Pythagorean theorem, is the square root of $1.5^2 + 2.4^2$, or $2.25 + 5.76 = 8$. The square root of $8 = 2.83$ inches.

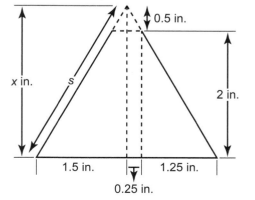

Answer Key

UNIT 4 *(continued)*

The inside surface area of the complete cone would be $SA = \pi rs = (3.14)(1.5)(2.83) = 13.33$ square inches. The small piece of the cone that is missing has a height of $(2.4 - 2) = 0.4$ inch. The slant height is equal to the square root of the radius squared of the smaller cone (0.25^2) plus the difference in height squared $(0.4\ in^2)$, so that $(0.25^2 + 0.4^2 = 0.2225$; the square root of 0.2225 is 0.47 inch. Next, you can use the formula for surface area so that $SA = \pi rs = (3.14)(0.25)(0.47) = 0.37$ square inch. Taking the difference and rounding to the nearest tenth gives $(13.33 - 0.37) = 13$ square inches (choice C).

7. D; DOK Level: 2; **Content Topics:** Q.2.a, Q.2.e, Q.5.b, Q.5.f; **Practices:** MP.1.a, MP.1.b, MP.2.c, MP.3.a, MP.4.a, MP.5.c
The surface area of the inside of the cylinder is $2\pi rh$, where $r = 0.25$ and $h = 0.5$. Substituting gives $SA = 2(3.14)(0.25)(0.5) = 0.785$ inch, which rounds to 0.8 square inch. Adding that to the result for the conical portion of the funnel (13 square inches, established in question 6) gives 13.8 square inches (choice D).

UNIT 4 REVIEW, *pp. 112–119*

1. B; DOK Level: 2; **Content Topics:** Q.2.a, Q.4.a, A.2.a, A.2.b; **Practices:** MP.1.a, MP.1.b, MP.1.e, MP.2.c, MP.4.a, MP.4.b
The area of a square is the square of the side length. Since the area is 64 square meters, $s^2 = 64$ and $s = 8$ meters. Answer choice A is the result of dividing the side length, 8, by 2. Answer choice C is the side length of a square with a perimeter of 64 meters. Answer choice D is the result of dividing the area by 2 rather than taking its square root.

2. B; DOK 2; **Content Topics:** Q.2.a, Q.2.e, Q.4.c; **Practices:** MP.1.a, MP.1.b, MP.1.d, MP.1.e, MP.2.c, MP.4.a
To find the side length of each placemat, first determine that a hexagon = 6 sides and two hexagons = 12 sides. From there, subtract the remaining 8 inches of ribbon from the total, 80 inches, for 72 inches of ribbon used in creating the placements. Next, establish the equation: $72 = 12(x)$ to find $x = 6$.

3. C; DOK Level: 2; **Content Topics:** Q.2.a, Q.2.e, Q.4.e; **Practices:** MP.1.a, MP.1.b, MP.1.e, MP.2.c, MP.4.a, MP.4.b
The ramp forms the hypotenuse of a right triangle whose legs are the horizontal length and the rise of the ramp. Substitute 12 for c and 2 for a in the Pythagorean Theorem and solve for b, the horizontal length of the ramp: $2^2 + b^2 = 12^2$. Multiply: $4 + b^2 = 144$. Subtract 4 from each side: $b^2 = 140$. Take the square root of each side: $b = 11.8$. Answer choice A is the difference between the ramp length and rise. Answer choice B is the difference between 12 and the square root of 2. Answer choice D is the result of subtracting 2 from 12^2 and then taking the square root.

4. B; DOK Level: 2; **Content Topics:** Q.2.a, Q.2.e, Q.4.e; **Practices:** MP.1.a, MP.1.b, MP.1.d, MP.1.e, MP.2.c, MP.4.a
The ramp forms the hypotenuse of a right triangle whose legs are the horizontal length and the rise of the ramp. Substitute 15 for a and 2 for b and solve for c, the new length of the ramp: $c^2 = 15^2 + 2^2$. Multiply and add: $c^2 = 225 + 4 = 229$. Take the square root of each side: $c \approx 15.1$ feet. Subtract the original ramp length from the new ramp length: $15.1 - 12 = 3.1$ feet. Answer choice A is the increase in the horizontal length. Answer choice C is the difference between the new horizontal length and the original ramp length. Answer choice D is the result of a computational error.

5. 5; DOK Level: 2; **Content Topics:** Q.2.a, Q.4.a; **Practices:** MP.1.a, MP.1.b, MP.1.d, MP.1.e, MP.2.a, MP.4.a, MP.4.b
The area of a square is equal to s^2. So, $s^2 = 25$. Take the square root of each side: $s = 5$ feet.

6. 7.1; DOK Level: 3; **Content Topics:** Q.2.a, Q.4.b, Q.4.e; **Practices:** MP.1.a, MP.1.b, MP.1.d, MP.1.e, MP.2.a, MP.4.a, MP.4.b
The diameter of the circle is equal to the diagonal of the square. The diagonal of the square is equal to the hypotenuse of a right triangle whose legs are the sides of the square. Since the area of a square is equal to the square of its side, $s^2 = 25$. Take the square root of each side: $s = 5$ feet. Substitute 5 for a and 5 for b in the Pythagorean Theorem and solve for c, the length of the diagonal of the square: $c^2 = 5^2 + 5^2 = 25 + 25 = 50$. Take the square root of each side: $c^2 = 50$, so $c = 7.07$ feet, which rounds to 7.1 feet.

7. 39.6; DOK Level: 3; **Content Topics:** Q.2.a, Q.4.b, Q.4.e; **Practices:** MP.1.a, MP.1.b, MP.1.d, MP.1.e, MP.2.a, MP.4.a, MP.4.b
The area of a circle is given by $A = \pi r^2$. The radius of a circle is one-half its diameter. The diameter of the circle is equal to the diagonal of the square, which is the hypotenuse of a right triangle whose legs are the sides of the square. Therefore, $d = \sqrt{5^2 + 5^2} = 7.1$. Divide the diameter by 2 to find the radius: $r = 3.55$. Substitute 3.55 for r and calculate the area: $A = 3.14 \times 3.55^2 = 39.6$ square feet.

8. 22.3; DOK Level: 3; **Content Topics:** Q.2.a, Q.4.b, Q.4.e; **Practices:** MP.1.a, MP.1.b, MP.1.d, MP.1.e, MP.2.a, MP.4.a, MP.4.b
The circumference of a circle is equal to the product of its diameter and π. The diameter of the circle is equal to the diagonal of the square, which is the hypotenuse of a right triangle whose legs are the sides of the square. Therefore, $d = \sqrt{5^2 + 5^2} = 7.1$. Multiply the diameter, 7.1, by 3.14, to find that the circumference of the circle is 22.3 feet.

9. 1st, 2nd and 4th figures; DOK Level: 2; **Content Topics:** Q.2.a, Q.4.c; **Practices:** MP.1.a, MP.1.b, MP.1.e, MP.2.c, MP.4.a
The perimeter of a regular polygon is the product of its side length and number of sides. So, the side length of a regular polygon is the quotient of its perimeter and its number of sides. For each polygon, divide the perimeter by the number of sides. For the pentagon (five sides), $s = 42.5 \div 5 = 8.5$ inches. For the octagon (eight sides), $s = 68 \div 8 = 8.5$ inches. For the heptagon (seven sides), $s = 59.5 \div 7 = 8.5$ inches.

10. **D**; **DOK Level:** 1; **Content Topics:** Q.2.a, Q.2.e, Q.4.a; **Practices:** MP.1.a, MP.1.b, MP.1.e, MP.2.c, MP.4.a
The area of a rectangle is the product of its length and width, or $A = lw$. So the area of wood used to create the table is $8 \times 4.5 = 36$ square feet. Answer choice A is the result of dividing the product lw by 2. Answer choice B is the perimeter of the table top. Answer choice C is the area of a table 8 feet long and 4 feet wide.

11. **B**; **DOK Level:** 2; **Content Topics:** Q.2.a, Q.4.b; **Practices:** MP.1.a, MP.1.b, MP.1.d, MP.1.e, MP.2.a, MP.4.a, MP.4.b
The area of a circle is given by $A = \pi r^2$. Substitute 254 for A and solve for r: $254 = 3.14 \times r^2$. Divide each side by 3.14: $r^2 = 80.89$. Take the square root of each side: $r \approx 9$ cm. The diameter of a circle is twice its radius, so $d = 2 \times 9 = 18$ cm.

12. **B**; **DOK Level:** 2; **Content Topics:** Q.2.a, Q.4.a, A.2.a, A.2.c; **Practices:** MP.1.a, MP.1.b, MP.1.d, MP.1.e, MP.2.c, MP.4.a, MP.4.b
Since the square and the parallelogram have the same area, use the side length of the square to find the area of each figure. The area of a square is equal to the square of its side length, so the area is $6^2 = 36$ square inches. The area of a parallelogram is equal to the product of its base and height, so $36 = 9h$. Divide each side by 9: $h = 4$ inches.

13. **C**; **DOK Level:** 2; **Content Topics:** Q.2.a, Q.2.e, Q.4.a, Q.4.e; **Practices:** MP.1.a, MP.1.b, MP.1.d, MP.1.e, MP.2.c, MP.4.a
The path through the park is the hypotenuse of a right triangle with legs of 50 yards and 120 yards. Use the Pythagorean Theorem to find the length of the path through the park: $c^2 = 50^2 + 120^2 = 2,500 + 14,400 = 16,900$. Take the square root of each side: $c = 130$ yards. If Wanda had taken the sidewalk, she would have walked $50 + 120 = 170$ yards. So, by walking through the park, Wanda walked $170 - 130 = 40$ fewer yards. Answer choice A is the length of the path through the park. Answer choice B is the difference between the length of the path through the park and the shorter side of the park. Answer choice D is the difference between the length of the path and the longer side of the park.

14. **C**; **DOK Level:** 2; **Content Topics:** Q.2.a, Q.2.e, Q.3.b, Q.3.c; **Practices:** MP.1.a, MP.1.b, MP.1.d, MP.1.e, MP.2.c
Write a proportion to represent the situation: $\frac{1 \text{ inch}}{3 \text{ feet}} = \frac{7 \text{ inches}}{x \text{ feet}}$. Cross-multiply to find that $x = 3 \times 7 = 21$ feet. Perform a similar computation for the other dimension of the garage: $\frac{1 \text{ inch}}{3 \text{ feet}} = \frac{8 \text{ inches}}{x \text{ feet}}$; $x = 3 \times 8 = 24$ feet.

15. **B**; **DOK Level:** 2; **Content Topics:** Q.2.a, Q.2.e, Q.3.b, Q.3.c; **Practices:** MP.1.a, MP.1.b, MP.1.d, MP.1.e, MP.2.c
Write a proportion to represent the situation: $\frac{1 \text{ inch}}{3 \text{ feet}} = \frac{x \text{ inches}}{5.4 \text{ feet}}$. Cross-multiply: $3x = 5.4$. Next, divide each side by 3: $x = 1.8$ inches.

16. **C**; **DOK Level:** 2; **Content Topics:** Q.2.a, Q.4.c; **Practices:** MP.1.a, MP.1.b, MP.1.d, MP.1.e, MP.2.c, MP.4.a
The perimeter of a trapezoid is the sum of its side lengths. To find the missing side length, subtract the known side lengths from the perimeter of the trapezoid: $58 - (11 + 13 + 13) = 58 - 37 = 21$ feet. Answer choice A is the result of including the height, 12 feet, in the perimeter of the figure. Answer choice B is the height of the figure. Answer choice D is the result of including the height, 12 feet, in the perimeter and including only one of the 13-foot sides in the perimeter.

17. **B**; **DOK Level:** 2; **Content Topics:** Q.2.a, Q.4.c; **Practices:** MP.1.a, MP.1.b, MP.1.d, MP.1.e, MP.2.c, MP.4.a
The area of a trapezoid is given by $A = \frac{1}{2}(b_1 + b_2)h$. Since the figure has a perimeter of 58 feet, the second base is $58 - (11 + 13 + 13) = 58 - 37 = 21$ feet long. Substitute 11 for b_1, 21 for b_2, and 12 for h to calculate the area: $A = \frac{1}{2}(11 + 21) \times 2 = 16 \times 12 = 192$ square feet.

18. **9.9**; **DOK Level:** 2; **Content Topics:** Q.2.a, Q.2.e, Q.4.e; **Practices:** MP.1.a, MP.1.b, MP.1.e, MP.2.c, MP.4.a
The distance between points A and C is the hypotenuse of a right triangle whose legs are segments AB and BC. Segment AB is 7 units long and segment BC is also 7 units long, so $AC^2 = 7^2 + 7^2 = 49 + 49 = 98$. Take the square root of each side: $AC \approx 9.9$.

19. **B**; **DOK Level:** 3; **Content Topics:** Q.2.a, Q.2.e, Q.5.a, Q.5.f; **Practices:** MP.1.a, MP.1.b, MP.1.d, MP.1.e, MP.2.c, MP.4.a
The set of steps can be accompased into three rectangular prisms. One way in which to decompose the steps is into one prism that measures 8 inches by 10 inches by 36 inches, one prism that measures 16 inches by 10 inches by 36 inches, and one prism that measures 24 inches by 10 inches by 36 inches. Find the volume of each prism and add them together and find the total volume of the set of steps: $8 \times 10 \times 36 = 2,880$; $16 \times 10 \times 36 = 5,760$; $24 \times 10 \times 36 = 8,640$. Find the sum $2,880 + 5,760 + 8,640 = 17,280$ cubic inches.

20. **D**; **DOK Level:** 2; **Content Topics:** Q.2.a, Q.4.b; **Practices:** MP.1.a, MP.1.b, MP.1.d, MP.1.e, MP.2.a, MP.4.a, MP.4.b
The length of the strip of lead is equal to the circumference of the circle. To find the circumference, begin by using the area of the circle to find its radius. The area of a circle is given by $A = \pi r^2$. Substitute 113 for A and solve for r: $113 = 3.14 \times r^2$. Divide each side by 3.14: $r^2 = 36$. Take the square root of each side: $r = 6$ inches. The circumference of a circle is equal to $\pi \times d$, or $\pi \times 2r$. Substitute 6 for r and calculate the circumference: $3.14 \times 2 \times 6 = 37.68$, which rounds to 37.7 inches.

21. **C**; **DOK Level:** 3; **Content Topics:** Q.2.e, Q.4.e, A.2.a, A.2.c; **Practices:** MP.1.a, MP.1.b, MP.1.d, MP.1.e, MP.2.c, MP.4.a, MP.4.b
The area of a triangle is equal to $\frac{1}{2}bh$. In a right triangle, the base and height are the legs of the triangle. Since the area of the triangle is 216 cm^2 and one of the legs measures 24 cm, $216 = \frac{1}{2}(24)h$. Multiply: $216 = 12h$. Divide each side by 12: $h = 18$ cm. Now, use the Pythagorean Theorem $(a^2 + b^2 = c^2)$ to find the length of the hypotenuse of a right triangle with legs that measure 24 cm and 18 cm: $c = \sqrt{24^2 + 18^2} = \sqrt{576 + 324} = \sqrt{900} = 30$. Finally, the perimeter of the triangle is the sum of its side lengths: $24 + 18 + 30 = 72$ cm.

Answer Key

22. **A;DOK Level: 2; Content Topics:** Q.2.a, Q.4.b; **Practices:** MP.1.a, MP.1.b, MP.1.e, MP.2.c, MP.4.a, MP.5.a, MP.5.b

The area of a circle is given by $A = \pi r^2$. The circumference of a circle is given by $C = \pi d$. Since the diameter of a circle is twice its radius, the circumference of a circle is also equal to $2\pi r$. Substitute each radius into the formulas for area and circumference to determine which radius describes a circle whose circumference is greater than its radius. For answer choice A, $A = 3.14 \times 1.5^2 = 7.1$ and $C = 2 \times 3.14 \times 1.5 = 9.42$. So, answer choice A demonstrates that the area of a circle is not always greater than its circumference.

23. **B; DOK Level: 2;** Content Topics: Q.2.a, Q.2.e, Q.4.a, Q.4.b, Q.4.d; **Practices:** MP.1.a, MP.1.b, MP.1.d, MP.1.e, MP.2.c, MP.4.a

The perimeter of the pool is equal to the sum of the perimeters of the two semicircles and the two exterior sides of the rectangle. Since the two semicircles have the same diameter, their combined circumference is equal to the circumference of a circle with diameter 4.5 feet: $C = 3.14 \times 4.5 = 14.13$ feet. Add the lengths of the two 5-foot sides: $14.13 + 2(5) = 24.13$ feet.

24. **Parallelogram: 5 cm; Triangle: 10 cm; Rectangle: 8 cm; DOK Level: 2; Content Topics:** Q.2.a, Q.4.a, A.2.a, A.2.c; **Practices:** MP.1.a, MP.1.b, MP.1.d, MP.1.e, MP.2.c, MP.4.a, MP.4.b

The only figure for which there is sufficient information to determine the perimeter is the square. The perimeter of a square is equal to $4s$, so the perimeter of each figure is $4 \times 6 = 24$ cm. The perimeter of the triangle is the sum of its side lengths, so subtract the known side lengths from the perimeter to find the remaining side length: $24 - (5 + 9) = 10$ cm. The perimeter of a parallelogram is $2(b + s)$. The side length is 7 cm, so $2(b + 7) = 24$. Multiply: $2b + 14 = 24$. Subtract 14 from each side: $2b = 10$. Divide: $b = 5$ cm. The perimeter of a rectangle is $2(l + w)$. The width of the rectangle is 4 cm, so $2(l + 4) = 24$. Multiply: $2l + 8 = 24$. Subtract 8 from each side: $2l = 16$. Divide: $l = 8$ cm.

25. **C; DOK Level: 2; Content Topics:** Q.2.a, Q.2.e, Q.4.a, Q.4.d; **Practices:** MP.1.a, MP.1.b, MP.1.d, MP.1.e, MP.2.c, MP.5.a

A composite plane figure can be decomposed in more than one way. Determine which answer choice is not the result of decomposing the polygon. Answer choice A is the result of extending the 5.5-foot side upward to create two rectangles. Answer choice B is the result of extending the 6-foot side to the left to create two rectangles. Answer choice D is the result of extending the 8-foot side to the right and the 4-foot side downward to create a large rectangle, and then subtracting the area of the extended portion. The rectangles described in answer choice C cannot be produced from the composite figure.

26. **C; DOK Level: 2; Content Topics:** Q.2.a, Q.4.c; **Practices:** MP.1.a, MP.1.b, MP.1.e, MP.2.c, MP.4.a

The perimeter of an irregular figure is the sum of its side lengths. The perimeter of Brendan's figure is $2 + 10 + 4 + 5 + 5 + 6 = 32$ cm. The perimeter of a regular polygon is the product of its side length and number of sides. For each answer choice, determine the perimeter of a figure with the given side length and number of sides. For answer choice A, $P = 8 \times 4 = 32$ cm. For answer choice B, $P = 5 \times 6.4 = 32$ cm. For answer choice C, $6 \times 5.4 = 32.4$ cm. For answer choice D, $P = 4 \times 8 = 32$. So, the wire could be bent into each of the regular polygons except the hexagon.

27. **A; DOK Level: 2; Content Topics:** Q.2.a, Q.4.b; **Practices:** MP.1.a, MP.1.b, MP.1.d, MP.1.e, MP.2.a, MP.4.a

The pie crust must extend 1 inch beyond the dish, all the way around, so add 1 inch to each end of the diameter of the pie dish to find the diameter of the crust: $9 + 1 + 1 = 11$ inches. So, the radius of the pie crust is $11 \div 2 = 5.5$ inches. The area of a circle is given by $A = \pi r^2$, so the area of the pie crust is $3.14 \times 5.5^2 = 95$ square inches.

28. **C; DOK Level: 2; Content Topics:** Q.2.a, Q.2.e, Q.3.b, Q.3.c; **Practices:** MP.1.a, MP.1.b, MP.1.e, MP.2.c

Write a proportion to represent the situation: $\frac{2.8 \text{ cm}}{98 \text{ km}} = \frac{1 \text{ cm}}{x \text{ km}}$. Cross-multiply: $2.8x = 98$. Divide each side by 2.8: $x = 35$. So, the scale of the map is 1 cm:35 km.

29. **B; DOK Level: 2; Content Topics:** Q.2.a, Q.2.e, Q.4.a, Q.4.d; **Practices:** MP.1.a, MP.1.b, MP.1.d, MP.1.e, MP.2.c, MP.4.a

The length of wood is equal to the perimeter of the figure. The perimeter of the figure is composed of 10 sides, each measuring 1.3 meters. Multiply the number of sides by the side length to find the perimeter of the figure: $10 \times 1.3 = 13$ meters.

30. **C; DOK Level: 2; Content Topics:** Q.2.a, Q.2.e, Q.4.a, Q.4.d; **Practices:** MP.1.a, MP.1.b, MP.1.d, MP.1.e, MP.2.c, MP.4.a

The total area of the figure is the sum of the areas of the pentagon and the five congruent triangles. The area of each triangle is equal to $\frac{1}{2}bh$. Substitute 1 for b and 1.2 for h to find the area of each triangle: $A = \frac{1}{2}(1)(1.2) = 0.6$ square meter. There are 5 triangles, so the total area of the triangles is $5 \times 0.6 = 3$ square meters. Add the area of the pentagon to the area of the triangles: $1.72 + 3 = 4.72$ square meters.

31. **A; DOK Level: 2; Content Topics:** Q.2.a, Q.5.b, Q.5.c, A.2.a, A.2.c; **Practices:** MP.1.a, MP.1.b, MP.1.d, MP.1.e, MP.2.c, MP.4.a, MP.4.b

The volume of a pyramid is equal to $\frac{1}{3}Bh$. The pyramid has a base area of $14 \times 11 = 154$ square inches and a height of 18 inches, so the volume of the pyramid is $\frac{1}{3} \times 154 \times 18 = 924$ cubic inches. The volume of a cone is $\frac{1}{3}\pi r^2 h$. The cone has a diameter of 18 inches, so its radius is $18 \div 2 = 9$ inches. Since the volume of the cone is equal to the volume of the pyramid, $\frac{1}{3} \times 3.14 \times 9^2 \times h = 924$. Multiply: $84.78h = 924$. Divide each side by 84.78: $h = 10.9$ inches.

32. **B**; **DOK Level:** 2; **Content Topics:** Q.2.a, Q.2.e, Q.4.a, Q.4.b, Q.4.e; **Practices:** MP.1.a, MP.1.b, MP.1.e, MP.2.c, MP.4.a, MP.4.b

The ladder forms the hypotenuse of a right triangle whose legs are the wall and the ground. Substitute 18 for c and 14 for a in the Pythagorean Theorem and solve for b, the distance between the wall and the ladder: $14^2 + b^2 = 18^2$. Multiply: $196 + b^2 = 324$. Subtract 196 from each side: $b^2 = 128$. Take the square root of each side: $b = 11.3$ feet.

33. **A**; **DOK Level:** 3; **Content Topics:** Q.2.a, Q.2.e, Q.3.b, Q.3.c; **Practices:** MP.1.a, MP.1.b, MP.1.e, MP.2.c

At the same time of day, shadows cast by the sun are proportional to the length of the object. Write a proportion to represent the situation. $\frac{24 \text{ ft}}{3.6 \text{ ft}} = \frac{x \text{ ft}}{4.5 \text{ ft}}$. Cross-multiply: $3.6x = 24 \times 4.5 = 108$. Divide each side by 3.6: $x = 30$.

34. **B**; **DOK Level:** 3; **Content Topics:** Q.2.a, Q.2.e, Q.3.b, Q.3.c; **Practices:** MP.1.a, MP.1.b, MP.1.e, MP.2.c

If the figures are similar, then corresponding sides are proportional. Write a proportion to represent the situation. $\frac{8 \text{ cm}}{20 \text{ cm}} = \frac{15 \text{ cm}}{x \text{ cm}}$. Cross-multiply: $8x = 20 \times 15 = 300$. Divide each side by 8: $x = 37.5$ cm.

35. **B**; **DOK Level:** 2; **Content Topics:** Q.2.a, Q.2.e, Q.5.b; **Practices:** MP.1.a, MP.1.b, MP.1.d, MP.1.e, MP.2.a, MP.2.c, MP.4.a, MP.4.b

The volume of a cylinder is given by $\pi r^2 h$. Since the volume of the cylinder is 3,740 cubic centimeters and the height is 17.5 cm, then $3,740 = 3.14 \times r^2 \times 17.5$. Multiply: $3,740 = 54.95 r^2$. Divide each side by 54.95: $r^2 = 68.06$. Take the square root of each side: $r = 8.25$ cm. The diameter is twice the radius, so it $= 2 \times 8.25 = 16.5$ cm.

36. **A**; **DOK Level:** 1; **Content Topics:** Q.2.a, Q.4.c; **Practices:** MP.1.a, MP.1.b, MP.1.e, MP.2.c, MP.4.a

The perimeter of an irregular polygon is the sum of its side lengths. To find the missing side length, subtract the known side lengths from the perimeter of the polygon: $42 - (9 + 12 + 7 + 8) = 42 - 36 = 6$ m.

37. **D**; **DOK Level:** 3; **Content Topics:** Q.2.a, Q.5.a, Q.5.d, Q.5.f; **Practices:** MP.1.a, MP.1.b, MP.1.d, MP.1.e, MP.2.c, MP.4.a

The figure is composed of two congruent square pyramids and a rectangular prism. Each square pyramid has a base area of $12 \times 12 = 144$ square cm and a height of 15 cm, so the total volume of the two pyramids is $2 \times \frac{1}{3} \times 144 \times 15 = 1,440$ cubic centimeters. Meanwhile, the rectangular prism has a volume of $12 \times 12 \times 22 = 3,168$ cubic centimeters. So, the volume of the figure is $1,440 + 3,168 = 4,608$ cubic centimeters.

38. **C**; **DOK Level:** 3; **Content Topics:** Q.2.a, Q.5.a, Q.5.d, Q.5.f; **Practices:** MP.1.a, MP.1.b, MP.1.d, MP.1.e, MP.2.c, MP.4.a

The surface area of the figure is equal to the sum of the four rectangular faces of the prism and the eight triangular faces of the pyramids. Each exposed face of the prism has an area of $12 \times 22 = 264$ square centimeters, so the area of the four faces is $4 \times 264 = 1,056$ square inches. Each of the triangular faces of the pyramids has an area of $\frac{1}{2} \times 12 \times 16 = 96$ square centimeters, so the area of the eight triangular faces is $8 \times 96 = 768$ square centimeters. The total surface area of the figure is $1,056 + 768 = 1,824$ square centimeters.

39. **C**; **DOK Level:** 3; **Content Topics:** Q.2.a, Q.2.e, Q.5.a, Q.5.c, Q.5.f; **Practices:** MP.1.a, MP.1.b, MP.1.d, MP.1.e, MP.2.c, MP.4.a

The house is composed of a rectangular prism and a triangular prism. The surface area of the exposed sides of the rectangular prism is $(12 \times 6) + 2(12 \times 8) + 2(6 \times 8) = 72 + 192 + 96 = 360$ square inches. The two rectangular faces of the triangular prism have a total area of $2(7 \times 6) = 84$ square inches. The two triangular faces of the rectangular prism have a total area of $2\left(\frac{1}{2} \times 12 \times 4\right) = 48$ square inches. Add to find the total surface area: $360 + 84 + 48 = 492$ square inches.

40. **48**; **DOK Level:** 2; **Content Topics:** Q.2.a, Q.4.a, A.2.a, A.2.c; **Practices:** MP.1.a, MP.1.b, MP.1.e, MP.2.a, MP.4.a, MP.4.b

The perimeter of a triangle is the sum of the lengths of its sides. Since the perimeter is 100 inches, $26 + 26 + b = 100$. Combine like terms and subtract 52 from each side: $b = 48$.

41. **10**; **DOK Level:** 2; **Content Topics:** Q.2.a, Q.4.a, A.2.a, A.2.c; **Practices:** MP.1.a, MP.1.b, MP.1.d, MP.1.e, MP.2.a, MP.4.a, MP.4.b

The area of a triangle is $\frac{1}{2} bh$. The base of the triangle is $100 - 26 - 26 = 48$ inches, so $240 = \frac{1}{2}(48)h$. Multiply: $240 = 24h$. Divide each side by 24: $h = 10$.

42. **A**; **DOK Level:** 2; **Content Topics:** Q.2.a, Q.2.e, Q.4.b; **Practices:** MP.1.a, MP.1.b, MP.1.e, MP.2.c, MP.4.a

The area of a circle is given by $A = \pi r^2$. The grass and fountain have a diameter of 22 feet, so the radius of the grass and fountain together is $22 \div 2 = 11$ feet. Substitute 11 for r to find the area of the fountain and grass together: $A = 3.14 \times 11^2 = 379.94$ square feet. Next, subtract the area of the grass to find the area of the fountain pool alone: $379.94 - 253.3 = 126.64$ square feet.

43. **D**; **DOK Level:** 2; **Content Topics:** Q.2.a, Q.2.e, Q.4.b; **Practices:** MP.1.a, MP.1.b, MP.1.d, MP.1.e, MP.2.c, MP.4.a

Since the fence must extend 5 feet beyond the pool and grass, the diameter of the fence will be $2 \times 5 = 10$ feet longer than the diameter of the fountain and grass. So, the diameter of the fence will be 32 feet. The circumference of a circle is the product of the diameter of the circle and π. Multiply to find the circumference of the fence: $3.14 \times 32 = 100.48$ feet.

44. **A**; **DOK Level:** 3; **Content Topics:** Q.2.a, A.4.a, A.4.b; **Practices:** MP.1.a, MP.1.b, MP.1.d, MP.1.e, MP.2.a, MP.4.a, MP.4.b

The area of a circle is given by $A = \pi r^2$. Substitute 314 for A and solve for r to find the radius of Circle A: $314 = 3.14 \times r^2$, so $r^2 = 100$ and $r = 10$. The diameter of Circle A is $2 \times 10 = 20$ cm. Since the radius of Circle B is equal to diameter of Circle A, the radius of Circle B is 20 cm. Since the circumference of a circle is equal to πd or $\pi \times 2 \times r$, the circumference of Circle B is $3.14 \times 2 \times 20 = 125.6$ cm.

Answer Key

UNIT 4 *(continued)*

45. **8**; **DOK Level:** 3; **Content Topics:** Q.2.a, Q.4.a, Q.4.b, Q.4.d, A.2.a, A.2.c; **Practices:** MP.1.a, MP.1.b, MP.1.d, MP.1.e, MP.2.a, MP.2.c, MP.4.a, MP.4.b
The perimeter of the figure is the sum of the lengths of three sides of the square and the perimeter of the semi-circle. The perimeter of a semicircle is equal to one-half the circumference of a circle with the same diameter, so the perimeter of the semicircle is $\frac{1}{2}\pi d$. Since the side length of the square is equal to the diameter of the semi-circle, the perimeter of the semicircle is $\frac{1}{2}\pi s$, and the total circumference of the figure is $3s + \frac{1}{2}\pi s$. Solve for s: $3s + \frac{1}{2}$ × 3.14 × s = 36.56. Multiply: $3s + 1.57s = 36.56$. Combine like terms: $4.57s = 36.56$. Divide each side by 4.57: $s = 8$.

46. **89.1**; **DOK Level:** 3; **Content Topics:** Q.2.a, Q.4.a, Q.4.b, Q.4.d; **Practices:** MP.1.a, MP.1.b, MP.1.d, MP.1.e, MP.2.a, MP.2.c, MP.4.a, MP.4.b
Since the side length of the square is equal to the diameter of the semicircle, the perimeter of the semicircle is $\frac{1}{2}\pi s$, and the total perimeter of the figure is $3s + \frac{1}{2}\pi s$. Solve for s to find that the side length is 8 feet. The area of the figure is the sum of the area of the square and the area of the semicircle. The area of the square is $8^2 = 64$ square feet. Since the diameter of the semicircle is 8 feet, the radius is 8 ÷ 2 = 4 feet and the area of the semicircle is $\frac{1}{2}\pi r^2 = \frac{1}{2}$ × 3.14 × 4^2 = 25.12 square feet. So, the total area is 64 + 25.12 = 89.12 square feet, or 89.1 rounded to the nearest tenth.

47. **C**; **DOK Level:** 1; **Content Topics:** Q.2.a, Q.5.d; **Practices:** MP.1.a, MP.1.b, MP.1.d, MP.1.e, MP.2.c, MP.4.a
The surface area of a sphere is $4\pi r^2$. Substitute 3.5 for r and calculate the surface area: 4 × 3.14 × 3.5^2 = 4 × 3.14 × 12.25 = 153.86. So, to the nearest square centimeter, the surface area is 154 cm^2.

48. **B**; **DOK Level:** 1; **Content Topics:** Q.2.a, Q.5.a; **Practices:** MP.1.a, MP.1.b, MP.1.d, MP.1.e, MP.2.c, MP.4.a
The volume of a cube with an edge length of 12 feet is 12 × 12 × 12 = 1,728 cubic feet. Determine which answer choice describes a rectangular prism with a volume of 1,728 cubic feet. Answer choice A has a volume of 4 × 6 × 10 = 240 cubic feet. Answer choice B has a volume of 4 × 16 × 27 = 1,728 cubic feet. Answer choice C has a volume of 6 × 9 × 16 = 864 cubic feet. Answer choice D has a volume of 6 × 12 × 18 = 1,296 cubic feet.

49. **B**; **DOK Level:** 2; **Content Topics:** Q.2.a, Q.2.e, Q.4.b; **Practices:** MP.1.a, MP.1.b, MP.1.e, MP.2.c, MP.4.a
The area of a circle is given by $A = \pi r^2$. The radius of a circle is one-half its diameter, so the radius of the blanket is 9 ÷ 2 = 4.5 feet. Substitute 4.5 for r and calculate the area: A = 3.14 × 4.5^2 = 63.585 feet, which rounds to 63.59 square feet. Answer choice A is the circumference of the blanket in feet. Answer choice C is the result of using the diameter to find the area, and then dividing the product by 2. Answer choice D is the result of using the diameter to find the area.

50. **C**; **DOK Level:** 2; **Content Topics:** Q.2.a, Q.2.e, Q.4.b; **Practices:** MP.1.a, MP.1.b, MP.1.e, MP.2.c, MP.4.a
The circumference of a circle is the product of the diameter of the circle and π. So, the circumference of the blanket in feet is 3.14 × 9 = 28.26 feet. There are 12 inches in 1 foot, so multiply the number of feet by 12: 28.26 × 12 = 339.12 inches. Answer choice A is the area of the blanket in feet. Answer choice B is the result, in inches, of multiplying π by the radius instead of the diameter. Answer choice D is the result of multiplying the area, in feet, by 12.

51. **1,413 cm^2**; **DOK Level:** 2; **Content Topics:** Q.2.a, Q.2.e, Q.5.b; **Practices:** MP.1.a, MP.1.b, MP.1.e, MP.2.c, MP.4.a
The amount of fabric Carmen needs is equal to the surface area of the cylinder. The surface area of a cylinder is the sum of the area of its two bases and its lateral area: $2\pi r^2 + 2\pi rh$. The diameter of the cylinder is 10 cm, so its radius is 10 ÷ 2 = 5 cm. Substitute 5 for r and 40 for h to calculate the surface area: 2 × 3.14 × 5^2 + 2 × 3.14 × 5 × 40 = 157 + 1,256 = 1,413 square centimeters.

52. **3,140**; **DOK Level:** 2; **Content Topics:** Q.2.a, Q.2.e, Q.5.b; **Practices:** MP.1.a, MP.1.b, MP.1.e, MP.2.c, MP.4.a
The volume of a cylinder is equal to $\pi r^2 h$. The diameter of the cylinder is 10 cm, so the radius is 10 ÷ 2 = 5 cm. Substitute 5 for r and 40 for h to calculate the volume of the cylinder: 3.14 × 5^2 × 40 = 3,140 cubic centimeters.

53. **C**; **DOK Level:** 3; **Content Topics:** Q.2.a, Q.2.e, Q.5.a, Q.5.e, Q.5.f; **Practices:** MP.1.a, MP.1.b, MP.1.d, MP.1.e, MP.2.c, MP.4.a
The volume of the rectangular prism is 30 × 20 × 15 = 9,000 cubic centimeters. The volume of the hemisphere is one-half the volume of a sphere with the same radius, or $\frac{1}{2}\left(\frac{4}{3}\right.$ × 3.14 × $12^3\left.\right)$ = 3,617.28 cubic centimeters. So, the total volume is about 9,000 + 3,600 = 12,600 cubic centimeters.

54. **A**; **DOK Level:** 3; **Content Topics:** Q.2.a, Q.2.e, Q.3.b, Q.3.c, Q.5.e; **Practices:** MP.1.a, MP.1.b, MP.1.d, MP.1.e, MP.2.c, MP.4.a
The actual diameter is 30 meters, so the actual radius is 15 meters. Write and simplify a ratio to represent the situation: $\frac{12 \text{ cm} \div 12}{15 \text{ m} \div 12} = \frac{1 \text{ cm}}{1.25 \text{ m}}$. So, the scale of the model is 1 cm = 1.25 m.

55. **A**; **DOK Level:** 2; **Content Topics:** Q.2.a, Q.2.e, Q.4.a, A.2.a, A.2.b, A.2.c; **Practices:** MP.1.a, MP.1.b, MP.1.d, MP.1.e, MP.2.c, MP.4.a, MP.4.b
The area of a rectangle is the product of its length and width. The area of the smaller plot of land is 5.6 × 3.8 = 21.28 square miles. The area of the larger plot of land is 4 × 21.28 = 85.12 square miles. The length of width of the larger plot is 2 × 3.8 = 7.6 square miles. Since $A = lw$, 85.12 = 7.6 × l. Divide each side by 7.6 to find the length of the larger plot: l = 11.2 square miles.

Index

Index

slope-intercept form of equation of a line, xiv, 74–75
slope of a line, xiv, 74–75
slope-point form of equation of a line, 74–75
standard form of quadratic equation, xiv, 64–65
surface area of cone, xiv, 108
surface area of cylinder, xiv, 106
surface area of prism, xiv, 28–29, 106
surface area of pyramid, xiv, 108
surface area of sphere, xiv, 108
volume of cone, 108
volume of cylinder, 106
volume of prism, 28, 106
volume of pyramid, 108
volume of sphere, 108
Fraction bar, 8
Fractions
converting to/from decimals and percents, 14
entering into calculator, xii–xiii
expressing probability as, 32–33
expressing values in circle graphs as, 36
operations with, 8–9
rational expressions as, 66–67
ratios written as, 10–11
Functions
comparison of, 82–83
evaluation of, 58–59, 80–81

G

GED® Mathematical Reasoning Test, x
GED® Test
on computer, vi–vii
subjects and question types, iv–v. *See also* Spotlight Items
Geometric patterns, 58–59
Geometric problems, 76–77
Geometry
area of quadrilaterals, xii, 28–29, 94–95
circles, 100–101
composite plane figures, 102–103
composite solids, 110–111
perimeter of polygons, 28–29
polygons, 98–99
prisms and cylinders, 28–29, 106–107
pyramids, cones, and spheres, 108–109
Pythagorean Theorem, xiv, 96–97
scale drawings, 104–105
solving problems with slope of a line, 76–77
triangles, 94–95, 104–105, 116
Graphing
coordinate grid, 70–71
inequalities, 68–69
linear equations, 72–73
quadratic equations, 78–79
Graphs
circle, 36–37
dot plot, histograms, box plot, 38–39

of functions, 82–83
line and bar, 34–35
of quadratic equations, 78–79
Greater than (>), 2, 68
Greater than or equal to (≥), 68

H

Hemisphere, 108–109, 119
Histograms, 38–39
Horizontal axis, 34
Hot spots, 34
Hypotenuse, 96–97

I

Improper fractions, 8–9
Incongruent sides, 98–99
Independent events, 32
Independent variables, 72–73
Inequalities, 68–69, 86
Input, 58–59, 80–81, 82–83
Inside the Items
check units, 28
perimeter of composite figures, 102
plotting points on coordinate grid, 70
signs of terms, 64
solutions to linear equations, 72
using formulas, 106
Integers, xii–xiii, 6–7
Intercepts
comparing functions with, 82–83
of functions, 80–81
of linear equations, 74–75, 76–77
of quadratic equations, 78–79
Interest, xiv, 14–15
Inverse operations, 52–53, 60–61
Irregular polygons, 98–99
Isosceles triangle, 94–95

L

Lateral area of a cylinder, 106
Length, 26
Less than (<), 2, 68
Less than or equal to (≤), 68
Like terms, 50–53, 56–57
Linear combination method, 62–63
Linear equations
graphing, 72–73
in one variable, 52–53, 60–61
in two variables, 52, 62–63, 72–73
Linear functions, 82–83
Line graphs, 34–35
Lines
parallel and perpendicular, 76–77
slope-intercept form of equation of a line, xiv, 74–75

slope-point form of equation of a line, 74–75
using slope to solve geometric problems, 76–77
See also **Linear equations**
Line segment, 70–71
Lower quartile, 38–39
Lowest common denominator (LCD), 8–9, 66–67
Lowest terms, 8–9

M

Making Assumptions,
finding the rule for patterns, 58–59
Mathematical patterns, 58–59
Maximum value
of data set, 38–39
of quadratic equation, 78–79
McDoniel, Huong, 92
Mean, 30–31, 38–39
Measurement
length, area, volume, 28–29
U.S. customary and metric system, 26–27
Median, 30–31, 38–39
Minimum value
of data set, 38–39
of quadratic equation, 78–79
Mixed numbers, xiii, 8–9
Mode, 30–31, 38–39
Multiplication
on calculator, xii
of decimals, 12–13
of exponential numbers, 56–57
of fractions, 8–9
of integers, 6–7
of mixed numbers, 8–9
of rational expressions, 66–67
by ten, 12
of whole numbers, 4–5

N

Negative numbers
absolute value of, 6–7
entering on calculator, xii–xiii
multiplying inequalities by, 68
operations with, 6–7
square and roots of, 54–55
Negative powers, 56–57
Number line, 68
Number patterns, 58–59
Number sense
decimals, 12–13
fractions, 8–9
integers, 6–7
operations with whole numbers, 4–5
percent, 14–15
ratios and proportions, 10–11
whole numbers, 2–3
Numerator, 8, 14, 66

O

Obtuse triangle, 94–95
One, as denominator, 10
One, as an exponent, 56–57
Operations, x–xii, 4–7. *See also*
  Addition; Division; Multiplication;
  Subtraction
Opposite Integers, 6–7
Ordered pairs, 70–73, 82–83
Ordering
  decimals, 12–13
  whole numbers, 2–3
Order of operations, 56–57
Origin, 70–71
Outcomes, 32–33
Output, 58–59, 80–83, 87

P

Parallel lines, 76–77
Parallelogram, xiv, 94–95
Parallel sides, 94–95
Pattern, finding rule for, 58–59
Parentheses, 50–51
Patterns, 58–59
Pentagon, 98
Percent
  converting to/from fractions and
    decimals, 14–15
  expressing probability as, 32–33
  expressing values in circle graphs as,
    36
  finding on calculator, xi
Perimeter
  of composite plane figures, 102–103
  of irregular polygons, 98–99
  of triangles and quadrilaterals, 28–29,
    94–95
Periodic functions, 80–81
Period of a function, 80–81
Perpendicular lines, 76–77
Pi (π), 100–101
Place value
  comparing and ordering decimals,
    12–13
  rounding numbers, 2
Plane figures. *See* **Two-dimensional**
  figures
Polygons, 98–99. *See also* **Composite**
  plane figures; Parallelogram;
  Quadrilaterals; Rectangle;
  Rhombus; Square
Positive numbers, 6–7, 54–55
Possible outcomes, 32–33
Power of a number, 56–57
Prism, xiv, 28–29, 106–107
Probability, 32–33
Proper fractions, 8–9
Proportions, 10–11, 14, 104–105
Pyramid, xiv, 106, 108–109
Pythagorean Theorem, xiv, 96–97

Q

Quadrants of coordinate grid, 70–71
Quadratic equation
  graphing, 78–79
  standard form of and formula for, xiv,
    64–65, 78–79
Quadratic formula, xiv, 64–65
Quadrilaterals, 94–95
Quartiles, 38–39
Question types on the GED® Test, v
  drag-and-drop, 55
  drop-down questions, 15–17, 42, 47,
    67, 117
  fill-in-the-blank, 5, 27, 51, 59, 63, 105,
    111
  hot spot, 34–35, 71
Quotient, 4, 50, 66

R

Radius, 100–101, 103, 106–109
Range, 30–31, 38–39
Rate, 14
Rate of change, 82–83
Rational equations, 66–67
Rational expressions, 66–67
Rational numbers, 66–67
Ratios
  percents as, 32–33
  in proportions, 10–11
  rate of change, 82–83
  scale factor as, 104–105
Reciprocal, 8–9, 56–57, 66
Rectangle, 94–95
Rectangular prism, xiv, 28–29, 106
Regular polygon, 98–99
Relationship of functions, 80–81
Relative maxima, 80–81
Relative minima, 80–81
Rhombus, 94–95
Right triangle, 94–95, 96–97
Rise, 74–75, 82–83
Root sign, 54–55
Roots of numbers, xiii, 54–55
Rounding
  decimals, 12–13
  whole numbers, 2
Rule, 56, 58–59
Run, 74–75, 82–83

S

Scale drawings, 28, 104–105
Scale factor, 104–105
Scalene triangles, 94–95
Scale of graphs, 34
Scatter plots, 34–35
Scientific notation, xiii, 56–57
2nd key, xii–xiii

Sides
  of incongruent polygons, 98–99
  of regular and irregular polygons,
    98–99
  of right triangles, 96–97
  of triangles and quadrilaterals, 94–95
Similar figures, 104–105
Similar to (~), 104
Simple interest, xiv
Simplified form
  of algebraic expressions, 50–51
  of rational expressions, 66–67
Slant height, 108
Slope
  finding, 74–75
  formula for, xii
  of functions, 82–83
  of parallel and perpendicular lines,
    76–77
  using to solve geometric problems,
    76–77
Slope-intercept form of equation of a
  line, xii, 74–75
Slope-point form of equation of a line,
  74–75
Solid figures. *See* **Three-dimensional**
  figures
Sphere, xii, 108–109
Spotlight Items
  drag-and-drop, 55
  drop-down questions, 15, 67
  fill-in-the-blank, 5, 51, 59, 63, 105,
    111
  hot spot, 71
Square, 94–95
Square of a number, x, xi, 54–55
Square pyramid, 108
Square roots, xi, 54–55
Standard form of quadratic equation,
  64–65
Subject areas on the GED® Test, iv–v
Substitution
  evaluating expressions and equations
    with, 52–53, 60–61, 64–65
  solving two-variable equations with,
    62–63
Subtraction
  on calculator, x
  of decimals, 12–13
  of exponential numbers, 56–57
  of fractions, 8–9
  of integers, 6–7
  of mixed numbers, 8–9
  order of, 50
  of rational expressions, 66–67
  of whole numbers, 4–5
Surface area
  of composite solids, 110–111
  of cone, xii, 108–109
  of cylinder, xii, 106–107
  of hemisphere, 108
  of prism, xii, 28–29, 106–107
  of pyramid, xii, 108–109
  of rectangular prism, 28
  of sphere, xii, 108–109
Symmetry, 78–79

INDEX

Index

T

Tables, 2, 82–83
Terms
  in expressions and equations, 50–51
  in patterns, 58–59
Test-Taking Tech
  computer-based tests, 4
  interpreting graphs online, 34
  scientific notation on calculator, 56
Test-Taking Tips, xv
  converting metric unit, 26
  graphing inequalities, 68
  independent and dependent events, 32
  integers, 6
  lowest common denominator, 8–9
  multiplication by ten, 12
  multiplying by π, 100
  proportions used to solve for parts of
    similar figures, 104
  representings of functions, 82
  right triangle, 96
  rounding, 2
  solving linear equations, 62
  taking square root of a number, 54
  writing multiplication in algebraic
    expressions, 50
Theoretical probability, 32–33
Three-dimensional figures
  composite solids, 110–111
  cube, 28–29
  prisms and cylinders, 28–29,
    106–107
  pyramids, cones, and spheres,
    108–109
TI-30XS calculator, xii–xiii
Toggle key, xii
Translation, 70–71
Trapezoid, xiv
Triangles, 28, 94–95, 104
Triangular prism, 106–107
Two-dimensional figures
  area of rectangle, 28–29
  area of trapezoid, xiv
  circles, 100–101
  composite plane figures, 102–103
  perimeter of regular polygons, 98
  quadrilaterals, 94–95
  scale drawings, 104–105
  triangles, 28, 94–95, 104
Two-variable linear equations, 62–63,
  72–73

U

Undefined numbers, 54–55
Unit rate, 10–11
Units of measure, 26–27
Upper quartile, 38–39
U. S. customary system, 26–27
Using Logic
  formula for x-value of maximum or
    minimum, 78
  formulas, 94
  fractions and percents, 14
  information for answering questions, 76
  interpreting circle graphs, 36
  interpreting dot plots, 38
  perimeter of regular polygons, 98
  proportions, 10
  solving linear equations, 60
  values in tables, 30
  viewing composite solids, 110

V

Variables
  in algebraic expressions, 50–51
  eliminating one in two-variable linear
    equations, 62–63
  independent and dependent, 72–73
  isolating on one side of an equation,
    52–53, 60–61
  solving linear equations with one, 60–61
  solving linear equations with two, 62–63

Vertex, 108
Vertical axis, 34
Volume
  of composite solids, 110–111
  of cone, 108–109
  of a cylinder, 106–107
  of a hemisphere, 108–109
  of a prism, 28–29, 106–107
  of sphere, 108, 109

W

Whole numbers, 2–3, 4–5, 36

X

X-axis, 70–71
X-intercept
  comparing functions with, 82–83
  of functions, 80–81
  of quadratic equations, 78–79

Y

Y-axis, 70–71
Y-intercept
  comparing functions with, 82–83
  of linear equations, 74–77
  of quadratic equations, 78–79

Z

Zeros
  as exponent, 56–57
  as an integer, 6–7
  as place holders, 4, 12

INDEX